AF694496

School Crisis Intervention

The Guilford Practical Intervention in the Schools Series

Kenneth W. Merrell, Founding Editor
Sandra M. Chafouleas, Series Editor

www.guilford.com/practical

This series presents the most reader-friendly resources available in key areas of evidence-based practice in school settings. Practitioners will find trustworthy guides on effective behavioral, mental health, and academic interventions, and assessment and measurement approaches. Covering all aspects of planning, implementing, and evaluating high-quality services for students, books in the series are carefully crafted for everyday utility. Features include ready-to-use reproducibles, appealing visual elements, and an oversized format. Recent titles have Web pages where purchasers can download and print the reproducible materials.

Recent Volumes

Executive Function Skills in the Classroom:
Overcoming Barriers, Building Strategies
Laurie Faith, Carol-Anne Bush, and Peg Dawson

The RTI Approach to Evaluating Learning Disabilities,
Second Edition
Joseph F. Kovaleski, Amanda M. VanDerHeyden,
Timothy J. Runge, Perry A. Zirkel, and Edward S. Shapiro

Effective Bullying Prevention:
A Comprehensive Schoolwide Approach
Adam Collins and Jason Harlacher

Social Justice in Schools:
A Framework for Equity in Education
Charles A. Barrett

Coaching Students with Executive Skills Challenges,
Second Edition
Peg Dawson and Richard Guare

Social, Emotional, and Behavioral Supports in Schools:
Linking Assessment to Tier 2 Intervention
Sara C. McDaniel, Allison L. Bruhn, and Sara Estrapala

Family–School Success for Children with ADHD:
A Guide for Intervention
Thomas J. Power, Jennifer A. Mautone, and Stephen L. Soffer

School Crisis Intervention: An Essential Guide for Practitioners
Scott Poland and Sara Ferguson

Classwide Positive Behavioral Interventions and Supports,
Second Edition: A Guide to Proactive Classroom Management
Brandi Simonsen and Diane Myers

Family–School Collaboration in Multi-Tiered Systems of Support
S. Andrew Garbacz, Devon R. Minch, and Mark D. Weist

Overcoming Test Anxiety:
Tools to Support Students from Early Adolescence to Adulthood
Alex Jordan and Benjamin J. Lovett

School Crisis Intervention

An Essential Guide for Practitioners

SCOTT POLAND
SARA FERGUSON

THE GUILFORD PRESS
New York London

Printed in the United States of America

This book is printed on acid-free paper.

Last digit is print number: 9 8 7 6 5 4 3 2 1

Library of Congress Cataloging-in-Publication Data

Names: Poland, Scott, author. | Ferguson, Sara, PsyD, author.
Title: School crisis intervention : an essential guide for school practitioners / Scott Poland, Sara Ferguson.
Description: New York : The Guilford Press, [2025] | Series: Practical intervention in the schools series | Includes bibliographical references and index.
Identifiers: LCCN 2024038841 | ISBN 9781462556175 (paperback) | ISBN 9781462556397 (cloth)
Subjects: LCSH: School crisis management.
Classification: LCC LB2866.5 .P676 2025 | DDC 371.2/07—dc23/eng/20241106
LC record available at *https://lccn.loc.gov/2024038841*

About the Authors

Scott Poland, EdD, is Professor in the College of Psychology and Director of the Suicide and Violence Prevention Office at Nova Southeastern University. Dr. Poland has served as president of the National Association of School Psychologists (NASP) and was the first chairperson of the NASP National Emergency Assistance Team, serving for 14 years. He is a nationally recognized expert on school crisis, youth violence, suicide intervention, school safety, threat assessment, and the delivery of psychological services in schools. Dr. Poland has personally responded to or consulted after hundreds of school crises and has led over 1,000 workshops worldwide. He has published numerous articles, book chapters, and books on crisis intervention.

Sara Ferguson, PsyD, is a clinical psychologist who provides psychotherapy and psychological assessment services to at-risk youth in a South Florida private practice. Dr. Ferguson leads suicide and violence prevention training workshops in school settings and has extensive clinical experience working with at-risk youth. She has also worked in trauma-specific clinics, providing individual psychotherapy services for individuals with posttraumatic stress disorder. Dr. Ferguson has coauthored a number of research publications on such topics as youth suicide and violence prevention, juvenile offending, school shootings, and the neuropsychology of crime.

About the Authors

Preface

This publication is a practical guidebook on the topic of crisis intervention in the school context. The primary goal of the book is to provide the most current information and tools to best help school practitioners to prepare for, prevent, and respond to crises at school. School crisis intervention can be complex and unpredictable, and many school personnel find themselves ill equipped to facilitate appropriate crisis responses. It is imperative that all school personnel have training in crisis intervention and that school mental health professionals (SMHPs) and administrators go above and beyond basic training in order to become competent in this area (to be discussed further). This book can be used in conjunction with your current crisis prevention and intervention training. It is meant to be a resource from which SMHPs can find guidance on best practices and obtain ideas for implementation in crisis response.

The guidebook begins by reviewing the general theory of crises and crisis intervention, along with your role in providing these services in the school context. Chapter 2 provides an in-depth review of crisis prevention, a critical part of crisis intervention, including best practices for creating a climate of safety and security at your school. School violence and suicide prevention are also explored in detail. Part I focuses on the intervention aspects of serious school crises, including unexpected death, suicide, school violence, and natural disasters. Specific guidance on best practices is offered. The aftermath of a crisis and how you can best meet the needs of your school community post-crisis are reviewed in Chapters 8 and 9. The topics discussed include procuring appropriate help, addressing victim mental health needs, returning to school, planning for memorials/funerals, and navigating financial, political, and media-related concerns. The book concludes with two chapters that focus on special issues in school crisis intervention, including diversity factors, such as culture and students with disabilities, and ethical and legal considerations. We close with final thoughts and future directions in Chapter 12.

Each chapter contains materials that are meant to be used in your crisis planning, intervention, and postvention. It offers user-friendly worksheets and checklists that will help to increase the accessibility of the content explored. Additionally, ideas for consideration are sprinkled throughout the chapters, including suggestions for activities and tasks that will enhance your crisis prevention and intervention practices. Lastly, pertinent resources are reviewed, and we highly recommend that you follow up on the resources discussed to ensure that you and your team are creating a comprehensive approach to school crisis intervention.

A unique aspect of this book is the incorporation of real-life experiences and professional perspectives from experts in the school crisis intervention field. I (SP) provide a number of valuable reflections that highlight a variety of relevant factors in crisis intervention. My 30-plus years of firsthand experiences have informed my breadth of knowledge and expertise. I have personally responded to 17 school shootings across the United States, including the tragedies at Columbine, Sandy Hook, and Marjory Stoneman Douglas, which occurred in my own backyard. "Professional Perspectives" go beyond my experiences and include excerpts from interviews with a number of well-known school crisis responders. *We are incredibly grateful to the experts and their generosity of time, and we want to thank them for their contributions.* The insight that they have shared is invaluable and will be a key part of this guidebook. We have included brief bios of each expert here so that the reader can be well acquainted with their backgrounds and experience in the field of crisis intervention.

Stephanie Crawford-Goetz, PhD, is Director of Mental Health for the Douglas County Schools in Colorado. She has 18 years of experience in responding to school crises, including those involving suicidal students, youth who threaten to harm others, and larger-scale crises that have impacted her entire school community. Dr. Crawford-Goetz led the district crisis response after the shooting at the STEM School in Highland Ranch, Colorado, in 2019. She has developed extensive crisis prevention, suicide prevention, and safety initiatives for the district and presents frequently on these subjects.

Franci Crepeau-Hobson, PhD, is Professor and Director of the School Psychology Program at the University of Colorado–Denver. She has over 15 years of response experience. Dr. Crepeau-Hobson has served on both national and state crisis response teams and has responded to multiple school shootings, including the Aurora theater shooting, as well as wildfires and floods. She has also consulted with a number of schools and school districts regarding crisis response and suicide prevention. Her research has focused on youth suicide prevention, crisis response and intervention, school violence prevention, and psychological assessment.

Cynthia Dickinson, EdS, is the program manager for crisis intervention and dropout prevention services for the Fairfax County Public Schools in Virginia. She has over 20 years of experience in crisis response, including hands-on experience in highly publicized events such as the 9/11 attacks on the Pentagon, the East Coast sniper case in 2002, and the Virginia Tech shooting in 2007. She has also responded to a range of youth suicide, violence, and death crises. Ms. Dickinson has been a member of the NASP National Emergency Assistance Team or Crisis Support Group for many years. She has also consulted with Gulf Coast schools in Mississippi, North and South Carolinas, Bahamas, and Texas. In addition, she has served as a volunteer in disaster recovery in multiple states.

Fulvia Franco, PhD, NCSP, is a licensed psychologist, a Program Specialist–Guidance, and Coordinator of the Jordan Family Education Center in the Jordan School District in West

Jordan, Utah. She is also the Training Director in the Jordan School District for the APPIC (Association of Psychology Postdoctoral and Internship Centers) predoctoral internship program. Dr. Franco has over 30 years of experience in crisis response. She served as a delegate to NASP for 14 years and also served as a Delegate Representative on the NASP Executive Council for 4 years.

Cathy Kennedy-Paine, EdS, is a retired school psychologist, educator, and special education administrator. She spent the majority of her career in the Springfield School District in Springfield, Oregon, where she was a school psychologist and special education coordinator, and also served as crisis team leader for the district. She has supported schools for 33 years in her district, throughout Oregon, and nationally. She has responded to well over 100 incidents, most of them the deaths of students, administrators, and other school staff members due to accidents or illness. She has also responded to student, staff, and parent suicides, long-term illness, familicide, and seven high-profile school shootings. Ms. Kennedy-Paine was a member of the NASP National Crisis Response Team (formerly the National Emergency Assistance Team) from 2007 to 2022, and she served on the NASP School Safety and Crisis Response Committee for 8 years.

Philip J. Lazarus, PhD, has served as Director of the School Psychology Program at Florida International University (FIU) in Miami, Florida for over 30 years. He is licensed as both a psychologist and a school psychologist in the state of Florida. Dr. Lazarus is a former President of NASP and founder and past Chairperson of the National Emergency Assistance Team of NASP. He has responded to a number of school crises and natural disasters, such as school shootings, tornadoes, and hurricanes. He has also consulted in cases of deaths in schools and schoolwide sexual abuse. Dr. Lazarus has authored over 10 chapters and edited NASP's first edition of the first text on crisis prevention and intervention in the schools: *Best Practices in School Crisis Prevention and Intervention* (2002).

Richard Lieberman, MA, NCSP, is a retired school psychologist and suicide prevention consultant. He worked as a school psychologist for an incredible 47 years, with 25 years as the coordinator of the Suicide Prevention Unit in the Los Angeles Unified School District in California. He has responded to a variety of crises, including death by suicide; suicide clusters; school shootings; natural disasters; death by accident, homicide, or natural causes; and civil unrest. He has authored numerous book chapters on suicide prevention, intervention, and postvention in the schools and has consulted nationally with districts experiencing suicide clusters. He was one of the founding authors of NASP PREPaRE. He currently teaches crisis intervention at the Graduate School of Education at Loyola Marymount University in Los Angeles.

Amanda B. Nickerson, PhD, NCSP, is Director of the Alberti Center for Bullying Abuse Prevention and Professor in School Psychology in the Graduate School of Education at the University at Buffalo, State University of New York. She is a licensed psychologist and a nationally certified school psychologist with 20 years of experience responding to crises. Dr. Nickerson has engaged in crisis response consultations for murder(s) of student/families, suicides, 9/11 terrorist attacks, bomb threats, and natural disasters such as floods and hurricanes. Her research focuses broadly on school safety and building the social–emotional strengths of youth, with a particular emphasis on bullying and other forms of violence and victimization. She is an author of NASP's

PREPaRE School Crisis Prevention and Intervention Training Curriculum and is Coordinator of Research for the NASP School Safety and Crisis Response Committee.

Michelle Pastorek, PhD, LP, LSSP, is a psychologist on the Mental Health Intervention Team in the Cypress–Fairbanks Independent School District. She has 10 years of experience in crisis response. For the past 4 years, she has been part of the Mental Health Intervention Team, a multidisciplinary team focused on safety and mental health. Team members provide training, consultation, and response in the areas of suicide prevention, threat assessment, and coordination with the crisis response team.

William "Bill" Pfohl, PsyD, is a nationally certified school psychologist and Psychology Professor Emeritus at Western Kentucky University in Bowling Green, Kentucky. He has been involved in crisis response to school-related crises since 1997, although his initial response to crises began in 1974, as a first responder/EMT in western New York. He has responded to a variety of school crises, both internationally and in the United States, including a number of school shootings, natural disasters (e.g., tsunamis, fires, tornadoes), and many deaths by suicide of students and teachers. Dr. Pfohl is a two-time president of NASP and is the recipient of the NASP 2010 Lifetime Achievement Award.

Jeff Roth, PhD, NCSP, is a retired nationally certified school psychologist, crisis coordinator, and author. He has over 30 years of experience responding to school crises. His experience is primarily related to crises involving the death of teachers or students. Dr. Roth is the author of *School Crisis Response: Reflections of a Team Leader*, lead editor of *Perspectives on School Crisis Response: Reflections from the Field*, and lead author of *Developing Comprehensive School Safety and Mental Health Programs: An Integrated Approach*. He also wrote a middle school crisis manual, helped initiate and lead a district crisis response team, and was named School Psychologist of the Year by the Delaware Association of School Psychologists.

Frank Zenere, EdS, is a school psychologist and District Coordinator of Student Services/Crisis Program for Miami–Dade County Public Schools in Florida, the nation's fourth largest district, serving over 340,000 students. Over the past 30 years, he has coordinated and assisted in the provision of crisis intervention support at schools impacted by a critical incident or disaster. He has responded to a number of severe and publicized crises, including earthquakes, tsunamis, the 9/11 terrorist attack on New York City, mass-casualty school shootings (e.g., Sandy Hook, Marjory Stoneman Douglas), and youth suicide clusters. Mr. Zenere has served on numerous state and national committees overseeing the development of school safety policies and procedures. He served as a 10-year member and former Chairperson of NASP's National Emergency Assistance Team and is a recipient of three Presidential Awards from NASP for his service to children and school psychology. He has been a member of the Florida Crisis Response Team for the past 25 years, currently holding the position of Co-Coordinator for Miami–Dade and Monroe Counties; has written numerous articles for national publications and journals regarding his expertise and experiences; and has provided two congressional briefings on Capitol Hill regarding school safety, threat assessment, and suicide prevention.

Contents

Purchasers of this book can download and print copies of the reproducible forms at *www.guilford.com/poland-forms* for personal use or use with students (see copyright page for details).

Prologue

The following are excerpts from a narrative regarding the unknowns and lessons learned from my (SP) initial responses to three school shootings early in my career (see Roth & Fernandez, 2018, for a more detailed narrative).

PROFESSIONAL PERSPECTIVE: Scott Poland

Early Responses

Millsap Elementary School

I remember my first encounter responding to a school shooting in my district, Cypress Fairbanks Independent School District in Houston, Texas. This was back in 1985, during which I was working as the Director of Psychological Services. I received notice that an 11-year-old boy had been shot while raising the flag at Millsap Elementary School and that students had been fired upon at two other elementary school locations. This was my first response to a school shooting and, to be honest, I really had no idea what I was supposed to do. At that point in my career, I had not yet received any training in crisis intervention; however, my gut told me that I had to respond in some way. I needed to figure out how I could help the school out, so I went to my office to think over potential options.

Upon arriving at my office, I received a phone call from a local news station, asking if I would agree to an interview with them. I remember them posing the question, "Dr. Poland, what do parents in the Cypress Fairbanks school district need to do to help their children in the aftermath of this tragic shooting?" I had no experience completing a media interview, nor was I familiar with the district's media policies. Initially, I deferred to the superintendent, telling the media that he would be the best spokesperson for this tragedy. However, soon after, the superintendent reached out to me and said, "Scott, we believe in being cooperative with the media. We believe it would be a good idea if you gave that interview. It will be helpful to our families, our students, and their parents."

In a matter of moments, a media crew arrived at my building. I gave one clear message in that interview; I said, "Parents, pay attention to your child's emotions. Please give them permission for a range of emotions and do not project all your thoughts and worries about the world onto your child."

I can recall speaking with the staff at Millsap Elementary School. Tension was still high, as the gunman had not been captured and we had decided to keep the school open. I said to the teachers, "I bet your students slept better than you did. Working together, we are going to get through the day, we are going to help each other, and then we'll be in a better position to help our students." Later that day, the perpetrator turned himself into the authorities. He claimed that he was mad at the world and that kids and schools were an easy target. Thankfully, the student who was shot made a full recovery. As the school community began to return to their normal routine, I couldn't help but think, "Did that really happen? Yes, it really happened! But nothing like that could ever happen again in our top-rated suburban school district. . . ."

First Shooting at Langham Creek High School

Approximately 1 year after the Millsap shooting, on a slow-moving Friday, I remember my office assistant running into the staff lunchroom exclaiming, "There was a shooting at Langham Creek High School!" My first reaction was denial. I learned additional details about the shooting; Marvin Webster, the assistant principal, was shot in the cafeteria in front of more than 600 students and colleagues. I felt my emotions bubble to anger, thinking, "How could this happen again in our district!?"

I was called to respond to the shooting, and I remember my anger turning to panic and anxiety. I recall having to give myself a peptalk, saying, "You can stay calm, you can be collaborative, you've helped people before, and you can do it again." I remember arriving to the cafeteria, the crime scene, and was met by all of the officials in my school district: the superintendent, security director, deputy superintendents, assistant superintendents. They were gathering facts and reviewing the timeline of the shooting. I remember one of them pointing out, "The 16-year-old gunman stood here, and Marvin was shot right here, here's where the ricochet bullet hit the wall and hit the injured student. . . ."

I approached the principal of the school, whom I did not know that well. I looked around the cafeteria and wondered where the students who had witnessed the shooting had gone. I knew it was important that we respond to their needs. So, I approached the principal with some ideas. I said, "I'd like to talk to you. I have some things, as a psychologist, that I think would be important to do right away." He turned to me and said, "Scott, I'm sorry but I don't have time to talk to you right now. Please, write down all of your ideas and I'll take a look at them." Initially, I thought I was being brushed off, but it was understandable, as he was trying to make sense of the response in the moment. I'm glad to say that the principal actually implemented all of the appropriate steps, even without hearing my recommendations. He gathered the faculty, reunited the students with their parents, and made a plan for Monday, as the shooting happened on a Friday afternoon.

Second Shooting at Langham Creek High School

These shootings prompted our team to spend the next five years engaging in crisis planning and training on crisis intervention. We also built crisis response teams in every school in the district. I was taken aback when yet again there was another shooting at Langham Creek High School on a Friday in 1992. This time, a teacher was shot whom I knew very well. Her name was Rita Wenzel, and she was the head of special education at the high school. Unfortunately, she and her husband had been having some marital difficulties. That Friday, Rita's husband showed up to the school and pulled a gun on her with the intention of kidnapping her. Rita tried to escape, but every school door was locked at that time, except the front door. Sadly, she was unable to make it to safe cover; she was shot to death, and her husband then turned the gun on himself.

Thankfully, only a small group of students witnessed the murder–suicide. At that time, I didn't know about the concept and term "Circles of Vulnerability," that is, geographic proximity to the traumatic event, those with the closest relationships to the victim, and other populations at risk—meaning those with a unique trauma history. While I didn't know the concept then, I was keen on the fact that we needed to provide extensive assistance to the students who had witnessed the crisis.

When I think back to that call, I remember the school psychologist at Langman relaying to me that he was not in a position to respond to the school staff due to his close relationship with Rita. He said, "I just can't go to the school and focus on the needs of anyone else." This moment pointed to the very real need for crisis responders to be attuned to their own psychosocial needs; sometimes, one may be too close to the situation.

During the response, we had to make plans for how to keep the scene secure and limit students' visual access. We had to arrange for a different dismissal process, as the bodies were left on the ground, covered by a sheet, close to the bus loop. The principal rehearsed an announcement that was to be given over the loudspeaker, which I've come to learn is generally not the preferred method of informing the school about a crisis. In order to support classroom processing, we were rushing to get scripts, notes, and handouts to every teacher.

We kept the regular schedule for the remainder of the day. I spoke at the press conference and made an announcement about the family/community meeting that would be held later that night. In my message to the parents of Langman students, I heavily stressed the school's commitment to keeping them informed: "Langham Creek High School will be open until 10:00 P.M. this evening. Counselors and school psychologists will be here. If you have particular concerns about your child, please come to school this evening, bring them, and we will assist you and your family."

Remaining response tasks included an afterschool faculty meeting and the difficult process of notifying Rita's family of her death. The principal and I went to the home of her brother, where we expressed our condolences, asked about funeral plans, and reviewed memorialization plans. It was a very emotional but necessary meeting. I know that her brother and family really appreciated the outreach from the school. Many faculty members, including the principal and me, attended her funeral.

We focused our support efforts on those who were close to Rita, including her colleagues in the special education department and students whom she worked with. This was especially important because we had learned that some of these people had been dealing with their own personal losses and family issues. Moreover, we recognized that students with disabilities are at an increased risk for trauma, requiring additional support.

Since those three school crises, I have responded to 14 additional school shootings, and each has brought unique challenges and lessons to be learned. It is my hope that my experiences in responding to these shootings and so many other school crises will be helpful in strengthening other crisis responders in the school context.

CHAPTER 1

Introduction

WHAT IS A CRISIS?

The term *crisis* has been defined in many ways throughout history. Erich Lindemann (1944) is credited with developing the first formal framework to outline the symptom presentation of a crisis. Lindemann's work was inspired by his evaluation and treatment of survivors and loved ones of victims from a deadly fire that took place in Boston's Cocoanut Grove Club. At the time, Cocoanut Grove was one of the most popular nightclubs in the area. The fire occurred as a result of overcrowding, fire-hazard violations, and an electrical short that was fueled by methyl chloride in the air conditioning unit. Tragically, 492 people died and another 166 were injured (Boston Fire Historical Society, 2021). Lindemann provided intervention in the aftermath and detailed many observations, including presentations of acute grief and specific symptoms that formed a distinct syndrome. These symptoms included somatic distress, preoccupation with the image of the deceased, guilt, hostile reactions, and the loss of patterns of conduct. He also offered treatment guidance, sharing that survivors must face their loss and readjust to their new normal, in which the deceased person is no longer present.

In the 1960s, Gerald Caplan and his Harvard colleagues expanded upon this guidance in their work with families who immigrated to Israel following World War II. Their work led to the development of crisis intervention theory and practice (Poal, 2009). As a result, many definitions of the term *crisis* have evolved from this foundation, notably,

"An obstacle that is, for a time, insurmountable by the use of customary methods of problem solving. A period of disorganization ensues, a period of upset, during which many abortive attempts at a solution are made" (Caplan, 1961, p. 18).

"A precipitator in the form of a hazardous event intrudes on the life of an individual or group, causing a state of tension that is subjectively uncomfortable and the person experiencing the hazardous event resorts to customary coping behaviors" (Janosik, 1986, p. 7).

"A perception of an event or situation as an intolerable difficulty that exceeds the resources and coping mechanisms of the person" (Gilliland & James, 1988, p. 3).

"An acute emotional upset; it is manifested in an inability to cope emotionally, cognitively, or behaviorally and to solve problems as usual" (Centers for Disease Control and Prevention [CDC]), 2020a; Hoff, 2009).

Throughout my (SP)* career, I have come to find that the "trilogy definition" is the best descriptor of a crisis event, in which three consecutive steps occur: (1) a person is involved in a precipitating event, (2) their perception of that event causes subjective distress, and (3) the person's usual coping methods fail, resulting in decreased level of functioning as compared to prior to the event (see Figure 1.1). These three components of a crisis must be recognized and understood because they are the elements that will lead to a successful intervention outcome. The perception of the event is by far the most crucial part to identify where your intervention can be most helpful. Survivor perception is the focus in this trilogy definition and the point that differentiates crisis intervention from most other forms of counseling.

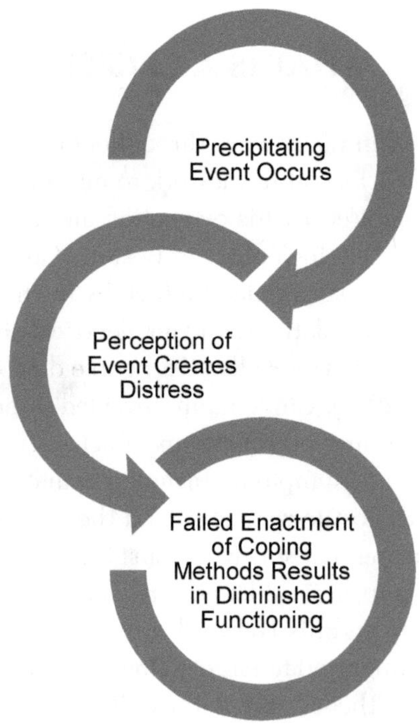

FIGURE 1.1. Trilogy definition of a crisis.

*Unless otherwise specified, first-person pronouns in text (e.g., *I*, *me*, *my*) indicate Scott Poland, and *we* indicates both Scott Poland and Sara Ferguson.

STAGES OF CRISIS DEVELOPMENT

Events preceding and following a crisis are predictable in some sense (Caplan, 1964), and they typically follow a general course of development. A crisis develops in four phases, and it is important that you become familiar with each stage prior to providing any crisis intervention services (see Figure 1.2).

Crisis theory highlights three possible outcomes of crisis: better than, similar to, or worse than precrisis functioning (Caplan, 1964). In some cases, the individual may return to precrisis levels of functioning in a relatively brief time. In more severe crises, this time period may be much longer. Regardless, crisis intervention greatly improves the recovery of survivors.

LEVELS OF CRISIS INTERVENTION

Ultimately, the goal of crisis intervention is to improve the survivor's level of functioning, to prevent future crises, or to manage them with improved efficiency. Crises represent an opportunity for growth and change. Individuals can grow emotionally and become psychologically stronger following well-resolved crises. While there are broad recommendations in crisis intervention, the process must be *site specific* and applicable to the context of the event. Crisis responses very quickly become personal, and victim responses will vary based on the unique characteristics of the individual and their family and community (see Chapter 10 for a deeper review of diversity needs). Crisis intervention approaches must therefore be tailored to meet individual needs.

Crisis intervention comes in differing formats, approaches, and levels, depending on the specifics of the crisis at hand. Intervention efforts are made on an individual or group basis and must be implemented to ensure safety and to mitigate potential harm of the victims. Crisis

Phase 1: Initial rise in anxiety/tension caused by the crisis event

Individuals are faced with a problem that is distressing. They attempt to implement their typical problem-solving skills to find solutions. This might be something that the individual has either never experienced or has not encountered with such severity.

Phase 2: Ineffective problem solving

In the face of the continued impact of the distressing event, the individual's attempts to use their past techniques are not working.

Phase 3: Heightened anxiety and fear

Anxiety, fear, and tension increase to even higher rates. The individual exhausts all possible resources, even those involving extreme means. If the individual can shift their goal from problem solving to coping, the crisis may be able to be resolved (or better dealt with). In some cases, this is not possible, and the fourth phase is enacted.

Phase 4: Breaking point

Tension and anxiety reach their breaking point and severe emotional dysregulation occurs. The individual has exhausted their own internal strength and skills.

FIGURE 1.2. Crisis phases.

intervention can often come in the form of psychological assistance, particularly in the case of suicidal or homicidal students. Caplan (1964) described three levels of crisis intervention:

1. Primary intervention: activities intended to aid in preventing a crisis (e.g., suicide and violence prevention programs)
2. Secondary intervention: actions taken in the immediate aftermath of a crisis to minimize the impacts of the crisis and to mitigate potential escalation (e.g., processing death with students who witnessed a crisis event).
3. Tertiary intervention: provision of long-term follow-up aid to the survivors of a crisis (e.g., ongoing mental health support) in order to strengthen the coping process and help the individuals return back to precrisis functioning.

Primary interventions are discussed at length in Chapter 2, which provides best practices for prevention. The chief emphasis of this guidebook, however, is on the secondary level of intervention, with detailed reviews of the steps to take when responding to specific crises (e.g., unexpected death, suicide, violence). Tertiary intervention recommendations are included throughout the crisis discussions, along with special considerations for crisis intervention.

SCHOOL-BASED CRISIS INTERVENTIONS

School-based crisis interventions have evolved over time, with fire-related incidences being the most common and publicized over the last 150 years. As a result, fire drills were one of the first crisis prevention strategies that were addressed in crisis planning (Heath, Ryan, Dean, & Bingham, 2007). In the early 1990s, increasing rates of gun violence in schools prompted a significant shift in the emphasis of crisis intervention (Poland & Ferguson, 2021a). School violence continues to be a significant concern across school systems. Since the Columbine High School massacre in 1999, over 311,000 students have experienced gun violence at school (Woodrow Cox et al., 2022). Moreover, suicidal risk for the youth population continues to rise, taking the lead as the second leading cause of death among middle school children in 2021 (CDC, 2024b). These statistics are tragic and justify the great need for prevention and intervention services in the school context.

The CDC's Youth Risk Behavior Surveillance System (2020b) is a comprehensive national survey that monitors priority health risks and experiences among U.S. high school students. The Youth Risk Behavior Survey (YRBS) results highlight the vast amount of risk facing the youth population, many of which will be present at your school. Moreover, the results point to the significant need for school crisis preparedness and intervention. The most recent data set, published in 2023, offers an important picture of the well-being of the young people in the United States. The data have been generated from surveys gathered in 2021. Among the topics reviewed is mental health, and a bleak picture emerges for our youth, revealing increasing trends of suicidality and feelings of hopelessness and sadness. The data reflect the strong need for crisis preparedness and intervention, as students are experiencing increased psychological difficulties. Additional relevant findings for crisis intervention from the 2021 YRBS are summarized in Table 1.1.

TABLE 1.1. YRBS Relevant Findings

Sexual risk behaviors (CDC, 2023)

- The percentage of high school students who have ever had sex has declined over the last 10 years (from 47% in 2011 to 30% in 2021).
- The percentage of students who had four or more sexual partners also declined from 15% in 2011 to 6% in 2021.
- Condom use among students having sex decreased from 60% in 2011 to 52% in 2021.
- *Implications:* Serious health risk for STDs, including HIV. This decrease follows a period of increased condom use throughout the 1990s and early 2000s.

Drug use (CDC, 2023)

- 12% of high school students reported current prescription opioid misuse.
- 18% of students currently use an electronic vapor product.
- 16% of students currently use marijuana.
- 23% of students currently drink alcohol.
- *Implications:* Substance use is linked to sexual risk behaviors, violence, poor mental health, and suicidality.

Violence and mental health (CDC, 2023)

- *Violence*
    - 15% of high school students reported being bullied at school.
    - 16% of students reported being cyberbullied.
    - 9% of students did not go to school because of safety concerns.
    - 11% of students reported experiencing sexual violence.
- *Suicide*
    - 42% of high school students experienced persistent feelings of sadness or hopelessness.
    - 22% of students reported seriously considering attempting suicide.
    - 18% of students made a suicide plan.
    - 10% of students engaged in a suicide attempt.
    - All measured items are trending upward over the last 10 years.
- *Implications:* Experiences of violence and poor mental health are factors that have been shown to be linked to sexual risk behaviors that can lead to HIV and sexually transmitted diseases, unintended pregnancies, and increased suicide risk.

Relatedly, in 2021, the U.S. Surgeon General published a General Advisory, which has brought attention to an urgent public health issue in the nation. The advisory was titled *Protecting Youth Mental Health* (2021), and it called attention to the sharply increasing mental health needs of U.S. youth. The advisory cited the 2019 YRBS findings (particularly the 42% increase in feelings of sadness and hopelessness in the last decade) as a driving force in our country's need to respond with swift action. The advisory elaborated that the concerns reported in 2019 have likely been compounded by the COVID-19 pandemic, given the fear, high death rates, economic strain, and isolation that it produced. The advisory emphasized that while mental health issues are rampant among our youth, they are *treatable* and *preventable*. Recommendations are provided to the institutions that engage with youth, including schools, community organizations, the government, health care systems, and media (U.S. Surgeon General's Advisory, 2021).

School-based crisis interventions can be thought of as an extension of the basics of crisis intervention applied to the school context. The goal of school crisis intervention has broadened from an individual to a group level, and the mission is to improve the well-being of the entire school community in the aftermath of a crisis (Anewalt, 2010). Primary and secondary interventions aim to maintain student well-being via prevention and targeted management of the crisis (Morrison, 2007). This aim is imperative, given that a traumatic event within a school community is a threat to students' optimal mental health and learning outcomes (Finelli & Zeanah, 2019).

SCHOOL CRISIS RESPONSE TYPES

Many students will encounter issues at school that are considered crises, though it is important to differentiate between occurrences that are stressful (e.g., failing a class) and those that are potentially traumatic. Moreover, crisis theorists note the difference between developmental crises and situational (or accidental) crises. *Developmental crises* commonly occur as individuals move through their developmental stages (e.g., from childhood to adolescence). They are generally more predictable in nature and create impact on an individual basis. *Situational crises* differ in many ways; they often occur without warning, and they can impact a larger group of people at once (Brock & Jimerson, 2012). As such, school crisis response typically focuses on situational crises, although developmental crises will be an important consideration throughout your planning and intervention.

Before reviewing the types of large-scale crises you may encounter, it is important to discuss the specific qualities of crises that may have traumatic implications. First, these types of crises are typically associated with extremely negative experiences and feelings. They have the potential to cause significant emotional pain and ongoing hurt. As mentioned, they often occur suddenly, with little predictability, creating a situation in which there is minimal time to adapt (behaviorally, cognitively, emotionally) to the issues the crisis has created. This characteristic is linked to another primary aspect of traumatic crises: they are typically out of one's control, generating feelings of powerlessness, helplessness, and/or a sense of being trapped. This loss of control can also create feelings of depersonalization, reducing one's feelings of self-worth and individuality. Lastly, large-scale crises have the potential for large-scale impact and require specific interventions, given the high number of people that can be traumatized in the aftermath (Brock & Jimerson, 2012).

In light of these characteristics, we must also consider the definition of trauma and/or a traumatic stressor. Trauma is generally thought of as an emotional response to a highly distressing event in which harm or the threat of harm takes place. Traumatic events are often associated with acts like physical and sexual abuse, accidents that cause serious injury, and deaths. The fifth edition, text revision of the *Diagnostic and Statistical Manual of Mental Disorders* (DSM-5-TR) defines a trauma event in its criteria for posttraumatic stress disorder (PTSD), describing it as an experience of death or, relatedly, the very real harm of death, serious injury, and/or violence of a sexual nature (American Psychiatric Association, 2022). The experience of trauma is also related to the lasting impacts (acute or prolonged) of the event. Exposure to traumas can result in impaired functioning, along with feelings of fear, paranoia, and helplessness,

TABLE 1.2. Crisis Types

- Weather related
  - Severe inclement weather
  - Flash flooding
  - Natural disasters (e.g., hurricanes, tornadoes)
- Fires
- Chemical/hazard spills
- Power outages/IT issues
- Medical emergencies
  - Mass allergic reactions
  - Outbreak of a disease
- Assaults and/or fighting
- Bus crashes
- Bomb threats
- Acts of terror or war
- Riots and demonstrations
- Armed intruder/school shooting
- Student and/or staff death (on or off campus)
- Suicide attempt or suicide
- Missing and/or kidnapped student or staff
- Hostage situations

Note. Based on *Vermont School Crisis Guide* (2017).

memory difficulties, and dissociative symptoms. Moreover, individuals who experience trauma can struggle with changes in their perceptions about themselves, others, or the world (American Psychiatric Association, 2022).

This guidebook focuses on situational crises that have the potential for traumatic impact, for example, those that may culminate in death or injury. There are also thorough discussions of the varying impacts of traumatic events across school-related populations. Table 1.2 provides a list of the range of significant crises that can occur in the school context.

While this list is comprehensive, it is not exhaustive, as crises are unpredictable and occur with variable circumstances. Our crisis expert contributors have responded to a number of different kinds of crises, some of which involved injury, death, or criminal activity.

PROFESSIONAL PERSPECTIVE: PHILIP LAZARUS

Probably the most challenging crisis I responded to was in 2010 at the International School of Curacao in Willemstad, Curacao, a Dutch island in the Caribbean. Typically, I will respond to a crisis along with a partner or a small team. For this crisis, I responded on my own.

A former teacher at the school, Stephen Wayne Sudduth, had been arrested in Texas for possessing and producing child pornography. Police had found more than 58,000 illicit images and videos on his computer, and some included very young children he had taught while serving as a kindergarten teacher at the International School. Prior to being employed there, he had also worked for the Hays consolidated school district near Austin and the Katy school district near Houston. The charges against Sudduth stemmed from an international investigation conducted by members of the Houston office of Homeland Security Investigations, the office of the Caribbean Attaché for Homeland Security, the Texas Attorney General's Cybercrime Unit, and the Public Prosecutor's Office in Curacao, a special task force unit comprised of Dutch and local law enforcement.

As would be expected, the entire school was in shock, and parents were concerned that their children may have been involved. I provided crisis intervention at the school and in the community on two different occasions, each for three days. I met with the school board, school administrators, all the teachers, the entire staff (e.g., bus drivers, custodians, cafeteria workers, teacher's aides). I met individually with every parent who was concerned about their child and with every parent who had a child in Sudduth's current or former classrooms. The perpetrator also had asked to babysit children at the school when their parents went out for an evening together. I met with members of the community and held evening presentations, which were covered by the media in three languages.

What made the situation so challenging was that parents at the school did not know, though some suspected, whether their children had been photographed or had been videotaped in compromising positions or partially or fully undressed. For example, children reported that their teacher took small groups of children into the bathroom and played "games" with them. I also provided a curriculum for the school called Good Touch, Bad Touch and other child abuse crisis prevention and intervention materials.

Every day was a long one. What helped was that I would often have a liaison who would guide me, and she would announce: "We are now going to meet with the school board in room xxx and I will take you there and bring you a fresh cup of coffee." Or "I will pick you up at your hotel at 6:00 P.M. and we will go to your presentation; the computer and all the equipment has already been set up for you." Therefore, I never had to be concerned about logistics and I could focus exclusively on delivering services and responding effectively with all parties and dealing with their specific concerns. I also had to learn about the staff of the school, the nation of Curacao, and the best interventions for child abuse, as well as read all of the reported news about the situation that had been reported in English prior to my arrival to the island.

Epilogue: Sudduth was sentenced to 360 months—30 years—in federal prison by U.S. District Judge Nancy Atlas, minus credit for the more than three years he had been in federal custody since his arrest. He will also serve 25 years of supervised release after he completes his prison term, during which time he will have to participate in counseling, have no contact with minors under the age of 18, and have limited access to computers and the Internet. He must also register as a sex offender.

PROFESSIONAL PERSPECTIVE: CATHY KENNEDY-PAINE

The Thurston High School shooting [was one of my most challenging responses. . . .]. When we responded to this crisis, we had a crisis plan, a crisis team, a superintendent who understood crisis response, and immense community and national support (NEAT, NOVA, U.S. Department of Education). Even with all of that support, we encountered enormous challenges in planning, communicating, responding to national and international media, obtaining mental health support, and trying to mitigate the impact of the trauma on every aspect of our lives. The entire community was affected in some way for years. However, having an organized team and plan in place did help people to feel a sense of confidence in a situation for which they otherwise felt little control.

Our community's response to the Thurston High tragedy was effective largely because of the district's preparation and our own connectedness. Community agencies such as the police, church groups, the American National Red Cross, other school districts, and county mental health workers all provided support because of our prior relationships. The district crisis team coordinated the help of more than 200 counselors, setting up a screening system for outside mental health workers to ensure they had experience with schools. Additionally, school resource officers began serving our high school campuses through one of the first such partnerships with local law enforcement in our county.

We were able to implement our plan, albeit with more resources and for a longer period of time than a usual response. With the aid of grant funds, our primary response—additional mental health support and follow-up, extended for the next 3 years, until the freshman class had graduated. Our permanent memorial was constructed at the 5-year point, and that became a natural concluding event for the community involvement in the tragedy. The media, of course, have since noted the 10-, 15-, 20-, and 25-year anniversaries.

While the large-scale crises discussed have the potential to create traumatic impact, it is not a guarantee, and you will need to be highly attuned to the common characteristics of a crisis state (i.e., an individual's crisis experience in the aftermath of the event). Simply enduring a crisis does not result in a crisis state; rather, it occurs when the individual's coping abilities fail and the issues created by the crisis are not able to be solved, prompting acute distress. Acute distress is the experience of intense and unpleasant feelings that cause impairment in functioning and occurs shortly after exposure to a traumatic event (American Psychiatric Association, 2022). The primary symptoms include reexperiencing (memories or flashbacks of the event), avoidant behaviors and related emotional numbing, and increased arousal states. If these symptoms persist in the aftermath, they can be diagnosed as an acute stress disorder. If they remain after 4 weeks, the individual will likely then be diagnosed with PTSD.

Individuals who are displaying these symptoms are considered to be in a crisis state, and so they certainly require intervention. Crisis states are typically time-limited occurrences in which individuals will work hard to cope with the distress that they experience, reducing their acute state of distress. While some aspects of the crisis may linger, the acute pain that individuals experience can typically be reduced within a few weeks to a few months. Crisis states also present individuals with the need for change (Caplan, 1964); most often, individuals are forced to find new ways to cope, and those who do so successfully are able to return to precrisis functioning. On the other hand, those who are unable to may develop maladaptive behaviors or strategies that result in a further decline in their functioning (Brock & Jimerson, 2012).

It is also important to understand that while crisis states come with many of the symptoms commonly associated with pathological presentations, they are not generally regarded as mental health symptoms. Rather, they are considered understandable reactions to atypical situations. However, it is possible that preexisting mental health symptoms can intensify the crisis state and result in a deteriorated state of functioning for a longer period of time. Moreover, while most crisis states are resolved in a relatively short period of time, some individuals will be unable to cope and may go on to experience chronic PTSD (Brock & Jimerson, 2012). Awareness of the common characteristics of the crisis state will help you to tailor your interventions in the aftermath of a serious crisis. Crisis states and associated traumatic and grief reactions are discussed further in later chapters, as they relate to specific crises.

WHAT IS YOUR SCHOOL'S ROLE IN SCHOOL CRISIS INTERVENTION?

> Responding to any crisis has prevention, preparedness, response, and recovery components.
>
> —RICHARD LIEBERMAN

> The initial response is only the beginning, not the end. Crises go on for a long time and one must be prepared for the entire event's impact, which can last years. School crisis response happens in phases and each phase has important interventions that help healing.
>
> —BILL PFOHL

Implementation of best practices for school crisis prevention, preparedness, and intervention is a critical component of efforts to mitigate the negative effects on students' learning and mental health. Your school must adopt these practices and ensure that you are equipped with a comprehensive crisis intervention approach. These efforts should generate ways for school personnel, students, and parents to return to precrisis functioning as quickly as possible in the aftermath of a crisis. They should address aftermath concerns, such as psychosocial issues, and identify preventative actions to enhance their preparedness for future crises.

Whatever policies are developed at the school level should be shaped by district policy and procedural guidelines. In most instances, the district's administration will provide your school with specific guidelines for handling major crisis events, such as a natural disaster. These guidelines should also include the district support resources (e.g., district crisis teams, medical and mental health support) that can be made available to your school. Regardless of what your district provides, it falls on your school to develop specific prevention and intervention approaches based on the needs of your school community.

Your school should collaborate with the district when beginning their crisis planning process. In order to plan effectively, the following must take place:

1. *Develop a school-based crisis team.* This team is a multidisciplinary group responsible for implementing appropriate crisis prevention and intervention. (This team is discussed in detail in Chapter 2.) In the best of circumstances, the district should provide not only policy and procedural guidelines but also support staff to help the school planning committee formulate a specific plan, organize and train the crisis team, and coordinate with relevant district and community resources.
2. *Create a written school safety plan.* This plan will outline all measures taken to ensure and maintain school safety, prevention efforts for potential crises, intervention procedures, and actions your school will take to help the school community return to precrisis functioning.

As a school mental health professional (SMHP), your role in school crisis intervention is critical. Your training and expertise are significant assets of the school crisis team. SMHPs were not a primary part of school crisis intervention prior to the 1980s; however, their role is now recognized as a major part of these procedures. Your specific role in the process is discussed in more detail in later chapters, although the overarching role is to use your expert knowledge to provide support and services for those at risk for mental health issues.

HOW CAN YOU BEST PREPARE FOR YOUR ROLE IN SCHOOL CRISIS INTERVENTION?

PROFESSIONAL PERSPECTIVE: FRANCI CREPEAU-HOBSON

[It is so important for] responders [to be] trained in school-based crisis response and intervention. [I have been involved in crisis responses where] the folks leading the response were not trained in crisis response and had never worked in schools. They had no idea how important it was to have and disseminate the verified incident facts, nor any idea about the power of psychoeducation in the context of crisis intervention. They were unaware of the importance of having an incident action plan, triage, offering a continuum of supports/interventions based on need, or what these interventions might even look like. These individuals were well trained in threat assessment, trauma, and trauma therapy and were well intentioned, but the whole response was a mess because they lacked the training needed to lead an effective school-based crisis response. The kids and the school community in general did not get their needs met and continued to struggle for quite a while after the incident.

Given the complexity of crisis events and reactions, best practices for crisis planning and intervention require special expertise and training. It is recommended that all providers involved in crisis intervention engage in professional training. There are a number of options across the country and, when selecting your training, it is imperative that you find one that is offered by verified crisis response experts/organizations. I have provided over 1,000 trainings on this topic, many of which our own crisis expert contributors have taken. Additionally, expert contributors such as Mr. Richard Lieberman and Dr. Philip Lazarus are well-known trainers in the field.

PROFESSIONAL PERSPECTIVE: CATHY KENNEDY-PAINE

About 9 years into my crisis response career, I was given the task of designing my district's mental health support following a mass school shooting in one of our high schools. I received "on-the-job" training from many counselors who came to help us, and especially from the highly skilled professionals from the National Association of School Psychologists [NASP] National Emergency Assistance Team and the National Organization of Victim's Assistance. Following our shooting I attended a 3-day NOVA crisis training. NASP has developed the PREPaRE School Safety and Crisis Preparedness curriculum over the past 15 years and I have been able to integrate those concepts with all of my experience.

One of the most well-known crisis intervention curriculums, PREPaRE (Brock et al., 2016), has been significant in school crisis training. It is the only comprehensive, nationally available training curriculum developed by educators (each of whom has firsthand school crisis response experience and formal training) for educators (NASP, 2021b). PREPaRE provides training to SMHPs and other educators on how to best fulfill the roles and duties they will have in the crisis planning and intervention process. The PREPaRE model incorporates guidance from the U.S. Departments of Education, including their Readiness and Emergency Management for Schools (REMS), and Homeland Security, including the Incident Command System (ICS) as described by the National Incident Management System (NIMS) from the Federal Emergency Management Agency (FEMA). It is based on a five-phase mission, including prevention, protection, mitigation, response, and recovery (Brock et al., 2016; see Figure 1.3). (If you are interested in participating in a PREPaRE workshop, contact the NASP PREPaRE Coordinator at *prepare@naspweb.org*.)

Experts agree on the top training courses available, and it is recommended that you engage in each of these continued learning opportunities as they will serve as the foundation for your crisis response. Top recommended training courses are reviewed in Table 1.3. Beyond the recommended training and programs, our contributors have shared what they have found to be most helpful in their careers responding to school crises.

Prevention

Take the necessary steps to prevent school crises (e.g., implementation of prevention programming)

↓

Protection

Secure the school campus and school members from potential crises (e.g., natural disasters or acts of violence)

↓

Mitigation

Assess the school's means to prevent or lessen crisis consequences (e.g., property damage and/or death) by decreasing the effect of a school crisis (e.g., implementing a lockdown procedure when an intruder is on campus)

↓

Response

The school's ability to appropriately address crises and create a smooth passage to recovery (e.g., implementing responses to a weapon on campus or a staff member death)

↓

Recovery

Return to normal routine and learning as soon as possible (e.g., reopen school quickly or provide alternative learning environments)

FIGURE 1.3. PREPaRE model's mission phases of a crisis. Based on Brock et al. (2016).

TABLE 1.3. Recommended Trainings

Program name	Key features	Training options and how to access
American Red Cross Trainings (2022)	Offers training for professionals in the areas of first aid, disaster response, and mental health support.	Visit American Red Cross online at *www.redcross.org/take-a-class* In-person workshops and online training
Critical Incident Stress Management (CISM; 2016)	Comprehensive, integrated, systematic, and multicomponent intervention system. While originally intended for emergency responders, with some modification, CISM is useful when applied to other populations at high risk for psychological injury or posttraumatic stress. Its approach is aimed at strengthening human resilience (Everly & Mitchell, 2016).	Visit Crisis Prevention Institute online at *www.crisisprevention.com/Blog/Incident-Management-Training* Verbal Intervention Training: In person Nonviolent Crisis Intervention: Hybrid (in person and online) Nonviolent Crisis Intervention with Advanced Physical Skills: Hybrid
Dr. Dewey Cornell's School Threat Assessment Training	School violence expert Dr. Cornell has a team that provides in-person and online threat assessment trainings to schools. He utilizes a model that he developed outlined in the Comprehensive School Threat Assessment Guidelines (CSTAG; School Threat Assessment Consultants, LLC, n.d.).	Visit School Threat Assessment online at *www.schoolta.com* In-person workshops and online training
National Organization for Victim Assistance (NOVA) Model (2023)	NOVA Crisis Response Team Training™ (CRT) has over 30 years of evidence-informed and field-tested best practices as a crisis management utility that includes trauma mitigation and education protocols. NOVA CRT training is an effective tool that can be instantly scaled up for mass-casualty critical incidents and has trained over 10,000 responders (NOVA, 2023).	Visit NOVA online at *www.trynova.org/training/overview* In-person workshops
PREPaRE (2009, 2014)	Trains school-employed mental health professionals and other educators on how to best fill the roles and responsibilities generated by their membership on school crisis response teams. PREPaRE is the only comprehensive, nationally available training curriculum developed by educators (each of whom has firsthand school crisis response experience and formal training) for educators.	Visit National Association for School Psychologists online at *www.nasponline.org/professional-development/prepare-training-curriculum/upcoming-prepare-workshops* Free materials available online In-person workshops available to the public and option to request trainings for your school Printed training curriculum: *PREPaRE, Second Edition* (2014), by Stephen E. Brock, Amanda B. Nickerson, Melisa Louvar Reeves, C. Conolly, Shane R. Jimerson, R. Pesce, and B. Lazzaro

(continued)

TABLE 1.3. *(continued)*

Program name	Key features	Training options and how to access
Readiness and Emergency Management for Schools Technical Assistance (REMS TA) Center (USDOE, 2006)	Created by the U.S. Department of Education's (USDOE's) Office of Safe and Supportive Schools to aid education agencies and related community partners to manage safety, security, and emergency management programs. REMS TA helps to expand preparedness efforts (including prevention, protection, mitigation, response, and recovery efforts) of schools, their districts, and community partners. Also serves as the main source of information dissemination for emergency preparedness.	Visit REMS TA online at *https://rems.ed.gov* Offers online and in-person training and prerecorded webinars on the following topics: • Hazards and Threats • Planning Basics and Principles • Emergency Exercises • Family Reunification • Bereavement

PROFESSIONAL PERSPECTIVES

What Have Been the Most Helpful Aspects of Your Training?

[. . .] learn[ing] specific skills and strategies for responding, [along with] tips and resources from experts and attendees about experiences.

—AMANDA NICKERSON

[. . .] using a model to navigate circumstances to help people (students and school staff members) address crisis-related problems and concerns and cope as effectively as possible. Also, using a structure to evaluate the response as it is ongoing, identify service gaps and improve what was offered.

—CINDY DICKINSON

[. . .] the ability to shadow and be mentored by a leading expert in the field.

—STEPHANIE CRAWFORD-GOETZ

[. . .] having a sense of what to expect (PREPaRE), making it easier to function and adapt/change in the noise and chaos. Triage and matching degree of trauma with needed (or not needed) intervention. Lots of "aha's" like not imposing intervention when not needed, using homogeneous groups having similar degree of trauma so as not to create vicarious trauma, keeping disengagement in mind.

—JEFF ROTH

Training of staff members is critical. It's important that mental health practitioners, crisis responders, and school administrators receive consistent training in response practices so they can use a shared terminology.

—MICHELLE PASTOREK

What has been helpful is learning from others in real-life situations. "Book" learning is not sufficient for being a good crisis responder.

—BILL PFOHL

BARRIERS TO CRISIS INTERVENTION

What helps brings us to a review of the barriers you might face in your crisis interventions. My experience has taught me that the greatest barrier to crisis intervention is lack of preparedness. Crisis planning is critical to the process and is discussed in detail in the following chapter. In the aftermath of crises, your school must always review the response, evaluating the good and the bad. This assessment will enhance the planning process, as it will aid in identifying specific barriers that prevented the provision of best practices. Sadly, many schools are faced with this consideration in the aftermath of a crisis in which their response went wrong. Experts agree on common barriers, and their experiences highlight these roadblocks in real time.

What Challenges May You Encounter in Crisis Preparedness?

One of the most prominent challenges in crisis preparedness is the limited access to resources in a number of domains, for example, staff, funding, and training programs. This situation is particularly true for underserved areas, such as rural and low-income communities. Additionally, staffing has become an increased concern in the context of the COVID-19 pandemic, with school staff shortages reported across the nation (Carver-Thomas, 2022). Moreover, federal funding for education is already a limited resource that must be carefully budgeted to meet the varied needs of student bodies; crisis preparedness, while important, is just one piece of the pie. Lastly, while there are training programs offered nationwide, their accessibility is limited, given their high costs and length of time required (e.g., weekend workshops that many school staff members must attend on their off hours).

Another challenge in crisis preparedness is the development of inadequate plans. While some states mandate crisis prevention training, many do not, nor do they provide best practice guidelines, leaving a large number of school districts to enact their own methods. This results in varied levels of crisis preparedness across school districts and states, along with inconsistent approaches that may not be well supported by evidence-based practices. We are sorry to share the fact that there are too many tragedies to point to wherein best practices for crisis response were not implemented.

Other barriers include potential territorial issues. I have found that initially, schools often want to handle things on their own, without the help of the community; however, they typically do not have enough SMHPs. Political issues and competitiveness among providers may occur. I have also found that school administrators consistently underestimate the impact of a crisis and do not always understand that they are in it for the long term. I recommend that schools decide in advance whom they would call on for assistance should a major crisis occur.

Moreover, often schools do not properly utilize mental health expertise, which is a key component of the crisis prevention process. SMHPs offer unique knowledge and skills that can aid in identifying environmental and individual risks, along with appropriate prevention and intervention strategies to help maintain school safety. It is imperative that schools utilize SMHPs in their crisis preparedness. Should your school not have an SMHP on staff, it is recommended that you create a relationship with the district SMHP assigned to your school. This SMHP can play an active role in your crisis prevention process.

PROFESSIONAL PERSPECTIVES

What Barriers Have You Encountered in Crisis Intervention?

"It can't happen here." Often, administrators are reluctant to provide training or address their safety vulnerabilities because of this belief. Breaking through this resistance can be very difficult.

—CATHY KENNEDY-PAINE

Sometimes administrators at the school or district level have been ineffective or even caused harm; sometimes some teachers have not understood the need and length of response; racial/ethnic barriers and mistrust on a particular occasion when we worked with Black students as a mostly White team; need for conflict resolution between two teacher teams after [the] teacher rape of student; dealing with media presents both barriers and opportunities during crisis response.

—JEFF ROTH

Administrators want to "handle it all," but do not know what to do. Families that do not wish to have their student's death confirmed or any close peer outreach to occur. Administrators who did not know how to use available resources effectively. Administrators who did not appreciate the scope of the work needed to restore schools to more normal functioning. Crisis teams coming in to support schools, and school colleagues returning to their normal activities/not helping.

—CINDY DICKINSON

School administrators are often reluctant to allow outside professionals to provide requisite services to their students and staff. Some district superintendents embrace outside experts in the field of crisis intervention and, in my state of Florida, I have worked in a number of districts with well-intentioned administrators who welcomed and appreciated support. However, we were not successful in helping the Sandy Hook community in spite of pleas from their own school psychologists for help. I believe if they had received more expert help, their response could have greatly improved.

—PHILIP LAZARUS

In my own experience, I've seen a range of skill and desire by onsite staff (school psychologists, counselors, social workers) impact the degree of their involvement and support in a crisis in their school.

—FULVIA FRANCO

The few barriers [I have encountered] include school administration and staff not having completed basic crisis response training to collaborate more effectively with district crisis teams. Another barrier is not having timely communication to the school and larger community now that social media can be used to post information, factual or not, so quickly to so many people. In schools we now feel we are trying to get out communications in a timely manner while still honoring the family that has lost their loved one and dealing with rumors by providing factual information.

—STEPHANIE CRAWFORD-GOETZ

[I have encountered barriers such as] administrative/parental direction not to proceed with intervention, media interference and messaging, and funding [issues].

—RICHARD LIEBERMAN

> [I have observed] inappropriate allocation of resources (over-responding or under-responding) and sometimes turf wars or people with different priorities (e.g., concern about their school "looking good" and avoiding bad press as opposed to being most concerned with the welfare of students and school community).
>
> —AMANDA NICKERSON

Lack of training and poor leadership on the part of administrators (e.g., not accepting help) appear to be a recurring theme across experiences and point to critical needs in the preparation for school crises. Moreover, these examples reiterate the imperative need for administrators to include SMHPs in crisis intervention. SMHPs have a significant responsibility, and you *must* advocate for your involvement in the process.

Crisis intervention in the school context is a complex approach that requires a considerable number of working parts, considerations, and collaborations. The purpose of this guidebook is to equip SMHPs and related school personnel to build their crisis intervention knowledge and skills and to ultimately help them to be best prepared to handle the challenges that come with large-scale school crises. This guidebook offers a number of best practices recommendations, guidelines, and unique professional reflections that give a window into the real-world experiences of experts. Ideas for consideration, hands-on activities, and recommended resources are reviewed. The guidebook brings you through considerations for prevention, intervention, and postvention (i.e., acts that should take place in the aftermath of a crisis) in the domains of unexpected deaths, suicide, and school violence. It offers guidance on important matters such as funeral planning and memorialization, media management, diversity issues, and legal implications. It is our hope that this guidebook can help to strengthen your practices in school crisis intervention and, ultimately, enhance the safety and well-being of your school community.

PART I

CRISIS RESPONSES AND INTERVENTIONS

CHAPTER 2

Crisis Preparedness

Getting Ahead of a Crisis

The very best form of crisis intervention is *prevention.* Your school will be best equipped to handle a crisis with proper preparedness. Postcrisis evaluations, expert reflections, and research have all shown us that many of the crises schools undergo are preventable. This fact is a driving force in the need for crisis preparedness. Moreover, large-scale crises are complex events that create a vast number of novel challenges in the response. The more your team makes efforts to prepare for potential crises, the better equipped they are to handle the curve balls that will inevitably come their way. This chapter takes a detailed look at crisis preparedness and the ways your team can get ahead of a crisis. It reviews general topics, such as school safety, and more specific preparedness, such as suicide and violence prevention. The guidelines discussed in this chapter are critical in ensuring that you are implementing best practices for crisis intervention at your school.

> [Crisis] response goes better when people are prepared and are on the same page (e.g., guidelines, resources, training).
>
> —AMANDA NICKERSON

> Engage in planning and preparedness before a crisis happens! We tend to be so reactive in this context. It often isn't until something happens in a community or a neighboring community that folks start thinking about how they might respond to a crisis.
>
> —FRANCI CREPEAU-HOBSON

> Many crisis events have the potential to overwhelm both adults' and students' coping capacities. The effectiveness of recovery is extremely dependent on the quality of prior planning and preparation as well as the character and connectedness of the school climate.
>
> —CATHY KENNEDY-PAINE

SCHOOL SAFETY PLANNING

Crisis preparedness cannot be successful without implementing best practices in school safety. The development and maintenance of student safety is essential to student health, well-being, and academic success and it is a key component of crisis prevention and intervention.

Your school should complete regular (annual, with quarterly check-ins) safety planning in order to create a climate of security for the students and school personnel, and the timeline of this planning should be outlined in your crisis plan.

School Safety Teams

The first step in school safety planning is to create a safety team. This team is responsible for developing and implementing comprehensive and appropriate school safety efforts in order to maintain a positive and secure school environment. Safety planning should be a collaborative, multidisciplinary, and comprehensive approach that incorporates members from the school setting (e.g., administrators, teachers, school psychologist) and the broader community (e.g., local police department liaison, parents/caregivers, mental health agencies). School and district providers are important contributors, for they can guide academic and extracurricular programming. SMHPs are another integral part of this process, as they serve to target important social, emotional, and psychological domains relating to school safety and prevention. Form 2.1 is a worksheet that your team can use to keep track of school safety goals and how you will meet them.

Your school safety teams' overarching goal is to ensure the safety of the school via prevention and protection efforts. In times of crisis, the school safety team will offer direction to others as needed for response and recovery. Moreover, the team will work in collaboration with the school crisis response team (CRT) to create comprehensive response efforts. The CRT differs from the school safety team in that the members have received specialty training related to mitigation efforts. Additionally, they will act as direct responders to crises; these individuals will provide firsthand aid and recovery interventions and support. CRTs also offer pertinent guidance to the school safety teams regarding prevention and protection strategies that can increase the overall safety of your school. Depending on the size of your school, your safety team and CRT may be made up of the same members or broken into two different teams.

Crisis Response Teams

CRTs should be developed strategically and must aim to include a mix of school personnel, outside agency employees, and community members. Team members should have a variety of knowledge and skills to offer. They should also be designed to reflect the diversity of your school community, including relevant cultural backgrounds and experiences. Ideal characteristics of team members include strong communication skills, calm affect, and a collaborative attitude. Examples of potential members include administrators, teachers, students, parents/caregivers, mental health professionals, law enforcement, and other relevant school personnel.

PROFESSIONAL PERSPECTIVES

Qualities of a CRT Member

There are many traits a crisis responder must have, perhaps the most important are empathy, flexibility, creativity, and the ability to communicate effectively. A crisis responder must think clearly, make decisions quickly, have integrity and courage, and must offer a vision of hope for the recovery of the affected community.

—CATHY KENNEDY-PAINE

[CRT members must have] flexibility, professionalism, openness to new circumstances, resilience in the face of potentially challenged "normal resources," [and] a healthy life focus.

—CINDY DICKINSON

[CRT members require] the ability to remain calm and collected. Awareness of one's own biases and the ability to set those aside in a response. Ability (and willingness) to engage in intentional self-care. This includes having an awareness of one's own triggers and limitations. And being able to give yourself permission to step back/away from a response and to say "no." Good communication and interpersonal skills. Being okay with taking a back seat and not being in charge or being at the center of a crisis (remembering this isn't about you!).

—FRANCI CREPEAU-HOBSON

[CRT members should be] compassionate, dedicated, collaborative, knowledgeable, resilient, and someone who values self-care.

—RICHARD LIEBERMAN

[CRT members need the] desire to do the work [and] to help and empower others, . . . resilience, regulated empathy, willingness to take and share leadership, basis in knowledge and skills, but ability to problem-solve, think on your feet, and address unique and unexpected situations.

—JEFF ROTH

[Qualities of CRT members include] flexibility, organization, being a lifelong learner, strong communication skills, ability to stay calm under stressful circumstances.

—MICHELLE PASTOREK

[CRT members should be] calm, confident, competent, and compassionate. [They also need to be a] problem solver and flexible ([with awareness that] it will not go the way you want it to go) and work well under stress and ambiguity.

—BILL PFOHL

I have outlined CRT structures for over 30 years (see Pitcher & Poland, 1992; Poland & McCormick, 1999), and they continue to be relevant today. CRTs can be established on three different levels—building, district, or community—and they are utilized based on the type and severity of the crisis, the size of the school and district, and the area in which the crisis occurred. Each level comes with its own advantages and disadvantages. The building level only requires the use of school personnel within the same school, which results in the least restrictive approach; however, it limits the variety of team members' skills/assets. Both district and community teams require the use of additional and outside resources (i.e., district personnel, police officers, mental health workers), which ends up making it more difficult to coordinate regular planning meetings and maintain close relationships. However, they offer a more diverse and comprehensive team (Erbacher, Singer, & Poland, 2015).

The role details of a CRT can be viewed in Table 2.1. Ideally, CRTs will be supervised by the district superintendent. Within the school, the principal most often serves as the crisis

TABLE 2.1. Crisis Team Member Roles

Crisis Coordinator: This person is preferably put in charge as the lead for the crisis process. Another option is for the administrator to take on the lead, or the administrator could pair with a school psychologist to co-coordinate the response team. This person will coordinate the crisis intervention and remain available and visible to the school community. This person must be calm and well versed in crisis intervention. They should be orderly and a clear thinker and someone who is able to delegate efficiently.

Medical Liaison: If your school has a nurse, then they are a logical person to fill this role. This person will administer first aid, triage the injured, keep a record of who is injured and where they are transported, and communicate this information to the parent/family liaison and serve as a liaison between the school and hospital personnel.

Media Liaison: If your school or district has a public relations (PR) representative, they are the logical person to fill this role. This person must have an authoritative, yet sympathetic, approach and preferably has training in public speaking. This person will hold a press conference to keep the media updated as the crisis unfolds. The press will likely want to hear from the head administrator of your school and the superintendent as well. If the media liaison is not also the head administrator, they can help the administrator to prepare for the press conference or interviews.

Security Liaison: Your school's security officer, constable, or a police officer is the appropriate person to fill this role. This person or persons will secure the crime scene and evidence until the police arrive. They will also limit media access to the campus.

Parent/Family Liaison: This person or persons will provide parents and other family members with verbal and written information about the crisis and make sure that the information communicated to them is consistent. This liaison delivers injury and death notifications, meets with parents and other family members when they arrive to the school, and plans the family/community meeting. Someone on your school's counseling staff or an administrator would be an ideal person to fill this role.

Counseling Liaison: The school psychologist or counselor is the obvious person to fill the role of counseling liaison. This person will work to calm students, staff, and family members during the crisis. They will also work to provide counseling sessions, both small groups and individual, for students and staff after the crisis, and they should advocate for opportunities for staff and students to express their emotions.

Campus Liaison: This person will communicate the specifics of the crisis to the school staff and will offer guidance on how the staff can assist in crisis management. The campus liaison will also greet and briefly interview any volunteers who come to your school, vet their intentions and skills, and assign each person to a task for the day according to their needs. Furthermore, this person will evaluate the scope of the crisis and will discuss the needs with the crisis coordinator. A member of your school's counseling staff or an administrator is a logical person to fill this role.

coordinator who directly oversees the following members/roles: counseling liaison, law enforcement liaison, media liaison, student liaison, parent/family liaison, campus liaison, and medical liaison. These teams must be appropriately trained in crisis intervention strategies, with an emphasis on prevention and intervention.

CRTs are established so that members can work to address crises that can be prevented and to prepare for those that cannot be avoided. The goals of a CRT are outlined in Table 2.2.

Needs Assessment

Once a safety planning team is established, the next step is to evaluate your current school safety practices; this process will inform your safety plan. Form 2.2 provides a worksheet that outlines a list of questions to guide your needs assessment in order to best capture the strengths and needs of the current safety practices at your school. While this list is not exhaustive, it is a solid guide to begin the needs assessment process and will open the doors to other questions and needs. Additional recommendations include the use of surveys to obtain a sense of school members' perceptions of safety and security in the school. Moreover, it would be helpful to collect and analyze data from school crime reports and administrative assessments of school safety, providing concrete examples of areas of concern and need.

School Safety Plan

Upon completing your needs assessment, a comprehensive school safety plan must be created. These plans provide guidance for implementing appropriate crisis preparedness, prevention, and safety efforts at your school. The creation of school safety plans must be driven by the data collected, including findings from your needs assessments, along with analyses of your school's safety, behavioral, and academic domains. This type of collection ensures that the plan is not formulated based solely on opinion, but rather is a thoughtful integration of team members and objective data.

TABLE 2.2. CRT Goals

- Prepare for crises.
  - Conduct recurrent reviews of school safety practices and complete needs assessments.
- Prevent crises.
  - Engage in prevention efforts:
    - Develop student resiliency.
    - Develop and maintain a climate of school safety.
    - Develop written school safety teams/plans.
    - Develop written crisis response plans.
      - Develop effective protection and mitigation strategies for safety and potential psychological trauma for victims.
  - Provide immediate and effective crisis responses.
  - Manage the immediate and long-term needs of the victims in the aftermath of crises.

Additionally, I believe that school safety is primarily an inside job and schools must get a commitment from students first. I implemented student safety pledges in my previous Texas school district where students pledged to report to school adults if someone threatened violence or brought a weapon to campus. I recommended that every classroom provide an activity to help students identify their go-to trusted adult at school and discuss when students must go to that trusted adult to avoid a tragedy.

Importantly, safety plans must outline the ways in which the team will foster a positive school climate, address the social-emotional well-being of school members, and ensure adequate mental health care support for all. Moreover, the team must detail the types of safety efforts and methods that will be used, including agreed-upon prevention and intervention strategies, or specific safety programming used, as well as detailed response methods to various crises. While suicide and violence prevention are the primary focal points of the safety plan, other crises must be considered as well, such as natural disasters and accidental deaths. Many states have school safety centers that provide a wealth of information for schools about safety issues and can offer exact guidance on what to include in your checklist. NASP (2015c) provides complimentary recommendations regarding safety planning. Form 2.3 presents a checklist of these recommendations that are ready for use by you and your team when you are creating your safety plan.

STRENGTHENING AND MAINTAINING SCHOOL SAFETY

Establishing your school's safety and crisis teams, along with their respective plans, is the first major step in ensuring that your school is safe. Safety planning must come with special considerations of *how* safety will be both strengthened and maintained over time. As mentioned, you must address a number of areas, including school climate, social-emotional well-being of the students, and the availability of adequate mental health support. Moreover, your school may consider the use of a formal school safety program. These areas are addressed in more detail below.

How to Create a Climate of Safety

Adequate school safety is not without a positive school climate. It is important that your team works to create a "climate of safety" on your campus. While your needs assessment can point to areas that require attention in terms of school climate, it is important to make an independent assessment of this domain. The U.S. Department of Education (USDOE; 2014, 2019) has published helpful tools that can aid in data collection and analyses of your school's climate (see the Recommended Resources section later in this chapter). Implementation of strategies is completed through use of the USDOE's Safe and Supportive Schools Model (U.S. Department of Education School Climate Surveys [EDSCLS] Measures, n.d.), which targets three domains of school climate: (1) *engagement* (i.e., school participation, relationship, and cultural and linguistic competence), (2) *safety* (i.e., emergency readiness/management, substance abuse, physical and emotional safety, and bullying issues), and (3) *environment* (i.e., physical and instructional environment, physical and mental health, and discipline).

Some of our contributors have highlighted many of these topics in a recent publication, "Fostering the Emotional Well-Being of Our Youth: A School-Based Approach" (Lazarus,

Suldo, & Doll, 2021). Their recommendations mirror those of the USDOE, including the use of a dual-factor conceptualization of youth mental and physical health. Key points for fostering the well-being of students, and thereby enhancing the climate of safety, are summarized in Table 2.3.

Many districts utilize formal programs that offer specific guidance on implementing appropriate steps to enhance your school's climate of safety. Positive behavioral interventions and supports (PBIS; Epperson, 2021), for example, is a widely used, data-driven, three-tier framework that targets behaviors for the entire school population, with the goal of helping students gain the skills necessary for success both in and out of school. The USDOE includes PBIS as a recommended resource for schools to use in conjunction with their model. Unlike most traditional disciplinary approaches, PBIS emphasizes positive behavior interventions, including teaching, modeling, and positive reinforcement for desired behaviors.

TABLE 2.3. Key Points to Fostering the Emotional Well-Being of Students

- Utilize a dual-factor model (i.e., integration of psychopathology and subjective well-being) within a multitiered framework for mental health services that incorporates early interventions and universal approaches.
- Incorporate culturally responsive approaches based on student population.
- Empower socially marginalized students (e.g., immigrant and economically disenfranchised youth).
  - Create programming, supports, and policies that promote well-being for all; target factors that place limitations on rights, privileges, and opportunities for students.
- Utilize the positive behavioral interventions and supports approach.
- Incorporate a trauma-informed approach of social-emotional learning for students.
  - Incorporate self-regulation tools, use of students' positive character building, enhanced sense of purpose, and positive emotions.
- Emphasize resilience and incorporate statewide practices that enhance student well-being.
- Promote healthy lifestyle practices (e.g., good nutrition, sleep, and engagement in exercise)
- Provide support for highly mobile students (e.g., homeless students, those in foster care, and those involved in the juvenile justice system).
- Incorporate screening methods for emotional well-being, academic, and behavioral needs.
- Target the needs of students dealing with depression and anxiety.
- Create increased access to targeted and intensive mental health services.
- Enhance school safety, including the use of school violence prevention measures.
- Foster increased student engagement and relationships.
  - Increase student and staff connectedness.
  - Target socially isolated students.
- Incorporate bullying prevention and intervention methods.
- Enhance preschool, childcare, and parenting practices.
  - Foster emotional well-being and positive behavior via parent engagement within the childcare context.
- Create strong family–school partnerships; enhance family engagement.
- Provide training for trauma-informed practices.
- Prevent school dropout and related academic failure.
  - Develop student competence and decrease behaviors that create barriers to achieving academic success.
- Ensure the provision of evidence-based supports in the aftermath of a crisis.

Note. Based on Lazarus, Suldo, & Doll (2021).

Below you will find more detailed recommendations for best practices in developing and maintaining a climate of safety at your school, along with "Ideas for Consideration" that can be used in everyday practice.

Build Positive and Respectful Relationships between Students and School Personnel

Staff should be encouraged to cultivate more individualized relationships with students, especially those who may be at risk for social rejection and/or isolation. Mentorships can be a valuable preventative strategy, as just one caring adult in a student's life can buffer their risk for future adversity. You and your staff are encouraged to practice and model nonjudgmental communication and an attitude of openness and acceptance.

Fostering positive student–staff relationships can be particularly helpful in the area of prevention. For example, it can aid in breaking any potential "codes of silence" that students may keep with their peers; for example, a student is self-harming and swears a peer to secrecy. If a strong and positive student–staff relationship is in place prior to a student learning of risk-related information, they are more likely to go to a trusted adult at school. Moreover, the established rapport deters worries that the student may be punished for their report, that it won't be taken seriously, or that swift action will not occur to mediate the threat (Bonnano & Levinson, 2014).

It is important to share these details with your staff, as it can enhance their motivation and buy-in to the process. As an SMHP, you can provide helpful psychoeducation materials or training to relay the social-emotional benefits of building strong student bonds as they relate to crisis prevention.

Ideas for Consideration

- **Develop a team-building day with volunteer staff members and students; this can be something like a collaborative field day with teacher and student participation or the use of a ropes-course instructor for integrated classes. You can also incorporate small-group meetings to facilitate opportunities for open communication and relationship development.**
- **Show every student's picture at a staff meeting and ask teachers their name and what they are involved in at school (which is easier to do in a smaller school).**
- **Place all students' names on a board at a staff meeting and have school staff sign up to create a relationship with students. Each teacher should take on a few students so that all students can be covered.**

Increase Connectedness among the Student Body

Case studies from previous acts of school violence, particularly school shootings, have revealed an important factor in school safety: connectedness. For example, research has demonstrated that school shootings are far more common at larger schools in which students are less connected to others and the school itself (Baird, Roellke, & Zeifman, 2016; Poland & Ferguson, 2021a). The larger the school, the less opportunity for connectedness, and the greater the sense of anonymity. Thus, enhancement of social connections and sense of belongingness is critical.

In your efforts to develop a climate of safety, consider ways to create more connectedness among your student body. This procedure will already be under way if you have taken the first step of building more positive and individualized relationships between students and staff. With that in mind, staff should be encouraged to facilitate these opportunities given the overall positive benefits related to crisis prevention.

> **Ideas for Consideration**
>
> - **Survey the students to find potential ideas for new clubs at school. Be creative in your ideas for extracurricular activities that can enhance peer relationships. This approach can also help to target students who may be otherwise disinterested in the common activities offered, for example, football, debate, theater, or chess.**
> - **Encourage group work and be thoughtful about pairings, utilizing a buddy system approach to creating increased connections.**

Openly Disavow Negative Behaviors Such as Bullying, Harassment, and Victimization

School environments where bullying occurs consistently and/or is not addressed by school personnel have significant detrimental effects. These environments can impact academic learning and increase social-emotional risks (i.e., isolation, negative self-esteem, feelings of disconnectedness, hopelessness, anger). Such factors often motivate students to engage in harmful acts against themselves or others. Research has consistently identified bullying as a significant risk factor in youth suicide and in acts of school violence, such as a school shooting (Hinduja & Patchin, 2019; Poland & Ferguson, 2021a).

In light of this research, your school should take a stand against bullying and harassment. It is recommended that your school implement formal antibullying programs. These programs are often helpful in making positive impacts across student culture and peer relationships (Bonnano & Levinson, 2014). See Recommended Resources at the end of the chapter for successful bullying programs that are available for use.

> **Idea for Consideration**
>
> - **Declare your campus a "shame-free zone" (Fein et al., 2002), where such behaviors are neither acceptable nor tolerated. Use visual messaging, such as advertisements on video announcements, posters/flyers, and buttons/ribbons for students and staff to wear.**

How to Enhance the Positive Social-Emotional Well-Being of Students

A climate of school safety is enhanced via the targeted support of positive social-emotional well-being in students of all ages. Increased social-emotional functioning helps students to better understand and regulate their own emotions, demonstrate empathic responses, and develop positive social connections (Berman, Chaffee, & Sarmiento, 2018). These are important protective factors that many students who are at risk for school violence or suicide do not possess. Your school's efforts to develop and support your students' social-emotional functioning will act as an overall prevention method and contribute to a positive school climate.

To date, there has not been a formal investigation on the effectiveness of social-emotional programming in reducing school crises. However, some studies have linked social-emotional programming to enhanced student social skills, emotion regulation, and connection to school (Durlak, Weissberg, Dymnicki, Taylor, & Schellinger, 2011). Moreover, specific program outcomes have demonstrated increases in students' problem-solving skills and impulse control, resulting in more positive connections to their peers and the broader school culture (e.g., *Lesson One: The ABCs of Life* [Oliver & Ryan, 2004]), all of which buffer the risks commonly observed in students who engage in violence to themselves or others.

Ideas for Consideration

- Utilize journal writing to enhance emotional expression and provide prompts that encourage students to reflect on their strengths and challenges in life. These will lead to an exploration of effective and ineffective coping and problem-solving skills. Prompt ideas might include:
    - *What has been the biggest challenge I have faced, and how did I overcome it?*
    - *What is my greatest strength, and how have I used it in life?*
    - *A friend comes to you and says that they have been really struggling; what would you say and do?*
- Encourage positive self-talk; utilize affirmations, and model positive self-esteem.
    - Pass an "affirmation" jar around the room every day; students can pick out a folded paper that has an affirmation printed on it, for example, *"I have the strength to overcome my daily challenges"* or *"I am worthy of the good things that come to me."*

How to Address Access to Adequate Mental Health Support at School

Among the many sections of your safety plan and relatedly, your crisis prevention efforts, the topic of mental health support remains one of the most, if not *the* most, important domain. A wealth of research has been done to provide evidence of the significant impact that the provision of adequate mental health support can have on student violence. Sandra Jo Wilson and Mark Lipsey of the Peabody Research Institute at Vanderbilt University (2007), for example, completed a large-scale meta-analysis on the effect of psychological intervention and student behavior.

Their findings pointed to a number of counseling program approaches (e.g., universal, individual, computer-based) and other psychological interventions (e.g., social skills training, cognitive-behavioral approaches) that have resulted in moderate to strong effects in improving student behavior and reducing student aggression. The most common and most effective approaches were found to be universal programs that were provided to all students in a classroom or school and targeted programs for selected/indicated students who engage in programs outside of their regular classrooms (Wilson & Lipsey, 2007).

As mentioned, it is imperative that you obtain the consistent involvement of SMHPs in safety planning and crisis preparedness. This recommendation is also important in the broader context of supporting mental health adequately across the student body. In order to do so, SMHPs must be regularly available to provide consultation, staff training, psychological and social-emotional student support, and necessary assessments (risk, safety, abuse).

Moreover, these professionals have an integral role in the development and implementation of social-emotional programs, prevention programs, and crisis responses, such as threat assessment procedures. Students who are at risk for violence often share common issues such as mental health concerns, suicidal ideation, and bullying/harassment victimization. Without appropriate mental health services in their reach, students with such risk factors often go unnoticed and untreated, resulting in potentially devastating consequences.

NASP (2022b) recommends a 500-to-1 ratio of students to school psychologists, while the American School Counselor Association (ASCA; 2022) recommends a 250-to-1 ratio of students to school counselors. The Violence Project (n.d.), a well-known nonprofit, nonpartisan research center dedicated to violence prevention and intervention, indicates that in actuality, the national average is 1,500 to 1 and 450 to 1, respectively. This stark reality points to the very significant need for increased SMHPs in our school system.

The availability of mental health services to students is a critical component of school safety, positive school climate, and overall crisis prevention. Students who are at risk for violence often share common issues such as mental health concerns, suicidal ideation, and victimization through bullying/harassment. Without appropriate mental health services in their reach, students with such risk factors often go unnoticed and untreated, resulting in potentially devastating consequences. In my experience, many SMHPs are bogged down with administrative duties and psychoeducation/eligibility testing. Students often view them as inaccessible. I recall asking my own daughter if she would go to her high school counselor if she had a personal problem, and her answer was "No, but I would go to her if I needed to get out of an AP class."

Ideas for Consideration

- **Advocate to have a portion of your schedule dedicated to outreach with the students. Outreach ideas might include:**
  - **Creating a mental health awareness club**
  - **Tabling during lunch or dismissal; offering information about suicide prevention and free healthy snacks**
  - **Participating in local fundraisers, for example, 5k races, where students can join as teams**

How to Choose a School Safety Program for Your School

The use of specific school safety programs is a helpful way to ensure that your school is implementing best practices. Schools across the nation have begun to use a variety of different school safety programs. These programs generally aim to target the areas discussed thus far, with an emphasis on building a positive and safe school environment. Some programs offer detailed manuals and toolkits, while others include more extensive training and hands-on collaboration.

At the time of this publication, there are no federal mandates regarding the use of specific safety planning programs. As a result, the use of such programs is left in the hands of school districts. Safety planning programming should be chosen with care; it is important that you review their goals, methods, and any associated research they may have published. Programs that implement best practices often craft their approaches under the guidance of evidence-based research. See the Recommended Resources section for examples of quality school safety programs that are used throughout the country. Components of successful school safety programs are outlined in Table 2.4.

Across these programs, one common thread is the incorporation of student involvement. This is a logical addition to safety planning because students can play a critical factor in preventing school violence. Moreover, student involvement creates an opportunity for increased student connectedness among peers and school staff. Your school is therefore encouraged to involve

TABLE 2.4. Successful School Safety Programs

- Raise awareness of safety concerns at your school.
- Incorporate school members and students.
  - Enhance their involvement and responsibility in prevention of school crises.
- Utilize a multidisciplinary approach that facilitates community collaborations.
- Provide guidelines for school safety that applies to all school members as it relates to crisis prevention, response, and postvention.
- Utilize evidence-based methods.
- Target the social-emotional and mental health needs of school members.

your students in the safety planning and prevention processes. Recall my suggestion regarding the use of student pledges.

Ideas for Consideration

- Involve your students in creative ways.
  - Create student safety task forces.
  - Elect student officials to serve as school safety representatives.
  - Develop and use student safety pledges.

PRACTICE AND UPDATE

Once your team has completed the appropriate crisis planning, the next step is to ensure that your processes and plans will work. Planning alone is not sufficient in crisis intervention, and it is imperative that your team outline procedures for how they can practice the crisis plans. Practice will allow your school to determine the strengths and weaknesses of your crisis planning and ensure that it is well matched to the current needs of your school. Importantly, it can bring to light any gaps or missed areas of planning that must be addressed. These findings will highlight areas of your crisis plan that require updating. Practice runs should occur on an annual basis, and planning sessions, which include a review of the practice run and how the team will address the needed updates, should be held afterward. Questions to explore might relate to concerns about adding more staff or incorporating additional prevention programming.

The discussed planning sessions should also be held in the aftermath of any serious crises that have occurred and that require the use of your crisis plan. These sessions are typically referred to as "debriefings." After your crisis plan has been enacted, debriefings will be held, as part of a critical process that ensures your school is well equipped to better handle future crises. These issues are discussed in further detail in later chapters in this book as they relate to individual crises and in Chapter 8's review of aftermath procedures.

Idea for Consideration

- NASP (2013) advises the use of "Tabletop Drills" in the planning and preparation process. These drills allow your team members to run through various crisis scenarios in order to brainstorm the best ways to handle the myriad of issues (e.g., how to handle the media, how to get information to parents/families quickly) that might arise. While these drills are typically used to target larger-scale crises (e.g., school shootings), they can be

> **helpful in addressing a variety of crises (e.g., robbery at a nearby bank, death on campus of a beloved teacher). Tabletop Drills are discussed further in the "Crisis Drills" section presented later in this chapter.**

Recommended Resources: School Crisis Preparedness and Prevention

- **Bullying: NASP's (2021a) Bullying Resources:** Found at *www.nasponline.org/resources-and-publications/resources-and-podcasts/school-safety-and-crisis/school-violence-resources/bullying-prevention.*
  - *A Framework for School Wide Bullying Prevention and Safety:* A publication for specific guidelines for best practices on implementing formal antibullying programs in your school.
  - *Bullying and Youth Suicide: Breaking the Connection:* A thoughtful article on the connection between bullying and youth suicide that includes guidance for best practices on how school staff can prevent and intervene at this intersection of concern.
  - *Cyberbullying: Prevention and Intervention Strategies:* Best practices for how school teams can address issues of cyberbullying and their impact on the student body.
  - *Preventing Bullying: Guidelines for Administrators and Crisis Teams:* Helpful guidance on how to incorporate bullying prevention in your crisis plans and enhance a school climate of safety.
  - *Supporting Victims and Perpetrators of Bullying Guidelines for Parents and Educators:* Guidelines for caregivers, families, and school staff on how they can appropriately intervene and provide support to those involved in harassment at school.
- **National Center on Safe Supportive Learning Environments, School Climate Improvement Resource Package Assessments, and school climate data collection tools:** Helpful tools for surveying your school climate and gathering information for your needs assessment. Found at *https://safesupportivelearning.ed.gov/edscls/measures#Topic%20Areas%20the%20EDSCLS%20Measures.*
- **U.S. Department of Education, *Guiding Principles: A Resource Guide for Improving School Climate and Discipline* (2014):** Offers evidence-based policies, practices, and programs that will help your team to create safe, inclusive, supportive, and fair learning environments to aid in your student body's growth and success. Found at *www2.ed.gov/policy/gen/guid/school-discipline/guiding-principles.pdf.*
- **U.S. Department of Education, *Parent and Educator Guide to School Climate Resources* (2019):** Offers general information about school climate improvement, recommendations for leading an effective school climate improvement effort, and a number of helpful resources. Found at *www2.ed.gov/policy/elsec/leg/essa/essaguidetoschoolclimate041019.pdf.*
- **School Safety Programs**
  - *Make Our Schools Safe (2018):* An organization founded by Lori Alhadeff, the mother of Alyssa Alhadeff, who was killed in the Marjory Stoneman Douglas (MSD) shooting. Its mission is to empower students and staff to help create and maintain a culture of safety and vigilance in a secure school environment. Found at *https://makeourschoolssafe.org.*
  - *Safe and Sound Institute:* A program that offers regional workshops, training, and national

school safety experts to help members of the community become more engaged in improving school safety. Found at *https://safeandsoundschools.org/safe-and-sound-institute.*

- *Safe and Sound Schools (2015):* A nonprofit organization founded by Michele Gay and Alissa Parker, two mothers who tragically lost their daughters in the Sandy Hook shooting. This tragedy inspired the Safe and Sound School Initiative in which Michele and Alissa have dedicated their efforts to provide communities with valuable resources to improve school safety. Their "Straight A School Safety Model" provides a number of recommendations and activities in the form of safety toolkits that outline the guidelines on maintaining school safety. Found at *www.safeandsoundschools.org.*
- *SchoolSafety.gov:* Created by the federal government to provide schools and their districts with actionable recommendations to create a safe and supportive learning environment where students can thrive and grow. Found at *www.schoolsafety.gov.*
- *Striving to Reduce Youth Violence Everywhere* (STRYVE; CDC, 2021): A national youth violence prevention program, founded by the CDC, that fosters youth safety and well-being through collaboration with community and organizational resources and encourages the development of positive relationships with supporting adults within the community. Found at *www.cdc.gov/violenceprevention/youthviolence/stryve/index.html.*
- *Students Against Violence Everywhere (SAVE) Promise Club:* A collaboration with National SAVE and Sandy Hook Promise (2022), its aim is to empower student leaders to take an active role in increasing school safety and preventing different forms of violence in schools and communities. Found at *www.sandyhookpromise.org/our-programs/save-promise-club.*

PREVENTION EFFORTS

> My greatest hope is the next generation of adult Americans will know how to prevent suicide.
>
> —PHILIP LAZARUS

> The best intervention plan is prevention.
>
> —SCOTT POLAND

Getting ahead of a crisis is best achieved through the use of well-researched preventative efforts. As discussed, these approaches will be detailed in your safety plan and will emphasize suicide and school violence prevention methods. Below you will find a discussion of the ways in which your school can work to reduce school-related violence, suicidal behavior, and deaths by suicide. These efforts will help to enhance a positive climate of safety in your school.

> Schools need to provide risk screening at school for early identification of risk for suicide, depression, violence, and other self-harm. These can supplement a foundation of supporting resilience, connectedness, positive behavior, and school climate.
>
> —CATHY KENNEDY-PAINE

Suicide Prevention

Suicide prevention in the school context is one of the most critical aspects of broader crisis intervention. It is well established that there are rising trends in youth suicidal behavior (Poland & Ferguson, 2021b). Moreover, the most recent Youth Risk Behavior Surveillance System (CDC, 2023) data has confirmed that these rates continue to grow and were likely exacerbated as a result of the COVID-19 pandemic. Of the limited data available at the time of this publication, it appears that pediatric emergency departments across the nation are observing increased rates of hospital admissions related to suicidal ideation and/or behaviors (Hill et al., 2021; Ridout et al., 2021).

Among school crisis concerns, suicide is one of *the most* preventable. Proper suicide prevention strategies can be a tool that makes the difference between the life and death of students. Suicide prevention begins with an understanding of common protective and risk factors and warning signs of youth suicide. *Risk factors* are specific characteristics, history, and circumstances that increase one's statistical risk for suicide. *Protective factors*, on the other hand, are the aforementioned specifics that decrease one's statistical risk for suicide. Warning signs are considered visible signs that are noticeable to peers, teachers, and loved ones. All staff should acquaint themselves with this information and can help to prevent suicide by (1) recognizing the risk, (2) weighing the protective factors, (3) taking the signs seriously, and (4) knowing how to respond to them (Erbacher et al., 2015). Table 2.5 outlines these factors.

The school setting is the ideal locale for suicide prevention, as youth spend nearly half of the total days of the year in school. Research has found that school is a significant influencer in the behavior and health of young people (Evans & Hurrell, 2016). Moreover, the school's access to resources (e.g., SMHPs) and community partners (e.g., nonprofit agencies) create opportunities for prevention that would be otherwise difficult to implement in other settings.

Much like school safety programs, a number of school-based suicide prevention programs are used nationwide. The use of a program can be a helpful way to eliminate some of the heavy lifting involved in the development of curriculum or strategies. The American Foundation for Suicide Prevention (AFSP; 2019) outlines four evidence-based frameworks for suicide prevention: gatekeeping (i.e., training those considered to be natural helpers to recognize signs and symptoms of suicide [Katz et al., 2013]); psychoeducation; restriction to access of lethal means; and provision of mental health treatment to at-risk students (Lieberman, Poland, & Kornfeld, 2014).

These recommendations are further supported by research, as highlighted in Cooper, Clements, and Holt's (2011) systematic review of high school–based suicide prevention programs in the United States. Results revealed that a hybrid prevention approach was the most effective. Cooper and colleagues recommended using prevention methods that include the following elements: curriculum base, enhancement of protective factors, use of screening tools, and incorporation of gatekeeper trainings.

There is little evidence to prove that these approaches are effective as stand-alone programs. As such, you are encouraged to create a suicide prevention approach that is designed with a combination of these recommendations. Moreover, you must decide whether to take a universal (i.e., those that target an entire population vs. selected individuals/populations) or individual approach. Currently, a large number of school prevention approaches emphasize the universal approach because it casts a broader net of psychoeducation and awareness.

TABLE 2.5. Protective and Risk Factors and Warning Signs of Suicide

Protective factors

- Life skills
  - Strong coping and problem-solving skills, enhanced impulse control, adaptability in times of change
- Positive self-worth and a sense of purpose in life
- Social connectedness and supports
- Strong connections to school, including extracurricular participation
- Academic success
- Family cohesion, acceptance, and stability
- Religious, spiritual, and/or cultural beliefs
- Ability to think flexibly
- Access to quality mental health care services
- Restricted access to lethal means
- Resiliency
- Internal locus of control (i.e., sense of being able to take control and make change in your life)

Risk factors

- Mental illness
  - Increased risk comes with depressive and substance use disorders
  - History of self-harm behaviors
- Previous suicide attempt
- Contagion effect
  - Exposure to suicidal behavior/attempts/completion of others
    - Known to the youth or figures in the public eye (e.g., celebrities)
- Intrapersonal factors
  - Difficulties with emotion regulation—mood variations and impulsivity
  - Limited problem-solving and coping skills
  - Poor self-esteem
  - Low sense of self-efficacy
  - Anger and aggressive behaviors
  - Affectional orientation—LGBTQ+ youth are at an increased risk for suicide and bullying
  - Ethnicity—Native American/Alaskan Natives are at an increased risk for suicide (Bilsen, 2018)
- Interpersonal factors
  - Limited social support, increased social isolation
  - Exposure to bullying and harassment
- Familial factors
  - Familial history of mental illness, especially depression
  - Living with a family member with mental illness
  - Conflictual environments
  - Exposure to neglect and abuse
  - Parental rejection—especially true for LGBTQ+ youth
- Specific life events
  - Break-ups
  - Divorcing parents
  - Peer conflict
  - Death of a loved one
  - School/academic stressors
  - Disciplinary trouble
  - Exposure to abuse

(continued)

TABLE 2.5. *(continued)*

- Access to lethal means
  - Living in the home with firearms, especially those that are not safely stored
  - Access to large amounts of medication

Warning signs

- Social withdrawal; increased isolation or distance from friends/peers
- Depressive and anxious symptoms; these can manifest as:
  - Irritability, sadness, sleep disturbances, tension, agitation, difficulties with concentration, low mood, limited motivation
- Loss of interest in activities once enjoyed or found pleasurable
- Making suicide/death references in conversation, jokes, or written assignments
- Self-defeating statements such as "I should be dead"
- Suicidal threats, notes, plans
- Researching lethal means; making plans to access such means
- Hopelessness about the future; feeling trapped
- Feeling helpless or worthless; poor self-esteem
- Preoccupation with suicide/death (e.g., comics, movies, music, literature)
- Increased emotion dysregulation (e.g., anger, aggression, hostility)
- Truancy
- Increased engagement in risky behaviors (e.g., drugs, alcohol, sex)
- Increased impulsiveness
- Recent loss (e.g., peer death) or intrapersonal struggle (e.g., being embarrassed or feeling humiliated)
- Marked changes in behaviors
- Giving away personal items (Erbacher et al., 2015).

Suicide Prevention Strategies

CURRICULUM-BASED. These strategies emphasize the importance of addressing mental health factors, including the use of training materials that educate school personnel on suicidality and at-risk youth.

- The main emphasis is on providing evidence-based psychoeducation and increased awareness regarding suicide via school curriculum.
- Many of these programs incorporate other methods, including screenings and enhancement of protective factors.

Recommended Resource: Curriculum-Based Strategies

- **Signs of Suicide** (SOS; Mindwise Interventions, 2019): Evidence-based, well supported nationally. This program includes curriculum, screening, and gatekeeper training, with an emphasis on (1) heightened awareness of risk factors/warning signs via psychoeducation, (2) a self-report measure that screens for the presence of depression and suicide risk, and (3) student gatekeeper training (Lieberman et al., 2014; Mindwise Interventions, 2019). Found at *www.mindwise.org/what-we-offer/suicide-prevention-programs.*

ENHANCED PROTECTIVE FACTORS. These factors aim to identify problem-solving skills, the means to adaptively cope, and the promotion of developmentally appropriate mental health.

- Utilize strategies that emphasize self-esteem and social support, two critical protective factors that buffer the risk of suicide.
- Incorporate peer-leadership programs that aim to enact changes from within the student population. Students are taught how to respond appropriately to a friend's report of suicidal thoughts, including when to seek a trusted adult. A key goal is to create positive coping norms within the school setting and a culture of prosocial and help-seeking behaviors (Wyman et al., 2010).

Recommended Resources: Enhancing Protective Factors

- **HOPE Squad (2018):** A "peer-to-peer"-based program that partners with local community and mental health agencies to train students to be empowered to take action to prevent suicide. Found at *https://hopesquad.com.*
- **Sources of Strength (n.d.):** Student leaders are recruited through nominations and are trained to model and encourage other peers to "(1) name and engage 'trusted adults' to increase youth–adult communication ties; (2) reinforce and create an expectancy that friends ask adults for help for suicidal friends, thereby reducing implicit suicide acceptability; and (3) identify and use interpersonal and formal coping resources" (Sources of Strength, n.d.; Wyman et al., 2010). Found at *https://sourcesofstrength.org.*

SCREENING TOOLS. These are used to gain objective measures of student self-report of suicidality and related risk factors, that is, depression and bullying. Screeners are an easy way to identify at-risk students and to keep a finger on the pulse of the school culture of safety.

- Implement a quarterly schoolwide screening procedure in which those who are found to be at increased risk are referred for treatment. Given the fluctuating nature of mental illness, it is important to have multiple screenings in order to best capture student reports.
- Utilize measures that examine specific risk factors (e.g., substance use, bullying, depression, past suicidal behaviors) and those that target suicidality directly (e.g., current suicidal ideation).
- It is critical to ensure the availability of adequate referral sources prior to screening.

Recommended Measures for Risk Assessment

- Schools are encouraged to survey students about the school climate and the prevalence of bullying. SchoolSafety.gov is a collaborative, interagency website created by the federal government that offers great resources for selecting a survey. Found at *www.schoolsafety.gov/bullying-and-cyberbullying.*
  - Schools must determine the locations where bullying occurs the most. A practical approach is to provide a floor plan to students and ask them to shade in the areas where they do not

feel safe and where bullying occurs frequently. This simple activity will identify where schools need more adult supervision.

- Brief Suicide Risk Assessment Questionnaire (Miller & McConaughy, 2005)
- The Columbia Suicide Severity Rating Scale (CSSRS; Posner et al., 2009)
- The Hopelessness Scale for Children (Kazdin, Rodgers, & Colbus, 1986)
- MAPS: Measure for Adolescent Potential for Suicide (MAPS; Eggert, Thompson, & Herting, 1994)
- Reynolds Adolescent Depression Scale—Second Edition (RADS-2; Osman, Gutierrez, Bagge, Fang, & Emmerich, 2010)
- Suicide Risk Screen (SRS)
- Suicidal Ideation Questionnaire (SIQ)

GATEKEEPING TRAINING. Through use of this training approach, school personnel and sometimes peers (i.e., gatekeepers) gain skills and knowledge related to identifying and responding to suicidal behavior in the school environment.

- Often combined with curriculum-based programs.
- Helps gatekeepers to improve their knowledge, attitudes, intervention skills, preparation for coping with a crisis, and referral practices.

Recommended Resources: Gatekeeping Training

- **LivingWorks:** A mission-driven organization to enhance suicidal awareness and prevention. Found at *https://www.livingworks.net.*
- **Yellow Ribbon International for Suicide Prevention (2021):** Dedicated to preventing suicide and attempted suicide by making suicide prevention accessible to everyone and removing barriers to help. Found at *https://yellowribbon.org.*

Recommended Resources: Suicide Prevention

- **USDOE National School Safety Center (NSSC; 2010):** Serves as an advocate for safe, secure, and peaceful schools worldwide and as an agent for the prevention of school crime and violence. NSSC provides school communities and their school safety partners with quality information, resources, consultation, and training services. NSSC identifies and promotes strategies, promising practices and programs that support safe schools for all students as part of the total academic mission. Found at *www.schoolsafety.us.*
- **Model School District Policy on Suicide Prevention: Model Language, Commentary, and Resources (2021):** The Trevor Project in partnership with AFSP, NASP, and ASCA developed a Model School District Policy for Suicide Prevention and I served as a reviewer. Found at *https://afsp.org/our-work/education/model-school-policy-suicide-prevention.*
- **Preventing Suicide: A Toolkit for High Schools (2012):** Created by the Substance Abuse and Mental Health Services Administration, this resource provides a plan for schools on how to

educate their personnel, students, and parents/caregivers on youth suicide and related behaviors. The toolkit targets the identification of at-risk youth and the use of appropriate protocols for these students. Additionally, it outlines suggestions for evidence-based suicide prevention programs that are well matched for the school setting. Found at *https://store.samhsa.gov/product/Preventing-Suicide-A-Toolkit-for-High-Schools/SMA12-4669*.

Prevention of School Violence

In the last 30 years, schools have made significant efforts to enhance school violence prevention. The occurrence of deadly school shootings and the related media exposure have fueled community members, school districts, and policymakers to enact changes to target school violence. The majority of efforts thus far have emphasized increasing and strengthening school safety. A number of studies (see Bonanno & Levinson, 2014; Curran, Fisher, & Viano, 2020; Jonson, 2017) have analyzed these methods, and their findings have pointed to a variety of recommendations, many of which continue to be debated today. The following section provides direction on the key best practices for how you can help to prevent violence in your school.

Threat Assessment

A core method for preventing school violence is threat assessment. Since the early 2000s, use of this method in the school setting has been recommended by prominent government agencies, including the U.S. Secret Service, USDOE, and the Federal Bureau of Investigations (FBI). Within the school context, threat assessment is used as a problem-solving approach in which assessment and intervention are conducted with students who have made threats of violence. The assessment process can guide school personnel in determining whether a student has made a threat or *poses* as a threat (i.e., has the intent and/or means to carry out the threat), as well as the level of the threat in terms of risk/danger (Butkus, 2020; NASP, 2015f).

The primary goal of threat assessment is to maintain ongoing school safety. It is recommended that specific preventive efforts be made to target potentially disenfranchised students, who are likely experiencing limited academic success and chronic feelings of anger, despair, disconnectedness, and hopelessness. Forensic clinical psychologist and leading expert in threat assessment Dr. Dewey Cornell notes that when applied in the school context, threat assessment must expand beyond the identification and management of threats of violence. Best practices should aim to mitigate and potentially resolve common intrapersonal and interpersonal issues that typically contribute to the escalation of violent acts. In this regard, threat assessments may be more appropriately thought of as "safety assessment and intervention" or "behavioral assessment and intervention" (Cornell, 2020).

Threat assessments have been an essential part of school violence prevention, particularly in the realm of school shootings. Analyses of school shooters have demonstrated that most students reveal concerning behavioral signs prior to the attacks. Moreover, it is well documented that these students will often share their plans with others. There have been several cases in which peers aided (indirectly or directly) in the act of violence. This information, often referred to as "leakage" (Langman, 2009), highlights that critical warning signs can be detected ahead of a school shooting, revealing an important window of prevention (see Table 2.6).

TABLE 2.6. Common Acts of Peer Involvement

- Offering encouragement to the attacker
- Engaging in joking banter about potential attacks
- Liking or sharing online content/social media posts about potential attacks
- Assisting in developing the attack plans
- Obtaining weapons/means for the attacker

One important consideration regarding threat assessment is that this process differs from student profiling. Unlike student profiling, threat assessment is initiated due to a student's own concerning behaviors (i.e., making threats) rather than because of a broad set of common traits of a student (i.e., gender, race/ethnicity, home dynamics). Threat assessment efforts should be focused on reviewing a student's behaviors to determine if they pose a threat, rather than attempting to match them to specific student profiles (Borum, Cornell, Modzeleski, & Jimerson, 2010; O'Toole, 2000).

Threat Assessment Implementation at Your School

In order to implement successful school-based threat assessments, policies and procedures must be developed and put into place in advance. A threat assessment team must be created with a diverse membership. Cornell (2020) recommends that schools build internal teams, rather than utilize external resources. Internal teams are able to respond to and monitor threats with greater ease and more immediacy. In cases in which serious threats of violence have occurred, it is recommended that internal teams collaborate with central administration and district-level consultants. Table 2.7 outlines a sample of a threat assessment team structure.

Why diversify your threat assessment team? A multidisciplinary threat assessment team offers a number of advantages. Most importantly, it aids in creating an accurate and fair evalua-

TABLE 2.7 Your Threat Assessment Team

- Administration team
  - Principals
  - Vice-principals
- School personnel
  - Teachers
  - Teaching assistants
- Mental health professionals
  - School psychologists
  - Social workers
  - School counselors
  - Guidance counselors
- Security
  - School resource officer (SRO)
  - Local law enforcement members

Student Threat Is Learned

↓

Ensure safety

Background Information Is Gathered

Interviews with Collateral

Investigation of Social Media

↓

Suspected Student Is Interviewed

Emphasis on Motive, Planning, Access to a Weapon

Determine Threat Level: Transient or Substantial?

↓

Actions Taken to Mitigate Threat

Address Psychological, Social, and Ecological Factors

Parental/Caregiver Notification

Referral to Resources/Supports

Disciplinary Procedures (if warranted)

↓

Resolution of Threat

Ongoing Monitoring of Student at Risk

FIGURE 2.1. Steps of threat assessment.

tion of and appropriate response to student threats of violence. Moreover, members will contribute varied skills and roles that will provide necessary resources and services that target factors and stressors that typically precede threats. Lastly, the use of a diverse threat assessment team will enhance current school safety procedures, instill confidence in students that their needs will be met, and increase the overall safety of the school environment. Figure 2.1 displays an overview of the steps for threat assessment implementation. The details of this process are subsequently reviewed.

Threat Assessment Team: Steps for Implementation

1. ***The team identifies a student threat to commit a violent act.***
2. ***Interviews with the student who made the threat and with other collateral (i.e., the person who reported the threat, other witnesses) are completed in order to gather details and pertinent information about the threat.***

Once a threat is identified, the team must gather information to determine the seriousness of the threat. Documentation is critical in this process, and it is recommended that the team obtain as much detailed information as possible, including a verbatim record of the threat made, the context in which it was made, and any events leading up to the threat, along with the motivation and intention behind the threat (Cornell, 2018b). All the people involved should be interviewed to ensure that the team develops a comprehensive understanding of the threat made.

3. ***An appropriate team member (SMHP, social worker, school psychologist) provides a psychosocial evaluation and risk assessment of the student.***

It is important to gain an understanding of the social-emotional and psychological factors that have contributed to the threatening behaviors. An appropriate member of the team should conduct a psychosocial evaluation and risk assessment. The assessment should include an exploration of the student's potential risk factors, current mental state, and stressors (i.e., recent interpersonal conflict), familial support and dynamics, along with any protective factors and coping methods (refer back to Table 2.5 for a list of risk and protective factors).

The use of structured protocols is recommended, including risk assessment measures, such as the Structured Assessment of Violence Risk in Youth (SAVRY; Borum, Bartel, & Forth, 2005). These measures assess for the presence of important risk and protective factors in a number of domains (i.e., social/contextual, clinical/individual) and provide helpful information to better understand the potential origins and contributors to the student's distress and the related threat. The evaluation process is an essential component of the threat assessment, as it provides the information necessary to inform your next steps, including the need for additional mental health intervention for the student (Poland & Ferguson, 2021a).

4. ***The team determines the seriousness of the threat: is it transient or substantial?***

Effective threat assessment emphasizes an approach that carefully evaluates the reasonableness and sincerity of the threat, along with the student's perceived ability to carry out the threat (O'Toole, 2000). Your threat assessment team must evaluate the level of the reported threat and consider if it is transient or substantial.

- *Transient:* short-lived, reactive, emotion-driven, "in the heat of the moment." Transient threats are not well thought out, and they often lack specificity (i.e., actual details of the plan, methods, victims). If details are provided, they typically are inconsistent or implausible (e.g., brainwashing all of the teachers to drink poison).
- *Substantial:* premeditated with specific details, realistic means and methods, and explicit intention of severe and imminent harm to others. Substantial threats are considered more serious events because they usually include specific details (methods, time, and place of the attack), along with realistic means and methods to carry out the plan. These types of threats indicate that the student has spent a considerable amount of time thinking about and planning for the attack, and they suggest imminent danger for others.

PROFESSIONAL PERSPECTIVE: SCOTT POLAND

Threat Levels

In the realm of threats, my mind goes to a 2017 case, *Wilk v. St. Vrain Valley School District*, in which I served as an expert on the side of the plaintiff. This case involved two high school students, Sean and Erik, who bragged to peers about violent interests. The following information is recalled from my time working as an expert in this case. I remember that the threat was reported to the administration and was taken seriously, with police notified. Sean denied that he would ever hurt anyone; however, he alleged that Erik was actually planning something serious. Local police interviewed both students separately. Erik denied ever saying anything about school violence and remarked, "I do not know why my friend Sean threw me under the bus." Sean recanted his story and said he was joking about Erik planning violence.

The police searched Erik's home and found no working weapons, only replicas. His Facebook page had over 200 photos, a few of which had violent themes, and he was pictured with reenactment rifles. School records indicated a few minor discipline reports years ago. He had reportedly turned in several papers about Nazism and had received good grades on them. Erik liked to draw, and his drawings often had violent themes. Additionally, he reportedly enjoyed fictional books about serial killers. On the positive side, Erik was almost an Eagle Scout. The police concluded their extensive investigation, which included a thorough search of Erik's home and computer. There were no working firearms, no identifiable grudge or anger toward the school, no evidence of planning a shooting, no hit list, and no social media posts about a school shooting.

The police determined that a threat by Erik was unfounded. At this point, however, the school convened its own threat assessment team composed of the principal, teachers, and the safety director. A counselor was not included on the team. In an interview only with the principal, Erik repeated that he did not make the threat and provided a written statement that he did not make a threat. The principal did not share the results of the police investigation with the team, nor did he share the written statement of denial from Erik or the fact that Sean recanted his statement. The counselor who knew Erik and had talked with him on several occasions was not included in the threat assessment. The school recommended expulsion and did not put any emphasis on a private evaluation obtained by his parents that had concluded Erik was very low risk for violent behavior.

The expulsion resulted in a civil suit in which the court concluded that the district had reason to fear school violence and acted reasonably in expelling the student (*Wilk v. St. Vrain Valley School District*, 2017). The court ruled on the issue of "qualified immunity," which provides protection for government employees in cases of liability. Specifically, it protects a government employee's discretionary actions taken in their public position from suits against them as individuals. The doctrine specifies that liability can be imposed only if procedures have violated constitutional law (Sherman, 2022). In this case, the court held that the evidence did not prove that the St. Vrain Valley School District violated constitutional law (*Wilke v. St. Vrain Valley School District*, 2017).

Upon reflection, I understand the importance of keeping all students safe but am disappointed that a student was expelled for a threat that, if it was ever even made, was a transient threat and not a substantial one. My experience has been that schools often overreact to threats that do not involve a weapon, planning, or an identified grudge.

5. ***The team considers key questions*** **(Borum et al., 2010).**
   - What are the students' motives and intentions?
   - Have there been any communications that indicate any ideas or plans to attack?
   - Has the student shown inappropriate interest in any of the following:
     - School attacks or related perpetrators?
     - Weapons (including recent procurement of any relevant weapon)?
     - Incidents of mass violence (terrorism, workplace violence, mass murders)?
   - Has the student engaged in attack-related or violent behaviors in the past?
   - Does the student have the means to carry out an act of targeted violence?
   - Is the student experiencing hopelessness, desperation, and/or despair?

- Does the student have a trusting relationship with at least one responsible adult?
    - Does the student see violence as an acceptable—or desirable—or the only—way to solve problems?
    - Is the student's conversation and "story" consistent with their actions?
    - Are other people concerned about the student's potential for violence?
    - Which circumstances might affect the likelihood of an attack?

6. ***The team develops a comprehensive understanding of the level of seriousness and the risk factors involved; this informs an appropriate response and safety plan.***

The team's plan of action will vary based on the threat, the level of harm it poses, and any other psychosocial factors involved. Transient threats will likely only require the provision of mental health resources and additional support at the school. Should the team determine that a substantial threat is at play, they must enact a more heightened response, including serious disciplinary actions, such as suspension or expulsion, or the involvement of law enforcement. If a criminal offense has been committed, law enforcement may enact a criminal investigation and pursue legal action against the presumed offender(s). In these cases, the team should ensure that their role is made clear and differentiated from those of law enforcement (Cornell, 2018b).

7. ***The team develops interventions and safety plans that seek to protect potential victims and target the underlying problem(s) that triggered the threatening behavior.***

The team must work to create intervention and safety plans that simultaneously aim to protect potential victims and target the underlying problem(s) that triggered the threatening behavior. Interventions should be chosen with care and tailored to the needs of the student, their family, and the community. The team's approaches must target the observed psychological, social, and ecological factors that have contributed to the student's threats of violence.

The team should provide guidance on whether the student(s) may return to school or whether they need to recommend alternative education placement. Should the team determine that the student(s) may return to school, the plan must outline conditions that will be met and show how these conditions will be monitored to ensure everyone's safety.

8. ***The team implements these interventions and safety plans and monitors their effectiveness over time.***

Recommended interventions include safety planning, parent education, and ongoing, consistent, and culturally sensitive mental health services. These interventions can be offered in the form of academic and social-emotional support, skills training (i.e., interpersonal, anger management), and mentoring programs. Intervention plans should also incorporate community services, including extracurricular groups such as recreational sports teams or mentoring programs.

Ultimately, the overarching goals of threat assessment are to keep schools safe and to help potential perpetrators address the underlying sources of their anger, despair, or hopelessness. Effective threat assessment will equip your school with critical information about a student's risks and personal resources. Additional student risks that can be identified and prevented are suicide, alcohol and drug use, physical abuse, criminal activity, and dropping out/truancy. Additionally, several other positive outcomes are associated with the use of threat assessment, including a reduction in bullying, perceptions of a more positive and supportive school climate, greater willingness to seek help, and fewer long-term suspensions (NASP, 2015f). These findings highlight the fact that your use of threat assessment can create a valuable opportunity to identify students at risk for a variety of mental health problems and guide appropriate interventions and supports.

Recommended Resources: Threat Assessment

- **Comprehensive School Threat Assessment Guidelines (CSTAG; Cornell, 2018a):** An evidence-based model for schools to use in conducting threat assessments in K–12 schools. Found at *www.schoolta.com/manual.*
- **NASP's Threat Assessment at School Handouts (2015f):** Provides helpful guidelines for school staff members on how to navigate threats of violence and complete threat assessment procedures. A variety of topics are covered (see below). Found at *www.nasponline.org/resources-and-publications/resources-and-podcasts/school-climate-safety-and-crisis/systems-level-prevention/threat-assessment-at-school/threat-assessment-for-school-administrators-and-crisis-teams.*
    - *Behavior Threat Assessment and Management in the Virtual Environment*
    - *Brief Tips and Facts*
    - *Protecting Students' Rights in Behavior Threat Assessment*
    - *Responding to Students Who Threaten Violence: Helping Handout for the School*

Crisis Drills

Crisis drill exercises as a means of prevention and preparedness have been used in schools for several decades. They are a recommended practice for school safety; however, it is imperative that your crisis drills are implemented in a thoughtful and careful manner, in which the psychological and emotional well-being of students and staff are heavily considered. Crisis drill types can vary from targeting natural disaster responses, for example, fire or tornado drills, to violent occurrences, such as an active shooter. Despite the relatively low risk of school violence, the gravity of its potential implications has prompted ongoing efforts for preparation. Our recommendations for crisis-based exercises and drills, along with the appropriateness of their implementation, align with those provided by NASP (2013).

1. *Orientations.* The crisis team leader and administrative team should facilitate a discussion with staff members regarding the school safety and crisis response procedures. You might coordinate this during a staff meeting and you should offer materials, such as handouts or PowerPoint slides. The following details should be reviewed: your school's emergency response procedures, crisis response coordination, member roles and responsibilities, and any resources that may be used in response to a school emergency.

2. *Seminars/workshops.* These types of exercises are lengthier (1 to 3 hours) and are designed to be more collaborative. They emphasize team building via multifaceted approaches (e.g., lectures, discussion-based exercises, and participant engagement). You are encouraged to create workshops for your staff members that provide the opportunity to exchange information and differing perspectives; brainstorm and experiment with new ideas, procedures, and/or policies; provide training on specific crisis response; and practice problem-solving skills (U.S. Department of Homeland Security [USDHS], 2007).

3. *Tabletop drills.* These drills require you to present a crisis scenario to your crisis response team and request that they identify their crisis response roles and what their duties would entail in the given situation. This type of exercise (lasting 1 to 4 hours) can enhance your crisis team's understanding of their roles and responsibilities. Tabletop drills should facilitate comprehensive, problem-solving discussions about current emergency response plans. You are encouraged to incorporate crisis "surprises" into the scenarios in order to increase the flexibility of your team's approach and to mimic the unpredictable and fluid nature of crises. These drills are designed to help participants to identify, investigate, and resolve issues in emergency responses (Reeves et al., 2012; USDOE, 2006).

4. *Emergency drills.* These drills are used to practice a particular crisis procedure (e.g., fire, lockdown, duck-cover-hold, evacuation, shelter-in-place) and should last approximately 30 minutes to 2 hours in duration (Freeman & Taylor, 2011). Emergency drills allow your school members to practice the required steps for specific emergencies. Prior to implementing emergency drills, you should confirm your state's mandates regarding the potential required presence of local public safety agency representatives at the time of these drills (USDOE, 2006).

5. *Functional exercises.* The purpose of these exercises is to test one or more functions of your school's crises protocols. These are lengthier drills (3 to 8 hours) that simulate real-life crises but do not require the use/movement of emergency equipment/personnel. These exercises are typically coordinated with your district office and require participants to fulfill a number of roles (e.g., exercise controller who manages and directs the exercise, crisis responders, crisis simulators/actors, evaluators). Functional exercises are recommended as they are cost-effective and easier to implement without the use of emergency equipment/personnel (Freeman & Taylor, 2010, 2011; USDOE, 2006).

6. *Full-scale drills.* These types of drills are used to test a number of emergency response procedures simultaneously. The real-life nature of the full-scale drills has been found to be extremely helpful in crisis preparedness; however, they are highly involved (i.e., high costs and time consuming—can last half a day to multiple days) and come with certain risks (i.e., participant psychological trauma, loss of instructional time). It is critical that full-scale drills are planned with caution and that they do not result in any harm for the participants (e.g., promoting high rates of fear). You must provide at least a month's notice about the drill to your local community and to your students' parents/families, and coordination with your district and multiple local public agencies (e.g., police, fire, mental health agencies, hospitals, utilities, transportation, health departments, and emergency management agencies) is imperative. These drills may cross multiple municipalities and jurisdictions (Freeman & Taylor, 2010, 2011; USDHS, 2007). It is recommended that you complete a vulnerability assessment that incorporates a local hazard analysis to identify which crisis scenario is appropriate for your needs

(Reeves et al., 2011). NASP (2013) has further provided concise guidelines for implementing full-scale drills:

- You should engage in comprehensive plan development that may take a year to 18 months to create.
- Prior to implementing a full-scale drill, you should have your team complete orientations, emergency drills, and functional exercises.
- Your full-scale drills are meant to be part of a long-term emergency exercise plan that begins with basic drills and evolves to the full-scale drill.
- You may need to collaborate with external experts/consultants in order to gain guidance on best practices.
- It is imperative that the full-scale drills are not mistaken for a real crisis event.
- You should avoid exposing participants to content that could be potentially harmful/traumatic (e.g., using fake weapons/blood). Such content could produce prior trauma for individuals or create distressing reactions.
- You do not need to involve the entire student body.
- You should ensure that participating agencies follow the district's policies for emergency operations and notification.
- Prior to beginning the drill, participants must sign in, they should obtain an initial briefing, and fashion identification on who they are and their specified role.
- Post drill, your crisis team should evaluate the procedures and identify issues that are to be addressed.
- You need to approach the evaluation process with a "no-fault/no-fail expectation" and utilize errors as learning opportunities to strengthen future crisis response.

7. *Active shooter drills.* These exercises are a subset of the full-scale drills and have become increasingly popular in recent times. These drills include the use of traditional lockdown methods but are tailored specifically to incidences of school shootings. They utilize emergency practices such as staying quiet, locking the door, and turning off lights, and they may also include tactics such as fighting back, distracting the shooter, and evacuating mock shootings in schools. Some drills even take it a step further and simulate a school shooting in action with masked gunmen. Active shooter drills have received mixed reviews, as there are significant concerns regarding the potential long-term consequences and wider community impacts such as trauma and mental health impairments. Given their broad use, Everytown for Gun Safety (2022), a nonprofit organization that advocates for gun control and violence prevention, has provided clear guidelines for active shooter drills:

- Detailed information and notification must be provided to parents/guardians well in advance about the dates, content, and tone of drills.
- Drills should be:
  - Developmentally and age appropriate
  - Created by a crisis team
  - Announced to school members prior to commencement of the drill
  - Coupled with trauma-informed approaches
- Drills should not simulate an actual shooting incident.

- The school should track the efficacy and effects of the drill, along with any indicators of participant trauma (i.e., reports of bad dreams, school avoidance, depressive symptoms).
- Drills *must* be reevaluated if school members exhibit any signs of posttraumatic stress.

> [When considering safety and security in schools,] the concept of psychological safety is critical—for both kids and adults. I've seen well-meaning administrators go above and beyond in regard to ensuring physical safety after a crisis without considering the importance of individuals actually feeling safe. Sometimes, focusing solely on physical safety has actually made the kids feel less safe. Psychological safety considerations should be built into the emergency operations plan, including in drills and exercises.
>
> —FRANCI CREPEAU-HOBSON

Security Methods

Another common effort to prevent school violence is increased use of security measures. These measures come in a variety of forms ranging from security cameras to student ID badges to the use of metal detectors. Among the available options, most schools utilize access control, given its ease of implementation and its relatively low cost. Access control refers to limiting the access of outside individuals to the school interior. Examples of access control include establishing just one point of entry, locked doors, gated campuses, and the requirement of visitor screeners and ID badges (Fox & DeLateur, 2013; Zhang, Musu-Gillette, & Oudekerk, 2016). Despite the widespread use of access control measures, only limited evidence supports their effectiveness. Tragic examples of school crises highlight these concerns. In the school shooting at Sandy Hook Elementary, for example, the perpetrator was able to bypass the locked doors via a window.

Another popular, long-established security method are metal detectors, which can help prevent the admittance of weapons, such as knives and guns. In some cases, metal detectors have been found to reduce the reported likelihood of students bringing a weapon to school (Ginsberg & Loffredo, 1993). However, similar to access control, metal detectors lack solid support as a primary means of reducing school violence. Moreover, metal detectors should be used in a thoughtful manner; while they can communicate an increased sense of safety, they can also increase perceptions of fear within your school (Jonson, 2017).

More recent efforts have focused on increasing the number of guns on campus, including the use of law enforcement or security personnel, such as an armed school resource officer (SRO). Proponents of SROs believe that the presence of security personnel will deter individuals from attacking school settings. The research on the SRO's effectiveness is limited, however, and the few studies that have been completed have focused broadly on the effectiveness of these officers in reducing school crime, rather than school shootings (James & McCallion, 2013). Opponents of SROs maintain that as the police presence in schools has increased, the number of suspensions and expulsions for minority students has increased. NASP passed a 2022 resolution, "Regarding Policing in Schools," which wisely called for more training for school police and strengthening the partnership between school police and SMHPs, which we support. However, the resolution went too far in stating that as an organization, NASP (2022a) does not support federal funding of school police.

The sad reality is that in many of the most recent school shootings, police have failed our schools. The SRO in the MSD shooting, for example, came under legal action for his negligent actions (see Chapter 11 for more details on his case). The police response to the shooting at Robb Elementary School in Uvalde, Texas, in 2022 also received widespread national criticism. My own experience with SROs, however, has been very positive, especially those officials who see themselves as part of the school team and who spend considerable time developing close relations with students and staff.

In the aftermath of the Sandy Hook and MSD shootings, many states began to seriously consider expanding the use of armed professionals to school personnel, such as teachers and administrators (Butkus, 2020). In fact, in 2019, Florida passed legislation to allow teachers to become armed, with appropriate training (Trotta, 2019). Experts generally oppose this idea, as an increase in guns creates an increase in accessibility and risk. Dr. Peter Langman, a school violence expert, spoke to this movement in our recent publication, *Lessons Learned from School Shootings: Perspectives from the United States of America* (Poland & Ferguson, 2021a).

PROFESSIONAL PERSPECTIVE: Peter Langman, School Shooting Expert

I think [the idea of arming teachers . . .] is a problematic approach for multiple reasons. Even if you're skilled with a firearm shooting at a target, which has very little relevance to handling a firearm in a crisis situation. It's very easy to make a mistake. When your heart is pumping and the adrenaline is flowing and your hand is shaking, to even get your gun out and aim it, especially with hundreds of students running wildly and maybe people bumping into you, it would be easy for a teacher to hit the wrong person.

In fact, there is a study of New York City police officers who engage in firing against a suspect on the streets of New York. Even trained police officers miss their target 82% of the time. If they're trained and it's that hard to hit a target in a crisis situation, you have to ask where those bullets are going. It obviously would be very devastating for teachers with the best of intentions to wound or kill a student or colleague. That's one big concern.

Another concern is when police show up in that situation, if the first thing they see is a teacher pointing a gun at a student, the police may likely shoot the teacher. They may not know who the assailant is, and that teacher may be gunned down by mistake. There are other concerns too, but those are just some examples of what can go wrong with what seems like a good idea. When we start thinking of how this can really play out, it becomes more problematic (Poland & Ferguson, 2021a, pp. 34–35)

Given the vast number of considerations, it will be important for your school safety team to review school security measure options and implement those that best address your needs. These options can be identified and discussed during your safety planning meetings.

Recommended Resources: Crisis Drills and Security Methods

- **NASP (2013): Conducting Crisis Exercises and Drills: Guidelines for Schools materials**
  - *Best Practice Considerations for Schools in Active Shooter and Other Armed Assailant Drills:* Guidance from NASP and the National Association of School Resource Officers on best practices for safely conducting drills related to armed assailant scenarios. Found at *www.nasponline.org/resources-and-publications/resources-and-podcasts/school-safety-and-crisis/systems-level-prevention/best-practice-considerations-for-armed-assailant-drills-in-schools.*

- *Conducting Crisis Exercises and Drills: Guidelines for Schools:* Step-by-step guidelines on how to implement the various crisis drills at your school. Found at *www.nasponline.org/resources-and-publications/resources-and-podcasts/school-safety-and-crisis/systems-level-prevention/conducting-crisis-exercises-and-drills.*
- *Mitigating Psychological Effects of Lockdowns:* Guidance on how to best prepare and implement crisis drills that will reduce the potential negative psychological impact on participants. Found at *www.nasponline.org/resources-and-publications/resources-and-podcasts/school-safety-and-crisis/systems-level-prevention/mitigating-psychological-effects-of-lockdowns.*

- **NASP (2016): School Violence Prevention handouts**
  - *Brief Facts and Tips:* A list of user-friendly tips and facts for adults to utilize when approaching school violence prevention and implementing best practices. Found at *www.nasponline.org/resources-and-publications/resources-and-podcasts/school-safety-and-crisis/school-violence-resources/school-violence-prevention.*
  - *Talking to Children about Violence: Tips for Families and Educators:* Guidelines for caregivers and school personnel for how they can address aspects of violence in order to help students feel safe by creating a sense of normalcy and security, reinforcing their innate resilience, and talking with them about their fears. Found at *www.nasponline.org/resources-and-publications/resources-and-podcasts/school-safety-and-crisis/school-violence-resources/talking-to-children-about-violence-tips-for-families-and-educators.*

The guidelines offered in this chapter should be used to strengthen your team's preparedness to handle major crises at your school. Your team must make efforts to create a climate of safety that is geared toward increasing student connectedness and meeting the mental health needs of your school community. Suicide and school violence can, in many cases, be prevented when appropriate practices are put into place. Implementation of suicide prevention programming and threat assessment procedures has been proven to be critical components of prevention and will ultimately help to keep your school and its students and staff members safe.

FORM 2.1

School Safety Team Goals

Instructions for use: The school safety team should utilize the following questions as a guide for creating a comprehensive safety plan. Review each question and brainstorm as to how your team will ensure that each goal will be achieved in order to create a safe school environment.

1. Develop and maintain a climate of safety in the school.

How will this be achieved? ______________________________

____

____

____

2. Provide school staff members with appropriate training and support.

How will this be achieved? ______________________________

____

____

____

3. Maintain ongoing prevention and preparedness efforts.

How will this be achieved? ______________________________

____

____

____

4. Complete frequent assessments of safety efforts to gather data.

How will this be achieved? ______________________________

____

____

____

5. Evaluate data gathered and modify safety efforts as needed.

How will this be achieved? ______________________________

____

____

____

FORM 2.2

Needs Assessment Questions for School Safety Planning

Instructions for use: Utilize the following questions to obtain information on the status of your school safety planning. Circle Y for Yes or N for No and record the answers to each question in the given lines. These questions will provide a guideline for areas that must be addressed further in your safety planning.

- What are my school's current school safety initiatives?

  ____

  ____

- Is school safety reviewed regularly with staff? **Y/N** If yes, how often?

  ____

  ____

- Are students involved in school safety? **Y/N** If yes, in what ways?

  ____

- Are all doors to the school kept locked? **Y/N**
- Does your school have a policy of a staff member greeting all school visitors? Provide details. **Y/N**

  ____

  ____

- Are visitors at your school provided with a visitor badge? **Y/N**
- Does your school have a crisis team and, if so, who are the key members of the team? **Y/N**

  ____

- Did your school have any crisis events in the last two years? **Y/N**
  - If so, outline the nature of those, your response, and lessons learned.

    ____

- Have you identified local community mental health resources? **Y/N** If so, list options.

  ____

- Do you have a bullying prevention program? **Y/N** If so, specify program(s) used.

  ____

(continued)

Needs Assessment Questions for School Safety Planning *(page 2 of 2)*

- Have you surveyed students about important and related issues (e.g., feeling connected to school, safety at school, bullying prevalence, depression, and substance abuse)? **Y/N** If so, detail how you have completed the surveys.

  ___

- Does your school have an anonymous reporting system for threats? **Y/N** If so, what is used?

  ___

- Does your school have a process to evaluate threats of violence against others? **Y/N** If so, provide details on the process.

  ___

- What are the cultural issues that have impacted crisis intervention or safety planning?

  ___

- If you have conducted an active shooter or intruder drill, did you gather pretest and posttest information to determine if staff and students felt safer after the drill was conducted? **Y/N**

- Did you avoid the use of dramatic props such as the sound of gunfire? **Y/N**

- Was it clearly announced in advance as a drill? **Y/N**
  - Were attempts made to identify staff or students with prior trauma that might be greatly impacted by the drill? **Y/N** If so, in what ways?

    ___

FORM 2.3

Safety Plan Components Checklist

Instructions for use: Utilize the following checklist as a way to verify that your safety plan includes the necessary components. Review each bullet, check off those that are present in your plan, and record the ways in which each is implemented.

☐ School mental health procedures

____

____

____

☐ Multitiered academic and social-emotional screening and interventions

____

____

____

☐ School security policies

____

____

____

☐ Multihazard/vulnerability assessments

____

____

____

☐ School disciplinary procedures

____

____

____

☐ Employment screening procedures

____

____

____

(continued)

From NASP (2015c).

Safety Plan Components Checklist *(page 2 of 2)*

- ☐ School crisis plan
  - ☐ Response, communication, and reunification protocols

    ___

    ___

  - ☐ Psychological triage and assessment

    ___

    ___

  - ☐ Multitiered crisis interventions

    ___

    ___

CHAPTER 3

General Response for Serious Crises at Your School

School crises can be unpredictable, not only in their occurrence but also in their aftermath. It is impossible to provide exact guidance for each and every potential need in the face of a crisis; however, reviews of those that have already occurred, the good and the bad, provide critical guidelines on how your school should be prepared to respond to a significant crisis. For the purpose of this guidebook, we focus on providing direction on responses to major crises rather than less serious school crises. Given the basic training and education required of SMHPs, each SMHP is likely equipped with the skills to handle smaller crises, such as school fights, minor injuries or illnesses, or bullying/harassment. While these types of crises are not reviewed, we recommend that your CRT define what your school considers a minor or major crisis. This determination should be completed during the planning process and should include details of your school's protocols for addressing less serious crises.

I have encountered a variety of crises throughout my career and have consulted with numerous schools, CRTs, and related professionals. I have found that guidance is most significantly needed for major crises and that schools are often ill prepared to respond appropriately to unexpected events, such as a school shooting or suicide contagion. This chapter focuses on best practices for your immediate response to a general crisis at your school, ranging from the first hour to the following 24 hours and beyond. Topics covered include the development of a Crisis Fact Sheet, appropriate dissemination of information and notifications, processing and debriefing, school closures, and navigating the media. This guidance is shaped by my extensive crisis response experience and collaboration with other professionals.

> Every crisis is unique. Responding to a crisis is a matter of not only how to DO, but how to BE. Leading through a crisis will not make you a great leader, it will show what kind of leader you are. Preparation is key.
>
> —Cathy Kennedy-Paine

THE FIRST HOUR

Among the many crisis responses that I have participated in, I have acted as an immediate responder in the first hour and subsequent day of a school crisis. I often reflect on the many moving parts of these events, particularly the chaotic nature of the environment. I emphasize the need for structured lists that include specific action steps to take in the first hour, day, and beyond in the aftermath of a crisis. In future chapters you will find similar action lists that detail specifics with each type of crisis. It is our hope that these action steps will help you to follow through on necessary components of a strong crisis response. Should a severe crisis occur at your school, there are six tasks that you must prioritize with urgency, and the first two should occur immediately in the aftermath of the crisis (see Form 3.1).

> Crisis response is ultimately about communication. Timely, factual information needs to be disseminated to all individuals involved—whether it is death notification and psychoeducation for students, meetings for staff members, and communication sent to parents/guardians.
>
> —MICHELLE PASTOREK

Keep in mind that you may not be completing all of these action steps yourself. Some of these tasks will be delegated to others on your CRT. Additionally, these tasks will likely take longer than an hour to complete and that is okay. Some of these items may be completed over the course of the first 24 hours. Let's take a look at these tasks in closer detail.

VICTIM SAFETY/MEDICAL AID

Helping the Injured

In the aftermath of a serious crisis, the primary task is to attend to any medical needs of injured individuals. This task is most appropriately headed by the medical liaison and can include others who are available to help. The goal is to assist victims of crisis while waiting for an ambulance and other medical assistance to arrive. Upon identifying injured individuals, you will want to send a responsible student or staff member to the front office to notify the nurse. If your school has a nurse, they will be trained in performing cardiopulmonary resuscitation (CPR) and in administering first aid. The medical liaison (if it is not the nurse) should be alerted to the crisis and should assist in getting the school's first aid kits to the scene as quickly as possible.

Schools should have automated external defibrillator (AED) devices that can be used in the event of sudden cardiac arrest. "Stop the Bleed Kits" should also be in the school's inventory, and both of these products will help officials to be better prepared for medical emergencies. In addition, many schools have begun to include naloxone in their first aid kits. This life-saving medication, when given in the proper amount of time, can reverse an overdose from opioids, including heroin, fentanyl, and prescription opioid medications (Lifesaving Naloxone, 2022). Proper training must be offered to individuals who are likely to utilize these products (e.g., medical liaison and school nurse), although much of your staff could benefit from training when feasible (e.g., teachers and coaches). The American Heart Association offers a helpful course commonly used in schools called CPR in Schools: First Aid (n.d.). This course covers the discussed methods, along with a number of other important first aid topics such as allergic reactions, concussions, heart-related illnesses, and diabetic concerns.

If an injury occurs and there is no one with medical training in your building, at the very least, offer the victim(s) comfort. Keep them warm, calm, and quiet. You might hold their hand and speak in a reassuring manner. Your school likely already has a set procedure to follow for first aid, and we recommend that you utilize Table 3.1 to ensure that all aspects are appropriately covered.

While you are waiting for medical assistance from others, begin to assess the situation and identify all individuals who are injured. The medical liaison can utilize identification wristbands on individuals who are wounded or who have passed. The individual's name can be written on the wristband and can be helpful for identification once they are admitted to the hospital. Identification is appropriate for particularly intense crises where there are many injuries or deaths. Many strategies offered are intended to help decrease the inevitable chaos that comes with a crisis.

If the victims are students at your school, request that the front office make copies of their emergency notification forms. Additionally, you will want to make a list of those who were killed

TABLE 3.1. First Aid Guidelines

- Survey the scene for safety, develop an initial impression, obtain consent (when possible, e.g., the person is responsive), and use personal protective equipment when available.
- If you observe that the person is responsive and/or fully awake and is not in a life-threatening condition, do the following:
  - Interview witnesses to the event.
  - Inquire about medical conditions, allergies, and current medications.
- If you observe that the injured person appears to be unresponsive, check for breathing and life-threatening injuries or bleeding.
- Call 911 and get appropriate equipment (e.g., AED) or ask someone else to.
- Refrain from moving the injured individuals unless there are concerns regarding immediate danger in that location.
- If you suspect that someone has a spinal injury, it is especially important to keep them in the position that you found them. Refrain from moving the person at all, even to cradle their head in your lap.
  - Signs of a spinal injury include weakness or numbness in an extremity, inability to move an extremity, and lack of feeling in extremity.
- Refrain from offering any injured individuals fluids or medicines/prescriptions.
- Torniquets should only be utilized if the blood loss is so severe that the person is in danger of losing their life.
- CPR is most effective when administered by someone who has been trained in the procedure. However, if there is no one available who has been trained and the victim is not breathing, you should begin to administer CPR. *Note:* CPR should only be completed if the person does not have a heartbeat; doing so with a heartbeat may cause the heart to stop (American Red Cross, 2018).

or wounded, including the extent of their injuries (from what you are able to determine). This list should be shared with the parent/family liaison. It is important to keep a copy of this list on hand should you accompany the victims to the hospital. The parent/family liaison will take charge of trying to reach the families of the injured students; however, if they cannot be reached immediately, medical attention should still be provided if needed.

Protecting Students and Staff

Providing protection and ensuring the safety of school members are top priorities. The safest place for victims to go will greatly depend on the circumstances at the time of the event. In the past, recommendations have been made for school members to shelter in place in times of acute crises, such as a school shooter. This recommendation has changed over time, however, as sheltering in place has resulted in deadly consequences. In some situations, school members who have barricaded themselves in classrooms prevented the ability to escape and potentially delayed access to medical attention. Moreover, there have been tragic examples in which students had access to viable escape routes but were told to shelter in place. For instance, in the aftermath investigation at Columbine, it was found that several students were shot and killed in

TABLE 3.2. Safest Response to an Active Crisis

- If evacuation is required, follow the procedures from your fire drill. Once students have evacuated and assembled in the designated area, teachers should take attendance to ensure that all of their students are accounted for.
- If gunshots are fired:
  - Follow the procedures outlined in your active shooter drill.
  - Immediately drop to the ground and roll to the nearest cover, such as a shelving unit, desk, or other heavy furniture.
  - Remain on the floor with your hands covering your head.
- If you're told to remain in the classroom, follow the lockdown drill procedures. Teachers should ensure that the classroom door is locked, and students should not be allowed near any windows and doors. The hard corner away from doors and windows is the safest place for staff and students and should be kept free from any stored items or furniture. Attendance should be taken, and students should be advised to remain calm and quiet until the threat has been lifted.
- It is helpful if teachers are prepared for the potential for shelter in place orders. This might include the development of shelter in place kits that include items like fidgets, snacks, or common comforts (e.g., pictures of student family members, stuffed animals). This type of approach is especially important for younger students.
- If a crisis occurs and students and staff are located outside of the classroom (e.g., in a courtyard, on the playground), they should either take cover if possible or lay on the ground until an all-clear announcement has been made. Efforts should be made to move these individuals back to their classrooms as soon as it is safe to do so.
- The counseling liaison should report to any crisis scene and provide direction on how individuals can obtain first aid (if needed) and that students should return to their classrooms. This will create an opportunity to obtain a count of students and better assess any medical or mental health needs.

the library, just feet away from an exit outside (Should We Change How We Teach Run, Fight, Hide?, n.d.)

In response to such concerns, The USDOE has adopted the Department of Homeland Security's (2007) advisement for schools to teach staff and students to do the following: "Run, Hide or Fight," depending on the circumstances or if there is an active shooter. This approach does not come without its own problems, particularly in the area of "fight." Staff members have little support, training, or tools to engage in a fight with an active shooter. Moreover, this is certainly not an appropriate advisement for younger children. Ultimately, the safest reaction to a crisis will vary based on the context. Given how hard these circumstances are to predict and how quickly a crisis can arise, it is helpful to have a few guidelines (see Table 3.2) that will lead to the safest response to a dangerous crisis.

CALLING FOR HELP

Certainly, if a severe crisis strikes your school, obtaining emergency services support is a paramount need. Your first call will be to 911, and it is likely that the crisis coordinator will direct a specific person to do so. Really, anyone can make this call; the important part is that it is done with immediacy and that clear details are provided. Such information is highlighted in a checklist format in Form 3.2.

Soon, emergency response teams will arrive at your school, and the medical liaison should be present to offer direction. Depending on the nature of the crisis, you should make efforts to escort the injured to the hospital. Before you do so, remember to bring the aforementioned emergency notification forms and the list of those injured or killed. Both the crisis coordinator and the medical liaison should reach out to appropriate family members to notify them of the status of the injured and to give them information on the hospital locations (this is discussed in detail later in this chapter).

NECESSARY NOTIFICATIONS

The crisis coordinator will want to alert your district's central office about the crisis as soon as possible. A number of individuals must be notified, including the superintendent, associate superintendents, district public relations department, other CRTs, the school board, and the facilities plant manager (this person will have access to all of the buildings and blueprints of the schools in the district). The supervisor of transportation should also be alerted to the event so that they can provide notice to the bus drivers prior to picking up students. Ideally, the district will then enact their own calling tree within the county and can assist in contacting necessary city agencies (e.g., emergency management personnel) and leaders (e.g., county judge or city mayor).

The crisis coordinator must then alert neighboring schools about the event. Albeit rare, there have been crisis events in which multiple schools have been targeted or in which a perpetrator ran from one school to another campus. Given this risk, it is imperative that a call is made to the area schools in your county to help maintain their safety. Calling trees should be part of your crisis response plan and are a way to ensure that information about the crisis can be systematically shared with your school community. Additionally, neighboring schools often house important individuals (e.g., siblings) who need to know about the crisis. Since it will likely be difficult for your team to make all of the necessary phone calls, it is recommended that you request that your central office take on that task. This is a time when asking for help (*the right kind of help*) is something that your team must not shy away from.

SECURITY TASKS

In the event of a violent crisis, your school quickly becomes an active crime scene. Your next major task will be to ensure that the locales where the incidents took place are as secured as possible; this step is taken for a number of reasons. First, it is done to prevent any tampering and to maintain the integrity of the scene, which aids the police in their investigation. Your security liaison should handle this task and may require the assistance of others. Once the police arrive at your school, they will take over this duty.

Securing the crime scene also helps to protect the privacy of victims; information should be kept confidential in the initial aftermath as your team continues to obtain the facts to share with family members. These efforts are linked to another prominent reason for securing the crime scene: keeping the media at bay so that only agreed-upon information is released. In most severe crises, particularly those of a violent nature, the media will almost immediately be present on your school grounds in the aftermath.

PROFESSIONAL PERSPECTIVE: SCOTT POLAND

Media Run-Ins

On one occasion when I responded on site to a school shooting in my district, I was surprised and frustrated to find that the media was roaming around the school and offering students $200 for last year's yearbook, as it obtained a picture of the school shooter. This example illustrates how important it is for schools to have policies to keep the media off school grounds. I also remember another example where after a school shooting was covered nationally, the media provided a camera and offered a student $500 to go inside the school and film anything that they could. Thankfully, this example has a nice ending, as the responsible student went to the principal's office and said, "Apparently we have an equipment donation to the school" and he handed over the camera.

The media liaison should take charge of messaging and all interactions with the media. Although it will be in your team's best interest to cooperate fully with the media beyond the first hour, initially, your main goal is to set up clear boundaries and provide brief feedback. The security liaison and the police should make efforts to seal off your campus and create barriers that limit media presence. The best scenario is to send the media to another location at a neighboring school where a press conference can be held.

One security concern that may not become immediately known is traffic issues outside of the school. In a major crisis, emergency response vehicles, families, and media trucks will be inundating the area within moments. Traffic can become chaotic and potentially dangerous.

The security liaison should coordinate with your school's security staff and the police to control the flow of traffic in front of and in the surrounding area of the school.

THE CRISIS FACT SHEET

All these discussed actions will likely occur within a matter of moments and some at the very same time. In the midst of all of this confusion, you will be taking in a massive amount of information, for example, *What happened? Who was hurt? Is the school safe? Who is the perpetrator? Who needs help? Did we call for help? Is the crime scene secure? Are the media being handled?* Soon after the initial tasks are completed, you will need to create one of the most important documents of your crisis intervention process: the Crisis Fact Sheet.

The Crisis Fact Sheet will be a living document utilized to record the critical facts of the crisis. It should be completed collaboratively with the crisis coordinator, media liaison, campus liaison, and parent/family liaison. The document should be updated frequently as facts are learned, confirmed, and/or modified. The principal and superintendent will also contribute and will need to provide final approval before any of the information is released publicly.

PROFESSIONAL PERSPECTIVE: Franci Crepeau-Hobson

Get—and share—the facts! I did not fully appreciate how important this was until I responded to a school shooting, and this didn't happen. Typically, responders meet in the morning prior to students and staff arriving, and they go through the incident action plan. This meeting has always included sharing a fact sheet with all responders. The fact sheet includes *all* verified details of the incident so that responders will be able to provide psychoeducation, dispel rumors, and effectively support the school community. At one response, the responders got nothing in terms of information. We knew as much as anybody else—what was on the news and in social media (much of which we [later] learned was inaccurate). Not knowing the facts made it virtually impossible to provide any kind of crisis intervention and to support students effectively. The facts were also not shared with the school community, and everyone—students and staff—were on edge and anxious because they didn't have the information [that] they needed to wrap their heads around what [had] happened. Rumors were swirling and making things worse, and I could do nothing to dispel those and reassure the kids (and adults).

There are a number of key points to include in the Crisis Fact Sheet (e.g., location and time of event, who was killed or injured; see Table 3.3). These points will guide several parts of your team's crisis response, including media consultations, parent notifications, and injury/death notifications. One important item on the Crisis Fact Sheet that we'd like to highlight is the information about the family/community meeting that your team will hold that evening or as soon as possible. It is imperative that when a significant crisis occurs at your school, your team provides an opportunity for the school community to come together to process the event and obtain helpful guidance and resources. This meeting is discussed in more detail later on this chapter. On the fact sheet, you will want to list the date, time, and location of the meeting and encourage all caregivers/family members to attend. Form 3.3 provides a template for you to use to ensure that you are including all the major points in your fact sheet.

TABLE 3.3. Points to Include in Your Crisis Fact Sheet

- All known facts that have been confirmed by reliable sources
- Date, time, location of the crisis
- Name, age, grade, other relevant details about victims/perpetrator
- The status of victims and suspected perpetrators
- School schedule: will it stay open for the rest of the day/tomorrow?
- Steps the CRT has taken to notify parents/school community
- Have parents been encouraged to pick up their children or not?
- Information about the counseling services that are being made available to the school community
- Information about the upcoming family/community meeting

Given the seriousness of the information found on the Crisis Fact Sheet (see Figure 3.1 for an example of a completed Crisis Fact Sheet), verification of these facts cannot be emphasized enough. Your team must be vigilant in your vetting of information, and you must ensure that it is coming from a reliable source. Additionally, crisis facts must be verified at the highest levels before any information is shared with the public. Do not hesitate to share with others that you don't know something; giving no information is better than giving incorrect information.

For crises that occur off campus, the crisis coordinator must make efforts to obtain details from family members. Even though it may feel as though you are intruding on the family during a private time, it is imperative that you make contact. Without this information, your team will not know how to appropriately respond, what information can be given out, and what rumors they can dispel. The crisis coordinator and the parent/family liaison should complete this contact collaboratively, and it is best to attempt it in person first. This initial contact with any family member of a victim is critical, as it sets the tone for the ongoing relationship with the school.

Last update: 9/28/22 at 5:30 P.M.

On September 28, 2022, at 2:35 P.M., it was reported by the head football coach, Mr. Tartarkin, that during practice, one of his players, James Doe, sustained significant trauma to his head during a tackle. James Doe is 17 years old and is a junior. He reportedly lost consciousness and was not breathing. CPR was performed by the head coach but to no avail. Emergency response services were contacted immediately. The school nurse was alerted to the injury, who then notified the administration. James was transported to the local emergency department and his family shared that as of 4:30 P.M., he was declared dead. No other players were injured.

School is expected to remain open tomorrow with a normal schedule of classes. A crisis counselor will be available to speak with any students who have been impacted by this event. This provider will also complete a debriefing session with the football team members and coaches. Additionally, the provider will check in on each class that James attended and will also connect with James's close friends.

The administration will be holding a family community meeting tonight in the school's cafeteria at 7:00 P.M. This meeting is free and open to the public and all who are grieving this loss (*with the exception of the media)*. Counselors will be available to provide support and will share guidelines with parents on how to best support your children through this time. Funeral arrangements will be provided as the information is shared with us.

A phone tree has been completed to alert parents and school staff about the family/community meeting. A parent/family letter has been sent home with details about the crisis event and upcoming meeting. Relevant information has been posted to our social media account. The media liaison has already made contact with the media and has provided a preapproved statement of James's passing.

FIGURE 3.1. Sample Crisis Fact Sheet.

FACT-SHARING TIMELINE

The CRT should provide clear and accurate updates as they are confirmed, and they should keep the school and public informed as the crisis unfolds. The only exception to this requirement regards sensitive information, such as the names of those injured or killed. It is advised that you do not release any victims' names to the public; names should be released only to the loved ones, who must be notified. Photos of the victims should not be shared without the permission of their caregivers/guardians. When sharing information, you must consider content that the media has already reported on (e.g., rumors about victims), along with what the caregivers/family members have told you and what the police say. While we have emphasized that it is important to be direct and to share facts, we also want to reiterate that it is okay to say things like "there is no additional information to share at this time" when appropriate.

Should a crisis occur after school hours or over the weekend or holiday break, your gathering and sharing of the facts become more complicated. Best practices are to alert school staff at home and to initiate the predetermined phone calling tree. This will enable the school community to have time to process their reactions prior to returning to school. In these instances, you will want to prepare for potential teacher absences by lining up substitutes if possible.

COMMUNICATING THE FACTS

We've gathered and recorded the facts; now, we have to broach the task of successfully communicating the information to the public. The overarching recommendation in this action step is to share all the facts; be accurate and tell everything that you know (with approval). I have had several experiences in which administrators offer little to no facts, keeping information limited to the public. I have found that this tendency typically makes things more chaotic, as people are left to presume the worst and end up using their valuable energy to try to figure out what has happened rather than being able to process their reactions to the crisis. Sharing information thoughtfully can help to lower stress and create a sense of calm in the midst of disorder.

With all that said, sharing the facts doesn't mean providing every detail of the crisis. You will want to provide information in a factual way with as little detail as possible (e.g., a student was shot off campus vs. a student was shot off campus and was left to bleed to death slowly on the street). When relaying the information, one important thing to be mindful of is the type of language you use. This information will be reiterated time and time again in this book as it is a significant part of a successful intervention process. Always utilize age-appropriate language and ensure that you consider the developmental age of the population that you are sharing the news with. Continuing with our example, with elementary schoolers you might say, "a bad man shot a student," whereas with high schoolers, you'd say something like, "a student was shot and killed at a location off campus."

An additional consideration regarding your sharing of the facts is the manner in which you do so. It is recommended that when sharing crisis information initially, it is done so in a small-group setting. It would be appropriate to hold a meeting with your entire faculty but not with the whole student body. We do not advise that you group even two or three classes together to share the news, as it can create an array of emotional responses and chaos. Students should be provided the information in a setting like their classroom, and it is recommended that their teacher, a counseling staff member, and the principal are present. This allows students to receive potentially traumatic information in a familiar environment with known people.

What Do You Say?

In almost every crisis that I have responded to, at least one person, if not several, have asked, "What do I say?" It is likely not surprising that we recommend that when you speak, you speak truths and that you relay the information in a calm and uncomplicated manner. Sharing these facts can be an overwhelming duty, and it is important to remember that you are not the one who caused the crisis: you are simply the person who is reporting the facts of the event. As you prepare for any statements, consider questions that may be asked of you, for example, "What is the status of the suspected perpetrator?" Review these types of questions and your potential answers; if you find yourself unable to provide an immediate logical answer, then you're likely filling in gaps that you do not have the facts for yet.

HOW TO SHARE THE FACTS

The key individuals who should be in charge of sharing information about the crisis are the crisis coordinator and the campus liaison. It is imperative that a meeting be held where the facts of the crisis are shared with the faculty and other school personnel. This meeting should also be a space for these individuals to share their emotions, ask questions, and discuss how to support their students. Even if the crisis occurs off campus and the staff members were alerted at home, a meeting should take place that allows for group processing and support. You should come to this meeting equipped not only with the facts of the crisis but also with information on how staff members can best support the student body.

I have led or performed a major role in these meetings, and I remember a statement that I made to the Columbine faculty after the 1999 shooting at the school to provide directions to teachers about how to help their students: *"Let your heart be your guide to help students."* I always emphasize to staff that we will get through by helping each other and that things will go better than you have imagined because of the strength of the faculty.

If a crisis occurs during school hours, it is recommended that the information is shared with each individual classroom. This may be difficult to do in a large school, and the way in which your team goes about it should be discussed in your safety plan. In some cases, you may be able to coordinate a meeting with staff members prior to sharing with students; in other cases, you may need to go class by class to alert the teachers. It may be helpful for the principal to make an announcement for teachers to check their email as quickly as possible; the email will provide the facts and a script for teachers to use when sharing the news about the crisis. If there's no time to alert the school staff first, the intercom can be used as a last resort. The statement should be prewritten with clear facts about the crisis. The crisis coordinator should provide the statement over the intercom and must be mindful of their choice of words, tone, and inflection. We recommend practicing the statement a few times so that the message is delivered with less emotion.

Students should be told the information in a calm, concise, and direct manner. It is recommended that use of religious symbols or language be avoided and that the focus should be on emotional expression and their thoughts about the crisis. It should be emphasized that counseling will be made available to any students in need. CRT members should make visits to those classrooms that were particularly affected (e.g., the classes that the deceased student participated in). This is the time to be closely attuned to the trauma reactions of students and their risk for self-harm or suicide. These reactions are discussed in detail in later chapters.

NOTIFICATION OF AN INJURY/DEATH

Undoubtedly, one of the most difficult tasks in crisis intervention is the notification of a death or injury to a loved one. These notifications are typically completed by the crisis coordinator and family/parent liaison. It is critical that notification be made in a calm, supportive, and respectful manner. School crises typically result in the need to share information not only with next of kin but also with other loved ones, friends, and other people who knew the victim. When sharing this information, it is always preferred that you do so face-to-face; however, it is realistic that this may not always be possible. Table 3.4 reviews general recommendations for how you can approach these difficult notifications in varied formats. I learned many of these recommendations from one of the suggested trainings, National Organization for Victim Assistance Crisis Response Team Training™ (2023). I emphasize the benefit of their training model.

THE FIRST DAY

The first 24 hours in the aftermath of a school crisis are a critical period of time; there is much to do in order to provide the most thorough and appropriate crisis response. My list extends far beyond just the first hour, and I recommend that you continue to take structured action steps to best support your school's needs. It is okay if you are unable to fully complete all of the discussed items in the course of the first day; however, every effort should be made to follow these guidelines in order to maintain best practices.

The First 24 Hours: Action Steps

1. ***The CRT must come together to discuss crisis response.***

In the immediate aftermath of a crisis, your CRT must meet as soon as possible. During this meeting, your team will review the predetermined action and response plans based on the current situation at the school. It's important to be attuned to your team members during this meeting. You may find that a fellow member could become incapable of meeting their duties. Check in on your team members, and if one member requests taking a step back from the team, do not ask for reasons; allow it, and obtain a replacement. You never know what a CRT member has gone through in the past and what events may be triggering for them.

2. ***Begin to create the Crisis Fact Sheet; update as necessary.***

TABLE 3.4. Injury/Death Notification Guidelines

General approach

Beforehand
- Gather as many facts as possible
- Obtain emergency notification name/contact information

During the notification
- Show compassion
- Be empathetic
- Display calm energy
- Be comforting
- Be nonjudgmental
- Be direct and factual
- Limit use of euphemisms
- Encourage the person to sit down, if possible
- Answer all questions as you can
- Confirm appropriate contact person
- Monitor signs of risk (e.g., suicidal ideation, access to weapons)

By telephone

- Attempt to arrange for another adult/loved one to be with the person who you are notifying
- If no other adult is available, ask permission to connect them to someone of comfort who can be with them at this time
- Stay on the phone with them until this assistance is provided
- If you are sharing with multiple individuals, inform each person whom you have already notified

In person/at school

- Find a private place to meet
- Obtain the assistance of other staff members (two per victim)
- Ensure that your clothing is not disheveled nor shows evidence of injury (e.g., blood on your pants)
- Ensure that someone stays with the survivors
- Escort the person to the hospital or have a staff member do so
- Address the media as needed; security liaison should direct them to an off-campus location

At the hospital

- Investigate to determine if a death notification has already been provided to the family members upon their arrival to the hospital
- Ensure that your clothing is not disheveled nor shows evidence of injury (e.g., blood on your pants)
- Attempt to help individuals connect with their loved ones' doctors/nurses
- Provide helpful information to doctors and nurses about the facts of the event
- Ensure that someone stays with the survivors
- Accompany the survivors to identify their loved ones if they make such a request
- Address any media that may have arrived at the hospital

Missing/unidentified loved ones

- Make it clear that you have been given evidence that a loved one has been killed, but the final determination of the identification is still being investigated
- Share that you will keep loved ones informed as the investigation continues

3. ***Determine the school schedule for the day; will you be staying open or will you be closing?***

The decision to keep your school open or closed will need to be made quickly. In some cases, there will be a clear answer (e.g., a school shooting), while in others, your team will have to weigh all of the facts. As is true of many things in crisis intervention, there is no black and white guidance on the matter. Questions to consider include the following: *Are school members afraid to go outside or to the location where the crisis occurred? Is it safe for the students to go outside or to move in the building?* For less severe crises (e.g., learning of the death of a staff member), it is recommended that the following be considered: *Is the majority of the staff able to attend to the needs of the students?* If so, then the best option is to keep the school open; it is typically in the best interest of the students to be on campus with their peers and teachers. However, should you and your team find that the staff's functioning is significantly impaired, then it would be appropriate to cancel school for the day and attend to the needs of staff members.

Should the need arise for your school to be closed for longer than 24 hours (perhaps due to damage and/or an ongoing police investigation), the subsequent task will be to arrange an alternate location where your students can gather in classroom groups (e.g., nearby college or other school campuses, stadiums, community recreation centers). Even though it is inconvenient to hold your school at another location, it is critical that you facilitate as much structure for students as possible, including a collective opportunity to process their reactions to the traumatic event. It is important to return your students to their school at the same location in a short time frame, preferably the next day, so that they are able to easily access the aid of trained SMHPs. Moreover, a quick return to school can help to decrease potential occurrences of "school phobia" among students.

If the decision is to keep the school open for the rest of the day, you and the team will have to discuss how to structure the bell schedule. A modified bell schedule may be required in order to provide students with extended time to process the crisis in the class where they learn the news of the event (e.g., they learn of a teacher's death halfway through first period). An extended period may be needed to allow time for them to ask questions and work through the news.

4. ***If you are keeping your school open for the remainder of the day, begin to attend to the needs of your students.***

Children are resilient, but it is imperative that they have the opportunity to talk about what has happened. My experience has shown me that the more a child can verbalize after experiencing a traumatic event, the better they fare in the future. It is important that you convey to the staff that students must have permission to express their feelings and obtain validation for their experiences.

You are encouraged to engage students in small-group discussions. These groups must be emotion focused and supportive in nature. *Note:* Prior parental permission is not required for this type of counseling. The discussion should take place within the students' classrooms with the assistance of the teacher and at least one counseling staff member or an administrator. One exception to this arrangement involves younger elementary school–age children, who should be reunited with their caregivers as soon as possible.

Providing students with the opportunity to process their reactions to the crisis is an excellent way for them to begin the journey to recovery (see Chapter 8 for a detailed review of processing). Throughout the day, it is important to follow the schedule of any student who died or was injured in the crisis, as each class may have their own reaction to the crisis. While leading the processing session, be attuned to student reactions and identify any students of concern who will require follow-up services. Be mindful of cultural considerations in these settings, as they will impact the presentation of trauma and grief (see Chapter 10 for additional information). These reactions to trauma are discussed in more detail as they relate to each specific crisis (i.e., suicide, violence).

The rest of the day will likely need to be modified in some manner. You may want to recommend that teachers set aside their planned curriculum for the day and instead facilitate alternative activities such as artwork, creative writing, or listening to music. You will also want to convey a message to students about dealing with the publicity of the event. Provide the students with a basic lesson on how to handle the media; help them to understand that they do not have to speak with any reporters who may approach them. Advise them to direct any media requests to the school's media liaison. Also review guidelines for social media; students should be encouraged to limit their sharing of any graphic content from a crisis and spreading of any rumors that have not yet been confirmed or dispelled.

5. ***Make emotional support available during the day and evening.***

Depending on the availability of providers at your school or in your district, you may have to utilize outside volunteers who hopefully have been identified in advance. Your CRT will have to determine the level of need and available resources in order to provide adequate mental health care for the school members.

6. ***Evaluate your need for outside assistance; vet volunteers and assign tasks.***

As mentioned, to meet the needs of the school members, you may have to incorporate outside service providers (e.g., mental health agencies, clergy members, national crisis responders). In a time of crisis, it is recommended that you request additional assistance sooner rather than later. An over-response to a crisis is always preferable to an under-response. Moreover, depending on the nature and publicity of the crisis, there will likely be an influx of community members who want to volunteer to help. The campus liaison should take charge of these responsibilities, and it is recommended that they complete a brief interview with any volunteers. The volunteers deemed appropriate should then be assigned specific tasks for the day. In vetting for help, you will also want to consider the cultural needs of your school community and make efforts to obtain assistance that can best match the diversity factors of the victims (see Chapter 10 for additional recommendations).

7. ***Coordinate a family/community meeting to be held that night. Ensure that the meeting information is publicized to the appropriate parties. Create an agenda for the meeting.***

The media liaison or the parent/family liaison should work to coordinate a family/community meeting to be held later in the evening so that all community members have the opportunity to attend. The meeting details should be made public to all interested parties, and it is recommended that the media liaison disseminate the information among student and parent leaders, the Parent Teacher Association, local churches, and other area schools. The media liaison can also share information by holding a press conference, sending mass emails, and enacting telephone chains.

Meeting participants should include relevant school staff and community members, such as law enforcement, school administrators, and members from the CRT. The purpose of the meeting is to relay the facts of the crisis, the school's response, available resources, and the next steps to be taken in the crisis response process. It is suggested that your team put together a family/parent information packet, which is reviewed in Form 3.4.

8. ***When the time is appropriate, the media liaison should coordinate a press conference and publicize an announcement about the crisis response details.***

The purpose of this press conference will be to share crisis facts and plans for the school schedule. Throughout the day, the media liaison should remain in touch with the loved ones of the victims if they are open to communicating with the school. Family members can provide facts and permissions for sharing certain information.

9. ***Provide updates to appropriate parties throughout the day.***

The campus liaison should take charge of providing updates to school employees. Teachers should then share this information with their students. As with all things, it's best to be direct and factual with this information as it can help to appease building tension. Utilize your calling tree to keep community members informed. Ensure that you maintain open lines of communication with intervening medical staff, the police, and family members of the victims. New information should also be shared with the superintendent, school board, and other area schools via the central office.

10. ***Clean up the location where the crisis occurred.***

Once you are given the all-clear from the police, you will want to coordinate the cleaning of the scene of the incident. In cases of violent crises, it is likely that the police will not allow any cleaning to occur for several days to many weeks. Be sure to clean up any evidence of injury (e.g., blood) but do not move any personal belongings of the students and staff. Do not rearrange the classrooms. Do not immediately fix all the damage, as members of the community may want to come see the environment as part of their grieving process. This clean-up of course will depend on the magnitude of the damage.

11. ***Send a notification home to the caregivers*** **(see Figure 3.2 for an example).**

A notification must be sent home to the families of the students at your school. This notification should be completed collaboratively with the parent/family liaison and the crisis coordinator; all other CRT members are welcome to contribute. The notification should clearly explain what took place and what the school's response has been and will be. It should specify

9/28/22

Dear Parents/Caregivers,

We are writing to share that the students and staff of our school experienced a tragedy today with the death of James Doe, a beloved football player. James died in a tragic football accident. A statement providing the complete facts of this crisis is included on the backside of this letter. As a school community, we are all mourning the loss of James. In order to support the student body and staff, a grief specialist crisis intervention team will be serving our school. We feel it is important to provide an increased level of psychological aid and we want you to know that counseling services will be made available to all who have been impacted by this loss. We will continue to provide the services to students for as long as they are necessary. Please contact the school if you believe your child is in need of these services.

We also want to share that it is important that you are aware of the intense emotional reactions that can come with such a crisis. Your child may experience a range of emotions, such as fear, anger, sadness, and worry. They may have difficulty sleeping or trouble attending to academic tasks. Please be available to your children and offer a supportive environment and the opportunity for them to share their feelings.

Tonight, at 7:00 P.M., we will be holding a family/community meeting in the cafeteria. All family members, friends, and community members who have been impacted by this tragedy are encouraged to attend this meeting. Please note that the media will not be present. This meeting will provide an opportunity for the school to share pertinent information about the crisis and our response, answer any questions that you may have, and provide guidance and resources that will help you to support your child during this difficult time. The school schedule will remain intact, and our doors will be open tomorrow. We encourage you to send your child to school and to maintain their routine as much as possible. Please keep us in the know of any needs that your child may have and please reach out if you are in need of any assistance.

FIGURE 3.2. Sample parent notification.

the school schedule and the date, time, and location of the family/community meeting that will be held. Caregivers should be encouraged to attend the meeting and to bring any other family/community members who are interested. Share that the media will not be present. Emphasize the need for caregivers to maintain their children's routines and encourage them to send their children to school, should your doors be open. Dispel any rumors that may be circulating and stick to the facts. Copy the Crisis Fact Sheet to the backside of this notification. This notification should be completed in all relevant languages, depending on the makeup of your school.

12. *Eat something.*

It may sound trivial, but it's an important action step that is many times forgotten. Ensure that you have a bite to eat around lunch and dinner time. This will be a long day or even several weeks for you, and it will be important for you to maintain your strength and mental clarity; this isn't possible without good nutrients. Also, be sure to hydrate. The crisis coordinator should task someone in the front office to make sure that the CRT members have food to eat throughout the day.

13. *Plan for dismissal.*

Dismissal will be handled variably depending on several factors. If your school has decided to close, caregivers will need to be contacted and students must be signed out appropriately to ensure safety. If any students leave early due to emotional upset, you will want to take note to ensure that you follow up on their needs in the future. You will also need to be sensitive to the media presence and school members' vulnerability to their filming/requesting of interviews.

14. ***Process the crisis with your faculty and support staff.***

Do not forget your school personnel in all of this. Many times, they can be just as greatly impacted by the crisis as students. They will also be better equipped to provide support to students if they have a chance to process their own reactions and emotions. The crisis coordinator and counseling staff should coordinate debriefing sessions that are mandatory for all staff members. The groups should emphasize that there is no one way for them to feel and that they can share their emotions in a nonjudgmental space. Coping skills should be offered, along with ways that they can best support others in their lives.

15. ***Meet with the CRT to plan for the next day.***

The CRT should meet prior to the following day to create a plan that outlines what responses they will follow and what action steps they must take. Your team should also review the things that worked and did not work, along with how they are managing the media and any other public relations issues. A review of the help needed/requested should occur, along with an update of the Crisis Fact Sheet.

16. ***If your school stays open, coordinate a mandatory faculty meeting for the next morning and prepare teacher materials.***

The crisis coordinator and campus liaison should complete a meeting with the faculty before school on the following day of the crisis. This meeting should be brief, and its goals are to discuss the schedule for the day and ways that the staff can support the students. The counseling staff should assist in developing these tips.

17. ***Visit the victims and their families.***

If there are victims from your school who are in the hospital, efforts should be made to visit them in the hospital. These visits convey the school's care and concern for the victims and their families and can be a physical support at the hospital. At times, students may be without their families for several hours (e.g., their caregivers commute for work), and your familiar face can provide some comfort. Moreover, you can gather and share facts with loved ones and the attending medical staff. However, it is important that you do not overwhelm the families with your discussions, as the main purpose of your visit is to provide support, care, and comfort.

It is our hope that the action steps reviewed in this chapter are accessible and helpful in your preparation for an inevitable crisis response. Crises can often result in a chaotic environment, and having a task list that you can refer to in the immediate aftermath and beyond is imperative. While it is difficult to cover every factor of a crisis, utilizing the reviewed action steps in the immediate aftermath of a crisis will ensure that you are providing high-quality crisis intervention services.

Recommended Resources

- **American School Counselor Association's (ASCA) The School Counselor and Safe Schools and Crisis Response (2019):** ASCA's guidance for school counselors on how to maintain a climate of safety and what their role is in school crisis response. Found at *www.schoolcounselor.org/Standards-Positions/Position-Statements/ASCA-Position-Statements/The-School-Counselor-and-Safe-Schools-and-Crisis-R.*
- **NASP's PREPaRE Training Curriculum (Brock et al., 2014):** Evidence-based resources and consultation related to school crisis prevention and response. Found at *www.nasponline.org/professional-development/prepare-training-curriculum.*
- **NASP's School Safety and Crisis Response Committee (2018a): School Safety and Crisis:** NASP offers a number of helpful resources that target the varied areas of school crisis intervention and prevention (see below). Found at *www.nasponline.org/resources-and-publications/resources-and-podcasts/school-safety-and-crisis.*
    - *Health Crises*
    - *Direct Crisis Support*
    - *Media and Social Media*
    - *Mental Health*
    - *Natural Disaster*
    - *School Violence*
    - *Systems-Level Prevention*
    - *War/Terrorism*
- **National Education Association's (NEA) *School Crisis Guide* (2018):** A free guidebook that offers a detailed sample of a school crisis guide modeled after the U.S. Department of Education's directives for school crisis preparedness and response. Found at *www.nea.org/sites/default/files/2020-07/NEA%20School%20Crisis%20Guide%202018.pdf.*
- **Office of Justice Programs: Model for School-Based Crisis Preparedness and Response (2003):** Guidance on how to create a preplanned, systematic organizational model to direct decisions in school crisis response. Found at *https://ovc.ojp.gov/sites/g/files/xyckuh226/files/publications/bulletins/schoolcrisis/pg3.html.*

FORM 3.1

Priority Tasks Checklist in the Immediate Aftermath

Instructions for use: Utilize this checklist as a guide for the action steps to take in the immediate aftermath of a crisis. The tasks should be completed in the order in which they are listed.

- ☐ Call for help.
- ☐ Immediately attend to human safety and offer medical assistance.
- ☐ If needed, secure the crime scene and create boundaries with the media.
- ☐ Verify the facts and create a Crisis Fact Sheet.
- ☐ Communicate openly with relevant family members.
    - ☐ Discuss emotionality of survivors/witnesses (e.g., students who were exposed to a fearful situation).
    - ☐ Indicate the impact of the crisis event (e.g., the day was severely disrupted).
    - ☐ In serious cases, deliver injury/death notifications.

FORM 3.2

Checklist of Information to Share with Your Call for Help

Instructions for use: Utilize this checklist as a guide for the content that should be shared when reaching out for help in the aftermath of a crisis.

- ☐ Name and location of the school
- ☐ Nature of the emergency (e.g., bomb threat, school shooting)
- ☐ Number of victims and their condition
- ☐ Details about the suspected perpetrator, if relevant
- ☐ Directions to the specific location (i.e., what part of school should the police come to)

FORM 3.3

Crisis Fact Sheet Checklist

Instructions for use: Collect and record the following facts as they relate to the crisis at hand.

☐ All known facts that have been confirmed by reliable sources

____

____

____

☐ Date, time, location of the crisis

____

____

☐ Name, age, grade, other relevant details about victims/perpetrator

____

____

☐ The status of victims and suspected perpetrators

____

____

☐ School schedule: will it stay open for the rest of the day/tomorrow?

____

____

☐ Steps the CRT has taken to notify parents/school community

____

____

☐ Have parents/caregivers been encouraged to pick up their children or not?

____

____

☐ Information about the counseling services that are being made available to the school community

____

____

☐ Information about the upcoming family/community meeting

____

____

The answers to these questions will be used to generate your Crisis Fact Sheet.

CHAPTER 4

Unexpected Deaths

Unfortunately, many students will experience the loss of a loved one at some point during their schooling years. It is estimated that millions of children in the United States will lose a parent or sibling before they turn 18 (Judi's House/JAG Institute, 2022). Sadly, in just our recent past, more than 1 million Americans died from COVID, and many of them were caregivers or parents of children (Kekatos, 2022). Moreover, there are many tragic cases of unexpected student and teacher deaths that greatly impact the student body and school professionals. These deaths will inevitably vary in their nature; some will be unexpected (e.g., car accident), while others will have more preparation (e.g., a teacher dying of a terminal illness). This chapter is designed to help you to be best prepared in responding to an unexpected death at your school. Best practices for interventions are discussed in detail, with specific recommendations on how to employ appropriate strategies. Grief reactions and related bereavement are reviewed, along with ways to properly intervene and meet the needs of your school community.

WHAT IS YOUR ROLE WHEN RESPONDING TO A DEATH AT YOUR SCHOOL?

The circumstances of an unexpected death will greatly determine the action steps that must be taken. In many cases of nonviolent, unexpected deaths, the crisis response falls primarily on the SMHPs and the administration. Of course, if there are severe circumstances (e.g., death on campus, death by suicide), your CRT should convene immediately. Figure 4.1 outlines the key action steps that important school personnel (e.g., school psychologist and principal) should take in the aftermath of an unexpected death in their school community. These points are discussed in detail, including specific guidance on how to implement each action and the order in which to do so.

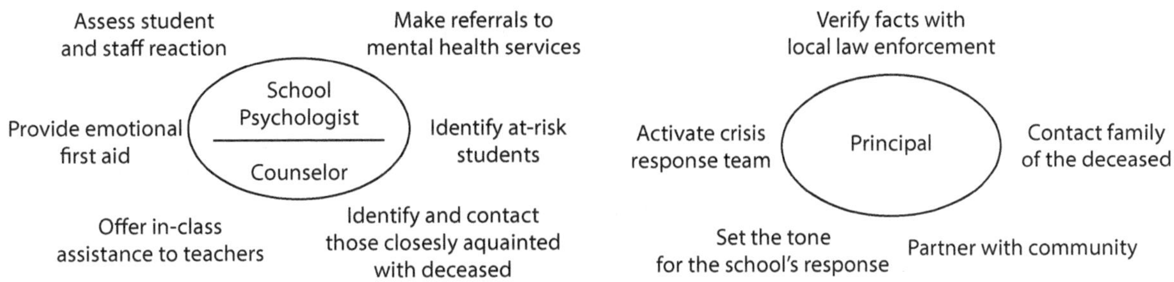

FIGURE 4.1. School personnel action steps in the aftermath of an unexpected death.

SMHPs are prominent figures in the crisis response of an unexpected death. You should be prepared to hold a number of responsibilities that range across the student community. When necessary, it is important to lean on other qualified professionals, particularly if you find that you are impacted by the unexpected death (e.g., a student you counseled in the past). If needed, collaborate with your principal to ensure that appropriate mental health support is available to the student body, even if that means utilizing district or other community resources.

HOW TO RESPOND TO A DEATH AT YOUR SCHOOL

> One of the most challenging was responding to an elementary school where a child was caught in a mechanical gymnasium door and crushed to death. There were multiple witnesses, and a teacher had activated the door to close the space. The after-school activity was overseen by a county, not school, program, and those employees were told "not to talk to anyone." Their after-school students were the most impacted. This was very difficult on many levels: the child was a teacher's child (another school), and only a third grader. To say that the loss was widely felt is an understatement. Crisis teams responded for days. End-of-year activities had to be relocated, and the gym was repainted (after school concluded). Laws got changed because of the lack of safety features on the door.
>
> —CINDY DICKINSON

As with all cases of crisis response, it is imperative that you first verify the facts of the situation. In the case of a death of a school member or a close community member, this will likely require consultation with law enforcement and loved ones of the deceased. Moreover, you will need to consider specific factors of the death to enact the most appropriate interventions. My responses to deaths in school communities have helped me to develop key questions you should be asking when faced with an unexpected death at your school.

These questions are helpful in two ways. First, the answers will help you to verify the facts. Second, they will provide the information needed to predict the level of emotional outpouring, along with the number of additional SMHPs that should be added to provide supportive services at your school. The questions are listed below, along with related professional reflections from my crisis response efforts. One important reflection features my response to an accidental death on campus. This narrative will be used to highlight the general steps to take when responding to unexpected death, and you will find notations that reflect recommendations for best practices. In Chapter 5, we provide detailed task lists that cover these steps, along with additional strategies specific to suicide.

KEY QUESTIONS TO ASK (AND MORE) WHEN RESPONDING TO AN UNEXPECTED DEATH

1. Who Was the Person Who Died?

- **Were they a staff member or a student?**
- **Were they a beloved member of the school community or were they new to the school?**
- **What type of extracurricular activities were they involved in (i.e., sports teams, debate club, either as a member or as a facilitator/coach)?**

Consideration of the person who died provides information regarding the magnitude of the death's impact. You will want to find out if this person was well liked and/or well known and how involved they were in the school community. Reactions to the death will vary based on these factors, and your response will be crafted around the information gathered.

PROFESSIONAL PERSPECTIVE: Scott Poland

In my career, I have responded to the deaths of three school principals. One example was the death of a high school principal at a school of over 3,000 students. While the principal's death was devastating to the school staff, it did not have the same impact on the student body. Given the large size of the school, very few students had a personal connection to her. The eight-member school administrative team was profoundly impacted as they worked closely with the principal. They needed a group processing session before they were ready to face the other staff members and share the plan developed to help the school cope with the death.

On another occasion, a high school student died, but she had only transferred to that school a few days before and was hardly known. Intervention and support to classmates and friends were really needed at her previous school.

Another example includes a high school band director who was killed in an accident. The band director had been at the school for over 30 years and was very popular. The school band numbered over 130 members, and almost every student had a strong connection with him. After his death, the entire band gathered during first period, and many of their parents also came to the band hall. Everyone wanted to reminisce about the band director and discuss whether the band concert would be held as scheduled the next week. The strong consensus was to hold the concert in the band director's memory.

2. What Happened to the Person Who Died?

- **What were the circumstances surrounding the death?**
  - **Accidental, due to illness, by suicide, homicide?**
- **Were there any violent or traumatic factors?**

An accidental death, a homicidal death, and a death by suicide are all sudden, unexpected, and often violent. The nature of these deaths is much more difficult for many to process, creating implications in your crisis response. Your response to each type of death should be similar in many ways, with the inclusion of varied strategies depending on the specific factors at hand.

PROFESSIONAL PERSPECTIVE: Scott Poland

Many types of unexpected deaths may be encountered in your school setting. Some deaths are easier to prepare for, such as a school member who has been ill in the hospital. I imagine that virtually everyone reading this book has lost a loved one to cancer or to another terminal illness, and when someone has an extended illness, we have some time to get used to the idea that we might lose our loved one. This type of death can create different complexities in your crisis response.

One example that comes to mind is the time I was asked to go into a second-grade classroom and notify students that their beloved teacher had died of cancer. Upon hearing the news, students became immediately upset. Several students said, "Just 2 days ago we were told she was getting better and now you're here telling us she died." I think it's very important that we be truthful with students and say things like "The doctors in the hospital did everything they could for her; she is no longer in pain; please keep her loved ones in your thoughts and prayers."

3. *Where Did the Death Occur?*

- **Was it on campus?**
- **Was it close to campus?**
- **Was it at a school member's home?**

Where the death has occurred is a primary factor to consider in your crisis response. If the death has occurred off campus, you will want to verify exactly where it took place, for that can have implications in terms of the impact on others. For example, if a student died in a car accident close to campus, many students may have witnessed the aftermath on their way to school. If a death occurs on school campus, then the extent of the traumatic impact will be very significant and so you must undertake a number of considerations. My response to an accidental death on campus highlights many of the special considerations and best practices in crisis response. The followings example can be used to outline the steps involved in this type of crisis response. **Bolded** text is linked to the <u>underlined</u> recommendations related to the actions.

PROFESSIONAL PERSPECTIVE: Scott Poland

Student Drowning on Campus

I received a call that a drowning accident had occurred to a student whom I will call "Sam" at the middle school across the parking lot from the offices of psychological services.

<u>Recommendation: In an ideal scenario and when possible, you would want to alert your CRT to the concerns so that they can begin to mobilize the crisis response plan for an accidental death.</u>

I reached this crisis quicker than any other crisis in my response history. I remember thinking, "Put your name tag on so that everyone will know who you are." I also grabbed paper, a pen, and my phone. An ambulance in the parking lot loaded up a student and quickly raced away with sirens blaring. The principal approached me and said he was following the ambulance to the hospital and that Sam's mom would be arriving soon. The principal asked if I would accompany Sam's mom to the hospital. I asked, **"Is Sam going to make it?"** and the principal replied, "We don't know as of yet."

Recommendation: It can't be emphasized enough: verify the facts.

I was then pulled in another direction by the assistant principal (AP), who asked what kind of information should be shared with students at the school. My reply was **"all we can say is that Sam is being taken to the hospital by ambulance. We will provide updated information about his condition as soon as possible."**

Recommendation: Share facts in a transparent and developmentally appropriate way. We can be honest about what we know, with thoughtful consideration of the audience, privacy, and safety. Refrain from sharing unnecessary details about the death.

I emphasized to the AP that it was important to ask staff and students to please think positive thoughts and/or prayers for Sam.

Recommendation: Remember that you are the model for reaction in a time of crisis; remain calm and focus on realistic, but positive messaging. This also encourages students and staff to turn to coping mechanisms, such as prayer.

Sam's mother pulled into the parking lot and immediately asked me if her son was going to be okay. I responded calmly that I did not know and offered to ride to the hospital with her. While driving to the hospital in the car with Sam's mom and his aunt, I found myself unable to answer many of the questions they asked. His mom and his aunt indicated that they were both devout and practiced a religion that I was unfamiliar with. I immediately thought, "What do I know about this religion and tragedy?" and I found myself in a place where the answer was not enough. **In reflecting back on this moment, it enhances the concept of how important it is that members of school crisis teams be knowledgeable about cultural and religious beliefs of the affected families**.

Recommendation: Consider diversity factors as they relate to the victims and the school community. These factors heavily influence trauma responses and grief.

When we arrived at the hospital, we met the school principal, and the doctors soon informed us that Sam had died. I will never forget the mother's screams, the scene of her pants unknowingly soiled in the midst of her trauma response. I asked if a nurse could get her some dry clothing. Soon after, the doctor asked the mother if she was ready to view her son's body. Sam's mother continued to scream. She kept yelling out, "Why did you let him die, why did you let him swim, why was he in the pool all alone!?" The school principal attempted to respond, providing a list of all the rules and all the procedures that were used whenever a student was swimming at school. I stopped him and let him know that this was not the time to reason with Sam's mother; this was the time to simply let her scream and cry. Sam's mother grabbed my hand and had me walk with her into the room to view Sam's body. This was not how I had ever expected to spend the day as a school psychologist, but I could tell that my presence provided support for her.

Sam had an older sibling at the high school, as well as a younger sibling at an elementary school.

Recommendation: Review who is closest to the victim and therefore most impacted. Find out if there are siblings in the same or nearby school. Reach out to their counselors to coordinate crisis responses and care.

Eventually, in the company of their father, the siblings arrived at the hospital. They were joined by the two respective principals. It was a testament to the care in our school district to have the other principals involved in making sure that the entire family was united. With the family now united, my school principal and I began communicating with the staff back at the middle school. **All the students had gone home for the day, but there was very important work to be done and the entire administrative and mental health support team was awaiting our arrival back at the school.**

Recommendation: Consider modifying the school schedule or closing for the day, depending on the severity of factors associated with the death. Should you decide to close school, you are encouraged to reopen and reestablish a normal routine as soon as possible.

A communication memo was drafted after consulting with the central office that notified all caregivers from the school that a student had unfortunately passed away as a result of drowning.

Recommendation: Staff should be notified first and provided with a prepared statement on how to share the news with students. Caregivers/families should be notified via email, letter, or phone call.

Caregivers were told to share the tragic news with their children and to contact the counseling office at school for support. They were also advised of the typical reactions that children have to a traumatic event, including academic and behavioral regression, sleeping problems, nightmares, irritability, and worries about the future. Caregivers were encouraged to be patient, tolerant, and loving and to maintain the routines for their child. They were told to primarily listen to their children and to give them permission to experience a range of emotions. The principal and I consulted and decided to use the school calling tree to update all staff that Sam died and to notify them of the **faculty meeting scheduled before school the next morning.**

Recommendation: Hold a faculty meeting either at the end of the day or the following day. This should be a place where facts are shared and teachers are given strategies to help support the students.

The faculty meeting was held before school the next morning, and we went over all of the facts about the tragic death. A great deal of support was provided to Coach B, who had supervised the swimming session. Coach B shared with the entire faculty that it was the first day of swimming for the school's eighth-grade football team. She had every student swim sideways across the pool so that she could make certain that every student could swim. The coach then asked every student to swim lengthwise across the pool. Sam went under the water about midway through the first lengthways lap; a student screamed for help. The coach jumped into the pool and brought Sam to the side and with the help of others placed him on the pool deck. Coach B immediately began CPR while the school nurse and ambulance were called. We could only imagine the feelings of guilt that Coach B was experiencing at that time, and we offered support and the message that she was not to blame. I consulted privately with the principal about providing additional support to Coach B. **The principal shared that another teacher had recently lost her son in a car accident, and he asked me to follow up and check in on her.**

Recommendation: Remember to be attuned to prior crises or traumas that survivors have gone through. Sometimes this is difficult to know but make efforts to find out when possible.

I was asked to speak to the entire faculty at the meeting before school. I stressed that it was important for each of them to reach out to their sources of support and to be supportive of the students. I also emphasized the importance of giving students permission to express and experience a range of emotions and noted that students often like to express their emotions through writing, music, artwork, projects, ceremonies, and rituals. I stated that each teacher chose to be an educator because of how much they cared about children and that in their heart, they had good ideas about how to help children during traumatic times. I emphasized that they should let their heart be their guide and that would help them to know what to do to help their students.

We decided that it was important to have the sixth-period football PE class begin the day by meeting with myself, the coach, and the eighth-grade counselor.

Recommendation: Mental health staff should be available to hold small-group meetings with students to process their reactions. These meetings should be held in all the classes the victim attended. In addition, individualized care should be provided to those most impacted, such as close friends and staff.

Nineteen members of the class were in the pool the day Sam drowned. We arranged the chairs into a circle and all the adults sat down. It was clear to me that the coach and the eighth-grade counselor wanted me to begin the session; that was challenging because none of the 19 students had ever seen me before. I introduced myself and said I was so sorry about the death of their classmate. I said I didn't know Sam, but that I had heard a lot of good things about him. I asked them to please tell me about their classmate.

Experience has taught me that what students want to do after the loss of a friend is to be allowed the opportunity to talk about them. I provided them with that opportunity, and they had a great deal to share about Sam. The students asked if they could make cards and share them with Sam's family. The cards identified all of the things they enjoyed about him. **I asked each of the students to think about who they had gone to before during troubling times and what had helped them through difficult times.**

Recommendation: Classroom meetings should emphasize healthy ways in which students can cope with their grief.

I encouraged each of them to think about how their caregivers could help, and I asked what they needed from caregivers and school personnel. I let the students know that the school counselor and I would be contacting each of their caregivers that day to discuss the tragic death. I emphasized that I would be stressing that their caregivers please reach out to their children, to truly be there and to listen to them during this difficult time. When the school bell rang to change classes, not a single student moved, as they knew the discussion we were having was very important. (One note: since that day, I have asked principals to check with all classes to see if students are ready to go to the next class before the bell rings.)

Before our session ended, I asked if any of the students would like to stay behind for some individual support. Two of them chose to do so, and they shared other sad things that had happened in their lives. One thing that I remember most about that intervention was how, at first, Coach B did not want to attend the session; however, she did come and it ended up being a helpful experience for her. She heard feedback from the students who told her over and over again that she had gotten Sam out of the pool quickly and that she was an obvious expert at CPR.

Sam's schedule was then followed by me and a school counselor for each classroom throughout the day. Desks were placed in a circle, and the primary focus was to provide opportunities for students to talk and reminisce, while the adults listened. The principal allowed the students to put a block of paper along the entire length of the eighth-grade hallway. The students used markers to write messages about Sam. They placed **makeshift memorials** around the school swimming pool, all of which were preserved until after Sam's funeral. Digital images were taken of the spontaneous memorials.

Recommendation: Temporary memorials are likely to pop up. You will want to decide on a reasonable time period for these to remain in place. It is suggested that you wait until the funeral is over. Permanent memorial policies should be put in place by the district and followed; in general, permanent memorials at school are discouraged in favor of raising funds for prevention or for a scholarship in memory of the victim.

Sam was an eighth-grade football player, and the coach asked me whether there should be practice that afternoon. My answer was **"Let's leave that up to the team members."**

Recommendation: Consult with students regarding scheduling changes and modifications to activities.

The entire team assembled on the bleachers around the football field at practice time. The coach gave the players the option to cancel practice. Their response was surprising: every football player got up off the bleachers and gathered in a circle under the goal post. They continued talking and processing the death of their teammate Sam.

By the end of the day, the eighth-grade counselor and I had reached the families of each of the 19 students who were in the pool when Sam drowned, and all caregivers were very appreciative. I told the families that I was a psychologist who was helping their child and that they must have heard what had happened. I emphasized that I was there to talk about the best way to support their child.

I was present at Sam's funeral, as were many members of his school.

Recommendation: Allow students and staff to attend the funeral.

For several days I followed up with those students who appeared to be the most deeply affected by Sam's death. In addition, I checked in with the school psychologists at his siblings' schools, and I made sure to have frequent check-ins with Coach B.

Recommendation: Continued follow-up with the most vulnerable is imperative. Trauma reactions can persist, and many people require ongoing support in the aftermath of a crisis.

I arranged for the 19 students to participate in a ROPES (Reality-Oriented Physical Experiences) course, a program that I developed that helps individuals to work on communication, problem solving, and belonging in a physical experience.

Recommendation: This is an example of the varied approaches you must take based on specific factors, for example, proximity to the death. These students certainly benefited from additional and more individualized support.

It also helps to build self-esteem and trust in others. I led the session with these students, and I found it to be a very powerful way for them to work together as a team through various obstacles. Moreover, they utilized the time after the session; sitting on tree stumps, they continued to process the loss of their friend and teammate.

A few weeks later, I received a call from the school superintendent asking me to join him, the school principal, and Sam's parents in a walk-through of the pool. Sam's parents had asked to be able to walk around the pool where their son had died. They asked us a few questions about where the coach was and the specific directions that were provided to the students that day before swimming. Sam's older sister and younger brother were also present. It seemed important to the three of them to simply be in the place where Sam had died.

An autopsy was completed, and we were hoping that there would be a clear cause of death that explained the quick nature of the drowning. Unfortunately, the report was inconclusive. According to the detailed account by the coach and all 19 students present in class that day, it appeared that Sam could not have been underwater more than 20 to 45 seconds and it did not appear that the school could have done anything to have prevented Sam's tragic death. Ultimately, Sam's parents sued the district. From my perspective, the school was not at fault; even so, the case was settled out of court for an undisclosed amount.

4. *Was Anyone Involved in or a Witness to the Death?*

- **Did anyone at school witness the death?**
- **Did anyone assist in the individual's death?**
- **Did anyone have knowledge of potential deadly behaviors beforehand?**

It is imperative that you consider the impact of the unexpected death in terms of the surviving crisis victims. It is not enough to simply consider the effects of death on the broader school population; you must think deeply about the detailed connections of impact. For example, if a student dies in a tragic accident, you'll want to consider things like: Who was in his inner circle of friendship? Who was his best friend? Was he on a sports team or part of a school club? Does he have a mentor or coach whom he's worked closely with? These questions will help you to connect the dots of who will be most impacted by the death and thus require more specific intervention.

It is recommended that you utilize the model of Circles of Vulnerability (Rosenfeld, Caye, Ayalon, & Lahad, 2005) in order to best complete this assessment. This model, which is typically utilized in the field of suicidology, will help you to identify individuals who could be more vulnerable to trauma impact. Your consideration will include three primary factors: geographic proximity (i.e., physical distance from the event), psychosocial proximity (i.e., level of connection to the deceased), and population at risk (i.e., mental health issues, previous trauma history, substance use issues, past suicide attempts). Form 4.1 provides a visual of the Circles of Vulnerability, with directions on how to implement the model. These factors are very helpful in determining how much support is needed and which staff and/or students will require support over an extended period of time.

> I remember a response where a student named Leroy was car surfing in the parking lot and three other students were in the car. Leroy was standing on the hood of the car as it traveled around the school parking lot. Unfortunately, Leroy fell off the car, hit his head, and died. Applying the Circles of Vulnerability model, it was important to note that three students were in the car that Leroy fell from, one of which was Joshua, his best friend. Additionally, other students in the parking lot witnessed the tragedy. The previous trauma history of the students who witnessed the accident was also a significant factor to examine. I came to find out that Joshua had just lost his mother to cancer a few weeks previously. Joshua was at the intersection of the three Circles of Vulnerability. Joshua was someone I knew would need longer-term support.
>
> —SCOTT POLAND

5. *What Else Has Impacted the School Community?*

- **Have there been any traumatic events in the community or at the school in the past?**
- **Has the school suffered any recent losses?**
- **Have the victims suffered any other recent losses?**

PROFESSIONAL PERSPECTIVE: SCOTT POLAND

Responding to the Death of a Teacher

I have received many calls for a consultation following a death in the school community. I always listen very carefully and take notes. I always ask, "Before you had this tragedy, what other trauma has your school been dealing with?" One case I was involved with was an elementary school where three fifth-grade teachers all died in the same school year. The third death was a teacher named Joe, who I happened to know personally. The morning after Joe's death, we had a faculty meeting before school, and the principal was crying as she shared information about Joe's death the night before. She apologized for her tears, but her staff told her it was okay and they were crying also. This was powerful to witness; the principal's acknowledgment of showing her emotions gave everyone permission to do the same, creating a shared experience of grief and connectedness in a time of loss.

We then went on to develop a response plan. We decided that all 100 fifth-grade students would be brought into the cafeteria and the principal would share the news of Joe's death. I arranged for additional counselors and the school psychologist to be present at the school. The principal asked all the fifth graders if any of them wanted to see a counselor that morning in the aftermath of Joe's death and approximately 80 hands went up. Luckily, we were prepared for this and had 10 additional SMHPs ready to provide services. Each SMHP counted off eight students and took them to their assigned room. In the future, I suggested that, when possible, students should be broken down into smaller groups for crisis intervention. I have been in a room before with 60 grieving students, and it can feel overwhelming for the crisis responders. In those instances, I had wished that I was providing support to only a classroom of students or even a smaller group.

As I progressed through my career concentrating on school crisis prevention and intervention, my focus shifted toward being with the superintendent or school principal to help plan the intervention for everyone. However, the morning after Joe's death, I did take on one of the groups of eight students who wanted to reminisce about Joe. They shared that Joe was a great teacher and spoke of many anecdotes regarding things he did in the classroom that they loved so much. They made cards to send to his family to share how much they cared about him and how he made them feel. I did of course ask a very important question: whether any of the students in my group had lost a loved one. One student, Jose, spoke of his father who was killed in a truck accident the previous month. After the meeting, I knew that I would be calling the caregivers of every single student in my group to talk about the support they needed. Importantly, I also scheduled a conference with Jose's mother to ensure that his needs were addressed more individually, and I made a note to follow up with the SMHP to let them know that Jose would need ongoing support.

BEREAVEMENT

Given the likelihood that you will encounter some form of death in your career, consideration of bereavement is a necessity. As a crisis responder, it is important that you develop a mature concept of death in order to best intervene with the bereaved. Death is many things; irreversible and final, nonfunctional (all life functions terminate), and a universal experience. Grief comes with death, but also with other losses in life (e.g., divorce, life transition, lost job). While there

FIGURE 4.2. Factors to consider in the grieving process.

are general concepts surrounding the grieving process, variability is observed in its manifestation. A number of factors impact the way one grieves (see Figure 4.2).

Consideration of these factors in the context of the grieving process is imperative and can give you important information on how to best respond to those in need. Additionally, it is helpful to become acquainted with the grieving process and the associated feelings and reactions across the lifespan. Grief is never linear. It is often likened to waves in the ocean, ebbing and flowing with memories of happiness and, conversely, overwhelming feelings of sadness. Grief manifests emotionally, physically, and cognitively and is an ongoing process with a varied duration; there is no timeline.

Grief is individualized and personal; there is no right or wrong way to grieve (NASP, 2015a). Acute grief is commonly marked by numbness, denial, feelings of sadness, fear, anger, and guilt, and it is often described in stages: *denial—anger—bargaining—depression—acceptance*. While these stages appear to be in consecutive order, those suffering from traumatic grief may cycle through these stages until their grief is resolved (Stanaway, 2020). Moving through grief requires an individual to meet specific milestones, including accepting the death, experiencing the emotional pain and feelings related to the death and one's separation from the person who died, and adapting to changes and a new environment that no longer includes the deceased (NASP, 2015a).

For a small number of bereaving individuals, the common experience of grief becomes more intense and prolonged and is clinically referred to as "complicated grief." Individuals with complicated grief are found to experience intense waves of grief symptoms, chronic rumination and worry about the death, excessive avoidant behaviors related to potential triggers of the death, and a persistent difficulty in comprehending the finality of the loss (Shear, 2012). Individuals experiencing complicated grief should be connected to a mental health provider experienced in treating bereavement.

Your understanding of grief symptoms is imperative and requires a review of the varied presentations of grief across age groups. As you can imagine, young children in elementary school are likely to grieve in a far different manner than a senior in high school. Given the range of ages that you may encounter in crisis intervention work, it's important that you are attuned to the varied developmental presentations of grief (see Table 4.1).

In the aftermath of an unexpected, nonviolent death at your school, much of your student body will likely be able to grieve appropriately without additional support. However, there will be some individuals (especially those within the Circles of Vulnerability) who will need additional support and should be followed on an ongoing basis. Students who demonstrate marked behavioral and mood changes require this type of follow-up and should be referred to additional mental health services. Signs of potential needs are summarized in Table 4.2.

You can be an important and helpful part of the grief process for students. Small-group meetings should be held in which students can express their thoughts and feelings about the loss. Ensure that you use developmentally appropriate language and be ready to answer student questions. Utilize these meetings to normalize the grieving process and provide information about its common course. Give students permission to grieve and advise them that it is best to maintain their normal routine and school schedule. Mental health resources should also be shared, including ways for students to follow up with the SMHP at school, if needed. Students should be encouraged to enact positive coping strategies and to avoid numbing mechanisms, such as drugs and alcohol (when age appropriate).

TABLE 4.1. Grief Reactions Based on Age

Preschool

May observe regressive behaviors, symptoms of anxiety, decreased verbalization

Elementary school

May observe decline in several areas:
- Academic performance
- Attention/concentration
- Attendance

May observe irritable moods, aggression, and acting out; somatic complaints; eating/sleep issues; social isolation; feelings of guilt, symptoms of depression and anxiety; repeated retelling of the event (NASP, 2015d).

Middle and high school

May observe a decline in several areas:
- Academic performance
- Attention/concentration
- Attendance

May observe avoidant behaviors, social withdrawal, engagement in high-risk behaviors or substance abuse and related emotional numbing, peer conflict/difficulties, nightmares, flashbacks, symptoms of depression and anxiety (NASP, 2015d).

Adults

May observe symptoms of depression, including issues with concentration; feelings of sadness, anger, and guilt; agitation; irritable mood (Mugahl, Azhar, & Mahon, 2020)

> Following an accidental student death in 1989, I was trained by a local grief counselor who taught me how to listen and how to be in the moment with a crisis victim—how to guide and support and not direct. She taught me about grief and loss, and how that affects learning and the emotional development of students and how to provide support and healing.
>
> —Cathy Kennedy-Paine

When you are intervening with bereaving students, it is important for you to be mindful of your approach, as it may differ from typical clinical support. NASP (2015a) has shared helpful tips for things to avoid in the context of bereavement. We agree with these recommendations of what to avoid, and I have included my suggestions, along with ideas for what to say instead (see Table 4.3).

TABLE 4.2. Signs of the Need for Additional Follow-Up

- Observed loss of interest in daily/pleasurable activities
- Changes in sleeping and eating patterns
- Voicing of desires/wishes to be with the deceased loved one
- Report of increased fears of being alone
- Significant decline in grades
- Increased somatic complaints (e.g., stomachaches, headaches)
- Attendance issues; skipping, intermittent attendance

TABLE 4.3. What to Avoid in Grief Processing

- Overidentification with the victims—for example, *"I get what you're going through."* You actually have no idea what they've gone through.
    - Instead, you can say, *"I am here to listen to you."*
- Statements that are minimizing and can be invalidating—for example, *"At least it was a teacher and not your family member."* Every death should be taken seriously.
    - Instead, you can say, *"This loss must be so hard for you."*
- Euphemisms about the deceased—for example, *"They went away for a long time."* Remember to be direct.
    - Instead, you can say, *"Person X died in a car accident."*
- Create a time frame for the grieving process—for example, *"It has been a few weeks, I think we can start moving on."*
    - Instead, you can say, *"There is no timeline for your grief."*
- Offering too much about yourself—for example, *"I've lost loved ones too."* Remember, the focus is on the victim, not yourself.
    - Instead, you can say, *"I'm here to support you."*

It is recommended that all professionals who provide crisis intervention services related to death become familiar with providing emotion aid to survivors. The National Child Traumatic Stress Network (NCTSN) and the U.S. Department of Veterans Affairs National Center for PTSD (NCPTSD; 2014) are excellent resources that provide online training in crisis response for mental health professionals. These agencies collaborated to create a well-known approach of "psychological aid" (Brymer et al., 2006), which is discussed in more detail in the response to severe crises, such as school shootings. Table 4.4 outlines guidance that is similar to NCTSN/NCPTSD's psychological aid, highlighting the ways you can provide emotional aid in your response to death.

TABLE 4.4. Providing Emotional Aid in Action

Reaching out physically	Reaching out emotionally
Position yourself at the person's side, at their level	Use brief comments: • *"This must be very painful for you."* • *"You are not alone. We are here for you."* • *"I'm sorry this happened. I am here to listen."*
Use the individual's name, using a soft, calming tone	Use brief suggestions: • *"It's okay, let your feelings out."* • *"It's okay to cry right now."*
Provide a comforting physical presence through the use of body language	Use brief questions: • *"How can I help?"* • *"What are you most worried about?"* • *"Who or what helped you in difficult times before, and what can help you now?"*

TABLE 4.5. NASP's Recommended Books for Grieving Children

Picture books

- *Badger's Parting Gifts* by Susan Varley; ages 3+
- *Bear's Last Journey* by Udo Weingelt; ages 4+
- *Dead Bird* by Margaret Brown Wise; ages 4–7
- *Everett Anderson's Goodbye* by Lucille Clifton; ages 5+
- *Goodbye Mousie* by Robie H. Harris; ages 4+
- *The Purple Balloon* by Chris Raschka; ages 3+
- *Remembering Crystal* by Sebastian Loth; ages 3+
- *Sammy in the Sky* by Barbara Walsh; ages 4+
- *The Scar* by Charlotte Moundlic; ages 5+
- *Six Is So Much Less Than Seven* by Ronald Himler; ages 5+
- *Someone Special Died* by Joan Pristine; ages 3+
- *Where Do People Go When They Die?* by Mindy Avra Portnoy; ages 5+
- *Where the Tomorrows Go* by Manoj S. Abraham; ages 6+

General books

- *A Terrible Thing Happened—A Story for Children Who Have Witnessed Violence or Trauma* by Margaret M. Holmes; more appropriate for older children
- *Bird* by Zetta Elliot; ages 7+
- *Chester Racoon and the Acorn Full of Memories* by Audrey Penn; more appropriate for older children
- *The Fall of Freddie the Leaf: A Story of Life for All Ages* by Leo Buscaglia; ages 4+
- *Good-Bye Sheepie* by Robert Burleigh; ages 6+
- *Her Mother's Face* by Roddy Doyles; more appropriate for older children
- *I Miss You: A First Look at Death* by Pat Thomas; ages 4+
- *The Invisible String by* Patrice Karst; ages 3+
- *Jenny Is Scared: When Sad Things Happen in the World* by Carol Shuman; ages 4+
- *Kaddish for Grandpa in Jesus' Name Amen* by James Howe; ages 4+
- *Lifetimes: The Beautiful Way to Explain Death to Children* by Bryan Mellonie Page; ages 5+
- *The Next Place* by Warren Handson; ages 5+
- *Old Pig* by Margaret Wild; ages 4+
- *Pearl's Marigolds for Grandpa* by Jane Breskin Zalben; ages 2+
- *Saying Goodbye to Lulu* by Corrine Demas; ages 3+
- *Sometimes I'm Scared* by Jane Annuziata; ages 5+
- *When Dinosaurs Die: A Guide to Understanding Death* (*Dino Guides for Families*) by Laurie Krasny Brown; ages 5+

Note. From NASP (2015d).

Ideas for Consideration

- Engage in creative group activities; ideas include:
  - Making a class scrapbook
  - Writing letters or cards to the deceased or their family members
  - Engaging in artwork; painting or drawing the emotions that students are feeling.
- Bibliotherapy: Make a group trip to the library to check out prescreened books on grief. Read these books as a group and have discussions about student feelings and reactions.
  - NASP (2015d) has an excellent list of recommended books about grief that are listed in Table 4.5.
- Hold a group processing session: While group processing sessions should be optional, those affected by the crisis should be encouraged to come into the room and be given an overview of what they have a chance to participate in.
  - Confidentiality should be emphasized, as well as the importance of one person talking at a time, and everyone who wishes to talk about the crisis will be given an opportunity.
  - It is best to have the group composed of individuals who had a similar experience with the crisis in the same group (i.e., those who were exposed physically to seeing injuries or a death should be separated from those not on campus or at the other end of the school building and did not witness injury or death).
  - The facilitator sets the tone and emphasizes the normal reaction to a crisis and says that no one should feel alone. The most important questions for the facilitator to ask are:
    - *What are you facing and what are you most worried about in the near future?*
    - *Who or what has helped you cope with sad things that have happened in the past, and who or what can help you now?*
  - The session should be closed with emphasis on resilience in the group. Additional available resources for the facilitator should clearly identify support that is available over the next few days, and immediate individual support should be offered for those who would like it. See the Recommended Resources section for ideas on what to share.

An unexpected death in your school community is an event you will likely encounter at some point in your career. Preparation for your response is the first step in ensuring best practices for intervention. Each response must be made in an individualized manner, with consideration of the manner of death, the location of the death, and those who will be most impacted. You must be attuned to the needs of your school community, including common grief reactions and vulnerabilities that may increase their risk for a heightened response. Processing is a key component of your response and should be implemented according to the guidelines discussed in this chapter. You will be a critical part of the response to an unexpected death, and so it is imperative that you employ best practices to ensure that the needs of your school community are met.

Recommended Resources

- **Compassionate Friends:** Connects families who are grieving the loss of their children to local support groups, with over 500 chapters nationwide. Found at *www.compassionatefriends.org.*
- **Federal Emergency Management Agency's (FEMA; 2009) Guidelines for Student/Staff Sudden Death:** Detailed guidance for best practices for school response to unexpected

deaths of school members. Found at *https://training.fema.gov/programs/emischool/el361toolkit/assets/suddendeath.pdf.*

- **National Child Traumatic Stress Network and National Center for PTSD:** A network of frontline providers, family members, researchers, and national partners whose mission is to change the course of children's lives by improving their care and disseminating scientific gains into practice across the nation. Found at *www.nctsn.org.*
- **National Alliance for Children's Grief:** Provides national resources and support for children who are grieving. Found at *https://nacg.org.*
- **NASP's Addressing Grief (2015d):** One of a number of helpful resources for educators, caregivers, and students. Found at *www.nasponline.org/resources-and-publications/resources-and-podcasts/school-safety-and-crisis/mental-health-resources/addressing-grief.*
    - Topics include:
        - **Tips for Caregivers**
        - **Tips for Teachers and Administrators**

FORM 4.1

Circles of Vulnerability

Instructions for use: Consider the graphic depiction of the Circles of Vulnerability. Ask the following questions and record the answers in order to make a solid assessment of victims who will likely require a higher level of care in the aftermath of a crisis.

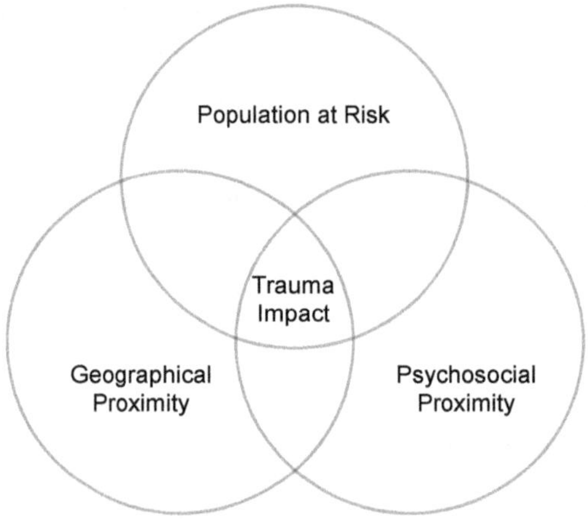

1. **Who witnessed the event? (Geographical Proximity)**
   Ensure that you are aware of all who have been exposed to major aspects of the crisis event. List staff members, students, or community members who bore witness to the event or the aftermath of the event. This includes seeing a dead body or blood from an injured person.

   ____

   ____

2. **Who is connected to the deceased? (Psychosocial Proximity)**
   Investigate those who had deeper relational connections to the deceased. List staff members, students, and/or community members who had a relationship with the deceased. Individuals to consider include peer groups, teammates, mentors, coaches, teachers, family members and loved ones, tutors, clergy members.

   ____

   ____

3. **What populations are at risk?**
   Consider risk factors for those who have been impacted by the death. Such risk factors include mental health issues, trauma history, substance use issues, relational conflict, victims of bullying/harassment, prior suicide attempts. List staff members, students, and/or community members who may be at a greater risk for trauma impact given their present risk factors.

   ____

   ____

Source: The Venn Diagram tool is provided by ReadWriteThink.org, a website powered by the National Council of Teachers of English.

CHAPTER 5

Suicide

SUICIDALITY IN YOUR SCHOOL

Considerations of suicidology in the school context are of utmost importance for all SMHPs. The school setting is a logical place for intervention, given the significant amount of time that the youth population spends engaged in the environment. Notably, research confirms that school impacts the behavior and health of young people (Evans & Hurrell, 2016). Moreover, seasonal variations of suicidal behaviors have been documented, in which the lowest incidence of suicidality is recorded during the summer months, with increasing trends in the fall and spring, coinciding with the school year (Plemmons et al., 2018).

The trends observed in the Youth Risk Behavior Surveillance System (YRBSS; CDC, 2023) data support these patterns, demonstrating high levels of youth suicidality and related behaviors from 2021. Note the most recent YRBSS findings on youth suicide at the high school level:

- 22% of students reported seriously considered attempting suicide.
- 18% of students made a suicide plan.
- 10% of students made a suicide attempt.
- Suicide attempts were the highest among females (13%), American Indians or Alaska Natives (16%), and students who identified as part of the LGBTQIA+ community (22% [CDC, 2023]).

These findings reveal alarming concerns regarding suicidality and our youth population, Moreover, it is important to note that the YRBSS trends over time indicate that these concerns are only getting worse. Notably, the percentage of every racial and ethnic group that felt persistently sad or hopeless increased from 2019 to 2021 (37 to 42%, respectively), along with those seriously considering a suicide attempt (19 to 22%), making a suicide plan (16 to 18%), and attempting suicide (9 to 10% [CDC, 2023]). Sadly, these reports are not surprising, considering the widespread difficulties experienced during the COVID-19 pandemic and related aftermath.

Among the crises discussed in this guidebook, suicidality is one of the most *preventable.* In fact, prevention is recommended as the best means for intervention. Identification of at-risk behaviors and warning signs is of the utmost importance and can mean the very difference between life and death. As discussed in Chapter 2, prevention of suicide should be a major focus in your CRT's planning approaches. However, despite your efforts, given the prevalent and increasing nature of suicidality, related behaviors are not unique occurrences in school settings. There will likely come a time in your career when you must intervene in the face of suicidal behaviors at your school.

As such, it is recommended that, in addition to your suicide prevention policies, you create related intervention guidelines. Comprehensive intervention policies and procedures ensure that your school personnel will have specific guidance in intervening with suicidal students. The AFSP (2019) emphasizes this recommendation, relaying that it will help to clarify your staff's roles and empower them to effectively intervene and support youth who are in need. Additionally, both the Substance Abuse and Mental Health Services Administration (SAMHSA; 2012) and the Trevor Project (2021) strongly recommend that protocols be provided in every school, outlining responsibilities and roles for each task in the event of a suicide risk, suicide attempt, or suicide. See the Recommended Resources section at the end of this chapter for more information on these helpful kits and policies.

This chapter provides lengthy guidance on how to approach suicide intervention in the school setting. We review best practices for suicide assessment, intervention practices, and postvention management in the aftermath of a student suicide. Having dedicated my career to suicide prevention, I have accumulated a number of helpful reflections and cases that will enhance your real-world understanding of how to appropriately approach suicidality in the school context.

AT-RISK BEHAVIOR IDENTIFIED

Recall the risk factors and warning signs that were discussed in Chapter 2; early identification of these factors is critical to the intervention process. While many youth who are at risk for suicidal behavior go unnoticed, the majority display clues to their distress in some form. These warning signs are the key reason why gatekeepers are an effective prevention tool. It is recommended that you and your staff consistently review the common warning signs associated with youth suicidality. Any recognition of signs for potential at-risk behavior should never go unaddressed as they are strong predictors for suicide.

Once you have established a student's potential risk, you must move forward with the intervention process. If an SMHP is not available, the administrator or school nurse should provide care for the student until an SMHP or outside professional can be reached to complete a thorough risk assessment. As a reminder, the student should *never* be left alone once at-risk behavior is identified (AFSP, 2019). Suicide screeners are a helpful first step that can be used to identify students in need of more in-depth risk assessment. Erbacher and colleagues (2015) developed a suicide screener, the *Suicide Risk Screening Form*, which includes five direct questions to ask students you suspect are suicidal.

1. Have you wished you were dead?
2. Have you felt that you, your friends, or your family would be better off if you were dead?
3. Have you had thoughts about killing yourself?
4. Do you intend to kill yourself?
5. Have you tried to kill yourself? (p. 95)

These questions are designed to investigate the presence and severity of suicidal ideation (SI). We also recommend use of the Columbia Suicide Severity Rating Scale (C-SSRS; Posner et al., 2009) as a basic screening tool. It is a free screener that provides a step-by-step questionnaire on how to properly navigate a risk assessment. If the questions on a suicide screener are positively endorsed, it is important to take a deeper look at the current state of their suicidality and inquire further about their frequency (how often the thoughts occur), duration (how long they last), controllability (intrusiveness of the thoughts and control of impulses to act on them), deterrents (barriers to acting upon the thoughts), and reasons for the ideation (Posner et al., 2009). Form 5.1 provides a detailed review of these questions and more that can be used in your suicide screening.

If the student completing the screener endorses any of the questions reviewed in Form 5.1, it is imperative that a comprehensive risk assessment be conducted, which ideally takes place in the community. Hopefully, there is at least one professional in the school setting who is trained to complete a thorough risk assessment. The risk assessment process is an evaluation aimed to elicit specific details regarding a student's intent to die by suicide.

Of note, the American School Counselor Association (ASCA; 2022) maintains a position that if counselors are required to use instruments to screen or assess suicide risk, then they cannot negate the level of risk, as students may tell counselors they are not suicidal to avoid scrutiny. ASCA stresses that counselors are part of a school collaborative team but cautions about the use of suicide assessment scales that classify risk as low, medium, or high. Additionally, counselors cannot guarantee student safety. ASCA importantly emphasizes that if a student is suspected of being at risk for suicide, parent notification is mandatory, not discretionary. Dr. Carolyn Stone, the Ethics Chair for ASCA, and I have been on the same side in several legal cases in which schools were sued after a student suicide. SMHPs must recognize that caregivers of a student at risk will look for any reason to deny the seriousness of the situation. You should therefore document in writing all steps taken for safety, including parent notification and recommendations for supervision and a community-based assessment (ASCA, 2022).

SMHPs vary widely in their training and confidence in suicide risk assessment and management. In order to become more competent in this area, we highly recommend that SMHPs practice through role plays where they ask students about suicidal thoughts. One compromise with the ASCA position discussed earlier is to utilize the risk level as a determinant of needed immediate supervision. We cannot overstate that caregivers should be notified regardless of the risk level. We recognize the position of ASCA, but we also note that school counselors comprise the largest number of SMHPs in schools and must be available to assess risk and connect students in need of help.

Specific items to review in your risk assessment include the student's plan, method, level of lethality, and availability, along with their history of SI, mental status, presence of support systems and other protective factors, risk factors, and levels of helplessness (AFSP et al., 2019). Kennebeck and Bonin (2019) incorporated important additional items to explore in the risk assessment, including the content and chronicity of the SI, developmental progress, functional impairments, and substance use. Lastly, it is imperative that you directly query whether the student is actively thinking about death.

Best practices for a proper risk assessment interview are outlined in Table 5.1 and are further explored in one of my personal experiences with a suicidal student, as follows.

PROFESSIONAL PERSPECTIVE: SCOTT POLAND

The school counselor administrative assistant let me know that an English teacher had escorted a student down to the counseling office due to concerns about suicidal behavior. Maria, a 13-year-old middle school student new to the school, had written on her English paper, "Hannah Baker Rocked and showed everyone and I can do what she did!" I knew that Hannah Baker was the main character in a very popular Netflix program, *13 Reasons Why*. Hannah died by suicide, and the program had many dangerous and incorrect messages about teen suicide.

Maria was safely supervised, but I needed to meet with her immediately. My preparation included a quick review of the SAMHSA Suicide Safe App that was on my phone, and I got out my Columbia Suicide Severity Rating Scale (C-SSRS) clipboard. The C-SSRS is standardized and asks questions beginning with thoughts of suicide, the development of a plan, and an attempt to act on that plan. It was important to gather additional detailed information from Maria. I made sure that I had a safety plan available on my desk as well as a parent notification form. I took a few deep breaths and remembered that students who are suicidal often deny being suicidal to avoid scrutiny from a counselor and parent notification. For the interview I used a conferencing model that has four steps:

1. **Get information.**
2. **Give information.**
3. **Make a plan.**
4. **End the conference with everyone understanding the plan and next steps.**

I had never met Maria before, and it was important to make a good initial connection, maintain eye contact, and be an active, nonjudgmental listener. Direct questions need to be asked about suicidal behavior. The three key questions were:

- **Have you ever attempted suicide before?**
- **Are you thinking about suicide now?**
- **How would you end your life?**

Maria's answers to the questions determined the need for continual supervision by a school adult until she was handed off to a parent, law enforcement, or local mental health personnel. Maria presented as unkempt, shy, with very little eye contact and lack of affect. She initially did not want to talk; however, when she was asked about *13 Reasons Why*, she opened up, as she was fascinated by the show and about how Hannah escaped a horrid life, took revenge by dying by suicide, and was then able to watch over everyone who had mistreated her.

Maria shared that she was experiencing family issues. She had not seen her mother since she was 8 years old. Maria did not understand why her mother did not want to be involved in her life. She had recently moved with her father and his live-in girlfriend, Babs, and so she was new to our school. Maria shared that Babs yelled at her frequently and that she thought Babs had a drug problem, as her behavior was so erratic. She reported that her father worked all the time in his new position in a law firm and had a significant commute to work each day. She relayed that Babs didn't work, that she was always home when Maria returned home from school and was consistently on Maria about her chores. Importantly, Maria also mentioned that she had been close to her 19-year-old cousin who died by suicide last year.

Maria relayed that she had not wanted to move to the new school and really missed her dog, Buddy. Her father made her leave Buddy behind because they were moving to a condo that did not allow dogs. Her father said that they might get a house, at which time Buddy could come live with them, but Maria didn't think that would happen. She reported that she missed her old friends in St. Louis and had tried to stay in touch via texting and social media, but her father and his girlfriend had told her repeatedly to move on and to get new friends. Maria had enjoyed participating in a church youth group in St. Louis, but she had no plans to attend church in her new town. Maria shared that all the eighth-grade girls at the new school seemed to be already matched up in groups and no one had welcomed her. She played basketball last year on the school team, but she was not good enough to make the team in her new school, which was much larger than her previous one.

Her younger brother, John, in contrast, thought the move was the best and had already made new friends. What is more, her father's girlfriend was not so hard on him. Maria, being so unhappy here, wondered what was wrong with her. She shared that she slept a lot, spent most of her time at home in her room, and had little appetite or energy. She was behind on school assignments even though it was only the second week of school. Maria admitted that she had thought of cutting herself the way Hannah did, and she acknowledged that she had watched *13 Reasons Why* three times. She also thought that if she couldn't cut herself like Hannah did, then she could pull the trigger on a gun. She mentioned that her father had a gun, and while she was not sure where it was, she had thought of looking for it when no one was home.

There were few protective factors and many risk factors for Maria. The next step was to develop a safety plan. I moved my chair next to Maria and said, "We need to keep you safe and let's write down your ideas for keeping yourself safe." A safety plan has two main components: internally what she could do to calm herself down and externally who she could contact when she had suicidal thoughts. Maria shared a few things that calmed her down, including listening to music, shooting baskets in the driveway, deep breathing, and drawing pictures of butterflies. Externally, she identified her dad, her English teacher, and me as people she could turn to when she had suicidal thoughts. She also cited two friends in St. Louis who she could call on the phone. I showed her how to access the National Suicide Prevention Helpline by telling Siri on her iPhone or by calling 988. The safety plan also included Maria agreeing not to look for her dad's gun and not to handle any instruments she could cut herself with. All these things were written on her safety plan, and we made her a copy and I kept a copy. Maria confided that she had not received any counseling before in the community and was open to it, but she thought her dad would not support counseling.

I then explained to Maria that I needed to contact her dad and ask him to come to school and confer with us. She was initially not supportive of the idea as her dad was busy at work, and so she thought he would be mad at her. I emphasized that I would do my best to get a supportive reaction from her dad and knew that he cared about her and would want her to be safe and to get the help she needed. She reluctantly agreed to the idea that her dad needed to come to school. I explained to Maria that she would remain in the counseling office and supervised while I contacted her dad to request that he come to school. In the call I made to her dad, I was very insistent that he must come to school for a conference. I refused to give him detailed information and repeatedly stated that Maria was safe, but that we needed to have a face-to-face conference at school. Her dad only reluctantly agreed to come to school for a conference. While waiting for him to arrive, I informed the principal that Maria was at risk for suicide and that I would be conducting a parent notification conference and asking her dad to sign a form that he had been notified of the suicidal concern for Maria. Additionally, I would be discussing suicide-proofing his home by securing any lethal means for suicide and would be recommending a comprehensive community-based assessment for Maria. I promised to share the outcome of the parent conference with the principal. The principal and I agreed that regardless of the dad's actions, I would be following up with Maria, and if her father refused to seek community-based services for Maria, then protective services would be notified.

This reflection outlines the items detailed in Table 5.1. As you can see, it is more than just asking the basic questions on a screener. I gathered a number of important details from Maria's life that helped me to formulate a better understanding of her risk level and potential protective factors. Memorizing the questions on a screener alone is not sufficient; you must be prepared to do a thorough investigation to determine a student's level of risk and their potential for suicidality.

These discussed guidelines must be considered in your intervention procedures. In order to ensure that best practices are employed across SMHP approaches, a step-by-step protocol should be put in place that guides a SMHP's review and assessment of all the critical items discussed above. Schools across the United States use a variety of risk assessment approaches; those that are most effective are comprehensive, multistaged, and designed with evidence-based tools. For example, my wife, former principal Donna Poland, and I collaborated with the Big Sky Council and National Alliance for Mental Illness (NAMI) in Montana to create a model suicide prevention program; the result: the Montana Crisis Action School Toolkit on Suicide (CAST-S; Poland & Poland, 2017).

The Montana CAST-S, which was updated in 2022, offers clear guidelines for risk assessment that encompass best practices. It recommends use of the C-SSRS (Posner et al., 2009) in order to assess risk factors and the presence of SI (see Recommended Resources for ways to access a free copy of this screener). A comprehensive interview follows, including a detailed collection of family history, psychiatric concerns, precipitating stressors, presenting symptoms, and access to lethal means. Protective factors, both internal (e.g., fear of death, ability to cope with stress) and external (e.g., beloved pets, engaged in work or school) should be identified, followed by specific questioning about thoughts, plans, and suicidal intent. The CAST-S recommends utilizing the C-SSR's Suicidal Ideation Intensity form, which includes direct and specific language necessary to determine the level of risk involved. See the Recommended Resources section for more information on how to access the CAST-S.

TABLE 5.1. Recommendations for Suicide Assessment

- Create connections with the student by providing empathy, support, and trust.
- Reflect others' feelings, maintain a nonjudgmental stance, and do not minimize the concerns.
- When collecting necessary information for consideration of appropriate community referrals, respect the student's developmental, cultural, and sexuality issues.
- Utilize a standardized suicide screener or assessment but know that suicide assessment is more than yes or no questions.
- Take peer reports of suicidal behavior very seriously.
- Remember that it is common for suicidal students to deny being suicidal.
- Develop a written safety plan jointly with the student.
- Notify parents, with the only exception being if abuse is suspected; then protective services must be immediately notified.
- Be direct in questioning the student, staff member, and/or parents when collecting information.
- Do not promise confidentiality.
- Keep detailed records and ensure that the principal is notified.
- Be sure to maintain the chain of supervision at all times.

SAMHSA has provided free materials clinicians can utilize in their risk assessment. We recommend utilizing their Suicide Assessment Five Step Evaluation Triage (SAFE-T) protocol (2009) in conjunction with the C-SSRS (Posner et al., 2009). These steps are outlined in the snapshot of the SAFE-T pocket card, which can be printed and used on the go for risk assessment needs at school (see Form 5.2).

Another important resource to review is a recent publication, STEPS (School Toolkit for Educators to Prevent Suicide, 2021), which I developed with one of my school psychology graduate students, Catherine Ivey. STEPS is designed to be utilized by K–12 educators in both public and private school settings and directly addresses the need for awareness to help stem the tide of mental health struggles and youth suicide. STEPS will now be shared across Florida due to the award of a 3-year grant from the Florida Blue Foundation and will train 500 administrators or SMHPs a year for the next three years. After the training, each participant will receive the 186-page toolkit. The STEPS manual offers user-friendly materials that can be utilized in your risk assessment process (see Recommended Resources for more information on how to access this free toolkit). Form 5.3 provides a snapshot from the manual "Tool 14B: Suicide Assessment: SAFE-T Protocol with C-SSRS Screening," which can be used to complete an expanded version of SAMHSA's SAFE-T (2009) protocol. You can find an additional copy of this tool (and other useful materials) on page 68 of the STEPS manual. As a reminder, it is recommended that Form 5.3 be used in conjunction with the C-SSRS.

I also helped to develop the After Suicide Toolkit for Schools for the AFSP and the Suicide Prevention Resource Center (SPRC) when it was first issued in 2011. It was revised in 2018 and provides critical recommendations for how schools can best respond to suicide. These toolkits were developed after extensive research and with input from many professionals who have focused their career on schools and suicide. Unfortunately, many school administrators and some SMHPs are still not aware of the excellent recommendations in the toolkit. The Recommended Resources section will have more information on how you can access this free toolkit to utilize in your practice.

One important aspect of the risk assessment process is *language*. It is recommended that you utilize direct language in your assessment, including phrases such as "kill yourself," "suicide," and "take your own life." Use of direct language helps to differentiate the type of at-risk behavior the youth is reporting. For example, a student who engages in nonsuicidal self-injurious behaviors (e.g., cutting) as a means of coping with overwhelming emotions or the absence of emotions may respond "yes" to a less direct question, such as, "Have you thought about hurting yourself?" Additionally, most youth will respond "yes" to the question "Have you had thoughts of dying?" given that it is developmentally appropriate to consider mortality (Poland & Ferguson, 2021b).

Another important consideration is the use of developmentally appropriate language. Increasing numbers of elementary-age children talking about and even threatening suicide have been documented. These threats must be taken seriously, and all school procedures should be followed. Language in these cases is particularly important, as we must ensure that children understand the questions they are being asked during a suicide screening.

I have heard from numerous school personnel that increasing numbers of elementary children are threatening suicide; each threat must be assessed, and caregivers must always be notified. It is challenging to use language that a young child will understand about death and suicide. Suggestions are to ask if they have thoughts of leaving and not coming back or not being here anymore. SMHPs must utilize all their skills and developmental knowledge in assessing young children for suicide risk.

The use of direct language also enhances your rapport with the student you are assessing. This approach conveys a nonjudgmental attitude that is open to discussing suicide with the youth. Moreover, a discussion can often serve as cathartic release for the suicidal individual, as they can share their pain with someone else.

While on the topic of language, it is important to review general use of language related to suicidality. The words you use when discussing suicide have great power and should be offered in a thoughtful manner. Language considerations have evolved over time, and you need to be mindful of a number of important recommendations. The SPRC (2021) has provided specific guidance on phrasing that should be utilized in any discussion or public messaging about suicidality. Figure 5.1 provides a summary of the common phrasing that is used and how to shift the language to more appropriate terminology. Among the recommendations, the most salient includes the modification of language from the common phrase "person *X* committed suicide" to "person *X* died of or by suicide." This is an important change in phrasing as the term *committed* is often associated with negative acts, for example, committed a crime.

Your suicide screening should include the above recommendations for language and is an important first step in helping the student in need. The initial screening at school is largely designed to determine the need for immediate and intensive supervision of the student who is at risk. The goal is to connect any students suspected of being suicidal to a more comprehensive suicide assessment in the community. SMHPs must keep school administrators in the loop as to what interventions they are taking to safeguard the student. This will include notifying the caregivers, which is a mandatory part of the intervention process.

PARENT/GUARDIAN NOTIFICATION

Should you determine that a student is at risk, your next step is to contact their parent or guardian. This is a *critical* and *imperative* step in the intervention process. SMHP failure to notify caregivers of risk concerns has been cited as a major factor of negligence in numerous legal cases after a student's suicide (see Chapter 11 for relevant legal cases). In fact, court rulings have determined that a SMHP is obligated to report any student who is suspected of suicidal behavior based on foreseeability. As such, if a student is ever referred to you for suspected suicidality, you *must* notify the caregivers or guardians, even if the student denies the SI. This should be

Don't Say This		Do Say This
Committed suicide	→	*Died of or by suicide*
Successful attempt	→	*Suicide death*
Unsuccessful attempt	→	*Suicide attempt*
Suicide ideator or attempter	→	*Person living with suicidal thoughts or behaviors*
Completed suicide	→	*Suicide*
Manipulative, cry for help, suicidal gesture	→	*Describe the behavior*
Dealing with suicidal crisis	→	*Working with*

FIGURE 5.1. Phrasing for Discussions about Suicidality. Based on Suicide Prevention Resource Center (2021).

the case for all students, ranging from elementary to high school, and even for students over 18 years of age. The only exception to this requirement is if abuse in the home is suspected, in which case you should be involving the Department of Children and Family Services (DCF).

Contacting caregivers can create unique challenges, which may be unexpected. This concept has become increasingly complex in recent years, particularly in the context of privacy and disclosure for LGBTQ+ students. This topic is discussed in more detail in Chapter 11 related to SMHPs' ethical and legal obligations as they relate to potential liability. My experiences have taught me that when it comes to risk concerns and potential suicidality, the bottom line is that parents/caregivers *must* be notified. Unfortunately, as I have noted earlier, I have found that caregivers often look for any reason to deny that their child might be truly suicidal. With this in mind, your notification must emphasize the seriousness of this concern, no matter what.

PROFESSIONAL PERSPECTIVE: Scott Poland

One case that comes to mind is when I was tasked with assessing an alternative school student at high risk for suicide and insisted that his father come to school to discuss needed support and interventions for his son, whom I will call "Raymond." When I told Raymond's father about his son's suicidal plans, he responded by saying, "He should just kill himself after all the trouble he's caused our family. He stole that car, ran from the police, and hit and killed two pedestrians. We are now being sued in civil court; it would be best if he just killed himself." I responded, "But you can't possibly mean that." The father further stated that I was "never to see his kid again." I informed the father that the school policy was that mental health professionals did not need parental permission to talk with students whenever they believed a student to be suicidal. The policy mandated that protective services must be notified when parents do not take the suicidal behavior of their child seriously, as it is negligence. I then called protective services and notified them of negligence.

Ideally, conferences with caregivers that notify them of suspected suicidal risk should be held in person and all communications should be completed in writing. If there are emergent needs, it is appropriate to contact the parent by phone; however, the nature of the phone call should be documented in a written note. If SMHPs do not follow through on this duty, they can be considered negligent in a court of law (*Eisel v. Board of Education of Montgomery County*, 1991; Lieberman, Poland, & Cassel, 2014). Given the legal implications, parental/guardian notification should always occur when suicidality is suspected (again, unless abuse is suspected, in such cases protective services should be notified). Moreover, notification ensures that the adults in the student's life are alerted to their child's risks and needs.

I recall an important example that highlights the need for parental/caregiver notification and the potential implications if notification is not carried out. A mother sued Howard County Schools in Maryland for negligence for their part in her son's death by suicide. The school psychologist had allegedly assessed one of the high school students, Matthew, as being at risk for suicidal behavior. As a result, the SMHP notified Matthew's mother. The school psychologist recommended that Matthew's parents provide increased supervision at home and obtain a community assessment. His mother agreed and was at home at the time of the phone call. She asked that her son be allowed to walk home. Matthew did arrive home, and his mother was present. Unfortunately, Matthew died by suicide later that day in his home. The case was eventually settled out of court for an undisclosed amount (Civil No. 201358). I refused to take the case on the side of the plaintiff, as Matthew's parents were notified and, from my perspective, Matthew was their responsibility once he walked into their house. This example emphasizes why it is most ideal that SMHPs hand off students who are at risk directly to caregivers, law enforcement, or mobile crisis teams.

CREATING A WRITTEN SAFETY PLAN

Your next step in proper suicide intervention is to collaboratively create a written plan with the student that will help to keep them safe. These plans emphasize coping skills and resources that the student can utilize when thoughts of death become active. Historically, the majority of schools have used no-harm/no-suicide contracts, which serve as a written documentation of the student promising not to act on thoughts of self-harm or suicide and to instead reach out to appropriate resources, for example, loved ones and police. Despite their widespread use, no-harm/no-suicide contracts have become controversial, with little evidence to support their effectiveness, and to date, there is no published data to support their impact on the reduction of suicide. These contracts focus on what not to do as opposed to how to keep safe. Safety plans are considered a better practice as they are strengths based and encourage the suicidal individual's input and agency (Erbacher et al., 2015; McMyler & Prymachuk, 2008; Rudd, Mandrusiak, & Joiner, 2005).

Collaborative creation of a safety plan between the student and SMHP is essential in the face of suspected suicidality and/or a reentry to school from a hospitalization. The design of this plan is flexible and can include a variety of components (Brent, Poling, & Goldstein, 2011; King, Foster, & Rogalski, 2013; Stanley & Brown, 2021). The plan should include input from students, especially in the areas of coping skills (e.g., doing an art project, going for a walk, taking a hot bath) and support (e.g., close friend, suicide hotline, trusted aunt) that they would readily turn to. You must share this plan with the student's caregivers/guardians. Additionally, you will want to emphasize to the student that they must be able to readily access the plan when in need. Relay to the student that in times of crisis it is often difficult to think clearly and that a safety plan can be a "go-to" list with helpful ideas. Table 5.2 provides guidelines for creating your own template for a safety plan.

It is important to expand upon a few components of a safety plan. First, creating an agreement in which the suicidal individual and/or their guardians remove lethal means is a crucial aspect of safety planning. Restriction of lethal means can have a significant impact on the trajectory of the student's future decision making when in crisis. Suicidal youth are often dysregulated emotionally and impulsively (Daniel & Goldston, 2009); any barrier to their access to lethal means is a critical part of prevention.

TABLE 5.2. Safety Plan Guidelines

- **Goal:** Provide a written document that includes helpful resources students can reference when in times of crisis.
- **Components:** Predetermined coping strategies, peer and adult supports, and professional resources, all of which can aid the student in working through the crisis.
- **Additional elements:** Identified triggers and related thoughts, emotions, and behaviors; internal and external coping resources; a plan of how to access such resources in times of distress; an agreement to remove lethal means; and the contact number of appropriate crisis hotlines.

This consideration leads to a common myth that we can dispel: that restriction of lethal means does not reduce suicide; that those whose access to lethal means has been removed will go on to pursue an alternative method to die by suicide. In fact, research has documented quite the opposite, finding that if a specific method is removed and unavailable, suicidal individuals are unlikely to seek another method (Poland & Poland, 2017). The Means Matter website at Harvard University (2019) provided data confirming that restriction of lethal means, such as raising the barrier on bridges, has decreased the incidence of suicide.

An additional aspect of the safety plan that should be reviewed further is your provision of both local and national suicide/crisis hotlines. These resources are a key part of safety planning and should be included in every plan. Moreover, you should ensure that these resources are easily accessible for students and staff (e.g., posters on school walls, monthly emails). Students should be provided with the phone number of the National Suicide Prevention Lifeline, 1-800-273-TALK (8255) and 911 (Suicide Prevention Lifeline, 2019). In 2024, SAMHSA's national crisis line was renamed "The 988 Suicide & Crisis Lifeline." Any person can dial "988" and gain access to trained crisis counselors who can help people experiencing suicidal, substance use, and/or mental health crisis, or any other kind of emotional distress. (Note that the original number continues to be in service; 988 is just a quicker way to access services [SAMHSA, 2022a].)

Relatedly, you should speak with your students and staff about alternative technical resources that can be used in times of crisis. Examples include the Crisis Text Line (2013), a program through which at-risk students can text "HOME" to 741741 to receive 24/7 crisis support via text. Other technical resources include Apple's "Siri," the application that enables users to complete tasks by speaking to their phone, which, over time, has modified its approach to questions about suicide and death. Prior to June 2013, if an iPhone user told Siri that they wanted to jump off a bridge, Siri would provide a list of bridge locations. However, Apple has since modified Siri to respond to suicide and death-related questions with the phone number for the National Suicide Prevention Lifeline. Furthermore, Siri will then ask if the user would like her to call the number or provide a more detailed list of local suicide prevention centers on a map (Erbacher, Singer, & Poland, 2023; Poland & Ferguson, 2021b; Stern, 2013). You are encouraged to share these avenues for help, as youth may be more willing to utilize technical resources.

We recommend that your CRT develop a template for safety planning that can be used in times of risk assessment. There are also existing templates that can be accessed for free online. We recommend utilizing the Stanley-Brown Safety Plan (2021), which encompasses all of the guidelines for safety planning that have been reviewed (see Recommended Resources for more information on how to download a free copy).

PROVIDING REFERRALS

Once risk is assessed, caregivers/guardians have been notified, and a safety plan has been put ino place, an action plan must be developed. This plan should be collaboratively developed with school personnel, family members, and outside professionals. The focus of this plan is to determine the next steps that should be taken to best support the student's needs and help to prevent further suicidal behaviors. A primary component of the action plan is the referral list for treatment providers. It is recommended that you maintain an active, up-to-date list of mental health resources and their specialties that can be used in times of crisis. Various factors such as developmental, cultural, socioeconomic (potential need for providers who offer sliding scale rates), and sexuality issues should be considered when making such referrals (Lieberman, Poland, & Cowan, 2006; Lieberman, Poland, & Kornfeld, 2014).

Both the SAMHSA toolkit (2012) and the Montana CAST-S (2017) advise schools to complete a prescreening process of your referral options in order to ensure the appropriateness of their care. Form 5.4 highlights a few helpful questions related to services and business logistics that you can ask in your prescreening.

It is imperative that you maintain thorough and clear written documentation of the events that have occurred. The documentation should be completed on the day that the incident took place, and it should include as much of the verbatim content that was collected in the interviews and risk assessment. School districts should provide specific documentation forms in order to guarantee that proper records are kept of their crisis responses, including the referrals made to a suicidal student and/or the individual's caregivers (Lieberman et al., 2008).

Addressing Reentry

After a student engages in suicidal behavior, reentry to school is an important consideration. Often, students report a reluctance to come to school when they are feeling depressed; however, in the aftermath of suicidal behavior, students are thought to be safer *in* school rather than *out.* Recommendations for a student's reentry to the school after they have engaged in suicidal behaviors are taken from AFSP's Model Policy (2019). While each school district may have a different approach, the Model Policy outlines key guidelines that should be followed (see Table 5.3).

Lieberman, Poland, and Kornfeld (2014) added to these recommendations, emphasizing the importance of completing a student's reentry in a "careful [and] precise manner" (p. 282). They recommended that prior to reentry, a meeting should take place that includes all individuals who can assist in mediating a successful reintegration into the school environment (e.g., caregivers, teachers, SMHPs, administrators, outside mental health professionals, medical staff). The Montana CAST-S (2022) provides a useful checklist for school reentry for administrators, SMHPs, and staff members. It includes a step-by-step guide for how each professional should approach the reintegration process for a suicidal student (see p. 83, Tool 20: Checklist for School Reentry of Suicidal Student [CAST-S, 2022]; the link to this resource is found below in the Recommended Resources section). Although these are guidelines for best practice for reentry procedures, it is always imperative that SMPHs review and adhere to their individual district's policies.

TABLE 5.3. Guidelines for Student Reentry

- A SMPH should coordinate with the student, family, and any outside mental health providers (if permission was granted) prior to reentry.
- The student's parents/guardians must provide appropriate medical documentation that indicates that the student is no longer a danger to themselves or others.
- The designated SMHP should then consider the types of support needed to assist the student in readjusting to the school community. This support will include recurrent meetings with the student to address any ongoing concerns and provide a mental health check-in (Vaillancourt & Gibson, 2014).

Suicide Attempt

Prior to addressing a death by suicide, it is important to consider how to best respond to a suicide attempt (SA), either on or off campus. If an attempt is made on school grounds, a number of immediate steps must be taken to ensure the safety and well-being of all students. Form 5.5 provides a task list that must be reviewed in the event a suicide attempt occurs on campus.

If you learn of a student who attempted suicide off school grounds, it is imperative, as with all crises, to obtain the facts. If you are not notified of the SA, but members of the student body are discussing the situation, you must contact the family of the student in question in order to verify the rumor. The crisis coordinator, counseling liaison, and/or another member of your CRT should speak with the family in person, if possible. It's understandable that this contact may create discomfort; however, it is important to hear the details from the family so that you can provide the appropriate interventions for the student and any other individuals involved. If the caregivers/guardians of the student are unaware of the rumored SA, you should outline the common risks and warning signs of suicide and ask them to be alert to their child's behaviors.

DEATH BY SUICIDE

> The most common precipitating event to a youth suicide is a loss of a relationship, loss of dignity, or a severe discipline sequence.
>
> —RICHARD LIEBERMAN

In the tragic event that a student or staff member dies by suicide, it is imperative to have a comprehensive response plan in place. This plan should focus on two primary tasks: (1) providing assistance to your students and staff in processing their crisis reactions and (2) working to mitigate any potential contagion effects, that is, additional suicides, by providing care to at-risk students. *Postvention*, a term created by Shniedman (1972), describes helpful and appropriate acts that should take place in the aftermath of a dire event. Postvention is used to outline the coordinated responses that schools should employ following a suicide in the school community. More specifically, postvention encompasses specific activities, events, and strategies that schools should implement following a suicide; these approaches help to evaluate the overall impact of the suicide, identify at-risk individuals, prevent a contagion effect from occurring, and help survivors to best cope with their losses/traumas (Lieberman, Poland, & Kornfeld, 2014).

In the realm of school suicides, postvention is just as important as prevention. The rationale behind postvention is that a timely response to suicide in the school community helps to reduce potential subsequent morbidity and mortality among exposed students, including reducing the onset of symptomology related to depression, posttraumatic stress disorder, and bereavement, along with suicidal behaviors (Gould, Greenberg, Velting, & Shaffer, 2003; Singer, Erbacher, & Rosen, 2018; Talbott & Bartlett, 2012). Your school should implement postvention programming in order to target the following goals: assist and support survivors in the grief process, identify and refer at-risk individuals, dispel myths and offer facts about the suicide, attempt to minimize suicide contagion, and create a plan for continued prevention efforts (Gould et al., 2003; Hazell, 1993; Lieberman, Poland, & Kornfeld, 2014; Underwood & Dunne-Maxim, 1997).

PROFESSIONAL PERSPECTIVES

Postvention

Visiting the family of the suicide victim in person has provided me the opportunity to express condolences, meet surviving siblings, and provide them with support. I have even discussed the timing of the funeral so that parents can attend with their children. I've also had the opportunity to discuss funeral concerns with clergy members, suggesting hopeful and preventative messages at the service. I have also been able to convince parents that we will not theorize about why their child died by suicide, but we can prevent further suicides by being able to tell staff and students the truth about the cause of death.

—SCOTT POLAND

Some schools get the message to do nothing after a suicide, but it is always recommended to help all concerned with their shock, grief, and confusion and increase suicide prevention awareness and resources.

—FRANK ZENERE

The best advice for school districts after a suicide is follow the recommendation in the After a Suicide Toolkit for schools from AFSP (2018).

—RICHARD LIEBERMAN

A student in a small Texas town during a postvention classroom intervention asked me why I was not there last week as then he would have known the warning signs and known to get help for his friend. I have often reflected on his statement and thought why we are not in classrooms teaching students the warning signs and how to get help for themselves or a suicidal friend.

—SCOTT POLAND

Crisis response is an opportunity for providing and building in additional support and connection for students, making the postvention effort a prevention effort.

—STEPHANIE CRAWFORD-GOETZ

One example of what not to do is the middle school principal who insisted on telling all students in an assembly about a student death by suicide. Many students immediately became agitated and blamed another student. It took hours to restore order in the school and several students were suspended.

—SCOTT POLAND

An important note: if a suicide occurs on your school grounds, a number of immediate steps must be taken: (1) call 911, (2) notify the school nurse, (3) implement a lockdown per school policy, (4) protect the area where the suicide occurred and ensure that no one is unnecessarily exposed to the body, (5) treat the area as a crime scene and do not touch anything, and (6) provide support to any individuals who have seen the body, including the school nurse, the janitors/custodial staff, and those who found the body. If possible, it is recommended that an outside agency be hired to clean the area where the suicide occurred in order to mitigate any potential traumatization for the custodial team, who may have known the deceased person or may have seen them in the halls frequently (Erbacher et al., 2015). The following section reviews a detailed task list of best practice guidelines you can utilize in the event you encounter a suicide on your school campus.

RESPONDING TO A SUICIDE AT YOUR SCHOOL: TASK LIST

1. ***Verify the suicide and the related facts.***
   a. *Who* is deceased?
   b. *When* did the death occur?
   c. *Where*, *why*, and *how* did it happen?
   d. Upon learning of a death by suicide, the crisis coordinator should contact the family to verify the facts of the death. In-person contact is preferred to the phone. The coordinator must approach contact with care and should be equipped with resources for mental health referrals and have the ability to offer support to the family they speak with.
   e. One important factor among many is the family's privacy. During the initial contact, the crisis coordinator should ask the family about what they feel comfortable sharing with the public at that time.
   f. If the family requests that limited information be shared, the crisis coordinator must relay this wish to the CRT and student body. The message should be something like this: *"At the request of [the deceased person]'s family, we are declining to release additional details at this time and are choosing to respect their privacy."* The After Suicide Tool Kit for Schools (AFSP & SPRC, 2018) has several sample letters, one of which addresses the family request that the death not be shared as a suicide but still encourages the important discussion of suicide prevention, as it is a leading cause of death for school-age youth.
2. ***Notify key personnel.***
   a. Administrators and the CRT must be notified immediately in order to respond appropriately.
3. ***Create a Crisis Fact Sheet.***
4. ***Follow the same school procedures that you would enact with any death of a school community member.***
5. ***Mobilize the CRT and create an action plan.***
   a. Part of your initial response must be to determine if the person has siblings who attend your school or another school close by.
   b. If the person who died by suicide is a student, review their schedule and arrange for an assigned person to meet with every class that the student attended for at least the first day in the aftermath.
   c. Remove the student's name from any electronic lists so that no phone calls or notices are automatically sent home and so that teachers do not see the name on the attendance rosters.
   d. Obtain feedback from students for decisions related to upcoming extracurricular activi-

ties. While getting back to normal routine is the goal, for some situations, holding scheduled activities may be inappropriate (Erbacher et al., 2015)

6. ***Notify your staff about the news of the suicide.***
   a. Coordinate a faculty/staff meeting as soon as possible so that you can share the facts, dispel any rumors, and help to prepare teachers to attend to students' reactions to the news.
7. ***Hold a class meeting and notify your students about the news of the suicide.***
   a. When you are ready to share the news of the death with the student body, you must first assess for proximal impact/Circles of Vulnerability. Siblings, family, and close friends of the person who died should be told about the death first and individually.
   b. For the remainder of the student body, a death notification statement should be provided to each classroom teacher. Students should be informed by school staff as soon as possible, as they will likely learn of the news quickly through social media and texting. Students feel most familiar with their own teachers, who can therefore provide the most comfort, particularly for younger children.
   c. The notification should utilize the languages spoken by the families in your school. Teachers should read the notification out loud in class to the students.
   d. It is *not* recommended that you share the death notification over the loudspeaker. This approach may cause confusion and hysteria, and it generally feels impersonal.
   e. Clarify to students that class meetings are not a time to share stories or to process deep emotions and that they will be provided with this opportunity in the future if needed. Note that these meetings are not intended as counseling sessions or therapy; however, they do have some psychoeducational components in which students are taught ways they can cope with crisis reactions. The meeting should be used as an opportunity to educate all students about managing crisis reactions regardless of how impacted they are by the particular event.
   f. Steps for the classroom meeting
      i. Make introductions (of any additional staff in the classroom).
      ii. Share crisis facts.
      iii. Clarify any rumors and answer student questions.
      iv. Normalize student reactions and prepare them for what to expect in the aftermath.
      v. Provide students with psychoeducation on effective coping strategies.
      vi. As needed, triage and refer students who are in need of more support.
      vii. Teach students how to recognize when their peers are in need of support and how to use self-referral strategies (Brock et al., 2014; Erbacher et al., 2015).
   g. Important note: how a child learns of a death by suicide can have a significant impact on their response. With this consideration in mind, it is important to be mindful of your presentation; try your best to maintain a calm demeanor, as children's understanding of the impact of a crisis is based on the adult's reactions that are modeled for them (Nickerson et al., 2015)

h. It is important to talk with students and to be truthful about suicide. Your efforts should be to focus on student shock, grief, confusion, and the ways everyone can work together to prevent further suicides. Discussions about suicide should not be held in a group size larger than a classroom. The After Suicide Tool Kit for Schools (2018) strongly recommends that suicide not be discussed in an assembly. The reasons are that in addition to glorifying suicide, students are unlikely to ask questions, and school staff will not be able to determine how students are experiencing the discussion of suicide.

The "Dos" for Communicating with Students about the Suicide of a Peer

- Utilize the Crisis Fact Sheet and provide facts about the death. If you do not know the answer to a question, tell the students that you are unsure and will try to follow up when you are informed and if you are able to share.
- Limit discussion regarding the method of suicide because sharing graphic details can create traumatic images. If asked, it is okay to give basic developmentally appropriate facts about the method. A specific statement such as "he shot himself" is enough detail about the method.
- You may find that students blame others and so they could desire revenge. You're encouraged to discuss this concept with them and the fact that no one person is to blame for someone's suicide.
- Students may share that they don't understand how someone could take their own life. You might say that perhaps it can be hard to understand because you have not experienced such a deep level of sadness or depression and that is a good thing.
- Students may voice feelings of guilt and share that they should have known about their friend's issues. You are encouraged to reassure the students that we can never predict someone's behavior and that their friend needed the help of a counselor.
- Students may ask, "Why did God allow this to happen?" You can explain that there are varied beliefs about this question, and then you can encourage the students to seek counsel with their clergy or parent/caretaker. I like the clergy response that emphasizes the afterlife and the idea that while God has embraced the deceased, God wishes they had stayed on Earth to do God's work over their natural lifetime. God does not choose young people to die by suicide.
- Focus on prevention; provide tips for students on how they can help themselves or friends in need. This help includes learning to recognize warning signs and common risk factors. Emphasize how important it is to tell an adult if they have concerns about a friend. Speak to the differentiation of snitching on your friend versus getting them the help they need.
- Encourage help-seeking behaviors for students who are feeling negatively impacted by the loss of their peers.
- Provide tips for coping strategies, including drinking enough water, eating and sleeping well, and connecting with friends and loved ones.
- Encourage students to engage in acts that help the deceased person's family, such as making condolence cards, offering to run errands, or making dinners.

- Emphasize that help is available for students in both the school and community. Provide students with the crisis hotline and relay to them that if they begin to have a hard time, they should connect with a trusted adult who can get them help.
- Be vigilant to the nonverbal signs from students in each class; should any students appear to be in distress, refer them for additional support.

The "Don'ts" for Communicating with Students about the Suicide of a Peer

- Do not provide any unnecessary details about the cause of death, such as how painful or gory it was, or what condition the body was in.
- Do not spend time contemplating why the person died by suicide. Students will invariably ask why, and the best response is to say that we will never know why that person died by suicide and that what we need to focus on most is the living and what their thoughts and feelings are in the aftermath.
- Do not glorify the death of the student in any way or communicate any kind of approval for their actions; that is, do not romanticize the suicide.
- Do not describe the person who died by suicide as mentally ill. Rather, state that they likely were experiencing significant feelings of sadness and loneliness. Emphasize that many students have problems and that our awareness and support can be the best help in the future.

8. ***Maintain the normal school schedule.***
   a. When possible, it is recommended that the school maintain as normal a schedule as possible. This helps to limit potential glorification of the death. In some cases, it may be appropriate to extend the class period in which the news is being shared with the students. Students will likely have questions during the class meetings, and it is recommended that if there is a need, teachers should forgo the lesson plans for that day.
   b. Some students may become highly distressed and will request to leave class and/or go home. These students should not be allowed to leave campus on their own. Their parents/caregivers should be notified and should be asked to pick them up from school. Once the parents/caregivers arrive, you will want to provide them with a copy of the Crisis Fact Sheet and encourage them to attend the upcoming family/community meeting.
9. ***Provide opportunities for your students and staff to process their reactions to the tragedy.***
   a. These opportunities are different from the classroom meetings. These meetings should be held by the counseling liaison or another member of your school's mental health staff, and they should be offered to any students impacted by the suicide, particularly those who were in the student's class. These meetings should be held in small-group settings.
10. ***Provide counseling services to those who need them, including those who were close to the deceased and those previously known to be suicidal.***
    a. These services should be conducted by the SMHPs at the school and by those trained in crisis response.

11. ***Plan and host a family/community meeting the night of the crisis.***
    a. Agenda points should include details from the Crisis Fact Sheet, dispelling any rumors, information about trauma reactions in children, and risk and warning signs of suicide, along with appropriate resources and mental health referrals.
12. ***Send a letter home to caregivers (see Table 5.4).***
13. ***Address media concerns, if any.***
    a. Should the suicide obtain media coverage, you will want to be on top of how information is shared, as it can greatly increase the chances of suicide contagion.
    b. The media liaison should take charge of any media coverage and should approach the media in a positive manner with an attitude of transparency and care for the student's privacy.
    c. Prior to the interview, the media liaison should make every effort to obtain specifics from the family and confirmation that they feel comfortable sharing with the public.
    d. Encourage the media not to cover the story. Instead, suggest that the media return to the school in a few weeks to do a story on suicide prevention. The media should be encouraged to follow media reporting guidelines from Suicide Awareness Voices of Education (SAVE; 2022) and Reporting on Suicide (2020) outlined in Table 5.5.
14. ***Allow funeral attendance.***
    a. Students and staff who would like to attend the funeral should be allowed to do so; however, school should not be canceled for the service. It is recommended that, when possible, the funeral occurs outside of school hours so that hundreds of students do not leave school all at once. This suggestion may be recommended to the family, with caution and respect for their emotional state.
    b. Students who wish to attend the funeral should be given information that will help them to prepare for what will occur, including cultural and religious considerations.
15. ***Follow memorializing guidelines.***
    a. A memorial committee can be established in advance; policies should be created on how deaths are memorialized at your school.
    b. All deaths should be memorialized in the same way, regardless of specific factors surrounding the death.

TABLE 5.4. Parent Notification Letter Details

- The nature of the crisis that occurred (e.g., a student has died by suicide)
- What the student body has been told
- Any funeral arrangements that are known
- Typical crisis reactions that parents may observe in their children
- Suggestions for how parents can best support their child
- Advisement on how to obtain additional support for any children who are having a difficult time
- Information on any parent/community meetings that will be held
- Relevant resources

Note. From Erbacher et al. (2015).

TABLE 5.5. Media Guidance

- Answer the media's questions but protect confidential information.
- Honestly acknowledge the suicide.
- Provide brief identifying information about the victim such as their age, grade, and gender.
- Limit details regarding the method of suicide.
- Read any statements that have been provided by the victim's family.
- Express sorrow and condolences on behalf of the faculty and student body.
- Relay information that the school is taking steps to help the students to cope with this tragedy.
- Share that students are being encouraged to maintain their regular schedules and activities as they are able to.
- Discuss the mental health services that are being offered to the students.
- Ensure that you publicize the details of the family/community meeting that will be held later that night, which will focus on prevention and helping parents to support their children.
- Acknowledge the widespread problem of youth suicide.
- Discuss any suicide prevention efforts that your school or district has implemented in the past.
- Ask the media to cover the risk factors and warning sides of suicide but not to print a picture of the deceased and not to share details on the method or to report the suicide as romantic or mystic.

c. Navigating memorialization can sometimes be difficult for school administrators, particularly if the student was well liked. See Chapter 9 for additional guidance on this topic.

d. It is imperative that you take caution to not sensationalize or glorify the suicide in any way. Suicides, particularly in the school context, can create a contagion effect that can result in subsequent suicidal behavior in other students. If any funds are donated in the name of the deceased person, these monies should be allocated to an appropriate cause such as suicide prevention or a school scholarship.

16. ***Continue to communicate with the family of the deceased.***
17. ***Implement postvention efforts in order to mitigate a potential contagion effect.***

CONTAGION EFFECT

We already know that exposure to suicide is a risk factor for future suicide, and this finding is even more relevant when we are discussing the concept of contagion effect. This concept in the context of suicidality is rooted in social learning theory and suggests that when someone is exposed to suicide (via peers, family members, celebrities, the media), they may develop the understanding that suicide is the only permanent and "successful" solution to their difficulties, creating higher risk for subsequent suicidal behavior (Lieberman et al., 2014). Young people have been found to be especially vulnerable to the contagion effect, resulting in *suicide point clusters* (i.e., suicides that are contiguous in time and space) in schools and communities across the nation, such as those that occurred in Fairfax County, Virginia (2014); Palo Alto, California

(2002, 2009, 2014); Salt Lake City, Utah (2018); and Colorado Springs, Colorado (2017) (Poland & Ferguson, 2021b; Poland, Lieberman, & Niznik, 2019).

Analyses of these point clusters have revealed common risk factors associated with this phenomenon. Such factors include male gender, mental health issues, history of SI/SA, self-harm (i.e., cutting) behaviors, substance abuse and relationship problems, a recent crisis, caregivers not recognizing the severity of the mental health needs of their child, sleep deprivation, academic pressure, sexual orientation, and intimate partner violence (Annor, Wilkinson, & Zwald, 2017; Garcia-Williams et al., 2016; Poland et al., 2019; Spies et al., 2014). It is critical that you are aware of these factors in the aftermath of a suicide, for they can assist in early identification of any students at risk and prevent potential contagions.

To mitigate the contagion effect, your school must focus on two main tasks: (1) take prevention steps with those known to be suicidal in the past and (2) identify others who are at risk for suicide. Postvention efforts must go into action quickly; timely implementation of a response plan in a school setting has been associated with fewer negative symptoms (Poijula, Wahlberg, & Dyregrov, 2001). Postvention should not be short in duration and should be targeted and yet broad in its scope (NASP, 2015b). The following postvention steps are likely to overlap with some of the crisis responses that have been discussed; however, they should be used specifically to target the potential contagion effect.

Postvention in Action: Mitigating the Contagion Effect

- Immediately begin networking efforts to connect students to mental health assistance. You will be offering help to two groups of students: those known to have been suicidal in the past and those who were close to the person who died by suicide.
- Instruct all school staff to be vigilant to student behaviors and about any talk about other students having attempted suicide in the past, feeling suicidal now, or being in distress.
- Ensure that all staff members understand who they should contact if they have concerns about an at-risk student.
- If your mental health team has not yet done so, immediately become familiar with the resources available in the community (i.e., police, mental health, fire-rescue) and begin to establish relationships.
- Tell students to talk with *any* trusted adult in the school community if they become concerned about a fellow peer.
- Take all threats of suicide seriously. Should you find a poem or paper that discusses suicide, report it to the appropriate official, as this may be an at-risk escalation point.
- Immediately refer a student known by an adult to be suicidal to the SMHP for a risk assessment. The parent/guardian must be contacted, and a written record of these efforts should be recorded.
- Be direct and do not mince words with caregivers when discussing access to lethal means. Advise them to remove any lethal weapons from the home, especially guns, and inform them of the increased risk of having the weapon in their home. You can also discuss gun safety and request that the caregivers keep the gun stored in a locked container that is not accessible to the children in the home.

- Make referrals for appropriate mental health practitioners in the community and follow up with the families to ensure that they have connected with the agencies.
- When possible and in the presence of a second school representative, ask the caregivers to sign an Emergency Notification Conference Form that documents their receipt of information regarding the school's concerns about their child. If the parent refuses to sign this form, document their refusal in writing. You must then consider the next steps, as refusal to obtain mental health assistance for a child in need may be considered negligent and require the involvement of child protective services.

I have led intervention efforts in schools and communities after 16 youth suicide point clusters. The following narrative includes a reflection that highlights many best practices in the case of a school suicide contagion.

PROFESSIONAL PERSPECTIVE: Scott Poland

Point Cluster Response

The Academy 20 school district in Colorado Springs tragically had five students who attended Discovery Canyon High School die by suicide in the spring semester of 2016. I was called to respond to this school after the fifth death, along with my colleague and expert contributor, Rich Lieberman. The following points list all the things that were put in place not just at Discovery Canyon but for the entire school district in the ensuing months. Rich and I led a session for parents that was standing room only at Discovery Canyon High School. Many points were made about the importance of parents being alert for warning signs of depression and suicide and increasing supervision for their children. It was also emphasized that mental health services for their child should be obtained without hesitation and that the school counseling offices be contacted for referrals.

It was stressed to find shared time when their children would truly talk to their parents. Parents need to be careful not to quickly say that they understand and that things are going to be okay; instead they need to help students work through their difficult issues and emotions. It was stated that guns are used in about 50% of all suicides and that parents must safeguard the guns in their homes. It was acknowledged that a youth suicide point cluster was occurring and that a comprehensive community response was needed.

The most difficult question a parent asked was: "What do you think about the fact that after the third suicide, the principal held an assembly for all students and allowed a grieving parent to talk about the suicide of their child?" I believe strongly that student suicide should be discussed in a group size no larger than a typical classroom. I was aware that the principal was standing a few feet away and did not want to throw the principal under the bus. My response was that the biggest problem was that we don't talk enough about suicide and about what everybody needs to look for and to do when someone is suicidal. However, the ideal way to have those discussions is in a classroom-size or even smaller group.

Discovery Canyon High School experienced a suicide of a sixth student the following January, about eight months later. Discovery Canyon mobilized quickly, and the second night after the sixth suicide, Rich and I conducted a Zoom session attended by over 750 Discovery Canyon parents. The session reemphasized many of the points made in the presentation the previous spring. Reflecting back on the intervention, a frustration for me and Rich was that local physicians did not get involved in the El Paso County Youth Suicide Prevention Coalition. It is well-known that the vast majority of suicidal individuals actually see a family physician in the month before their suicide. The existence of a point cluster should make screenings of adolescents a priority. Many years ago, the U.S. Prevention Task Force recommended that every adolescent seeing a physician for any reason should be screened for depression and suicide.

TABLE 5.6. Best Practices in Responding to a Suicide Cluster

- Expert assistance and advice were obtained.
- A parent meeting was conducted.
- All school personnel were taught the suicide warning signs, and prevention information was posted on the district website.
- All administrators attended a 3-hour suicide prevention training.
- Schools and the broader community formed a coalition for identification and treatment of suicidal youth.
- School provided counseling assistance over the summer.
- SMHPs received extensive 6-hour training suicide assessment.
- The Signs of Suicide (SOS; n.d.) Program and the Sources of Strength Program (n.d.) were implemented at all secondary schools.
- Hope Squads were established in 2018.
- Application for a Project SERV grant from the USDOE was made.
- Riding the Waves (Crisis Connections, n.d.) was implemented in fifth grade.
- A prevention coordinator was hired.
- There was quick mobilization after the sixth suicide, almost one year later.

The steps in Table 5.6 list all of the measures taken at Discovery Canyon and throughout Academy 20, which truly represent best practices in comprehensive suicide prevention and intervention in schools as it relates to a suicide cluster.

My responses to suicides in school settings have been varied in many ways (i.e., populations, risk and protective factors, readiness for crisis response), with common threads observed across events. When reflecting on the many responses, a number of commonly asked questions stand out. Many of these questions have already been answered in our "dos and don'ts" list for communicating with students about suicide. The remainder are discussed below and can be utilized for role-play scenarios with your staff to better prepare for suicide intervention at your school.

IN THE AFTERMATH OF A SUICIDE AT SCHOOL: COMMONLY ASKED QUESTIONS AND WAYS TO RESPOND

Q: *What should I say about my friend now that they have made the choice to die by suicide?*

A: It is important to remember the positive things about this person. In relaying details about them, we want to respect their privacy and that of their family. Remember to be sensitive to the needs of this person's close family and friends. Also, remember that the person who died by suicide is often feeling so low that they believe they have no other choice but to die as an escape from their pain.

Q: *Didn't they make a poor choice and is it okay to be angry with them?*

A: In all honesty, yes, they did make a very poor choice that has forever impacted many people who loved and cared for this person. In fact, research has shown that many youth who attempt and survive suicide report being very glad to be alive and regretful of their attempt. You have permission for any and all your feelings in the aftermath of suicide, and it is okay if you are feeling angry toward this person; that is also a normal part of grief.

Q: *Isn't someone or something to blame for this suicide?*

A: In times like these, we often search for answers as to why, or we look to someone or something to blame. However, the person who died by suicide made this decision on their own, and there is no one person or thing to blame. The decision to die by suicide involved every interaction and experience that this young person had throughout their entire life, up until the moment they died. It is the fault of no one. No one person, no one thing is ever to blame. Where we can take ownership is in making sure that any future suicides are prevented.

Q: *How can I cope with this suicide?*

A: I want you to think about what or who has helped you cope in the past when you have had to deal with hard things. Please turn to these things or people in order to best help yourself to deal with this distressing time. Important adults, like teachers, parents, aunts, or uncles, can help you to process some of your feelings about what has happened. Also, it is important to uphold your normal routines, keep up with proper eating and sleeping habits, and engage in regular exercise. In times of distress, we may want to turn to numbing agents, like drugs or alcohol; please do not do so, as it will only prolong the experience of grief and make it that much harder to deal with your emotions. In times of trauma, we often find that we can be very resilient, which is the ability to bounce back from adversity. This can only happen when we take care of ourselves and connect with positive support systems.

Q: *What should I do if I believe that someone may be suicidal?*

A: You want to be there for the person and ensure that they get help. You can listen to them, support them, and let them know that they are not alone, nor are they the first person to feel this way. Let them know that help is available. Offer to facilitate the help; escort the person to the nurse's office or offer to call a trusted adult. One note: *you* are not the person who should intervene; mental health professionals, such as counselors and psychologists, have special training to help young people who are suicidal. Do *not* keep a secret about suicidal behavior. You can help to save this person's life by obtaining help from an adult. Connecting your friend to the resources they need is what a good friend does, and someday your friend will thank you.

Q: *How does the crisis hotline work?*

A: I'm happy to share with you that we have a number of nationally certified crisis hotlines in many cities that are available 24 hours a day and are manned by trained volunteers. Individuals in need can also contact the 24-hour national suicide hotline, which can be reached via 1-800-Suicide or 1-800-273-TALK (8255) or simply dial 988. Upon calling, you will be connected to live crisis support; this person will help to keep you safe and determine if you need to seek further assistance. In addition, you can also utilize the crisis text line by texting 741741 from anywhere in the United States. A live crisis counselor will then respond to you via text and provide support and resources as needed.

Q: *I feel helpless right now; how can I make a difference in suicide prevention?*

A: It's understandable that you are feeling helpless right now. I think we all feel that way after an unexpected loss of a loved one. One thing that we can focus our energy on is the fact that future suicides *can* be prevented. Know the warning signs, listen to your friends carefully, take what they say seriously, and do not hesitate to get adult help. High school students can volunteer in some cities and be trained to answer the Teenline. Please contact the local Crisis Hotline (dial 988) for more information. One person can make a difference and prevent a suicide!

Q: *How can we memorialize the person who died?*

A: The most appropriate memorial is a living one, such as a scholarship fund or contributions to support suicide prevention. While we may want to create a physical memorial for this person on school campuses, it is better not to. The AFSP and SPRC's After a Suicide: A Toolkit for Schools (2018) is available for free on both of their websites. The publication provides specific guidelines for memorialization and balances the need for students wanting to do something after a suicide, while not glorifying the suicide victim.

Suicide intervention in the school setting is a complex matter, and it always begins with *prevention*. Given the unfortunate common presence of suicidality, you must become knowledgeable in best practices for intervention. It is recommended that you utilize the guidelines in this chapter to strengthen your approaches to risk assessment and the related responses that are required. Your interventions will vary, based on the concerns at hand, though they will always need to be implemented with best practices in mind. Postvention involves a number of considerations and, as with prevention and intervention of suicide, appropriate employment of strategies can mean the difference between the life and death of another student. We strongly recommend that you download the toolkits discussed in this chapter (see Recommended Resources below for where to find the materials) and utilize them in conjunction with this chapter. These guidelines are critical to your planning, response, and postvention practices.

Recommended Resources

- **American Association of Suicidology (AAS; 2022):** AAS is a not-for-profit organization that promotes evidence-based practices and training in order to prevent suicide worldwide. Found at *www.suicidology.org*.
- **American Foundation for Suicide Prevention (AFSP; 2019):** AFSP is a voluntary health organization that gives those affected by suicide a nationwide community empowered by research, education, and advocacy to take action against suicide. Found at *https://afsp.org*.
- **AFSP and SPRC's After a Suicide: A Toolkit for Schools (2018):** A free, evidence-based model suicide prevention program. Found at *https://afsp.org/our-work/education/after-a-suicide-a-toolkit-for-schools*.
- **Columbia Suicide Severity Rating Scale (C-SSRS; 2011):** Brief suicide screener that is recommended to utilize in risk assessments. Found at *https://cssrs.columbia.edu*.
- **Crisis Action School Toolkit on Suicide for the Montana Schools (CAST-S; 2022):** A free, evidence-based model suicide prevention program. Found at *https://dphhs.mt.gov/assets/suicideprevention/cast-s2022.pdf*.
- **Nova Southeastern University's Suicide and Violence Prevention (2022):** University-based

team composed of faculty, staff, and students who are passionate about suicide and violence prevention. Provides free training and resources for school and community members. Found at *www.nova.edu/suicideprevention.*

- **School Toolkit for Educators to Prevent Suicide (STEPS; 2021):** A free, evidence-based model suicide program geared for school staff members. Found at *www.nova.edu/suicideprevention/students.html.*
- **Stanley–Brown Safety Plan (2021):** Free safety plan template that can be used during your risk assessment to assist in keeping a suicidal individual safe. Found at *https://bgg.11b.myftpupload.com/wp-content/uploads/2021/08/Stanley-Brown-Safety-Plan-8-6-21.pdf.*
- **Suicide Prevention Resource Center (2019):** Organization with a vast number of resources for individuals, community members, educators, and related professionals. Found at *www.sprc.org/settings/schools.*
- **The Jason Foundation (2019):** Foundation whose mission is to prevent youth suicide through educational and awareness programs that enable youth, educators/youth workers, and families with the tools and resources to help identify and assist at-risk youth. Found at *http://jasonfoundation.com.*

FORM 5.1

Risk Assessment Screening Questions

Instructions for use: Utilize these screening questions to obtain information regarding an interviewee's potential risk for suicide. Remember to be mindful of your interviewing style (tone, body language). Circle Y for *Yes* and N for *No* and record additional details in the lines provided. Any endorsement of Yes is considered a positive screen and safety planning should immediately ensue.

Investigate severity of ideation:

- Have you wished you were dead or wished you could disappear or go to sleep and never wake up? **Y/N**; if yes, provide details:

  ____

- Have you had any thoughts of killing yourself? **Y/N**; if yes, provide details:

  ____

- Have you been thinking about specifics of how you might kill yourself? **Y/N**; if yes, provide details:

  ____

- Do you have any intentions of acting on these thoughts? **Y/N**; if yes, provide details:

  ____

- Have you begun to figure out or have you figured out all the details related to how you will kill yourself? **Y/N**; if yes, provide details:

  ____

- Do you intend to put your plan into action? **Y/N**; if yes, provide details:

  ____

- Have you ever done anything, started to do anything, or prepared to do anything to end your life? **Y/N**; if yes, provide details:

  ____

Look deeper into thoughts, plans, and suicidal intent:

- **Frequency:** How many times have you had these thoughts?

  ____

  ____

- **Duration:** How long do the thoughts last?

  ____

  ____

(continued)

Source: Posner et al. (2009).

Risk Assessment Screening Questions *(page 2 of 2)*

- **Controllability:** Are you able to stop thinking about killing yourself or wanting to die?

  ____

  ____

- **Deterrents:** Is there anything (e.g., family, religion, pain of death)—that stopped you from wanting to die or acting on thoughts of suicide?

  ____

  ____

- **Reasons for Ideation:** What reasons do you have for wanting to kill yourself?

  ____

  ____

FORM 5.2

SAMHSA's SAFE-T Protocol (2009)

Instructions for use: The following protocol can be used in your risk assessment for suicide. Follow the steps to ensure best practices in completing a thorough assessment of suicide. *Note:* Step 3 should be used in conjunction with the Columbia Suicide Severity Rating Scale (C-SSRS; Posner et al., 2009).

SAFE-T

Suicide **A**ssessment **F**ive-step **E**valuation and **T**riage

1
IDENTIFY RISK FACTORS
Note those that can be modified to reduce risk

2
IDENTIFY PROTECTIVE FACTORS
Note those that can be enhanced

3
CONDUCT SUICIDE INQUIRY
Suicidal thoughts, plans, behavior, and intent

4
DETERMINE RISK LEVEL/INTERVENTION
Determine risk. Choose appropriate intervention to address and reduce risk

5
DOCUMENT
Assessment of risk, rationale, intervention, and follow-up

U.S. DEPARTMENT OF HEALTH AND HUMAN SERVICES
Substance Abuse and Mental Health Services Administration
www.samhsa.gov

RESOURCES

- Download this card and additional resources at **http://wwww.sprc.org**
- Resource for implementing The Joint Commission 2007 Patient Safety Goals on Suicide **http://www.sprc.org/library/jcsafetygoals.pdf**
- **SAFE-T** drew upon the American Psychiatric Association Practice Guidelines for the Assessment and Treatment of Patients with Suicidal Behaviors **http://www.psychiatryonline.com/pracGuide/pracGuideTopic_14.aspx**
- Practice Parameter for the Assessment and Treatment of Children and Adolescents with Suicidal Behavior. Journal of the American Academy of Child and Adolescent Psychiatry, 2001, 40 (7 Supplement): 24s-51s

ACKNOWLEDGMENTS

- Originally conceived by Douglas Jacobs, MD, and developed as a collaboration between Screening for Mental Health, Inc. and the Suicide Prevention Resource Center.
- This material is based upon work supported by the Substance Abuse and Mental Health Services Administration (SAMHSA) under Grant No. 1U79SM57392. Any opinions/findings/conclusions/recommendations expressed in this material are those of the author and do not necessarily reflect the views of SAMHSA.

National Suicide Prevention Lifeline
1-800-273-TALK (8255)

http://www.sprc.org

A Life in the Community for Everyone
SAMHSA
Substance Abuse and Mental Health Services Administration
U.S. Department of Health and Human Services

HHS Publication No. (SMA) 09-4432 • CMHS-NSP-0193
Printed 2009

FORM 5.3

STEPS (2021) Tools for Suicide Assessment

Instructions for use: Tool 14b from the STEPS (2021) manual is a helpful tool to complete a comprehensive risk assessment. It combines pertinent information from SAMHSA's SAFE-T Protocol (2009) and the C-SRSS (Posner et al., 2009). Follow the steps in order and utilize it as a guide for your questions with the individual who is at risk. Step 1 will help you to identify the potential risk factors that inform your assessment of level of risk. Step 2 will help you to identify protective factors that can mitigate the risk level. Step 3 is a guide for deeply querying about ideation and severity of ideation. Step 4 provides guidelines to determine the level of risk and appropriate interventions.

Tool 14b

Suicide Assessment: SAFE-T Protocol with C-SSRS Screening

Suicide **A**ssessment **F**ive-step **E**valuation and **T**riage

Use in conjunction with the C-SSRS Brief Screening questions (Tool 14a).

Step 1: Identify Risk Factors (based on reports and observances during the brief screening)

Current and Past Psychiatric Dx

- ☐ Mood disorder
- ☐ Psychotic disorder
- ☐ Alcohol/substance abuse disorders
- ☐ PTSD
- ☐ ADHD
- ☐ TBI
- ☐ Cluster B personality disorders or traits (i.e., borderline, antisocial, histrionic, and narcissistic)
- ☐ Conduct problems (antisocial behavior, aggression, impulsivity)
- ☐ Recent onset

Presenting Symptoms

- ☐ Anhedonia
- ☐ Impulsivity
- ☐ Hopelessness or despair
- ☐ Anxiety and/or panic
- ☐ Insomnia
- ☐ Command hallucinations
- ☐ Psychosis

Family History

- ☐ Suicide
- ☐ Suicidal behavior
- ☐ Axis I psychiatric diagnoses requiring hospitalization

Precipitants/Stressors

- ☐ Triggering events leading to humiliation, shame, and/or despair (e.g., loss of relationship, financial or health status) (real or anticipated)
- ☐ Chronic physical pain or other acute medical problem (e.g., CNS disorders)
- ☐ Sexual/physical abuse
- ☐ Substance intoxication or withdrawal
- ☐ Pending incarceration or homelessness
- ☐ Legal problems
- ☐ Inadequate social supports
- ☐ Social isolation
- ☐ Perceived burden on others

(continued)

Change in Treatment

- ☐ Recent inpatient discharge
- ☐ Change in provider or treatment (e.g., medications, psychotherapy, milieu)
- ☐ Hopeless or dissatisfied with provider or treatment
- ☐ Noncompliant or not receiving treatment

☐ **Access to Lethal Methods:** Ask specifically about presence or absence of a firearm in the home or ease of accessing.

Step 2: Identify Protective Factors (protective factors may not counteract significant acute suicide risk factors)

Internal

- ☐ Ability to cope with stress
- ☐ Frustration tolerance
- ☐ Religious beliefs
- ☐ Fear of death or the actual act of killing self
- ☐ Identifies reasons for living

External

- ☐ Cultural, spiritual, and/or moral attitudes against suicide
- ☐ Responsibility to children
- ☐ Beloved pets
- ☐ Supportive social network of family or friends
- ☐ Positive therapeutic relationships
- ☐ Engaged in work or school

(continued)

Step 3: Specific Questioning about Thoughts, Plans, and Suicidal Intent (Reference brief screening results from tool 14a.)
If a semi-structured interview is preferred to complete this section, clinicians may opt to complete C-SSRS Lifetime/Recent for comprehensive behavior/lethality assessment.

C-SSRS Suicidal Ideation Intensity (with respect to the most severe ideation 15 identified above)	Month
Frequency ***How many times have you had these thoughts?*** (1) Less than once a week (2) Once a week (3) 2–5 times in week (4) Daily or almost daily (5) Many times each day	
Duration ***When you have the thoughts, how long do they last?*** (1) Fleeting—few seconds or minutes (2) Less than 1 hour/some of the time (3) 1–4 hours/a lot of time (4) 4–8 hours/most of day (5) More than 8 hours/persistent or continuous	
Controllability ***Could/can you stop thinking about killing yourself or wanting to die if you want to?*** (1) Easily able to control thoughts (2) Can control thoughts with little difficulty (3) Can control thoughts with some difficulty (4) Can control thoughts with a lot of difficulty (5) Unable to control thoughts (0) Does not attempt to control thoughts	
Deterrents ***Are there things—anyone or anything (e.g., family, religion, pain of death)—that stopped you from wanting to die or acting on thoughts of suicide?*** (1) Deterrents definitely stopped you from attempting suicide (2) Deterrents probably stopped you (3) Uncertain that deterrents stopped you (4) Deterrents most likely did not stop you (5) Deterrents definitely did not stop you (0) Does not apply	
Reasons for Ideation ***What sort of reasons did you have for thinking about wanting to die or killing yourself? Was it to end the pain or stop the way you were feeling (in other words, you couldn't go on living with this pain or how you were feeling) or was it to get attention, revenge, or a reaction from others? Or both?*** (1) Completely to get attention, revenge, or a reaction from others (2) Mostly to get attention, revenge, or a reaction from others (3) Equally to get attention, revenge, or a reaction from others and to end/stop the pain (4) Mostly to end or stop the pain (you couldn't go on) (5) Completely to end or stop the pain (you couldn't go on living with the pain or how you were feeling) (0) Does not apply	
Total Score	

(continued)

Step 4: Guidelines to Determine Level of Risk and Develop Interventions to LOWER Risk Level
"The estimation of suicide risk, at the culmination of the suicide assessment, is the quintessential **clinical judgment,** since no study has identified one specific risk factor or set of risk factors as specifically predictive of suicide or other suicidal behavior."

From the American Psychiatric Association's *Practice Guidelines for the Assessment and Treatment of Patients with Suicidal Behaviors*, page 24.

RISK STRATIFICATION	TRIAGE
High Suicide Risk Suicidal ideation with intent or intent with plan **in past month** (C-SSRS Suicidal Ideation #4 or #5) **OR** Suicidal behavior **within the past 3 months** (C-SSRS Suicidal Behavior)	• **Initiate local psychiatric admission process.** • **Stay with patient until transfer to higher level of care is complete.** • **Follow up and document outcome of emergency psychiatric evaluation.**
Moderate Suicide Risk Suicidal ideation with method, **WITHOUT plan, intent, or behavior** in the past month (C-SSRS Suicidal Ideation #3) **OR** Suicidal behavior more than 3 months ago (C-SSRS Suicidal Behavior Lifetime) **OR** Multiple risk factors and few protective factors	• **Directly address suicide risk, implementing suicide prevention strategies.** • **Develop a safety plan.**
Low Suicide Risk Wish to die or suicidal ideation **WITHOUT method, intent, plan, or behavior** (C-SSRS Suicidal Ideation #1 or #2) **OR** Modifiable risk factors and strong protective factors **OR** No reported history of suicidal ideation or behavior	• **Develop a discretionary outpatient referral process.**

FORM 5.4

Prescreening Questions for Outside Mental Health Support

Instructions for use: Utilize the following questions as an interview script for your screenings of individuals/agencies that may be able to provide mental health support in the event of a crisis. Record the answers below. Should you decide to establish a relationship with the individual/agency, keep this screener on file, as it will provide you with helpful information should you need to utilize their services in the aftermath of a crisis.

1. What process do you follow in the event of a suicide crisis?

____

____

2. Have you had specific training in suicide risk and assessment? Please explain.

____

____

3. Do you have experience working with LGBTQIA+ students and other groups that are disproportionately at risk for suicide and, if so, please elaborate?

____

____

4. How do you go about completing a written safety plan with your suicidal client?

____

____

5. Do you see the importance of sharing information with school personnel when students are suicidal?

____

____

6. Do you offer a sliding scale fee/take insurance/private pay?

____

____

7. What is your typical wait time to see a new client?

____

____

Based on Poland and Poland's Montana CAST-S (2017).

FORM 5.5

Responding to a Suicide at Your School: Task List

Instructions for use: Utilize the following task list as a step-by-step guide for responding to a suicide at your school. Mark each check box as you complete each task to ensure that you are following best practices in crisis response. See pages 113–118 for guidance on each task item.

☐ Verify the suicide and the related facts.

- *Who* is deceased?
- *When* did the death occur?
- *Where, why, how* did it happen?

☐ Notify key personnel.

☐ Create a Crisis Fact Sheet.

☐ Follow the same school procedures that you would enact with any death of a school community member.

☐ Mobilize the CRT and create an action plan.

☐ Notify your staff about the news of the suicide.

☐ Hold a class meeting and notify your students about the news of the suicide.

- Steps for the classroom meeting:
  1. i. Make introductions (of any additional staff in classroom).
  2. ii. Share crisis facts.
  3. iii. Clarify any rumors and answer student questions.
  4. iv. Normalize student reactions and prepare them for what to expect in the aftermath.
  5. v. Provide students with psychoeducation on effective coping strategies.
  6. vi. As needed, triage and refer students who are in need of more support.
  7. vii. Teach students how to recognize when their peers are in need of support and how to use self-referral strategies (Brock et al., 2014; Erbacher et al., 2015).

☐ Plan and host a family/community meeting the night of the crisis.

☐ Send a letter home to caregivers (see Table 5.4).

☐ Address media concerns, if any.

(continued)

Responding to a Suicide at Your School: Task List *(page 2 of 2)*

☐ Allow funeral attendance.

☐ Follow Memorializing Guidelines.

☐ Continue to communicate with the family of the deceased.

☐ Implement postvention efforts in order to mitigate a potential contagion effect.

CHAPTER 6

School Violence

School violence is an important part of crisis intervention that creates unique considerations for you and your CRT. Recall the 2021 YRBSS school violence trends: 7% of students reported that they were threatened or injured with a weapon at school, 9% of students reported that they did not go to school because of safety concerns, and 15% reported being bullied at school (CDC, 2023). Given these findings, it is likely that you will encounter some form of violence and related concerns throughout the school year. Violence considerations range widely from bullying and harassment to weapons on campus, threats of violence, gang presence, and active shooters. Best practices for responding to school violence have many of the same tenets as previously discussed interventions, including *prevention*. Much like suicide, acts of school violence can be mitigated through implementation of solid prevention efforts. Your prevention planning is equally as important as your intervention planning and should include the specifics discussed in Chapter 2.

Given the range of potential violence that your team may have to address, there are a number of important concerns that your team must consider in the prevention, intervention, and aftermath (e.g., safety, trauma reactions, potential publicity) processes. Moreover, your response to school violence will vary given the type of violence (e.g., physical fight vs. armed intruder) and the severity of the outcome (e.g., multiple injuries, deaths). Your response to threats of school violence, such as a bomb or a school shooting, should be outlined in your crisis response plan. Any threats you encounter should be dealt with as directed in Chapter 2's discussion of threat assessment.

> The most challenging school crisis that I've responded to involved the murder of a mom and her three children. The father survived and was charged with the murder but was acquitted. This crisis impacted the school and community for months, not only in terms of the loss, but also the fear that someone had committed this horrible crime in their stable and quiet neighborhood.
>
> —Fulvia Franco

> [The most challenging school crisis] was Beecher Elementary School in Michigan (movie: *Bowling for Columbine*). It was the youngest in-school shooting (2000) of a 6-year-old girl who was shot and died at the hands of a fellow classmate. Few knew how to respond to a child related shooting and death. (My EMT training in facing young death was an asset.) Using my knowledge of child development and school psychology background, I was able to navigate a very sad situation and school dynamics. The community was outraged, and the superintendent was being fired (he was great to our response). We had to provide outside leadership in what was chaos. The local mental health professional had no training in trauma or crisis response. And it was my first national response!
>
> —BILL PFOHL

WHAT IS YOUR ROLE IN RESPONDING TO SERIOUS SCHOOL VIOLENCE?

In any case of serious school violence, the CRT should be mobilized immediately, and each member should be utilized to appropriately respond to the crisis. Figure 6.1 highlights the primary action steps you should take when you are alerted to a serious incidence of school violence on your campus. Each step is discussed, along with details regarding best practices for implementation.

This chapter will help to prepare you and your team on ways to appropriately respond to common instances of school violence. In keeping with the theme of this guidebook, the guidelines focus on more severe crises that can result in serious implications. As discussed, most SMHPs are equipped with the skills to handle smaller crises, such as a physical fight on campus, and they are in greater need of guidance on more serious areas of crisis, such as gang violence and school shootings.

HOW TO RESPOND TO GANG VIOLENCE IN YOUR SCHOOL

If your administration suspects a gang presence at your school, it cannot be ignored. Best practices for intervention in gang issues begin with prevention, including many of Chapter 2's recommendations for preventing school violence and enhancing school safety. Additional

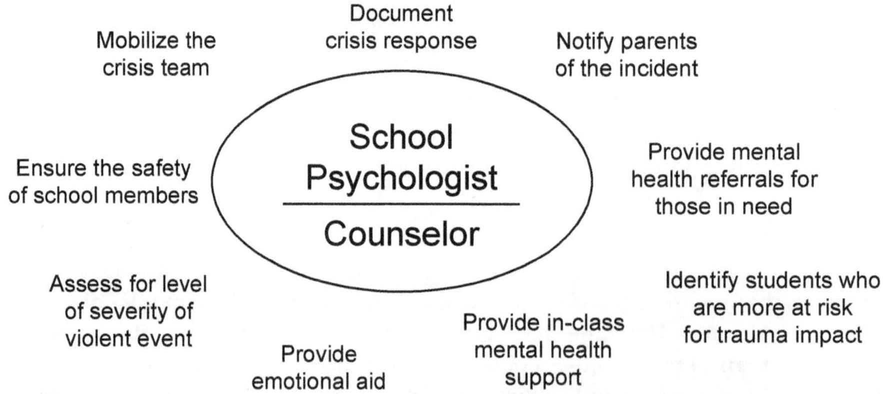

FIGURE 6.1. Actions to take in response to school violence.

recommendations for effective interventions include increased understanding of gang culture and the related issues at your school. Discipline approaches for gang-related behavior must be consistent. Additionally, your CRT should outline specifics for how to respond to gang issues in their crisis planning.

Gang intervention in schools can be tackled via whole-school or individual approaches (Office of Justice Programs, 2020). The whole-school approach, not surprisingly, targets all students, setting strict expectations for behavior, such as establishing a dress-code policy that forbids gang identifiers or paraphernalia. This approach requires your staff to be trained in gang culture and to become aware of common gang signs or trends, especially those in your community. Clear disciplinary procedures are set forth, including school suspicion or expulsion for any dress or behavioral code violations (depending on the severity; Office of Justice Programs, 2019).

Should your school use this approach, it is recommended that you also incorporate a reentry program for students who have been suspended/expelled. The design of these programs can vary but should include some element of family/caregiver involvement (i.e., training or classes), mental health support, and a set of social-emotional goals that the student must achieve prior to transitioning from alternative to traditional schooling (Office of Justice Programs, 2019). You may also want to consider offering a student-assistance program that can help students gain the skills necessary to meet the school's behavioral codes.

On the other hand, the individual gang intervention approach is more targeted and aims to divert gang-involved students away from their gang. Dress and behavioral codes should still be enforced, and identified students will be provided the skills and support necessary to distance themselves from their gang. This may look like a pull-out program in which students are pulled out of class on a rotation (as a means to limit regular class absences). Other designs might be a lunchtime or weekend program and an opportunity class, or it can be used during an on-campus suspension (Office of Justice Programs, 2019).

These approaches are not all encompassing, and other general recommendations should be applied when students suspected of being involved in gangs are identified. It is suggested that you make efforts to get to know these students and attempt to determine their member involvement/commitment. This will help guide your individualized approach.

Moreover, establishing rapport with these students can open the door to providing basic intervention techniques such as academic support, mentoring, and creation of support systems to help the student distance themselves from the gang. Upon establishing a relationship, you can begin to monitor and document the student's progress and behaviors (i.e., grades, attendance). This will alert you to any additional interventions needed (e.g., behavioral) that can be pulled from school resources.

Increasing your awareness of gang culture in your community will help you to be more attuned to potential violence in your school. Your team should make efforts to respond to any gang-related tensions, particularly if violent acts have occurred outside of school. In the aftermath of such occurrences, gang members of the groups who were involved should be separated and provided with mental health services. Ground rules should be set in order to maintain the safety of all students. Law enforcement should be alerted, and your team should closely monitor the situation (Arciaga, Sakamoto, & Fearbry Jones, 2010).

Any rumors of weapons on campus should be reported to the administration immediately, and you should follow up on every rumor and investigate them. If you have confirmed that a weapon has been brought onto campus, law enforcement should be contacted immediately. School staff members should not attempt to intervene (i.e., disarm the student) without the presence of law enforcement. It is imperative that you do not assume that a positive relationship with a student can protect you from a student's potential aggression (Arciaga et al., 2010).

Gang presence at your school can bring varied violent concerns, and your preparedness for how to intervene is critical. While physical fights are a common occurrence, violence can escalate to more serious incidents, such as attacks with weapons (i.e., with a knife or firearms). Your team must consider these potential crises in your planning and ensure that your crisis response plans outline how you will respond to larger-scale crises of violence.

HOW TO RESPOND TO A SHOOTING AT YOUR SCHOOL

In the rare event that you are faced with the horrific occurrence of an active shooter on your campus, your crisis preparedness could mean the difference between life and death. Your response to a school shooting will have a major impact on the well-being of your school community. There is no one specific way on how to respond to a school shooting. Much of the current guidance comes from studying the aftermath of past shootings. These reviews have highlighted both positive and negative examples of crisis response and have emphasized the grave need for crisis preparedness.

PROFESSIONAL PERSPECTIVE: SCOTT POLAND

The aftermath of a school shooting is very challenging. Many schools have wisely sought out counsel from experts in school shooting response in order to learn the lessons for returning to school and helping the school community. This book reviews many positive examples. One particular positive example that stands out to me is a school shooting that occurred in Brazil. I had the opportunity to assist in the aftermath, and I was incredibly impressed with the principal of the middle school where it occurred. He had planned to retire at the end of the year but said he wasn't able to now because, as he put it, "my school community needs me." I do not speak Portuguese, so communication was done only through a translator. The principal made the following points, which highlight best practices in crisis response for a school shooting:

- "Yesterday we worked with the staff all day to provide them support."
- "We will not be turning down any sources of assistance and we know we're in this for the long haul."
- "Three shifts of psychologists are coming to the school in the morning, afternoon, and evening to help students and their families."
- "Most of the affected students are about to finish the eighth grade in two weeks, and we need support for them over the summer and when they transition to a high school next fall."
- "We are using mapping, that is, Circles of Vulnerability, to determine who might need the most help."
- "We will not be focusing on the perpetrator."
- "All of the focus will be on the victims and the survivors."

While schools generally aim to do the right thing, many are ill equipped to do so. I can recall a few examples of decisions and responses in school crises that were not ideal:

- One teacher who had been shot in the school shooting shared that while she was at the hospital no one from the school district called or visited. After she was released from the hospital, she went home and again no one called or visited. She received an email telling her when to be back on campus. She indicated that support was provided at school, but she was frustrated that the same thing was not done for everyone. She was shot and witnessed the death of others at her school, and the red tape to get counseling services through the district was so complicated that she sought it out in the community and paid for it herself.

- In the many examples of shootings, several students have shared with me on numerous occasions that counselors who were brought to school to help were very well meaning, but that they were largely volunteers who were only there for a short period of time. The students reported that since their counselor changed frequently, they always felt they were starting over with each new counselor.

- A parent had two daughters at a high school where a school shooting occurred with multiple deaths. She was frustrated that a parent meeting to provide assistance on how to support her daughters was not held for 11 months.

- The principal of a school where multiple people died in a school shooting told me, "I understand you are the leader of a national crisis team, but we had counselors here the first morning after the shooting and we won't need anything else. Our motto is to keep a stiff upper lip."

- After a shooting, a school district closed the school for 13 school days and began planning for the students to start at a nearby high school due to the extensive damage done to the school during the shooting. The district felt it was important to have all the academic tools (i.e., books, materials for labs) available, overlooking the most important consideration: getting all the students back together with each other and getting the school staff the help they needed. If you close school for a significant amount of time, children are left unsupervised, given that in most cases their parents have to go back to work.

- One school where a shooting occurred has not held school on the anniversary date for many years, even though students currently attending the school were not even alive when the shooting occurred. The better arrangement would be to hold a meaningful day for the students by including a short remembrance of the tragedy and a focus on prevention efforts and service projects.

- A father told me that his child knew three of the victims in a shooting at her school. He felt that she needed help, but she refused to go to counseling. I advised the dad that this was not a decision a 14-year-old should be allowed to make. I suggested that she be given a choice of seeing a male or a female counselor but not be allowed to opt out of counseling altogether.

- In one case, I pointed out that in a few days it would be the anniversary of the death of the sibling of a student, and I encouraged the school psychologist to reach out to the sibling and offer support. The school psychologist disagreed on the basis that it would upset them. In turn, I stated that they surely knew the anniversary was approaching and that they would remember the exact date for decades. I urged the psychologist to reach out and support them.

- After a shooting in the school community, the lead counselor for the high school stated that school was out for the summer and it was not the school's responsibility to help the traumatized students. I responded: "School staff are still on duty, and you know which students you will be most concerned about. Let's set up the school as a place students can get help over the summer."

I have directly responded to 17 school shootings, for some of which I arrived as quickly as within 24 hours of the shooting. My firsthand experiences have prompted me to develop key recommendations that are critical in the aftermath of a school shooting. These recommendations have evolved over time, as each response has taught me something new. These guidelines are not exhaustive, and some aspects will be expanded upon further in this chapter. It is important to share the following recommendations with your school principal and superintendent.

My Key Recommendations for Responding to School Shootings

- Help the school staff and families first.
  - We like to use the analogy that if an adult is traveling on an airplane with a small child and there is a problem with the oxygen level in the cabin of the airplane, whose mouth does the oxygen mask go over first, the adult's or the child's?
- Hold a family meeting within a few days of the incident and just before the reopening of school. Valuable information should be offered to families/caregivers, including how to help their child cope and the typical reactions children have to a traumatic event. Families should also have the opportunity to walk through the school and process the event.
  - Children are likely to regress academically and behaviorally, have nightmares and sleeping problems, and may hold worries about the future.
  - Families/caregivers need to be careful not to project their own worries onto their children and instead should let their children express a range of emotions.
  - It is essential that families/caregivers find the time to speak with their child, giving them space to emote and be supportive. This is the time to reach out to your children, not to preach to them.
  - Families/caregivers should not tell their children that they understand what they're going through but should adopt an empathic perspective:
    - "Please help me to understand, as I can't imagine everything that you're going through in experiencing a shooting at your school."
- Accept help that is offered to staff and students, although help should be screened appropriately to ensure that the individuals/agencies are equipped to provide the appropriate help.
- Reopen your school as soon as possible and hopefully within a few days of the shooting.
  - The primary reason to keep the school closed after a shooting is to maintain the integrity of the crime scene. While police will be conducting an investigation, they almost always wrap up within a few days. It is far better for your child to return to school and get back into their routine than to stay home alone for days on end. Schools are the student's greatest source of assistance. If you close a school for weeks after a school shooting, the families/caregivers of the students will have to keep going to work, thereby leaving students to their own devices in working through their issues.

- Designate a recovery coordinator, whose sole job should be to plan recovery for the school district.
  - The recovery coordinator should of course possess a mental health background, along with excellent organizational and speaking abilities.
- Utilize the Circles of Vulnerability model (2016) to identify those who may be at most risk (see the worksheet, Form 4.1, in Chapter 4).
- Ensure that you individualize your interventions based on needs.
- Apply for a Project School Emergency Response to Violence (Project SERV; 2014) grant from the U.S. Department of Education (see the Recommended Resources section for more information).
  - These short-term grants are very easy to get and can provide invaluable initial support to schools.
- Be mindful of the long-term impact of the school shooting and the ongoing aftershocks (e.g., political issues, criminal trials, legislative changes).
  - It's important that the primary focus always be on helping staff and students get the support they need.
- After a school shooting, offer students a concrete symbol of increased safety and security.
  - One example would be clearing the trees around the school where the perpetrators had fired their weapons. Other examples would be building a fence around the school and having an increased police presence at school, as well as additional security cameras.
- Recognize that there is an increased risk for suicide after a school shooting; make efforts to prevent suicides (see Chapter 5 for guidance).
- Recognize that following a shooting, school communities have a long road ahead, which should include offering support to siblings and close friends on the victims' birthdays and on the anniversary date of the tragedy. Other important dates include school milestones, such as transitioning to a new school and graduation dates, along with the criminal prosecution, trial, and sentencing of perpetrators.
  - For example, it was 4-plus years after the shooting at Marjory Stoneman Douglas High School (MSD) before the punishment phase of the trial for the perpetrator started. In addition, civil suits have been initiated after school shootings, and in some cases, those suits have taken years to resolve. Not surprisingly, many emotional issues have surfaced at different stages of the legal process. One example was *Cleveland vs. Taft Union School High School District* (2019) in Taft, California, where a student shot and severely injured Bowe Cleveland, another student. I served as an expert witness on the side of the plaintiff (see Chapter 11 for a review of this case).
- When physical or structural damage occurs to the school, make repairs rather than tear the building down.

Among my many responses, the MSD shooting was one that hit close to home, as it occurred in my current place of residence, Broward County. In the aftermath of the shooting I was asked to consult with MSD. My guidance reiterates many of the points that have been discussed thus far.

PROFESSIONAL PERSPECTIVE: Scott Poland

I was invited to come to the first major planning meeting for the Broward schools in the aftermath of the tragic shooting at MSD. Because of my extensive experience in responding to many school shootings, I was asked to share my ideas with the leadership team first. I emphasized the following:

- Broward needed to apply for a U.S. Department of Education Project SERV Grant, Schools Emergency Response to Violence, to fund the needed additional mental health positions for the schools. I further shared that previously schools that experienced a shooting used SERV funds to bring trailers to campus so that the increased number of mental health personnel would have a confidential place to provide support services.

- I strongly advised the school teams that extensive efforts needed to be made to help the school staff prior to students returning to school. I also stressed the importance of the school district not turning down any sources of assistance, as we knew that we were in it for the long haul.

- I recommended that a parent meeting be held as quickly as possible to give them information about how to help their children cope and to prepare them for the typical reactions children have to traumatic events. I emphasized that parents needed to respond with patience, structure, and love.

- I recommended that the district identify one staff member with the right qualifications and background to become the recovery coordinator and that their sole job should be to chart the course for recovery, not just for MSD but for the entire district. I advised the teams to utilize the Circles of Vulnerability model to idenify those staff members and students who were likely to be most affected by the tragedy.

- I also recommended that the school should resume as soon as the staff received the needed support. I shared that when schools are closed for weeks after a shooting, students are largely left isolated and unsupervised, as their parents cannot stay home from work more than few days. I emphasized the importance of students being connected to their peers and mentors and maintaining structure in their day.

- Regarding mental health care, I mentioned that staff and students in the aftermath of previous school shootings have been frustrated because the counselor assigned to them changes frequently. I suggested that they strive to create consistency and connectedness among those providing mental health services to the victims. I shared the message that everyone needed the opportunity (if they wished) to talk about the tragedy. I emphasized the importance of psychological first aid and the need to help everyone affected to identify their existing sources of support. Lastly, I stressed the importance of offering students the opportunity to talk about the experience, write about it, and express their emotions through music and artwork.

Mass casualty events are fluid and complex; they require adaptive approaches that are flexible to the needs at hand. As you can imagine, a school shooting creates an incredibly chaotic environment, where it may be difficult to implement intervention procedures. As with many crisis responses, it is helpful to have a go-to checklist that can guide your action steps. These checklists should be outlined in your crisis response plan ahead of time. Dr. Crawford-Goetz's experience in responding to a school shooting highlights the critical need for your team's crisis preparedness.

PROFESSIONAL PERSPECTIVE: STEPHANIE CRAWFORD-GOETZ

The most challenging school crisis was responding to a school shooting. This crisis took a tremendous amount of preplanning in a very short amount of time to be able to offer immediate crisis response. The response was over multiple days, and the follow-up and recovery work has been over years and will be ongoing. When this happened, a separate site was needed to provide the immediate crisis response. The crisis response needs to be over multiple days due to the large volume of people coming in for crisis counseling. We also needed to pull in support from other school district crisis teams to have the capacity to support people.

The school served grades K–12, and this meant additional components were needed for the crisis response. We had a large space for young children staffed by people specially trained to work with young children and who could provide a variety of activities to meet their needs. We also needed to provide parental services as they were also impacted significantly by this event. There was a large amount of security needed as kind and well-meaning community members were flooding the crisis response site to offer their services and staff that were well versed needed to be in place to thank them and explain to them the process and vetting that needs to happen to support schoolchildren.

We also needed support from security and communications due to all the media presence. We had to navigate requests for support at the multiple vigils that community members were holding. There were also practical needs that had to be organized, including providing food at the response site for all the staff volunteering their time. The police were doing an active investigation and wanted to collaborate in talking with witnesses who were also people in need of crisis support. Staff also needed a lot of personal needs met as they had evacuated the school and were not allowed to return for several days due to the police investigation. We had to work with victim advocates and businesses to provide them with transportation, food, cell phones, and computers. We also worked with district leadership and other schools to find space to resume classes as soon as possible since the original school could not be accessed.

The work during this time was intense, and we worked over 12-hour days and on weekends for weeks as we continued to provide both crisis support and practical support. Crisis work is not my full-time role, and while we have a crisis team lead, this person also has multiple roles in addition to crisis response; this meant that we both needed other people to do all our other duties during the weeks that we devoted to the response and immediate recovery process.

Although it has been years since this event occurred, recovery work continues and collaboration is not just with the people at the school but all of the staff in the district, all students, community responders, and community mental health agencies. As a community, we continually provide resources and opportunities for support to anyone impacted by the event.

NASP (2020b) has issued critical guidelines that are universally applicable in the immediate aftermath (i.e., 1 to 24 hours) of a school shooting. These guidelines align with those that I have offered, and both of us (SP and SF) agree with their recommendations. It is important to note, however, that this guidance is not a substitute for comprehensive crisis planning in advance. Form 6.1 is a user-friendly checklist of the guidelines that you should be implementing within the first two hours after a school shooting.

How Can You Address the Mental Health Needs of the Victims?

Addressing mental health needs will be an immediate priority in the aftermath of a school shooting. Services offered should promote recovery and resiliency in order to support the psychological well-being of those impacted. You are encouraged to utilize a *psychological triage* approach in which you identify and attend to individuals who are most in need of services. Successful triage models will also help you to identify those who are at high risk for ongoing trauma. Recall the Circles of Vulnerability (see Chapter 4); individuals at greater risk are those with physical and emotional proximity to the event, including staff, individuals with precrisis vulnerabilities, and those who exhibit more severe crisis reactions. Additionally, this approach will help you to determine the level of follow-up needed, including long-term provision of trauma-oriented services.

Best practices for this approach are thoughtfully outlined in the National Child Traumatic Stress Network and National Center for PTSD's (NCTSN/NCPTSD) Psychological First Aid crisis intervention program (Brymer et al., 2006). This program seeks to promote resiliency, improve adaptive functioning, and lessen the symptoms of trauma-related distress. Psychological First Aid can be implemented in both individual and group formats and is made up of the eight core actions summarized in the checklist in Form 6.2.

After the initial shock and crisis response to a school shooting is complete, you will be faced with a barrage of tasks and responsibilities. Your efforts will be split in many directions, with a focus on implementing best postvention practices. Much like your response in the immediate aftermath of a school shooting, it is helpful to have a checklist that can guide you through this next stage of recovery. Form 6.3 includes a checklist worksheet for you to utilize in the first 24 hours after a school shooting.

How Can You Be Best Prepared to Support the Ongoing Mental Health Needs of Your School Community?

Given the traumatic nature of school shootings, the ongoing mental health implications are of serious concern. As discussed in the aftermath of all severe crises, students and school personnel must be given the space to express the broad range of emotions they are experiencing. Group processing should occur, in which each participant is provided the chance to share their personal experience, immediate and current reactions to the tragedy, and concerns about the future. These groups should include psychoeducational components in which students are encouraged to explore the coping skills they have used in the past, along with ways they can help themselves to feel safer.

As with all interventions, you must be attuned to the psychological needs of your school members. Trauma creates varied emotional and physical implications. In the aftermath, many individuals may be struck with overwhelming emotions, while others may be devoid of emotions, unable to feel anything at all. These varied reactions highlight the significant post-trauma emotion dysregulation that can be experienced. Moreover, many individuals experience somatic concerns (e.g., stomach and body aches, headaches) and major sleep disturbances (e.g., nightmares, difficulty sleeping).

Trauma reactions, much like bereavement, will vary based on age, particularly in the case of persistent reactions. It is imperative that you and your staff be on the lookout for any of these reactions in your school community; the level of their severity will guide your response. See Table 6.1 for a review of trauma reactions by age in the event of a severe violent crisis.

TABLE 6.1. Trauma Reactions Based on Age

Preschool[a]

May observe loss of developmental skills, regressive behaviors, symptoms of fear and anxiety, decreased verbalization, feelings of helplessness, and nightmares

Elementary school[a]

May report feelings of:
- Concern regarding safety of self and others
- Worry/fear/anxiety
- Guilt and shame
- Sadness
- Somatic complaints

May observe:
- Concentration difficulties
- Academic decline
- Acting-out behaviors
- Retelling of the event

Middle and high school[a]

May report feelings of:
- Vulnerability
- Embarrassment/self-consciousness
- Worry/fear/anxiety
- Shame and guilt
- Revenge and retribution

May observe:
- Self-destructive or acting-out behaviors
- Social withdrawal

Adults[b]

May observe exhaustion, confusion, sadness, anxiety, agitation, numbness, dissociation, confusion, physical arousal, and blunted affect

[a] NCTSN (n.d.).
[b] Center for Substance Abuse Treatment (2014).

In the case of a school shooting, most survivors will require ongoing support to assist them in processing the traumatic experience. Referrals should be made to appropriate mental health agencies, including providers who specialize in treating trauma. Your school should also be mindful of triggering dates, such as the anniversary of the shooting or the birthdates of victims. Mental health support and services are typically high in the days and week following a school shooting but are lessened and maybe even nonexistent around these events when the emotional needs tend to peak again for survivors. Long-term connection to mental health support is critical.

Additionally, you should make efforts to involve families/caregivers in your ongoing response. Maintain open communication with them throughout the postvention process. Continue to encourage them to support their children, speak with them about the tragedy, and provide encouragement for the children to return to school. Families/caregivers should share the specific role that their own child plays in school safety. These discussions should include talking points provided by the school administration about the serious consequences of threats of violence, direction to use an anonymous reporting system if one is in place, and/or immediate disclosure to an adult when they learn of a threat of violence.

When consulting with schools on their crisis preparedness, I have engaged in many Q&As with administrators, CRTs, and school personnel. My summary of the key questions and answers is presented in the following section and highlights the critical points of your crisis intervention process in the aftermath of severe school violence.

After a School Shooting: Commonly Asked Questions and Ways to Respond

Q: What advice do you have for schools to prepare for the mental health needs of staff, students, and families/caregivers if a school shooting occurs?

A: *The wise superintendent would encourage the district to plan who they would call on for mental health support. This should include identifying local mental health professionals as well as individuals with experience responding to a school shooting.*

Q: How could a school district decide who to accept volunteer help from after a shooting, as many well-meaning mental health professionals are likely to volunteer?

A: *If these individuals have not been identified in advance as in the previous question, then it would seem necessary to ask them to provide certification that they've been trained in crisis intervention, which would include the American National Red Cross, National Organization of Victim Assistance, Critical Incidence Stress Management or NASP PRePARE.*

Q: Can a community totally recover from a school shooting?

A: *The community can recover, and the emphasis needs to be on caring, connections, and compassion for all those affected. It is helpful to recognize that things will never be quite the same; there is a new normal and everyone should be hopeful for the future and advocate for ongoing support for those who need it.*

Q: Is there a ballpark figure or an estimate about how staff, students, and families/caregivers are going to do after a school shooting with regard to recovery?

A: *Estimates are that about 60% will be okay because they've turned to their existing support systems and 20% will have minor problems. Importantly, estimates are that about 20% will have major problems.*

Q: What are the typical behaviors that we need to be concerned about for adolescents who have been traumatized?

A: *Traumatized adolescents are unfortunately more at risk for substance abuse, reckless behavior, depression, and suicide.*

Q Is the school shooting life-altering for families and close friends of the victims?

A: *Many close friends and family members have channeled their grief in a search for meaning, which has resulted in many foundations and prevention efforts being started in memory of their lost loved one. Essentially, these individuals are not going to give up, and they want changes so that this doesn't happen to anyone else's loved one.*

Q: What should we say to someone in the months and years after they lost a loved one to a school shooting?

A: *We should always be there for them and should avoid saying that we understand. Rather, emphasize that we are there to listen anytime they want to talk about their loved one.*

Q: What processing opportunities should be provided to those affected by school violence?

A: *An opportunity to talk about it, write about it, music, artwork, projects, and rituals. Younger students are more likely to express emotions through artwork and drawing. Older students will talk about it more and search for the "gift of hope" and how to make the world better!*

Q: Should processing a crisis take place in a large group?

A: *Whenever possible the group size should be no larger than a typical classroom. Chairs should be in a circle, and the facilitator should sit down with the group. Processing is voluntary with the facilitator encouraging group members to stay and letting them know that previous participants in crisis processing reported it helped. Confidentiality should be stressed.*

Q: What are other ways to support our student and staff mental health in the aftermath of a school shooting?

A: *One idea that I have seen be very successful is the use of therapy dogs. Therapy dog visitations at school can be an excellent coping tool.*

Crisis intervention does not end there; effective intervention continues long after the initial response to a school shooting. Your postvention efforts are just as important as your prevention efforts and should continue to address the ongoing needs of the surviving victims and the school community. Chapter 8 will explore the postvention process in deeper detail.

School violence is a complex aspect of crisis intervention and covers a variety of potential crisis events. Preparation is key to mitigating the very serious impact of violent crises at your school. Your response to significant violence, such as school shootings, must be carefully detailed in your crisis plan and include step-by-step ways in which you will intervene. The aftermath of a violent crisis brings a number of concerns and is an ongoing matter that must greatly emphasize the emotional and mental health needs of your staff and student body that will undoubtedly be present in the aftermath. Your approaches must be implemented in line with the expert recommendations offered in this chapter in order to best meet the needs of your school community and enable a safe return to the "new normal" of life postcrisis.

Ideas for Consideration

- Gang-related prevention activities (Communities in Schools of North Carolina, 2015):
  - Individual approaches: help students to define their roles and responsibilities in multiple settings (i.e., family, school, community). Help them to recognize that they serve important roles across domains of their lives, which can decrease the interest in gang involvement. This also helps a student to understand that their responsibilities and roles will be at risk if they were to join a gang.
  - Small-group approaches:
    - Engage in exercises in critical thinking and building empathy (i.e., perspective taking, recognizing verbal and nonverbal cues, increased use of empathy).
    - Provide anger management strategies (e.g., deep breathing, taking a time-out, using "wise mind" vs. "emotional mind").
    - Engage in deescalation exercises: help students to problem-solve and use their skills in the moment of escalating tensions.
- School violence response and trauma processing ideas:
  - Engage in role plays with your team members. This is very helpful in creating comfort in the crisis response. Create scripts that include common questions that may be asked of you. The questions in the Q&A above can be used as a script during your role play.
  - Encourage emotion elicitation in students and staff. Create a box that school members can drop index cards into that include their needs and feelings and how you might best address them.
  - Encourage teachers to hold activities that promote resilience and connectedness in their classrooms. Ideas include (SoulShoppe, 2021):
    - Compliment circles: Each student has the opportunity to pay a compliment to everyone else in the class.
    - Affirmation language circles: Everyone gets a chance to say something affirming or encouraging about everyone in the class, for example, that they are strong and resilient in the face of tough times.
    - Community circles: Every student has the opportunity to offer an idea of something that builds community, for example, discussing shared interests that create deeper bonds.
  - Teachers can also enhance their classroom environment to be warmer and welcoming for students. Ideas include:
    - Bringing in plants or a class pet that the students can attend to.
    - Creating a "calm corner" where students can go to relax and decompress. Include coping tools such as helpful books, stuffed animals, or sensory toys.
    - Playing calming music and taking brain breaks with the lights off.

Recommended Resources

- **NASP (2020b): Responding to a Mass Casualty Event at a School: General Guidance for the First Stage of Recovery:** Best practices for your team to follow in the immediate aftermath of a major violent crisis. Found at *www.nasponline.org/resources-and-publications/resources-and-podcasts/school-safety-and-crisis/school-violence-resources/responding-to-a-mass-casualty-event-at-a-school-general-guidance-for-the-first-stage-of-recovery.*
- **Recovery from Large-Scale Crises: Guidelines for Crisis Teams and Administrators:** Effective crisis response and intervention for your team in the days and weeks following

a large-scale, violent crisis. Found at *www.nasponline.org/resources-and-publications/resources-and-podcasts/school-safety-and-crisis/school-violence-resources/recovery-from-large-scale-crises-guidelines-for-crisis-teams-and-administrators.*

- **National Gang Center:** A project funded by the Office of Juvenile Justice and Delinquency Prevention, the Office of Justice Programs, and the U.S. Department of Justice. The goal is to implement practices that engage and empower those in local communities with chronic and emerging gang problems to create comprehensive solutions that will prevent gang violence, reduce gang involvement, and suppress gang-related crime. Found at *https://nationalgang-center.ojp.gov/spt/Programs/53.*
- **National Child Traumatic Stress Network:** Provides resources, support, and connections for families and their children who have been exposed to significant trauma. Found at *www.nctsn.org.*
- **School Emergency Response to Violence (Project SERV, 2014):** Provides grant funding to schools in need in the aftermath of a severe crisis. Found at *www2.ed.gov/programs/dvppserv/index.html.*

FORM 6.1

School Shooting Response Checklist: The First 2 Hours

Instructions for use: The following checklist should be utilized as a guide to ensure that best practices are implemented in the immediate aftermath of a school shooting. Check off each item as the tasks are completed. *Note:* These tasks do not have to be completed in the exact order provided, and some may not be addressed within the first 2 hours; however, they should be prioritized within the first several hours after a school shooting.

- ☐ Contact law enforcement; begin collaborative relationship.
- ☐ Ensure that your campus is safe and that all threats have been addressed.
- ☐ Work to identify and account for all members of the student body and staff.
- ☐ Convene district and school CRTs immediately.
- ☐ Review your crisis plan and steps for implementation.
- ☐ Establish a site of family reunification and coordinate an organized process for students to reunite.
- ☐ Coordinate with community agencies, such as the police (state and local) and fire departments, the city manager, and the FBI.
- ☐ Your media liaison from the CRT must coordinate with the media.

  Relevant media-related steps:

  - ☐ If you do not have a media liaison yet, you must designate a media spokesperson; this is often the school/district public information officer.
  - ☐ Make careful consideration of what is publicized. Media can be helpful in providing information about emergency responses and how victims are coping; however, it can also enhance trauma or the potential for another threat.
  - ☐ Limit the media exposure of the campus; set clear boundaries for the media as to where they can set up shop.
  - ☐ Find an alternative place to have press conferences so that they are not held on campus. Find a place away from the school to hold the media interactions.
  - ☐ Present a message that is consistent, coordinated, and clear across all parties (e.g., administrators, law enforcement).

- ☐ Maintain open communication with any survivors and their families; offer resources and support.
- ☐ Communicate with law enforcement regarding any injuries or fatalities.
- ☐ Use additional phone lines, the district website, local media, and social media to publicize need-to-know details regarding the response and answers to important questions.
- ☐ Plan for technology failure. When it rains it pours—ensure that you have options for communicating beyond land lines and cell phones, should these become unavailable. In some cases, radio systems may be the only way to communicate in the initial aftermath.

(continued)

Source: Based on material in NASP (2020c).

- ☐ Dispel and/or verify rumors; confirm the facts.
- ☐ As needed, implement immediate mental health crisis intervention triage.

  Triage Steps:

  - ☐ Work to create a space where immediate crisis intervention services can occur. When possible, these services should be conducted by a SMHP.
  - ☐ Utilize a structured triage model from a research-based approach, such as the PREPaRE model.
  - ☐ Identify and assess the level of trauma that the survivors are experiencing.
  - ☐ If your school has been damaged or is broadly considered a crime scene, you should move your crisis intervention to an off-site location (e.g., community center, church, another school).
  - ☐ Check in with the adult survivors and help them to manage their own reactions.
    - ☐ Suggestions: practice mindfulness, diaphragmatic (i.e., deep) breathing, and the use of other coping and self-regulation strategies.
    - ☐ Reaffirm the need to focus on the current tasks and to draw upon their crisis training.

- ☐ Ensure that you have a district mental health professional in place who can respond to and manage outside support resources (e.g., volunteer counselors) that come to offer their assistance.

FORM 6.2

Checklist for Psychological First Aid

Instructions for use: The following checklist should be utilized as a guide to ensure that your team is providing the key components of appropriate psychological first aid. This can be used to prepare your staff for providing psychological aid and as a review to reflect on the implementation of the aid.

Make Contact and Engage

- ☐ Create a helping relationship with the survivor by responding with an empathetic and compassionate manner.
- ☐ Start by introducing yourself.
- ☐ Then move on to asking questions that help to assess the concerns and needs of the survivor.
- ☐ Maintain confidentiality and privacy.

Provide Safety and Comfort

- ☐ Ensure physical safety and attend to physical needs of the survivor.
- ☐ Attend to children separated from a parent or caregiver.
- ☐ Share information about the disaster response.
- ☐ Make efforts to protect survivors from additional trauma exposure.
- ☐ Encourage social engagement and connections with others.
- ☐ Attend to and help survivors who are missing a loved one.
- ☐ Intervene with survivors who are experiencing acute grief reactions due to the loss of a loved one.
- ☐ Support survivors when death notifications are received or during body identification.
- ☐ Be thoughtful of spiritual issues.
- ☐ Share information and provide assistance in planning funeral arrangements.

Stabilization

- ☐ If needed, calm, stabilize, and orient survivors who appear to be emotionally distraught or disoriented.

Gather Information: Current Needs and Concerns

- ☐ Nature and severity of traumatic experience
- ☐ Loss and death of a loved one
- ☐ Address concerns regarding immediate and ongoing danger
- ☐ Preexisting medical and mental illness and current medications
- ☐ Loss (person, place, property, pets, belongings)

(continued)

Source: Adapted from Brymer et al. (2006).

- ☐ Recent or prior exposure to loss and trauma
- ☐ Extreme negative emotions (e.g., shame or guilt)
- ☐ Self-harm thoughts or desires to harm others
- ☐ Past substance abuse
- ☐ Accessibility of social support
- ☐ Specific concerns regarding developmental impact of the trauma

Provide Practical Assistance

- ☐ Identify the most pressing needs.
- ☐ Clarify the need with the survivor and ask them to share details about the issue.
- ☐ Create an action plan.
- ☐ Help the survivor to enact the action plan.

Establish Connections with Social Supports

- ☐ Model appropriate social and emotional support.
- ☐ Help survivors gain access to primary support persons.
- ☐ Encourage survivors to use immediate available support.
- ☐ Discuss survivors' willingness toward giving and accepting support.

Share Information on Coping

- ☐ Discuss post-trauma reactions; normalize and provide information.
- ☐ Provide information regarding stress reaction and psychological reactions to trauma exposure.
- ☐ Talk with children about bodily and emotional reactions.
- ☐ Provide information to encourage adaptive coping techniques.
- ☐ Introduce relaxation techniques.
- ☐ Provide family coping techniques to encourage stability and recovery.
- ☐ Assist with physical, emotional, cognitive, social, and developmental issues.
- ☐ Introduce anger management techniques.
- ☐ Address sleeping difficulties.
- ☐ Address alcohol and/or substance use.

FORM 6.3

School Shooting Response Checklist: The Remaining 24 Hours

Instructions for use: The following checklist should be utilized as a guide to ensure that best practices are implemented within the first day after a school shooting. Check off each item as the tasks are completed. *Note:* These tasks do not have to be completed in the exact order provided and some may not be addressed within the first 24 hours; however, they should be prioritized in the aftermath of a school shooting.

- ☐ Continue to handle the media and methods of communications using the aforementioned guidance.
  - ☐ Continue to maintain strict boundaries and guidelines with the media and their ability to access the school grounds.
  - ☐ Prohibit the media from filming any damaged part of the school, as that can cause trauma reactions.
  - ☐ Take steps to ensure that students and staff are not faced with potentially harmful media attention and interactions that can be triggering in nature and can also contribute to misinformation spreading widely.
  - ☐ Relay the potential risks of media interviews to students, their families, and the community.
  - ☐ Emphasize that minor interviews should only take place with a legal caregiver or SMHP present.
  - ☐ *A note to consider:* When students and their community are bombarded with media coverage, it hinders their ability to heal, and it can give the public a sense that the victim survivors are not coping well.
- ☐ Provide clear, consistent, and coordinated messaging across all parties involved (i.e., school administrators, law enforcement, and medical personnel).
- ☐ Dispel and/or verify rumors, as always, and confirm the facts.
- ☐ Monitor social media posts both to track responses to official district posts and to be aware of and respond as necessary to posts from others in the community.
- ☐ If you have not already done so, expand space (on or off campus) and staff to provide immediate crisis intervention services as needed; this may look like going to a nearby school or community recreation center or bringing portables/trailers onto campus.
- ☐ Continue to communicate with and support victims' families and staff in all areas that may be impacted in the district. Specifically, widespread support is important so that you can connect with staff or students (e.g., relatives, close friends) who may be more severely affected by the crisis. These communications must be ongoing, and you need to be alert to the various trauma reactions.
- ☐ Continue to address mental health needs of victims.
- ☐ Utilize a research-based, structured model of triage to address the psychological needs of victims over time. Integrate any new information that you learn and its impact on triage decisions.
- ☐ Ensure that you reaffirm the physical health, comfort, and safety of school members, while continuing to attend to any medical needs.

(continued)

Based on material in NASP (2020b).

School Shooting Response Checklist: The Remaining 24 Hours *(page 2 of 2)*

- ☐ Continue to share information about the crisis facts, minimize public exposure to crisis scenes, and begin assessment of intervention efforts.
- ☐ Utilize outside agencies to address mental health needs should the level of support be beyond what your team is able to meet.
- ☐ Depending on the level of publicity, your school may be flooded with numerous offers to help. You may need this assistance; however, there needs to be a proper screening procedure in place in order to ensure the legitimacy of their assistance.
- ☐ Recognize and emphasize that there is no timeline for healing; recovery is individualized and depends heavily on the factors of the crisis at hand.
- ☐ Adults should be cognizant of their own reactions and what they are modeling to children, as it will influence their kids' perceptions and sense of safety. You should encourage families and caregivers to help their children to manage their feelings by modeling healthy coping strategies and being attuned to their own emotional state and that of their kids.

CHAPTER 7

Natural Disasters

> All schools need to be prepared to handle the unthinkable. Effective crisis intervention is critical for the well-being and mental health of our students and staff. It is not a matter of IF but WHEN a crisis will strike.
>
> —CATHY KENNEDY-PAINE

Crises typically come in unexpected ways and are typically linked to individuals or groups of people. There is, however, a type of large-school crises that are brought on entirely by our environment, climate, and nature: natural disasters. School communities across the nation have been affected by a variety of natural disasters. In fact, these events represent a significant and rising threat to the physical and emotional well-being of the youth population. Globally, approximately 175 million children are impacted by natural disasters on an annual basis (Lai & La Greca, 2020; Save the Children, 2007), including an estimated 25% of adolescents in the United States (Paul et al., 2015; Ruggiero, Van Wynsberghe, Stevens, & Kilpatrick, 2006). The most common experiences include hurricanes, tornadoes, floods, earthquakes, and wildfires. Natural disasters appear to be growing in their severity, intensity, and frequency, creating an increased risk of destruction and harm (Ornes et al., 2018). Their aftermath can be riddled with major destruction and potential for deaths, injuries, and traumatization. Moreover, some natural disasters (e.g., floods) create extended periods of aftermath, where individuals are left without the necessary resources to live and are exposed to ongoing traumatization. This chapter provides a detailed review of the most common natural disasters that schools encounter, along with the unique implications that accompany each event. Best practices for preparedness, interventions, and postvention are discussed in detail, including a review of related crises such as acts of terror and infectious disease epidemics.

NATURAL DISASTER PREPAREDNESS

Given their broad reach, natural disasters are events that every school *must* be prepared for, particularly those in vulnerable states (e.g., midwestern states at risk for tornadoes). While some natural disasters happen without notice (e.g., earthquakes) or can be difficult to predict (e.g., flooding in the aftermath of a hurricane), your school can still act to be prepared and to mitigate the harmful effects and potential losses. Proper preparedness includes maintaining your school's safety plan (as discussed in Chapter 2). Key preparedness recommendations regarding natural disasters are highlighted in a user-friendly checklist format found in Form 7.1.

Schools will serve a number of roles in the crisis response to a natural disaster, and the approaches will vary greatly given the range of potential aftermath concerns. Your school's responses to natural disasters should be determined in advance and under the guidance of government expertise, such as the Federal Emergency Management Agency (FEMA). FEMA has a number of helpful resources (see the Recommended Resources section) that all schools should refer to in their preparation process. Keep in mind that depending on the nature of the natural disaster, your school may be a critical part of the crisis response not only for your school but for the general community.

CONSIDERATIONS FOR SPECIFIC DISASTERS

Hurricanes

Hurricanes certainly have the potential for significant disaster and damage to a school community, although they offer the unique opportunity of time and some predictability. Hurricanes are typically tracked weeks to days in advance of their landing. This gives community members ample time to prepare for potential disaster factors; for example, they can stock up on supplies like water, canned goods, and gasoline. However, with that preparation comes the anticipation of the event, creating a wave of anxiety and fear as the storm creeps closer to land. Supplies can become limited, people can feel unprepared (e.g., they have no shutters for their windows), and tensions can begin to run high.

Moreover, while meteorologists can provide general predictions for landfall and the strength of a hurricane, there have been deadly examples of times when a hurricane made a last-minute shift in its path, taking out everything in its way. For example, Hurricane Ian made landfall in Fort Myers, Florida, in 2022, demonstrating a rapid shift in the direction of the eye. Initially, meteorologists had predicted a direct hit to Tampa, causing many in Fort Myers to be less worried about the severity of the landfall. Total destruction was observed across this beach community, and the after-effects were devastating.

The experience of a hurricane is unlike that of any other natural disaster; it comes with significant weather conditions, including rain, thunder, lightning, and wind. As the hurricane passes over your location, the sound of the wind is often likened to the sound of a freight train. My coauthor (SF), a native Floridian, can recall this very distinct sound that has rung through her shuttered windows during past hurricanes. Depending on their speed, hurricanes can take up to several hours to pass over a location, destroying the structures and nature in their path. In some cases, flooding can become a significant concern in the aftermath of a hurricane; recall the environmental conditions in the aftermath of Hurricane Harvey in Houston in 2017, which lasted 5 days, resulting in weeks of devastating flooding (WYTF Staff, 2021).

Certain emotional effects and reactions are specific to hurricanes. In cases of extreme disaster, many individuals suffer from emotional and physical exhaustion. For example, homes and cars may have been damaged or lost; sleep may be unattainable for survivors who are working to deal with the damage. Much as in other crises, survivors may feel emotional guilt as it relates to their reaction to or preparedness for the hurricane (e.g., the home was not properly shuttered, and someone was hurt by a projectile that flew through their window). Relatedly, survival guilt is commonly experienced in the aftermath of a hurricane, particularly in the case of significant disasters such as Hurricane Katrina in 2005, which caused the loss of over 1,800 lives (University of Rhode Island, 2020).

Although a hurricane may only last a relatively short period, its emotional toll can have lasting effects. Startle reactions are particularly severe in the months following a hurricane, and even ordinary rain/storms may trigger a panic response (Brock, Lazarus, & Jimerson, 2002). Moreover, depending on the level of destruction, property damage in the aftermath of a hurricane can be significant and may spread far and wide. Clean-up and reconstruction can take years to complete.

For example, in 1992 Hurricane Andrew brought nearly total destruction to many parts of South Dade County, Florida, where over 125,000 homes were destroyed or damaged (Victor, 2017). Families were left without homes, and those whose homes remained standing dealt with ongoing mold and mildew issues and the loss of electricity and air conditioning for months. Those who were most impacted were forced to evacuate their homes, and thousands lost their homes in the storm. In severe cases, recovery does not come quickly in the aftermath of such an intense disaster. The lengthy duration of time that is required to return to "normal life" is said to create significant mental health concerns for the victims, including depression and disillusionment (Lazarus, 1993).

Mental health implications are significant in the aftermath of a hurricane, including high rates of PTSD, worsened preexisting mental health conditions, and increased rates of suicidal ideation (Rathner, 2018). For example, after Hurricane Maria in 2017, calls to Puerto Rico's suicide hotline reportedly skyrocketed (Jervis, 2018). Moreover, victims from Hurricane Katrina were found to have symptoms of PTSD and increased suicidal ideation in the year after the storm (Reardon, 2015). Importantly, studies of childhood trauma reactions in the aftermath of South Carolina's Hurricane Hugo in 1989 have pointed to correlative findings between higher number of symptoms and more frightening experiences of the storm, paired with more significant damage to their homes (Brock et al., 2002).

Tornadoes

While tornadoes present with similar inclement weather conditions to hurricanes, their timing greatly differs. Moreover, their destruction can often be more significant and even deadlier. In just minutes, tornadoes can form and hit an area, bringing mass destruction. Their rapid formation leaves individuals with little, if any, time to prepare.

In many ways, reactions in the aftermath of a tornado are similar to those associated with hurricanes. Startle reactions to rain and storms and resulting panic/anxiety may be observed. Additionally, it can be difficult to cope with the sights (e.g., demolished homes) and smells (e.g., rotting food or death) that result. Survivors' guilt is found to be especially more common in the context of a tornado. First responders have pointed to examples of children expressing guilt that their home was still standing while their friend's home next door was not (Lazarus, Jimerson, & Brock, 2003). Studies have highlighted the most vulnerable populations in the aftermath of a tornado, including those who were in the impact zone, have been injured, and have experienced the death of relatives, as well as first responders and recovery workers (Bloch, Silber, & Perry, 1956; SAMHSA, 2022d). Additional common responses include overwhelming feelings of anxiety, sleep disturbances, and other depression-like symptoms. Other signs of emotional distress in the aftermath of a tornado include:

- Chronic worry or feelings of guilt while also feeling unsure as to why
- Feelings of hopelessness and/or helplessness
- Fear that something bad is going to happen with any forecast of a storm
- Relational conflict (i.e., yelling) with family and friends
- Experiences of nightmares or intrusive thoughts/memories related to the tornado (SAMHSA, 2022d)

Floods

All schools should be well equipped with a response to floods, as they are one of the most common natural disasters (National Weather Service, n.d.). Floods may wreak havoc on your school community in a number of ways (e.g., aftermath of a slow-moving storm, flash floods, and dam failures). Some floods may provide individuals with more time to prepare (e.g., in an area with slow-rising flooding), whereas other floods may occur quickly and with little warning. Flash flooding, for example, commonly occurs in urban areas where water runs off quickly to low spots, without ample area to infiltrate the ground. Flash flooding can be extremely dangerous, and the fast speed of the water can cause significant destruction. Water can rise quickly, trapping people in their homes or cars (National Weather Service, n.d.). Additionally, flooding can present the dangers of other disasters, such as mudslides.

Coping with floods presents unique challenges, as their duration can be lengthy, particularly in areas in which drainage is poor and the water is unable to recede. This delays the cleanup process for days or even weeks and often results in significant damage to standing buildings and homes. The psychological impact of enduring a flooding disaster is similar to that observed after hurricanes or tornadoes, including high rates of PTSD, depression, and anxiety (Mason, Andrews, & Upton, 2010). Inclement weather can trigger fears and worries, although the content of those anxieties tends to be more specific to the potential of future flooding (Babel, 2010).

Earthquakes

Earthquakes occur when there is a shift in the Earth's tectonic plates, creating a major shaking of the ground that typically lasts from seconds to minutes. The intensity of the shaking can vary, ranging from mild to violent. Earthquakes are a unique natural disaster in that they do not have a specific endpoint. The aftermath of earthquakes includes aftershocks (i.e., periods of tremors) that create an environment of ongoing distress. Additionally, unlike any other natural disaster, earthquakes occur entirely without warning, creating significant implications for the response and aftermath of their occurrence Many states on the West Coast of the United States are more vulnerable to earthquakes, given their location on fault lines (SAMHSA, 2022c).

The majority of earthquakes are mild and cause little destruction. However, even minor earthquakes can create emotional distress for the victims. The aftershocks may continue for months and can be triggers for anxiety and panic. Earthquakes are associated with a number of common fears, including worries of being buried alive, being pinned down, suffocating, and of not being rescued (Young, 1997). Moreover, victims of earthquakes may be exposed to major destruction amid sounds of explosions, smells of smoke and toxic fumes, and tastes of soot, smoke, and rubber (Lazarus et al., 2003). As with all natural disasters, an increase in psychological conditions such as PTSD, depression, and anxiety can be observed. Specifically, common symptoms experienced in the aftermath of an earthquake include a heightened startle response, recurrent nightmares, intrusive thoughts and memories about the event, and changes in sleeping patterns (SAMHSA, 2022c).

Wildfires

Wildfires can be triggered in a number of ways, from lightning to accidents and purposeful igniting (i.e., criminal intent). In many cases, wildfires may initially go unnoticed, leaving time for them to spread quickly across a given area. Forest fires, or fires near rural locales, mountains, and other woodland settings, are particularly vulnerable to quick spread and total destruction (U.S. Department of Agriculture, n.d.). Wildfires can become highly dangerous for school communities, as is often witnessed in high-risk areas, such as California. In fact, 2020 proved to be a record-setting year for wildfires in California; its August Complex fire has been labeled the nation's first "gigafire" (Milman, 2020). Statistics reveal that the fire burned over 1 million acres across seven counties in 2020, resulting in the destruction of over 10,000 structures and billions of dollars in damages (Moffitt, 2020).

While wildfires typically can provide some warning, they remain unpredictable when uncontrolled and they can shift directions abruptly. This can result in limited time for evacuation, leaving individuals only minutes to gather their most important belongings and to flee from the danger of the fires. Evacuation can be a traumatic event for young children and can spur fear and tension among all involved. Psychological impact will vary, depending on the severity of the fire and damage. Victims commonly experience symptoms of anxiety (e.g., chronic worry), sleep disturbances, and other depression-like symptoms. Other signs of emotional distress related to wildfires include:

- Intrusive thoughts, memories, or nightmares related to the wildfire
- Chronic worry or feelings of guilt while also feeling unsure as to why
- Excessive absences from work or school (SAMHSA, 2022e)

Other Crisis Events

War and Terrorism

Throughout history, students have been affected by issues related to war and terrorism. When compared to other war-torn countries, the United States has had limited exposure to the horrors of war; nonetheless, the need for response preparation is vital. The terrorist act that took down the Twin Towers of the World Trade Center in New York City will forever be etched into the memories of those who were alive in 2001. This horrific act was a stark reminder that our county is not immune to such acts and that preparedness must take place.

PROFESSIONAL PERSPECTIVE: AMANDA B. NICKERSON

My first crisis response was probably the most challenging; I was doing my predoctoral internship at a school for students with emotional and behavioral disorders in the greater Philadelphia area when the 9/11 terrorist attacks occurred. The school did not have a crisis team nor any idea of best practices in response. The principal thought it was not the school's job to inform students about what happened, yet some teachers were wheeling TVs into their classrooms and letting the kids watch while they screamed things like "we need to nuke them." Buses from neighboring schools started arriving to pick students up as many schools had early dismissal. It was a very chaotic scene, and the school turned to me as I had the most up-to-date knowledge about how to respond. We ended up creating a script for classroom teachers to share with students, but it was quite late. The next day a student made a bomb threat, the school was evacuated, and chaos ensued, and the parents of the student were extremely upset that the school treated him like a criminal instead of with care and concern. After that we started a crisis team for the school!

Young people can be exposed to war and terrorism in indirect ways as well, namely, through social media and news coverage. Moreover, they may become displaced from their home countries due to violence or oppression and may become refugees in foreign lands. While children are resilient, trauma and extreme stress and anxiety can impair their functioning and ability to learn. Crisis response in a time of war and terrorism can be particularly difficult to plan for.

The general recommendations are the same as those outlined in this chapter, along with many that were reviewed in the school violence chapter (Chapter 6) as well. Families and school personnel should make every effort to create a strong sense of safety and security. Students should be encouraged to process their thoughts and feelings, and their strengths and resilience should be emphasized. Efforts must be made to establish positive connections within the school community and to connect students to appropriate mental health supports. Schools should also be attuned to the needs of students who could be vulnerable to unfair stigmatization due to a perceived resemblance to perpetrators of violence, for example, because of the color of their skin or clothing attributed to their culture (e.g., hijab, turban). Your school should emphasize the value and importance of diversity in your school community and the broader country (NASP, 2021b).

COVID-19 Pandemic

In March 2020, the United States faced one of the most significant crises in recent history. Within a matter of weeks, our businesses, workplaces, and schools shut down following the outbreak of COVID-19. Schools were forced to take on the insurmountable challenge of transitioning all of their students to virtual learning. As a society, we became isolated and afraid and had limited access to the resources that we relied on. While young people initially cheered for the cancellation of school and the use of online learning, the reality soon became grim, with many complaining about the long hours on screens, eye strain, technical difficulties, and lack of peer interaction.

Not long into the pandemic, mental health needs skyrocketed, with little availability for intervention. My coauthor (SF) recalls a conversation with a representative from one of the national suicide hotlines, who shared that they were experiencing quadruple the number of calls than the year prior. She also remembers having to stop formal psychological services at a university clinic due to the lockdown closures, creating an abrupt termination to the therapeutic process and leaving patients without the care they needed.

Given the unique circumstance of the pandemic, school crisis intervention became difficult to exercise. I recall an example of an intervention that I had to facilitate in the midst of the lockdown.

PROFESSIONAL PERSPECTIVE: Scott Poland

During the pandemic, I was shocked to hear in our large graduate college monthly meeting (held on Zoom at that time) that G, a very well-known member of the administrative team, had died suddenly over the weekend. My colleagues and I were all shocked at this news, with many questions but no answers provided as the business agenda for the meeting quickly continued. I started receiving emails and text messages during the meeting from devastated students who worked closely with the deceased, and they were asking what, if anything, was going to be done in her memory.

I spoke up before the end of the monthly staff meeting and said that I felt it was important that we hold a voluntary session via Zoom for all staff and students as a remembrance. I enlisted the help of one other person, and we made contact with her family and arranged to have some pictures of her and found out about the arrangements for her funeral. There were still no specifics as to the cause of death as she fell ill suddenly and died. There was no ability for anyone to attend the funeral due to the height of the pandemic. I've had the opportunity of responding to many school tragedies, but when it's at your own school and it is a person you knew well, it becomes much more complicated.

On the day of the Zoom memorial, I was amazed and pleased to have more than 300 staff and students in attendance. G had been a very big Miami Dolphins football fan and knew her X's and O's. I wore my Miami Dolphins football hat and commented how much she liked to talk Dolphins football with me. I talked about her as a person, her loud booming voice, her friendliness, and how she got things done in our college. I shared that I was nervous about what to say about her and that I was afraid that my voice might break or things might not come out as well as I had planned. I hoped to help everyone be more at ease and not be so worried about whether they might cry as we all remembered her.

I introduced her husband and her son and felt that it was so important for them to hear how much we appreciated G, and that the session would be recorded and that all of the statements put in the chat box would be shared with them. I provided an opportunity for her husband and son to share some of their thoughts. The service lasted 75 minutes, and at least 40+ people spoke up and shared memories. Almost every one of over 300 people put something in the chat box. I concluded the meeting with the music that we had carefully selected and showed a picture of G. I shared our college's plans to provide a scholarship for her surviving son.

I closed with this quote: "There are some who bring a light so great to the world that even after they have gone the light remains." I emphasized that G's presence would be felt in our college for a long time. I remember watching the numbers as the participants signed off and the numbers dropped really rapidly all the way down to nine and on my computer screen, I saw a few of my colleagues and her son and husband staring at their computers and crying. I wished that I could've reached out and hugged them but that was simply not possible during the pandemic. It was very important for our college to have a Zoom memorial for G and many people thanked me for making it happen.

> I remember attending the memorial service for G. It was both heartbreaking and comforting and particularly difficult given the virtual context and pandemic circumstances. However, Dr. Poland made us feel connected to G and to our school community. The service felt like a chance to say goodbye and bond over the memories of what we loved most about G. The response reflected G's impact on our school community and so many of us were thankful to Dr. Poland for coordinating it.
>
> —SARA FERGUSON

Throughout the pandemic, recommendations were ever evolving and varied greatly depending on the needs of the school community. NASP (2021) provided ongoing guidance on school response to the pandemic, highlighting the unpredictable nature of the pandemic and the need for schools to be prepared for local and community-wide infectious disease outbreaks. They advised schools to work collaboratively with their local and state health departments and to follow any guidance from the CDC regarding medical and environmental safety. Key guidelines covered the following topics: communication, public health, medical, and mental health.

Regarding the mental health response, NASP (2021) advised the school to share information with parents/caregivers on how they could best support their child during the pandemic. NASP also included tips for managing stress and common reactions to anxiety and stress. The school was also advised to share contact information for the parents/caregivers to use, should their child become distressed. It was advised that parents/caregivers be encouraged to find ways to make the child's life stable and safe. Parents/caregivers should be advised to discuss the pandemic with their children in a developmentally appropriate way that would help the children to (1) accurately understand the threat of the disease and (2) decrease their risk of getting ill. Students should be encouraged to engage in physical activities and coping techniques that could aid in reducing stress.

We recommend that you review a recently developed emergency operations plan titled "Preparing for a Pandemic Illness: Guidelines for School Administrators and Crisis Teams" and its companion book, *Preparing for Infectious Disease Epidemics: Brief Tips for School Mental Health Professionals* (see Recommended Resources). NASP (2020a) created these guidebooks in response to the recent pandemic, and they detailed suggestions for the immediate school response to the threat presented by COVID-19. Key points are listed in Table 7.1.

Among the recommendations provided, we want to further expand on the concept of self-care and its importance in the context of a pandemic and other related natural disasters. Self-care is often confused with the idea of generally doing things to make yourself feel good (e.g., getting your nails done, taking a bubble bath). While these things can be helpful in setting a more positive frame of mind or reducing stress, self-care is much more than that. It is an intentional practice that includes taking the time to do things that will aid in building a more positive mindset and lifestyle and, ultimately, will help to increase your physical, emotional, and mental health. My experiences as a school psychologist during the time of the pandemic highlight important concepts of self-care, along with ways in which you and your team can best support your school during a time of uncertainty and great need.

TABLE 7.1. Key Points in Responding to a Pandemic to Help Children

- Ensure timely distribution of facts.
- Protect children from graphic and scary television coverage of pandemic deaths.
- Encourage positive adaptive action (e.g., frequent handwashing, social distancing, and wearing a mask).
- Emphasize to children that scientists all around the world are working on developing a vaccine.
- Emphasize to children that the adults are working to keep them safe and that if someone in the family gets sick, then they will get medical treatment.
- Adults should be careful not to project their own fears onto children.
- Adults need to monitor coping for children and promote self-care activities in families and at school.

PROFESSIONAL PERSPECTIVE: Scott Poland

Early on in the pandemic, I received a request from one of my friends to complete much-needed training on self-care. I was initially unsure about this request, as my entire career had been spent focusing on prevention of youth suicide and school violence. Intervention in a pandemic was not really my expertise; however, my friend insisted that I could do it. As a result, I developed the C.A.L.M. model of self-care. I wanted every letter to stand for something important to help children, families, and schools deal with an unprecedented pandemic. It was very important to help the adults first and to emphasize that adult modeling of coping would be critical to the reaction of children.

- The **C** stands for **coping** and remembering what we can **control** is our reaction to event.
- The **A** stands for being **available** to children, friends, and families and being alert for significant changes in their behavior.
- The **L** stands for truly **listening** to others and for **limiting** horrific television coverage of the pandemic.
- The **M** stands for **modeling** of coping, but also **management**, as all children do best when they are in a routine.

I conducted countless Zoom webinars throughout the pandemic that emphasized that self-care is not selfish. I shared with audiences that self-care is about taking care of ourselves, so that we will be in the best position to help others. Self-care needs to start at the top of an organization. Among the training offered, I provided one for Tennessee school superintendents that emphasized a top-down modeling approach. I directed the superintendents to develop a self-care plan that could be shared with their principals. I advised the audience to encourage their principals to develop their own plans and to model self-care for their building staff. The concept would be expanded, whereby teachers would then develop their own plans and help students to create individualized self-care plans.

In another training for school-aged children, I remember interacting with one student who had been learning virtually for months who raised the question, "Why, after I sit in front of my computer for hours, does my teacher give me more academic homework? Why can't the homework be on developing a self-care plan?" It was clear that the students were in need of self-care and seeking direction from their school leaders.

Over the course of the pandemic, I provided countless training on the topic of self-care, reaching well over 100,000 educators and families via Zoom. Time and time again I emphasized key elements of self-care: getting proper rest, proper diet, and regular exercise; letting go of self-criticism; engaging in creative outlets and hobbies such as music, artwork, journaling, gardening, yoga, and meditation; and so on. Training also emphasized a spiritual side. Many Americans received extensive support through their regular attendance at a synagogue, mosque, or church. Mindful that not every American goes to a place of worship, I pointed to a common set of values that include always interacting with others in a helpful, friendly, compassionate, kind, and respectful manner. I also shared that it is important to find humor when we can.

Moreover, self-care is something that even small children can understand. A first grader, for example, could draw a picture of themselves in the center of a poster and then draw surrounding pictures of being helpful to others, getting exercise, getting proper rest, and eating healthy foods. The argument can be made that self-care was never more important than in the recent pandemic years. It is my hope that self-care will become an enduring and major part of life in our workplaces, homes, and schools.

GENERAL SCHOOL CRISIS RESPONSE TO NATURAL DISASTERS

Crisis response in the context of natural disasters is complex and requires unique approaches and considerations. It is imperative that you seek the guidance of experts in your responses and be thoughtful about the chosen interventions based on the needs and vulnerabilities of your school. The following section provides guidance on how your team can best respond to the possible natural disasters in your school community.

What Is Your Role in Responding to a Natural Disaster in Your School's Community?

SMHPs will have duties to attend to in the immediate aftermath of a natural disaster that are similar to those associated with previously discussed crises. First and foremost, you should make every effort to ensure the safety of all students and school personnel and provide first aid when necessary. Your next step is to alert the CRT and to implement the steps outlined in your safety plan. You will then complete an assessment of the safety of those impacted by the natural disaster. Additionally, you should assist in the relocation of students and school personnel when an environment is deemed unsafe.

As time progresses, your role will shift, based on the needs of your school population. Initially, you will spend time making contact with the school community members to ensure their safety and well-being. You will provide appropriate resources and referrals. When your school reopens, your focus will be on the well-being of the students and staff, providing classroom discussions, debriefing sessions, and psychological screenings and aid.

How Can You Respond to a Natural Disaster in Your School Community?

As with every crisis, roles will vary across school personnel. Natural disasters create unique school responsibilities that must be considered. For example, schools will often be utilized as a shelter for safety during the event or to house displaced individuals in the aftermath. Schools are often large in size and have the amenities necessary to meet basic living needs (i.e., locker rooms with showers, a cafeteria with a kitchen). Moreover, schools can provide a sense of familiarity and safety and can serve as a place to connect with the broader community in a time of need.

Similar to other crisis responses, your team will want to rely on predetermined steps that should occur in the aftermath of a natural disaster. As mentioned, these tasks should be outlined in your school's safety plan and must detail the steps that must be taken pre and post the reopening of your school. At the end of the chapter you will find two user-friendly action checklists (Forms 7.2 and 7.3) that provide concise guidelines for your team's response both before your school reopens and after the return to school. These checklists are not exhaustive and are generalized to capture the needs commonly observed in the aftermath of a natural disaster.

NATURAL DISASTERS AND THE EMOTIONAL IMPACT

Among the crises discussed, natural disasters have the potential for the greatest amount of death, destruction, and traumatic impact. The emotional impact can be significant, and there are a number of factors that influence the victims' well-being in the aftermath. The following sections outline these concerns and provide guidance on how to best intervene and support survivors of the crisis.

Relocation

Depending on the aftermath circumstances of the natural disaster, relocation is a serious implication that many must endure. Relocation for disaster survivors presents novel crisis issues, including increased social, environmental, and psychological stress. Studies (Najarian, Goenjian, Pelcovitz, Mandel, & Najarian, 2001; Uscher-Pines, 2009) have revealed that relocation has been associated with increased rates of psychological morbidity, along with higher levels of ecological stress, crowding, isolation, and social disruption (Lazarus, Jimerson, & Brock, 2002).

I have extensive experience helping schools in the aftermath of Hurricane Katrina. Hurricane Katrina damaged many thousands of homes and killed more than 1,000 people. It caused the greatest relocation in modern history in the United States (Sastry & Gregory, 2014). In 2005, I was working as the Director of Psychological Services for the Cypress-Fairbanks independent school district (ISD) in Houston, Texas. My professional reflection of this time offers unique considerations and factors that come into play when relocation is required in the aftermath of a natural disaster.

PROFESSIONAL PERSPECTIVE: SCOTT POLAND

Relocation Considerations

Back in 2005, after the tragedy of Hurricane Katrina, thousands of students were relocated to the Cypress-Fairbanks ISD in Houston, Texas. My wife, Donna, was a principal at a middle school, and 115 new students were enrolled at her school. The school's goal was to truly make every student and family feel welcome. During enrollment, families were all told that there was no need to stand in line and that their names would be taken so that they could then go into the cafeteria for free food and refreshments until it was time to enroll their child. The school dress code was relaxed because many of the families had only been able to bring along a few belongings when they evacuated. Training was conducted for all school staff and emphasized the common reactions that children have to a crisis (i.e., academic and behavioral regression, nightmares and sleeping problems, and worries about the future). Teachers were encouraged to be patient and not to initially assess new students' abilities in subject areas. The goal was to meet students where they were academically, with an understanding that the hurricane and the relocation would significantly impact their learning. It is noteworthy that after a few weeks, several teachers felt that some students should be referred for a special education evaluation to determine if they had a disability. The response from the principal was to point out that their previous school did not identify a disability, and therefore teachers needed to meet students where they were academically, at the present moment.

I conducted many interviews with relocated students, and the common themes voiced by many were that they missed their old school, they worried about their loved ones and pets they had left behind, and they did not have the same position academically in the new school. It was recognized that many of the students lost more than material possessions: they lost the place they had had in their previous school, where they might have been on a volleyball team, a cheerleader, or the president of a student organization. Every effort was made to connect students with school extracurricular activities, but many of the spots they had had in their old school were already filled, as the middle school already had more than 1,000 students. The school teams and leadership positions, for example, were largely already filled.

Donna and I decided to conduct a meeting for the parents of all of the new students. I knew that the key to getting a large audience for a parent meeting was the inclusion of food and babysitting services. Donna and I arranged for a local restaurant to donate food for 115 families and for high school students to provide babysitting for children of all ages. The meeting gave the families the opportunity to introduce themselves, though we quickly found that it was going to be so much more than that. The parents did not just give their names: they also felt the need to tell the story about how the hurricane affected them, the damage their homes received, and what it was like to move to a new city. Many of them shared how difficult it was to be a single parent, at least for the foreseeable future. The fact that each parent felt the need to tell their story underscores one of the basic principles of crisis intervention: to provide an opportunity when someone wants to share their experience and to feel truly listened to.

I shared the typical reactions that children have to a traumatic event and emphasized the importance of modeling coping skills, finding the time to speak with their children, and the importance of listening in those moments. The meeting lasted several hours. The parents, extremely appreciative for the opportunity to speak, gave hugs of gratitude and comfort rather than handshakes. The church next door to the school collaborated with the school, offering resources to parents, including clothing, access to computers, and general information to help them adjust to their new city.

After the first grading period, Donna noted that the new students were struggling academically. I encouraged the school to do more than send home information about tutoring, emphasizing that these families were overwhelmed and underlining the importance of counselors having personal conversations with the parents about needed academic interventions. Clearly, as their grades reflected, the students were experiencing difficulties in the relocation process. I continued to emphasize to the administration that students were continuing to try to manage their emotions and deal with loss.

Interestingly, within weeks of relocation, the superintendent suggested a plan to again relocate the 2,500 students, this time to an abandoned warehouse on the campus of Hewlett Packer's national headquarters. This created significant concerns among all the principals in the district; thankfully, the idea was canned before it got off the ground. However, it underscored the reality that disastrous ideas and decisions can be made in a time of crisis. Unfortunately, I am not a stranger to potentially damaging ideas that are considered with good intentions during a crisis. While it was a challenge to welcome so many students who were relocated because of Katrina, I emphasized to the school staff that these students deserved the same enthusiastic welcome shown to students returning from summer break. Schools must stand firm in their commitment to welcome and serve all students regardless of the circumstances. Once they move to the community, they are all ours!

MENTAL HEALTH IMPLICATIONS OF NATURAL DISASTERS

The potential for emotional and psychological harm in the aftermath of a natural disaster is well documented (Vujanovic & Gallagher, 2017). As we know, children can be particularly impacted by experiences of trauma, and their endurance through a natural disaster is no different. In fact, research has demonstrated that children who are exposed to significant natural disasters experience high rates of physical and mental health and learning issues in the aftermath (see Table 7.2). Young people are considered at greater risk due to a number of factors, including physicality (i.e., higher breath rates, thinner skin, greater risk of fluid and body heat loss) and the potential loss of their support system/care team (i.e., parents/caregivers who are unable to provide care for their children [Lai, Auslander, Fitzpatrick, & Podkowirow, 2014; Pfefferbaum, Jacobs, Griffin, & Houston, 2015; Tang, Liu, Liu, Xue, & Zhang, 2014]).

Research has shown that youth are especially vulnerable to mental health difficulties because during the event, they are more likely to think that their lives were in danger. Moreover, they may have been exposed to life-threatening damage (e.g., power lines falling), and additional violence or traumatic events (e.g., community violence). This is especially true for marginalized communities that are already struggling economically to meet basic living needs (Lai & La Greca, 2020). Additionally, research has found that children are at greater risk when they belong to families experiencing constant conflict or when they have limited parental/caregiver supervision and support (La Greca, Silverman, Vernberg, & Prinstein, 1996). Lastly, in the aftermath of a natural disaster, girls have been found to be more symptomatic than boys (Lai et al., 2021). These findings point to important factors that SMHPs should consider when providing crisis intervention in the school setting.

Personal Reflection

As mentioned, Hurricane Katrina caused extensive damage in Louisiana and Mississippi and over 2,500 students from those affected states moved to Cypress-Fairbanks ISD. One of the relocated students mentioned in my previous reflection wrote this poem after her relocation:

TABLE 7.2. Natural Disaster Impact in Youth

Physical Health Problems	Mental Health Problems	Learning Problems
Increases in: • Acute illnesses (e.g., fever, diarrhea, respiratory illnesses) • Somatic symptoms (e.g., lethargy, nausea, headaches)	Increased mental health concerns, including: • Estimated 50% of children report PTSD symptoms in the aftermath • Reports of depressive and anxious symptoms • Reports of chronic mental health symptoms for up to 4 years postevent	• Disruption of academics (e.g., loss of power or significant damage) • Higher rates of absenteeism • Concentration and memory difficulties associated with PTSD and depressive symptoms • Lower achievement testing scores

Source: From Lai & LaGreca (2020).

THE STORM INSIDE MY HEAD

She comes in late almost every night into my bedroom
Not at all concerned with how tired and depressed I am
I know she's been in someone else's bedroom tonight
I do not want anything to do with her, she comes in stealthily disturbing my sleep and interrupting my peace
I toss and turn through the night; I want to put her out but there's so much between us
I cannot seem to let her go, so many people talk about her and they curse her
They say how much they hate her and call her evil but I cannot seem to let her go
She's a part of me now, when I speak of her to others, that we have a history their expressions range from pity to admiration
When I speak of her they can see the pain as it all comes back to me the Louisiana Superdome, the water and the bodies
I shudder to say her name Katrina

This poem illustrates the challenge of recovery for children after a natural disaster. Given the significant impact, it is imperative that adults are alerted to the potential mental health implications that children may endure in the aftermath. They should be encouraged to respond to children with love, patience, and tolerance, all while incorporating structure and routines.

Trauma Reactions by Age

> Not everyone has PTSD and should not be labeled as such. Social support networks can be activated in the healing process. Connecting people involved with their natural social support networks WORKS.
>
> —BILL PFOHL

Studies of large-scale disasters (Aseervatham, Born, & Lohmaier, 2017; Parkinson & Zara, 2013; Vujanovic & Gallagher, 2017) have highlighted that some populations (i.e., the elderly, people with chronic medical conditions and mental disorders, and children) are especially vulnerable to trauma. However, it is also well documented that all victims who are exposed to a significant natural disaster are at risk for depression, anxiety, and PTSD (Vujanovic & Gallagher, 2017).

Additionally, you are encouraged to be alert for signs of child abuse, as an increase has been documented in the aftermath of these events. Traumatized adolescents are also at increased risk for reckless behavior and substance abuse. As in the previous chapters of this book, it is recommended that you become familiar with the age-specific trauma reactions related to natural disasters. See Table 7.3 for the common trauma reactions observed in the aftermath of natural disasters.

How Can You Support the Mental Health Needs at Your School?

Your postvention at school should emphasize resilience and coping skills. Depending on the nature of the incident, the process for a return to school and the mental health needs of your student body will vary. General recommendations are similar to those that have been discussed

TABLE 7.3. Trauma Reactions to Natural Disasters Based on Age

Preschool	May experience a significant increase in • Social withdrawal • Anxiety • General behavioral problems • Regressive behaviors (NASP, 2017a)
Elementary	May experience • Nightmares and sleep issues • Irrational fears • Irritability • Extreme withdrawal • Depressive and anxious symptoms • Emotional numbing • Disruptive and acting-out behaviors • Attentional issues • Somatic complaints (e.g., stomachaches, headaches) • Specific phobias related to the disaster (e.g., fear that something bad will happen to others, of being separated from family, of being left alone) (NASP, 2017a)
Middle and High School	May report • A sense that the world is less safe • Lack of trust in adults • High-risk behaviors • Social anxiety • Feelings of being overwhelmed • Revenge and retribution May observe • Self-destructive or acting-out behaviors • Social withdrawal (NCTSCN, n.d.)
Adults	May experience • Nightmares or other intrusive memories of the disaster • Extreme distress triggered by reminders or flashbacks • Panic attacks and anxiety symptoms • Strong startle reactions • Avoidance of conversations, news, or memories of the disaster • Changes in their perception of themselves, others, and the world • Sleep and eating issues • Irritability • Low mood • Loss of interest in previously enjoyed activities/people • Increased use of substances (e.g., alcohol)

Sources: Based on Lazarus et al. (2002); Vujanovic & Gallagher (2017).

in previous chapters. Your two primary goals are to support the mental health needs of the students and staff and to screen for those who are in need of additional support. We want to stress the importance of your school's provision of psychological aid and the need to identify students who struggle over a longer period of time, ensuring that they are connected to a referral for a more comprehensive assessment in the community.

Students should be encouraged to discuss the events related to the natural disaster. Their engagement and expression should be facilitated in a number of ways (i.e., verbal and nonverbal) using varied methods (e.g., creative writing, art, sketches, dance). Be prepared to offer ideas to teachers so that they have a range of options to implement with their students. Encourage staff members to be honest and age appropriate in their discussions. Students should learn problem-solving skills connected to the stressors they have experienced due to the natural disaster (e.g., students may report difficulty completing homework and can work together to create a study group during a free period).

Similarly, students should work to develop coping skills that aid in reducing distressing symptoms commonly experienced in the aftermath of a natural disaster (e.g., incorporation of mindfulness activities, such as a visualization of a "safe space"). It is important to facilitate a discussion in which students identify ways they have coped with difficult times in the past and to brainstorm new ways to enhance their current coping methods. In addition, students should be provided with a repertoire of strategies they can apply to different contexts (e.g., diaphragmatic breathing, grounding techniques). Strong efforts should be made to emphasize student resiliency and hope. You should also talk about other communities that have endured, coped, and recovered from major disasters and provide hope for their own community's progress. And you need to encourage students to turn their attention to the successes in their daily lives (e.g., getting to school, being a friend to others) and in other times of distress.

Appropriate coping in the aftermath of a natural disaster can help reduce long-term mental health issues. Research on youth responses in the aftermath of natural disasters (Limacher, 2020) points to four different coping styles that children engage in: (1) catastrophizer, (2) sensitizer, (3) minimizer, and (4) denier. Other styles have been noted; for example, 3 months after Hurricane Andrew, children endorsed using wishful thinking as the most frequently used coping style, followed by positive coping, social withdrawal, and blame and anger, respectively (Lazarus, Jimerson, & Brock, 2008). A child's ability to cope can be impacted by a number of factors, and it is important to be attuned to these considerations. Tables 7.4 and 7.5 cover these considerations and provide helpful approaches to employ when working with children in the aftermath of a natural disaster based on their style of coping.

Additional recommendations include an emphasis on strengthening relational connections. Important related considerations for students are the potential for them to experience friendship disruptions (due to relocations) and decreased availability of parental/caregiver support (due to their own issues of distress). It has been well documented that children who have a solid emotional support system from others are able to cope more successfully than those without it (American Psychological Association, 2009). Furthermore, enhancing peer support can act as a model for coping and can help to buffer issues of isolation and feelings of loneliness. You should suggest to teachers that they increase the use of group activities to create organic opportunities for peer connection. Teacher–student relationships can also serve as a major source of support and is yet another reason why it is critical to develop those connections before a crisis.

TABLE 7.4. Significant Factors that Impact Student Coping after a Natural Disaster

Familial Reactions and Support	Familial dynamics, such as disruptions in family functions, separation of family members, and ongoing maternal preoccupation with the trauma are associated with higher levels of PTSD symptoms in children than the level of their exposure to the natural disaster.
Familial Relocation	Relocation is associated with higher levels of ecological stress, crowding, disruption of social supports, and isolation.
Level of Emotional Reactivity	Children who have struggled with anxiety prior to the natural disaster are considered to be more vulnerable to the risk of a greater trauma impact.
Coping Style	Attunement to student coping style is important as it can inform you as to what resources the student/family require, which can be helpful in buffering further risks. There are four broad coping styles and ways to approach each (see Table 7.5 for more details): • Catastrophizer • Sensitizer • Minimizer • Denier (Limacher, 2020)

Source: Adapted from Brock et al. (2002).

Ideas for Consideration

- Obtaining help from the community in the aftermath of a natural disaster
  - Parent–teacher associations and/or student councils can utilize funds to purchase gift cards for food and household items that are needed.
  - Volunteers from the school community can assist with outreach (e.g., babysitters, transporters).
  - Professionals in the community can be contacted to see if they would be willing to offer needed services pro bono (e.g., legal consultations, mental health services).
- Emphasizing resiliency
  - School personnel
  - With young children, emphasize that resiliency is about bouncing back; use a big rubber ball or even a wobble doll, the kind that when you knock it down, it then bounces back to life.
- Doing something positive with your children or students to help others in need. Taking action is one of the most powerful ways to help children feel more in control and to build a stronger sense of connection. Suggestions include making individual donations to international disaster relief organizations, holding a school or community fundraiser, or even working to support families in need within the community (NASP, 2017a).

Large-scale crises that are caused by acts of nature or other elements (e.g., war or infectious disease) present novel challenges in your crisis intervention approach. As with all other crises, preparedness is the key to appropriate intervention and postvention. Your individual school community needs must be taken into account, along with consideration for the specific disasters discussed. Emotional and mental health are severely impacted by natural disasters, and the risk for PTSD and related symptomology is high, especially for children. The information in this chapter should be utilized to build your awareness of the trauma reactions and coping styles you may encounter, along with learning how to best intervene and provide support to your school community in the aftermath of a large-scale natural disaster crisis.

Recommended Resources

- *FEMA's Natural Disaster–Related Resources*
  - **Government Assistance (FEMA, 2022):** A number of different assistance programs for individual citizens via public groups such as government agencies and private nonprofit organizations. Found at *www.fema.gov/assistance.*
  - **FEMA's FEMA for Kids (2021):** Resources, guidebooks, and classroom and home materials that can be used to help children prepare and best respond to a natural disaster. Found at *www.fema.gov/blog/fema-kids.*

TABLE 7.5. Coping Styles and Approaches to Use

Coping styles	Approaches to use
Catastrophizer: "worst-case scenario"; typically present as highly anxious and overwhelmed	• Create space for the child to talk about their feelings. • Explore ways that they have dealt with negative scenarios in the past. • Limit judgments and minimizations; validate their feelings and offer a differing perspective. • Engage in distracting activities to shift their focus.
Sensitizer: seek details and information; answers to questions ease their anxiety	• Provide information as requested. • Check in to ensure that the child is processing details appropriately. • Offer concrete answers when possible; using statistics can be helpful. • Help them to find answers.
Minimizer: downplay a situation in order to better cope with their anxiety	• Provide information in smaller parts rather than all at once. • Go slow and be prepared for these kids to take longer to process. • Allow the child to take the lead and offer information as requested.
Denier: avoid information as a means of coping with their anxiety	• Take things slow. • Give details in small parts. • Do not force information. • Engage in reflection exercises; Example: "What would you do if . . ." and explore situations similar to the one at hand, helping the child to gently reflect on how to handle the situation.

Source: Limacher (2020).

- *NASP's Natural Disaster–Related Resources*
  - **Preparing for Infectious Disease Epidemics: Brief Tips for School Mental Health Professionals (2020a):** Guidelines for SMHPs on how to approach crisis intervention in the context of a major outbreak of infectious disease. Found at *www.nasponline.org/resources-and-publications/resources-and-podcasts/school-safety-and-crisis/health-crisis-resources/preparing-for-infectious-disease-epidemics-brief-tips-for-school-mental-health-professionals.*
  - **Large-Scale Natural Disasters: Helping Children Cope (2017a):** Specific guidance for intervening with children who are impacted by the trauma of a natural disaster. Found at *www.nasponline.org/resources-and-publications/resources-and-podcasts/school-safety-and-crisis/natural-disaster-resources/large-scale-natural-disasters-helping-children-cope.*
  - **Relocating to a New School: Tips for Families (2017b):** Helpful guidelines that SMHPs can offer families when having to relocate after a major natural disaster. Found at *www.nasponline.org/resources-and-publications/resources-and-podcasts/school-safety-and-crisis/natural-disaster-resources/relocating-to-a-new-school-tips-for-families.*
  - **Resources to Assist States/Territories Recovering from Natural Disasters (2017c):** A resource guide that provides guidance on a number of topics (see below). Found at *www.nasponline.org/resources-and-publications/resources-and-podcasts/school-safety-and-crisis/natural-disaster-resources/resources-to-assist-states/territories-recovering-from-natural-disasters.*
    - **Caring for the Caregiver**
    - **Assistance for Reopening of Schools after a Natural Disaster**
    - **Guidance for Educators in Helping Children after a Natural Disaster**
    - **Prevention of Childhood Trauma**
- **SAMHSA's Disaster Distress Helpline (2022b):** A resource guide that provides 24/7, 365-day-a-year crisis counseling and support to people experiencing emotional distress related to natural or human-caused disasters. Found at *www.samhsa.gov/find-help/988/faqs.*

FORM 7.1

Key Natural Disaster Preparedness Checklist

Instructions for use: The following checklist should be utilized as a guide to assist your team in preparing for a natural disaster. Review each item and check off the tasks as they are completed or confirmed.

- ☐ **Alternative communication:** Ensure that your team has made a plan for how you will connect with each other in the event that regular means are unavailable (e.g., cellular phones). In many cases of natural disasters, traditional methods of communication are unavailable due to loss of power/internet and damaged telecommunication machinery.
  - ☐ Use two-way radios
  - ☐ Designate a specific location for posting important information ahead of time
- ☐ **Create a partnership with nearby schools:** In some cases, your school may endure such significant damage that the use of a neighboring school will be required. Collaborate with these schools in advance to have a plan in place for potential relocation needs.
- ☐ **Have emergency kits on site:** These kits should go above and beyond those that are used for an injury. Emergency kits should include survival items such as food, water, first aid supplies, and a two-way radio.
- ☐ **Practice natural disaster–specific drills (e.g., tornado or fire drill):** School members should feel well equipped to follow the evacuation plan set forth. This will greatly help in reducing potential chaos if a building becomes unsafe/damaged and requires its members to evacuate.

FORM 7.2

Natural Disasters: Before School Opens Actions Checklist

Instructions for use: The following checklist should be utilized as a guide to ensure that best practices are implemented prior to the school opening in the aftermath of a natural disaster. Check off each item as the tasks are completed. *Note:* These tasks do not have to be completed in the exact order provided; however, they should be prioritized and implemented prior to reopening the school in the aftermath of a natural disaster.

- ☐ School staff should follow the process determined in the safety plan for making contact with the CRT and students.
  - ☐ School personnel should reach out to the previously determined contact person to report their status and condition.
  - ☐ Faculty members should make effort to contact their students to confirm their safety and any potential needs that they may have (i.e., relocation).
  - ☐ Should it be determined that an individual is missing and/or unidentified, loved ones should receive a "missing notification" and the parent/family liaison or medical liaison should follow the same procedures as for giving an injury/death notification.
  - ☐ If death is determined after a missing notification, notification of death should be made immediately.
  - ☐ If you are unsure about the identification of a loved one, be clear that you have been given evidence that someone has been killed but that additional investigation is needed to make a final determination.

    Example: *"I need to speak with you about your child. We believe that they were in a building where the tornado caused significant destruction, but this has not yet been confirmed. Is there any way you or a close friend of your child can help us figure out their location?"*
- ☐ Complete a brief assessment of the damage and provide appropriate accommodations when able.
- ☐ Administrators and teachers should complete an inventory of any damages in their buildings and classrooms.
- ☐ Determine the level of response that is needed to meet the needs of the victims and based on the severity of damages.
- ☐ School superintendents should consult with CRTs across the impacted county to determine what types of resources are needed, particularly in the context of mental health assistance.
- ☐ Ensure that the emotional and survival needs of your school's staff and student body are addressed.
- ☐ Crisis services must be accessible to victims prior to school reopening.

(continued)

Natural Disasters: Before School Opens Actions Checklist *(page 2 of 2)*

- ☐ The media liaison should take on any media consultations and feedback. Utilize the media to create a positive relationship between the school and community.
- ☐ Assess and address any staff needs, especially basic living needs such as food, clothing, and shelter. Contact FEMA, as they will typically be the best resource to turn to for these needs.
- ☐ All families related to the school should be contacted. Like your outreach with staff members, you will want to connect students and their families to any necessary resources. See Ideas for Consideration for suggestions.
- ☐ SMHPs should have the opportunity to debrief with parents and should provide helpful materials and guidance for coping in the aftermath of a natural disaster. These groups will not only provide the support needed but also will create the opportunity to identify anyone in need of additional assistance.

FORM 7.3

Natural Disasters: School Reopening, First Day and Beyond Actions Checklist

Instructions for use: The following checklist should be utilized as a guide to ensure that best practices are implemented in the aftermath of a natural disaster. Your school should review this checklist in preparation for the reopening of your school. Upon reopening, check off each item as the tasks are completed. *Note:* These tasks do not have to be completed in the exact order provided; however, they should be prioritized as your school begins to resume its daily activities.

- ☐ Obtain additional administrative support; this may come from the district or neighboring counties that are not as impacted by a natural disaster. Additional administrative support can help in a number of ways (e.g., handling the routine duties while the primary principal attends to disaster-related issues).

- ☐ Upon returning to school, every student should be personally greeted by a school team member.

- ☐ Your principal should stop by each classroom to share their concern for every student, their families, and the school staff.

- ☐ Teachers should utilize creative instructional approaches and incorporate lessons learned in the aftermath of the disaster (e.g., real-life examples that can be used to teach about science, math, weather, and other related subjects).

- ☐ Coordinate activities at school that promote healing and resiliency (see Ideas for Consideration).

- ☐ Each classroom should have the opportunity to engage in a debriefing session with an SMHP. Goals of the session:
  - Provide a space for students to process their experiences
  - Give students the opportunity to express their reactions and emotions
  - Create a shared experience among the students and faculty
  - Provide validation for students and their feelings
  - Share helpful coping tools and resources
  - Encourage students to enhance their sense of connectedness among peers
  - Assess for any additional mental health needs/students who may be at risk for self-harm, suicidality, or PTSD

(continued)

School Reopening, First Day and Beyond Actions Checklist *(page 2 of 2)*

☐ It is imperative that you identify students who are at high risk for mental health issues. These students must then be referred to a higher level of care such as individual and/or family therapy.

Students who are considered more vulnerable are those who:

- *Had a high level of exposure*
- *Thought they might die during the disaster*
- *Were physically injured*
- *Witnessed significant/gory destruction*
- *Suffered major losses*
- *Are grieving for victims*
- *Relocated following the disaster*
- *Had preexisting anxiety disorders or other mental health problems*
- *Have inadequate parental support*
- *Are using inadequate coping strategies (Brock et al., 2002)*

☐ Mental health support options should already be outlined in your crisis plan; however, in times of natural disaster, it may be difficult to secure enough providers. Consult with community members, government agencies, and larger mental health agencies to ensure that enough support is in place in the aftermath.

☐ It is important that a debriefing session occurs with the CRT and all other volunteers who participated in the crisis response. Oftentimes these individuals are already experiencing their own difficulties associated with the natural disaster and are continuously exposed to more harm with their roles as crisis responders.

PART II

CONSIDERATIONS IN RESPONDING

CHAPTER 8

The Aftermath and the Return to School

In the weeks after a crisis, a number of considerations will be on your team's plate. The primary duty will be to ensure that you are meeting the mental health needs of those who have been impacted by the event. In a severe crisis, survivors may be experiencing significant posttraumatic stress on top of potential grief over others' lives lost. Processing the crisis, traumatic reactions, and related emotions is imperative and is a critical part of your role in the aftermath. You will also be a significant part of other important processes, such as funeral planning, memorialization, and the eventual return to school. This chapter reviews these roles in more detail, providing helpful guidance for best practices in an uncertain time. Moreover, it offers direction on how to handle the inevitable return to school, ensuring that your school members can be properly integrated into their new normal postcrisis.

> Recognize that healing takes a long time (weeks, months, years) and everyone goes through it in their own way and on their own timeline. The tragedy that entered all of our lives will always be there and we will never feel "normal" in the way that we did before the crisis. However, what will bring us to healing is to find our "new normal" and integrate the tragedy into our lives as we move forward.
>
> —CATHY KENNEDY-PAINE

PROCESSING THE CRISIS

In previous chapters, we have discussed the very important need and benefit for crisis survivors to process the trauma they have endured. We want to reiterate this recommendation, as it is paramount to recovery. Crisis often causes an upheaval of emotions that are generally difficult to resolve. The trauma of a school crisis can result in significant impairments in student and staff functioning, and it can be difficult to return to the normal school routine. In these cases, schools, in some part, have a duty to provide the support necessary to help victims process their grief and fears associated with the crisis.

Experience has found that when the victim is a longtime member of the school community, a significant level of emotionality can be expected in the aftermath. Additionally, if the death was the result of an accident, suicide, or homicide, if it is sudden, unexpected, or violent, there will be enhanced emotionality. It is also clear that when a death occurs on school campus, there is a great deal of emotionality. Particularly challenging for crisis intervention is a homicide of a student, staff member, or family member of a student, or when everyone in the school knows the perpetrator. Additionally, when consulting with schools after a tragedy, at some point I always ask, "What else has happened prior to the most recent tragedy that may be still affecting the staff and the student body?" It is helpful to understand prior conditions in terms of the school's existing vulnerabilities.

SMHPs should ask specific questions to help estimate the degree of traumatization and the need for additional school mental health professionals and support services. The Circles of Vulnerability worksheet (see Chapter 4, Figure 4.1) will be a helpful tool to utilize in this process. Form 8.1 includes an additional worksheet that outlines further questions your team should ask, along with a place to document the answers.

The benefits of engaging in processing are apparent almost immediately. My experiences in leading many processing sessions have shown me the power of this approach. It is imperative that you provide survivors with the opportunity and space to express their feelings about the crisis. The validation and shared experience of their feelings are critical parts of the initial steps in recovery. An additional advantage of offering processing groups is that they create a structured and safe place for survivors to share. Without this asset, they may turn to less desirable sources to share their story, including the media, which is typically not in their best interests. When working with child victims, school personnel should keep certain key recommendations in mind (see Table 8.1).

Familial/caregiver support is a significant part of youth recovery, and your aid to them will be an indirect help to the students at your school. You will want to emphasize that families/caregivers must also take care of their own mental health and reactions to the crisis. We have likened this approach to the emergency procedures observed on an airplane: If the cabin becomes depressurized, caregivers are always instructed to put on their own oxygen mask first and to assist their children after. Caregivers must work from a position of strength and compassion in order to best support their children in the aftermath of a crisis (more on this in Chapter 9).

Resilient caregivers have resilient children, and that is why it is so important that you provide families/caregivers with the information to understand their child's reactions (refer back to Chapters 4, 6, and 7 for crisis-specific grief and trauma reactions). General reactions to be mindful of are academic and behavioral regressions, sleeping issues, fears, and worries about the future. We reemphasize the need for caregivers to respond to their children with structure, tolerance, and love. I have shared these recommendations many times with families of survivors of school shootings.

> When children live in a stable home and are shown unconditional love in every way, every day, by their parents, I believe that they can overcome almost anything.
>
> —Scott Poland

TABLE 8.1. Key Recommendations for Working with Children in Crisis

1. Continue to remember that children are resilient, particularly in the face of significant adversity.
2. Mental health support/providers should be visible and easily accessible in the aftermath.
   a. Clear information on how victims can access mental health services should be offered.
   b. Providers should be present on campus or in a designated nearby location and readily available to provide support services for those in need.
3. Mental health personnel should connect with those who are in need of help rather than waiting for survivors to seek them out.
   a. Group processing and individual processing opportunities should be readily available.
4. Engage with the children and their families/caregivers, when possible.
   a. Even inquire about well-being and offer encouragement.
   b. Sit with the families, offer a hug, inquire about basic needs (e.g., water or food).
   c. Engage in mental health support and offer contact information.

This brings us to another important consideration in the processing portion of your postvention. While much of your response efforts are focused on the students, it is important that you do not neglect the needs of affected adults. Many adults in your school community will require assistance in processing their crisis experiences. This falls in line with the discussed airplane safety analogy; if school personnel do not have the opportunity to properly process their trauma reactions, they will be ill equipped to support their students in need. Others who will likely need help are listed in Table 8.2.

It is very important for schools to help the faculty first in a processing session, and the administration should ask all staff members to come into a private room where staff will have the opportunity to process. The emphasis is on the fact that no one is alone, and it is important for everyone to identify their existing sources of support. Confidentiality is strict, and staff members are encouraged to attend the session but are given the choice. If they do attend the

TABLE 8.2. Individuals at Risk for Trauma Reactions

- Any individuals who have recently experienced the death of someone close to them
- Witnesses to the crisis/death
- Witnesses to the incident
- Friends and family members of the victims or suspected student perpetrators
- Parents/caregivers and other family members of your students
- Family members of school staff
- First responders on the scene
- Volunteers (i.e., persons who offer support in the aftermath, e.g., mental health providers, community members, friends of victims)
- Media personnel who may have borne witness to or have been affected by the crisis

session, it is totally up to them to decide whether they want to share their thoughts and emotions or whether they simply want to listen to what their colleagues are saying.

> School administrators . . . need to focus on the long-term impact of the event, not just the short-term crisis. Moreover, they need to pay attention not only to the mental health needs of their students but the needs of their faculty as well. Oftentimes, these issues can easily be overlooked.
>
> —PHILIP LAZARUS

I have encountered situations in which administrators are reluctant to initiate processing sessions and, instead, they hold meetings just to relay facts/information. For example, an administrator may hold a staff meeting in which they discuss when the students will return to school or what the bell schedule will be like, but they do not allow staff members to process their emotions. Lack of processing will send the message to your school personnel that they are simply expected to do their jobs and that their emotions do not matter. This will impact their ability to not only return to their jobs but also to be a proper support to their students. A final reason that administrators may skirt away from processing is that they minimize the severity of the crisis. However, all crises that involve any injury or death should be processed. In some cases, administrators may coordinate the processing but find that they are unable to run effective or appropriate groups. Best practices in implementation can be achieved by following basic guidelines, discussed next.

It is recommended that administrators take part in the processing. Their willingness to share some of their thoughts with school staff after a tragedy sets the tone for school staff to have that opportunity. I remember encountering school staff 8 months after leading a national crisis team in Paducah, Kentucky, where a school shooting occurred. They commented to me that the session he led in the Heath High School library after the shooting changed everything for them. They shared that they were not only allowed but *encouraged* to talk about the impact the shooting had on them. They reported that they felt supported by the administration.

Processing Guidelines

> It is very important to start and end with all staff members in crisis processing at the same time; if someone comes late, they miss the ground rules and if they leave early, they miss the summation at the end and information about additional support available.
>
> —SCOTT POLAND

> Crisis response [is] more about actively listening to [survivors'] words versus the words I would say.
>
> —MICHELLE PASTOREK

- When possible, enlist the involvement of outside CRT members who are providing aid to your school. *Note:* The session should *always* include adults from the school as well.
- Hold multiple processing sessions to ensure that all members of your school community are able to process the crisis. Hold separate processing sessions for the students and staff. The exception to this is the family/community meeting where adults and children can process at the same time.

- The goal of the session is to provide a place for the victims to process their experiences.
- Sessions should be held in every student classroom, and at least one counseling staff member and the teacher should be present. The administrators should make efforts to attend.
- Cultural considerations are imperative and should be integrated into all processing approaches (see Chapter 10 for further recommendations).
- Staff crisis sessions should occur either at the end of the day or the next day (if the school remains open), and they can be led by the counseling liaison.
    - Staff session attendance should be strongly encouraged. Emphasize that attendance is important for the short-term functioning and long-term recovery of your school community.
- Process the crisis at a location that is as close as possible to where the crisis occurred (i.e., at your school or a nearby location).
    - Choose a location that is large enough for a group and can maintain the privacy of the participants (i.e., doors present, limited windows, quiet environment).
- Provide drinking water and tissues. If possible, it would also be helpful to offer a healthy snack.
- Ensure that you allot ample time for the session. Processing should not be done under a time constraint. Try your best to allow the processing to end organically, so that all participants feel that they have had the opportunity to express themselves. If you must have an end time, you should make the time frame clear from the beginning of the meeting.
- Communicate the importance of processing. School administrators and CRT members, especially the crisis coordinator or counseling liaison, should participate in the processing and act as a model of strength, resilience, and leadership. This will also break down potential barriers that come with the hierarchical structures of the school. All participants should feel equal in their experiences and able to share without judgment.
- Recognize that every story is valid. Do not minimize others' experiences. Everyone has a story that is important and that should be heard. The teacher who was in a different building from the attack has a story that is every bit as important as that of a person who was in the classroom next door.
- Provide permission for a range of emotions to be expressed and emphasize the importance of emotional expression and its benefits in the aftermath of a traumatic experience.
- Be attuned to trauma reactions of the population you are engaged with and begin to identify those who may need additional mental health support. Refer to previous chapters for individual responses based on the need and type of crisis.
- Recognize that not all participants need to speak during the processing session. Do not force everyone to participate. Those who remain quiet will still benefit from the process, as it enhances a feeling of shared experience and normalizes the range of emotions they are likely feeling.
- Allow time for prayer for those participants who may wish to pray during or after the processing session. But emphasize that prayer is not required.

Processing the crisis is a critical part of your postvention practices. It is the beginning steppingstone to the recovery process. Furthermore, it creates a space of calm and connected energy that best helps victims to prepare for the next steps in the healing journey.

FUNERAL PLANNING

Soon after a significant crisis, survivors must begin to make plans on how they will honor the lives that have been lost. If the crisis that your school endures involves the death of a school community member or their loved ones, it is likely that their family will handle the funeral arrangements. Funerals are a ritual that allows loved ones to say goodbye to the deceased. The ceremony also creates a shared experience of grief and support and helps survivors to face the loss openly and realistically. While you must be respectful in your approach, offering input to the family about the funeral can be helpful in the process. Often, the family members are not in the position to consider the many other individuals who have been impacted by their loved one's death. My experience has been that most caregivers and family members are generally receptive to school input on this matter.

Some basic recommendations that you may offer relate to timing. You may suggest that the funeral be held after school, in the evening, or on a Saturday, so that as many families/caregivers and students possible can attend. Moreover, the change in timing may allow a strong presence of adults at the funeral, which will be necessary if there is a large youth presence. Additionally, having the funeral after school hours will allow students to keep to their regular routine and will also allow their families/caregivers to attend after work hours. This is especially important in the context of a death by suicide, as discussed in Chapter 5. Student attendance should be a choice, and no students should be made to feel bad if they decide not to attend the funeral. Ultimately, it will be up to the caregivers to decide if their child will attend the services. For the students who do attend, teachers can help to prepare them for what to expect and show them how to act appropriately (i.e., funeral etiquette).

PROFESSIONAL PERSPECTIVE: Scott Poland

I recall a case I was involved in at a large high school where a star football player died by suicide. The school decided to hold the funeral in the school cafeteria shortly after the end of a school day. This resulted in hundreds of students attending the service, as the expectation was that they should attend the funeral. Very few family members and caregivers were in attendance, as many were still at work at that time and so were unable to attend. I advised the school that holding the funeral on campus would dramatize the death and glorify the suicide victim. I emphasized that the potential to glorify a death by suicide could create a contagion effect and potentially encourage other students to die by suicide. Unfortunately, this high school experienced the suicide of another student just three weeks later. In response, the school chose not to hold that student's funeral at school. While that decision was in line with best practices, friends of the second suicide victim did not understand why their friend's funeral was not given the same treatment or attention as the first. This example reiterates how important it is for schools to treat all deaths the same, regardless of the cause of death or the popularity or socioeconomic status of the victim. Funerals for suicide victims or student funerals after death by any cause are best held in a community setting, not at school. I encouraged this school to develop a policy that would clearly define how the school would handle any school member death and indicate that funerals would not be held on the school campus.

In the aftermath of a school member's death, you ultimately must respect the family's decisions and, in some cases, they may ask you to consult with clergy members or funeral directors. If you are made aware that a clergy member or religious leader will be involved in the funeral service, it is recommended that you try to coordinate a meeting beforehand in order to discuss appropriate messaging. I recall a case that highlights the importance of this effort in the aftermath of a student death.

PROFESSIONAL PERSPECTIVE: SCOTT POLAND

A high school student died by suicide at a school where I was working as the school psychologist. I attended the funeral, along with numerous administrators and school counselors. The funeral was held after school at a local church, and it was estimated that over 700 students attended the service. Very few family members or caregivers were in attendance to support their children. I remember thinking that schools must use all means possible to encourage families and caregivers to attend funerals with their children so that they can support them through the process.

The suicide victim was buried in a casket that allowed students to write their goodbye messages to their friend on the exterior. I was very interested in reading the messages that were on the casket so that I could better gauge the students' emotional reactions to the suicide. It was especially important to learn if any students were feeling guilty about their last interaction with the victim or, more importantly, whether they had any thoughts of joining them through suicide. I will never forget the statement from the clergy representative who was conducting the service: "Her burdens were so great and she had to come to God, and if your burdens ever become too great then you too must come to God." I remember wanting to scream, "Tell them to come to God through Bible study, service, and worship—*not by suicide*!"

This example highlights how helpful it could be for SMHPs to consult with religious leaders prior to leading funeral services. SMHPs should advise these leaders to avoid emphasizing that students need to come to God through suicide. Since the date of this example, I have been successful in coordinating in-person meetings with appointed religious leaders and encouraging them to utilize phrases such as, "God tried to sound the alarm, but God could not prevent the suicide. God has embraced them in the afterlife, but God wanted them to stay on this earth to do God's work over their natural lifetime."

These perspectives review some of the important guidelines that should be implemented when planning a funeral for a school member's death. Additional advisements regarding funeral planning in school crisis are listed in Table 8.3.

Funeral planning requires a thoughtful approach, and the hope is that it can be a somewhat collaborative process among families of victims, community members, and your CRT. Cultural considerations should also be included in the funeral planning, as a family or community's cultural identification will greatly shape their desires and needs for this ritual aspect. The funeral is yet another crucial part of the recovery process that creates the opportunity to properly grieve lives that have been lost. The healing journey does not end here, however, as many times, survivors of loved ones who have died yearn to further honor the lives of those they lost.

TABLE 8.3. Key Advisements in Funeral Planning

- A joint funeral may be appropriate if more than one student was killed; if there are multiple funerals, it may be appropriate to hold a joint funeral or have a community-wide memorial service. This will help to create a sense of community support post tragedy.
  - Note: Communitywide services should be held separate from funerals
- Funerals at school are strongly discouraged; in small rural communities, a school gym may be one of the only appropriate places size wise, and if this is the case, it should be done after school hours.
- School personnel should participate in funerals; their attendance will be helpful to students and families.
- Funerals and memorial services should be individually determined by families and the community.
- Allow students to bring a paper banner on which they can express their affection for the victims. Seeing the messages of friendship and love may also be comforting for the family of the deceased.
- If music is to be played, ensure the selections convey a sense of hope, peace, and love.

MEMORIALIZATION

In cases of death, particularly multiple deaths, the school community often seeks to memorialize the loss. Memorialization is another helpful ritual in the grief process. It promotes healing by creating an opportunity for the survivors to come together in shared support and remembrance of their lost loved ones. It can also serve as a tool for closure and as a symbol that the community can start to return to regular school activities.

Memorialization should be developed with thoughtful consideration and planning from a multidisciplinary district team and under the guidance of a districtwide policy about permanent memorials at school. It is highly recommended that all memorials be the same regardless of cause of death, socioeconomic status, or popularity of the deceased. Unfortunately, few school districts have developed such policies and individual administrators have made decisions about memorials that have varied considerably.

PROFESSIONAL PERSPECTIVE: SCOTT POLAND

I provided a school safety and crisis intervention training session at Arapahoe High School in Littleton, Colorado. A school shooting had occurred there a few years before and, tragically, a student named Claire Davis was killed. While on campus, I was shown the Claire Davis Memorial, which is located east of the front door of the school and is visible to everyone arriving at the school. Claire Davis and her horse were carved in a large granite statue, surrounded by benches and hopeful phrases on a brick walkway.

A leader in student services asked me what I thought about having such a dramatic memorial of the school shooting victim on campus. Choosing my words carefully, I said, "I noted that your campus is only approximately seven miles away from the Columbine Memorial in Clement Park." The student services leader pointed out the difference in that their memorial was erected on campus instead of in the community. They shared that all the funding came from the community and that the school members had very little say. The school leader asked me to walk with him and, about 20 yards away, he showed me a small plaque in the ground in memory of another student who had previously attended the school who had died. The difference between the two permanent memorials was glaring.

I certainly acknowledged that decisions about permanent memorials at school are very difficult, but they are especially complicated when a school shooting is involved. I shared that the best advice is for a school district to develop a policy that treats all deaths the same regardless of the cause of death or the popularity or socioeconomic status of the victim and their family. If there must be a memorial on campus for the victim of a school shooting, then the school should choose the location carefully. A remote location and one behind the school building is recommended.

Decisions about memorialization are significant, for they can have an impact on the school community for many years to come. Moreover, they are difficult to plan given the varied opinions of people in the community; it is hard to satisfy everyone's desires in planning a memorial, and so having a policy developed in advance will help a lot. Students often create a spontaneous memorial at school, which should be allowed on campus until after the funeral. The spontaneous memorial should then be removed but should be preserved digitally. Students often find meaning after the loss of a classmate by raising funds for prevention and mental health; SMHPs can be invaluable in guiding this process.

> It's important to be consistent in how deaths are treated because a lack of consistency can inflict more pain on survivors.
>
> —Fulvia Franco

We cannot overstate that schools should strive to treat each death the same. It is recommended that you refer to the AFSP and SRPC Toolkit (2018) that was discussed in Chapter 5 on suicide response for key guidelines schools should follow when memorializing a death by suicide. I utilize these guidelines in all of my consultations, and I emphasize the need for consistent responses across schools (see Table 8.4).

PROFESSIONAL PERSPECTIVE: Scott Poland

A vast number of considerations can be reviewed in the context of memorialization. In one particular case, I received a call from the district communications director asking for advice about the memorialization of a student who died by suicide. The director relayed the fact that over 9,000 students and community members had signed a petition to request an empty chair at the upcoming high school graduation in memory of the suicide victim. The principal had publicly stated that there would be no empty chair in the student's memory. He felt strongly that having an empty chair at the graduation was the wrong thing to do and might further contribute to the problem of teen suicide. I shared recommendations from the After Suicide Toolkit for Schools from AFSP that I had helped to develop, emphasizing the importance of treating all deaths the same way, regardless of the cause of death. I asked if there had ever been an empty chair at a graduation ceremony before in memory of a student who died. The answer was yes, but they had died in an accident, not from suicide.

> After much thought, I relayed to the school that the empty chair was obviously very important to thousands of school and community members. Moreover, the graduation ceremony would be over in 2 to 3 hours, and the empty chair would be much different than having a permanent memorial at school in memory of the suicide victim. I suggested that if the principal allowed the empty chair, then perhaps the 9,000 people who had signed the petition could be encouraged to get involved in raising awareness and funding for mental health and suicide prevention. I further suggested that the school develop a policy to treat all the deaths the same. Ultimately, my suggestions were not followed, and no empty chair was present at the graduation.

While memorializing can come in many forms, it is typical that when a school community experiences a significant loss (e.g., school shooting), they will come together for a memorial service. These services should be conducted with the same care and thought as any other memorialization. Table 8.5 summarizes the recommended guidelines for holding a memorial service; a worksheet that your team can use when planning for a memorial service (see Form 8.2 at the end of the chapter).

There are many examples that we can look to for guidance on permanent memorials. Some have been completed with best practices and others have not. Many times, it takes many years to decide how to memorialize those who have passed. Table 8.6 highlights two such examples that reflect appropriate memorialization practices.

TABLE 8.4. Memorialization Considerations

- School districts should form a committee and develop a memorialization policy; if something permanent is done, it should be minor.
- All deaths should be treated in the same way, and memorialization policies should be set in place prior to a school community member's death.
- Any monies donated should go toward a scholarship or mental health organizations rather than a physical memorial (e.g., a statue). Any money raised or donated should help the living in memory of the deceased school members.
- In cases of a loss of life in other circumstances (e.g., violence), the policy will differ, although you must still exercise caution.
  - Reflect on what your school has historically done to memorialize students and staff who have died.
  - A scholarship is preferable to any physical statue or plaque.
- Involve students, staff, community members, and loved ones of the deceased in the planning, especially those who were close to the deceased.
- Do not rename the school in honor of the deceased.
- Be cautious about accepting any monetary gifts from the family and have an open discussion about the plans for memorials.
- Take your time planning any type of permanent memorial.
- Be mindful of the placement of the memorial. It should be in a place where students can choose to look at it, without being bombarded by its presence.

TABLE 8.5. Guidelines for a Memorial Service

- Should preferably take place in a different location than the school.
- When possible, should be held within a week of the death and after school hours.
  - Involve family members, students, and staff in the planning.
- The parent/family liaison can coordinate the family's involvement. They do not have to be involved or attend; however, it is respectful to share the details of the service.
- Allow varying amount time for the service: 15–20 minutes for elementary students and 30–40 minutes for secondary students.
- Carefully select musical pieces to be played or performed; emphasize messages of hope and resilience.
- Include several relevant speakers (e.g., school district or city and state representatives, administration, family members, and friends). Ensure that your school community is adequately represented.
- Limit the amount of religious focus if your school is public.
- Allow students to contribute by creating a banner that can be signed by the attendees.
- Incorporate physical symbols, including lighting of candles or release of doves.
- Prepare students for the high level of emotions that may be experienced and the appropriate behaviors to demonstrate.
- Do not make attendance mandatory. For those who do not attend, an alternative activity should be offered (see Ideas for Consideration section).

TABLE 8.6. Memorializing Examples

Stockton Children's Museum

In 1989, an assailant opened fire on Cleveland Elementary School's playground, killing five students and injuring 30 others. One of the survivors, a teacher named Janet Geng, joined other community members to create a living and physical memorial that the entire community could benefit from. They designed a children's museum, in a 22,000-square-foot facility, one of the largest children's museums in the country at the time. This museum is open today and continues its mission to provide children, families, and schools with a safe and fun center of discovery and learning (*childrensmuseumstockton.org*).

Sandy Hook

Nearly a decade after the deadly shooting at Sandy Hook, the community has only just recently come to a decision on their permanent community memorial. Sandy Hook's journey of memorialization points to the many issues that can arise in this context. The community struggled to agree on various aspects of the memorial, including its design and location. The Sandy Hook Permanent Memorial Commission was formed and included various community members, such as family members of victims, school personnel, emergency responders, community leaders, and townspeople. Their goal was to plan the memorial project. Trustees of the Boys Social and Athletic Club of Sandy Hook donated a five-acre site, a short distance from the new Sandy Hook Elementary School. The plan is to build a park with a reflection pool. The Commission accepted over 200 submissions for design renderings, eventually coming to a vote on its approval in 2021 (Williamson, 2021).

Ideas for Consideration

- Memory books: ask the students to create a "memory page" that might include poetry, magazine clippings, or drawings. Teachers can bind these into books for each class (Safe Crossings, n.d.).
- Balloon ceremony: Have each student hold a balloon, reflect on the memory of the deceased, and then let it go into the sky. This can serve as a physical symbol of letting go in the process of grief.
- Memory ribbons and other decorations: ribbons that symbolize the loss might be worn by school members, or students may decorate a space in their classroom (e.g., adding construction paper stars or hearts that represent each lost life).
- Websites: creating a memorial website with photos and narratives about the deceased. This website can also link to important resources about suicide and violence prevention and mental health support.
- Plan a fundraiser to raise money for the school and victims; the donations should go toward scholarships, mental health support, basic needs of victims, and prevention programming.
- Organize workshops to educate the community on warning signs of suicide and violence. Help to connect community members to helpful resources.

RETURN TO SCHOOL

> After a school shooting in early April, the building principal told me, "It is so sad that the seniors will not return to their school before graduation." I emphasized the importance of resuming school and stressed that even if parts of the school could not be utilized, the senior class needed to return, as it would be a place of support. I am pleased to share that the seniors did return, and the principal commented that things went better than they ever imagined.
>
> —Scott Poland

The return to school will differ depending on the circumstances of the crisis at your school. As discussed in previous chapters, it is recommended that your students and staff return to school and their routines as quickly as possible. However, this should only take place once an appropriate location is available. When there is significant physical damage, your return will likely have to occur in an alternative place, like another school. If there are limited options for relocation (as was the case in the COVID-19 pandemic), efforts should be made to distribute educational materials and/or online learning for students to engage in.

In the cases of crises that cause major damage to campus buildings, or in places where many deaths occurred, there are often calls for structural modifications or even total demolition of the locales. This decision has come under debate among survivors of school shootings. This was the case at Sandy Hook Elementary, which was torn down entirely 10 months after the shooting. Michelle Gay, the mother of Josephine Gay and cofounder of Safe and Sound Schools (2015; see Chapter 6 Recommended Resources), spoke to these issues in an interview with us in our 2021 publication *Lessons Learned from School Shootings: Perspectives from the United States of America.*

> For the most part, families were behind tearing it down and it was, in our case, a very practical decision. The building had gone past its life expectancy. I think it was maybe 60 years old,

> so it was not a brand spanking new building. There were a lot of difficulties with the building process in that early post tragedy journey. I guess the community hadn't yet figured out how important it would be to have the victims' families there or at least invited to every one of these critical decisions. So, there were things that were overlooked, that would cause pain, you know, sort of like the area, that latitude and longitude where the attacks happened, where our children and spouses were lost; that was very sacred to us.
>
> I'm connected with several of the families that lost children in Parkland and they're kind of bumping up against similar things like that; it is so hard for a community to navigate. They want to try to do the right thing, the best thing. And they're going to make missteps. Sometimes they're going to make the right choice, but it's still going to upset or hurt someone else. And how to handle that is so very difficult and painful. That's why a crisis support network is so needed, it's so important that you have somebody else to talk through, to think through. Are we going about this the right way? What would you suggest? So those kinds of things. (Poland & Ferguson, 2021a, p. 53)

While tearing down the school may be a desired outcome in some communities, it is a very expensive venture; remodeling or providing a new look to the school would be far more affordable and importantly would open up monies that could go toward mental health prevention and support.

The return to school will come with important considerations that can have a major impact on your school community. Of course, safety will be the number one priority, and all buildings on the campus should be safe, secure, and ready for student and staff return. Prior to returning to school, your team must create a plan for the reopening. Leading personnel should be agreed upon in advance (e.g., superintendent, mental health team, administration, budgeting), and these individuals will ensure a systematic return to school. The CRT should detail how they will continue their response, particularly in the areas of debriefing and processing sessions and ongoing mental health support. The day before school begins, I have found that it can be helpful for schools to hold a walk-through in the evening for families and students. NASP's School Safety and Crisis Response Committee (2018) offers guidance on the key actions that should be taken in the weeks after the crisis, during which you will begin to return to your regular school routine.

- Maintain open communication with survivors and their families, along with the family members of those who died.
- Continue to provide mental health support and intervention for those impacted.
- Develop a system for how you will return personal property to students and staff members.
- Attend any funerals/memorial services.
- Establish a Family Assistance Center that will be a primary source of support for the long-term needs of effected families. Resources will be offered (e.g., counseling, financial). The American National Red Cross, FBI, and community agencies can assist your staff in finding these resources.
- Determine how to communicate with staff, families, and the community about school district operations. Use both traditional and social media resources to provide information.
- Stress the importance of self-care for school personnel, especially those who were directly impacted by the crisis and/or responded to the crisis.

- Continue to manage communications and media using the guidance from the Actions Step List reviewed in Chapter 3.
- Be responsive to any family/caregiver concerns; provide direct and individualized responses when necessary. If there appear to be groups of concerns, it can be appropriate to respond in a written manner or in the context of a family/community meeting.
- General information can also be shared on the school's website.
- Maintain strict boundaries with the media and continue to limit their access to the school campus.
- Monitor and respond to social media posts. Strive to provide accurate and up-to-date information frequently.
  - Post up-to-date information on a frequent basis.
  - Share verified facts.
  - Avoid blaming or being defensive online.
  - Reach out to individuals who are expressing frustration online.
  - Share details on how the school community is coping and supporting each other.
  - Highlight the steps that the school has taken in the response process and the intervention and prevention programs that will be in place to assist survivors.
- Offer messages of growth and healing to the school community.

CRISIS EVALUATIONS

> Evaluating the response and updating policies and procedures are often forgotten pieces to crisis prevention and intervention.
>
> —RICHARD LIEBERMAN

> It is important for staff members to have protected time devoted to crisis intervention. This allows individuals, during times in which they are not responding to a crisis, to research and train on preventative strategies.
>
> —MICHELLE PASTOREK

While there are many aftermath considerations, one important area to discuss further is the concept of postcrisis evaluations. These evaluations are part of the longer-term crisis response and the prevention process. They assess the crisis response, including what worked and what didn't work. They are an imperative part of the postvention process, as they inform your school and others as to how to best prepare for and prevent similar crises in the future.

Crisis intervention research echoes Mr. Lieberman's concerns regarding the lack of postcrisis evaluations. While schools have begun to implement more structured prevention and intervention approaches, still little systematic efforts are being made to evaluate the aftermath. A number of issues may impact a school's effort to complete a postcrisis evaluation. A primary barrier is that schools typically develop a crisis intervention plan without the immediate need to deploy it. Additional challenges might include lack of training on evaluation methods, limited time and resources, and fears of litigation (Sokol et al., 2021). It is recommended that your team collaborate with the district to implement an in-house postcrisis evaluation in all crisis aftermaths. The systematic approach should be detailed in the safety plan in your initial crisis planning.

The considerations and guidelines presented in this chapter should be an integral part of your crisis response. There are many difficult aspects of the aftermath and implications for the social-emotional and psychological well-being of your school community. In all cases of a significant crisis, processing the event must occur for all individuals who have been directly or indirectly impacted. Processing initiates the journey for recovery and creates the first shared experience for survivors to work through the grief and trauma associated with a significant crisis. When there are tragic losses of life, funeral and memorial planning serve as rituals for healing and for saying goodbye to victims who lost their lives. Services must be planned with thoughtful approaches that are guided by expert recommendations. When possible and after appropriate processing has taken place, your school must try to help your staff and student body to return to school and to acclimate to their "new normal." In the case of large-scale crises, your support will be needed on an ongoing basis. Additionally, postcrisis evaluations must take place so that your team can properly reflect on the misses and the wins of your crisis planning and to ensure that you are better equipped to handle any future crises you may encounter.

Recommended Resources

- ***AFSP and SRPC After a Suicide: A Toolkit for Schools, Second Edition*** **(2018):** Thoughtful guidance on memorialization with key recommendations. Found at *https://afsp.org/our-work/education/after-a-suicide-a-toolkit-for-schools.*
- **National Center for School Crisis and Bereavement: Guidelines for Responding to the Death of a Student or Staff:** Guidelines for schools on how to best approach the death of a school member. Found at *www.schoolcrisiscenter.org/wp-content/uploads/2020/08/Guidelines-Death-Student-or-Staff-Booklet-Format.pdf.*
- **NASP's Recovery from Large-Scale Crises: Guidelines for Crisis Teams and Administrators (NASP School Safety and Crisis Response Committee, 2018):** Detailed recommendations for schools on how to handle recovery for your school community. Found at *www.nasponline.org/resources-and-publications/resources-and-podcasts/school-safety-and-crisis/school-violence-resources/recovery-from-large-scale-crises-guidelines-for-crisis-teams-and-administrators.*

FORM 8.1

Questions to Consider for the School's Trauma Impact

Instructions for use: Utilize the following questions to assess the potential trauma impact of the crisis event on your school and its members. Record the answers to the questions in the lines provided. These answers can also be helpful to utilize with the Circles of Vulnerability (Form 4.1).

1. Who was the person(s) who died?

   ____

2. Was this person a longtime member of the school community?

   ____

   ____

3. What happened to the person?

   ____

   ____

   ____

   ____

4. Where did the death occur?

   ____

   ____

5. What other crises or tragedies have previously impacted the school?

   ____

   ____

   ____

   ____

   ____

FORM 8.2

Memorial Planning Worksheet

Instructions for use: Utilize the content provided in this worksheet as a guide for memorial planning. Record the answers in the lines provided.

Memorial location: ______________________________

Time and date: ______________________________

Length of service: ______________________________

Publicization of service: ______________________________

Music selections: ______________________________

____

Speakers to be included: ______________________________

____

____

Symbolic actions to be taken during the ceremony (e.g., candle lighting): ______________

____

____

Suggestions from family members, students, and staff: ______________________

____

____

____

____

____

____

CHAPTER 9

Ensuring Your Team Secures the Right Supports

In a time of crisis, asking for and accepting help is imperative. There are unfortunate examples in which administrators have been reluctant to obtain help, hoping to keep the crisis "in-house." Administrators likely fear that they'll lose control of their own school and that a leader from the community might take charge. However, it is unlikely that anyone from outside of their immediate school community would attempt to take charge of the crisis response, unless the school clearly had no plan of action. This is yet another reason why preparedness ahead of a crisis is so critical. This chapter provides guidance for your team on the ins and outs of best practices for utilizing helping aids in the aftermath of a severe crisis. We first discuss external resources of help, such as mental health providers and financial aid, and then we move into a review of internal approaches, including how your team can stay actively involved in managing the aftermath of a crisis.

The best crisis responses for severe instances are those that are comprehensive and include helpful outside resources. In previous chapters we have touched on various areas that will require outside assistance, and there are additional considerations to take into account. Do not hesitate to ask for outside help and remember that an overresponse to a crisis is always better than an underresponse. Moreover, severe crises require the assistance of outside helpers no matter what, including the central office and the police and emergency responders.

> Organizations such as NASP can provide expert guidance in crisis intervention. However, school leaders can be overwhelmed with outside offers to help, particularly after major crises that generate a lot of media coverage. This can lead to confusion and, in some cases, reluctance to accept any outside support even when their expertise is truly needed. Administrators who are most effective are those who listen to their own mental health support staff about the type of help needed and the appropriate personnel to fill these roles. Having trained school mental health and crisis team members, trusted community partnerships, as well as an openness to outside guidance is critical.
>
> —Cathy Kennedy-Paine

In a severe crisis there will be people who can really help you. Table 9.1 outlines the many resources and providers that are available to schools to work collaboratively with their CRTs in the aftermath of a crisis. Many of these options for aid should be predetermined and documented in your crisis plan. In the aftermath of a crisis, chaos can often occur, so it is important that your team has a readily accessible list of contacts so that help is easy to obtain.

The main advisement in accepting this help is that you must be cautious about whom you are taking the help from. In the aftermath of a crisis, you must carefully consider the scope of the event and evaluate the need for additional resources. Moreover, you must ensure that the help is knowledgeable, qualified, and trustworthy; many people will offer help who are well meaning but are none of these things. Additionally, there are some individuals/agencies that respond without good intentions. For example, therapists in private practice may have an agenda: they may want to obtain publicity for their crisis response efforts, or some nonprofits may simply be looking to get their name out in the media. Form 9.1 at the end of the chapter provides a worksheet that can be used to screen any private providers you are considering accepting help from. As mentioned earlier, it is best to establish relationships with any private providers ahead of time, although in the aftermath of a major crisis, you may require additional helping hands beyond what is listed in your crisis plan. Take caution with this process and be sure to utilize the screening form. This form can also be used during your planning process when you are vetting private providers to add to your crisis plan.

TABLE 9.1. Help Available in the Aftermath

- Local caregivers/agencies
  - School psychologists/counselors
  - School-based teams
  - Other schools that have experienced crises
  - Regional/state mental health workers
  - Emergency management services for your city/county
  - City officials
  - University/college psychologists
  - Public relations firm
  - Telephone company
- Judicial/governmental involvement
  - Red Cross
  - Victims' advocates
  - National Guard/State Police
  - Governor/state attorney general
- National crisis response teams/organizations
  - National Organization of Victim Assistance (NOVA)
  - National Emergency Assistance Team (NEAT)
  - Community Crisis Response (CCR)
- State crisis response teams
  - Not every state has a team, and it is the responsibility of each individual school district to investigate in advance whether your state has one that can assist in the aftermath
- NASP crisis support groups

Additionally, any key consultants who are brought in should be verified experts in their area of knowledge. For example, my background and expertise are easily verified with a few clicks of a mouse on the internet.

> On one national crisis team that I served on I recall that the school district had more than 100 local mental health professionals who volunteered. The school district made the decision to only accept the volunteers who had an identifiable crisis certificate.
>
> —SCOTT POLAND

The campus liaison should be in charge of determining who the school can work with. Table 9.2 outlines guidelines that can help determine whose help is appropriate to accept and whose help you should promptly decline.

TABLE 9.2. Guidelines in Screening Helpers

- The best individuals to assist you are other school people. Logistically, they are most familiar with school operations and climate. In a large school system, you may have all the help that you need within your own district (outside of a specially trained state or national crisis response team). However, smaller school districts will require outside assistance in almost all cases of a significant crisis.
- Accept the assistance of any county or regional mental health association without checking references. It is safe to assume that any providers from a state-funded agency have gone through the appropriate background checks and are fully qualified.
- Do not use private therapists unless you already have an established relationship with these professionals and that they are well known in the community.
- Incorporate the use of psychologists and therapists rather than psychiatrists. While these professionals can provide valuable services in the aftermath through psychiatric care and medication, they are not typically trained with the hands-on experience needed in the aftermath of a crisis.
- If you think you need the assistance of a private mental health practitioner that you do not have a relationship with prior to the crisis, utilize Form 9.1 to complete a proper screening of the provider.
- Rural communities that have fewer options for assistance may need to utilize members of the clergy from their local churches.
  - Even larger communities may benefit from clergy involvement. For example, I recall that after the school shooting in Jonesboro, a deeply religious community, a local minister was part of every classroom team following the crisis.
  - Clergy members who are involved in the response should minimize their religious work and focus on providing support and a calming presence.
  - If you do decide to invite clergy members to your response process, be thoughtful of the denominations present at your school.
  - Similarly, you will want to be mindful of other religious/spiritual leaders who could provide aid, such as rabbis or imams.

MENTAL HEALTH RESOURCES

Given the common need for outside mental health assistance, it is important to review this type of help in more detail. As emphasized in previous chapters, it is critical that school districts determine in advance who they would call on from the community for mental health help after a traumatic event. This involves identifying private practitioners or agencies in the community that have staff members well versed in crisis intervention for a K–12 student population. These resources should be included in your safety plan and must be updated on an annual basis.

In my career, I have been frustrated to find that in the aftermath of a crisis, some schools have been ill prepared to meet the mental health needs of the students. I recall examples when schools have closed and have made statements that families and caregivers must look to the community for mental health support and services. One case that comes to mind is a crisis in which a deadly car accident took the lives of three high school students. The crash occurred immediately after graduation, and the school offered no support to the student body. As a result, the students gathered together the next day at the high school parking lot and made efforts to support each other and cope with the losses.

My experiences are not all negative, however, and I know many positive examples of appropriate mental health responses in the aftermath of a crisis. One example that comes to mind involves both successful prior planning and the school's recognition that it needed to be a source of assistance for affected students, even though the event occurred during summer vacation. On July 4, 2023, there was a shooting at a community parade in Highland Park, Illinois. Seven residents were killed, and 17 others were wounded. Highland Park School District was able to respond in a prepared and thorough manner. They already had established prior relationships with key mental health professionals in the community. School was opened the next day, and community mental health professionals began providing free services to members of the community regardless of their age. The sessions were hosted at the high school, and nearly 3,000 community members received assistance over the next seven days.

I was very pleased to provide extensive consultation to the Highland Park School District and to serve as the keynote speaker when staff returned in August. I also provided a session for caregivers on helping their children cope with a crisis. Highland Park's preparedness ensured that the victims were able to meet with others as quickly as possible to discuss the tragedy. This assistance helped the victims to better cope and to not feel alone.

PROFESSIONAL PERSPECTIVE: SCOTT POLAND

In 2001, I responded to a school shooting at Santana High School in California. At the time, I was sent there as the USDOE representative to assist the California Association of School Psychologists (CASP) crisis team that had been dispatched to Santana High School in the aftermath. The event posed many challenges, an initial one being how to respond to the 75 community-based mental health professionals who had volunteered to help provide crisis intervention to the survivors. The school district coordinated with the crisis team and made the decision to only accept volunteers who had a recognized certificate in crisis training. The specific certificates well known at that time were from the American National Red Cross, the National Organization of Victim Assistance (NOVA), and Critical Incident Stress Management. The NASP PREPaRE curriculum had not yet been developed. The Director of Safe and Drug Free Schools for the USDOE came to the affected high school and provided congressional funds through Project SERV (Schools Emergency Response to Violence). These funds were obtained quickly with little paperwork and provided funding to move trailers onto the campus to create a confidential place for the additional mental health staff volunteers to provide services. At the recommendation of the CASP team, the school district designated a crisis recovery coordinator (CRC), who already had a mental health leadership position in the district. The CRC agreed to greatly reduce normal school duties and provide a salary increase to the SMHPs, as their work hours were extended into the late afternoons and evenings. Support services were coordinated and provided well beyond the school day to students and staff. CASP team members and I stayed in close contact with the school and provided ongoing consultation and support to the CRC. We coordinated a meeting at a conference several months later and continued to emphasize the need for self-care for the SMHP staff members.

FINANCIAL AID

Financial assistance will be provided to your school or district in the event of a severe crisis, such as a school shooting or a major natural disaster. In most cases, community members will begin to collect emergency funds on their own. If your school's crisis is nationally publicized, your school/district will likely become the beneficiary of many donations from across the country. Additionally, your state's board of education may offer funds for the ongoing crisis response, or monies might be allocated from your state's disaster funds. One potential source of federal funding is the Department of Education. For example, I recall that the Westside school system received $100,000 in funding from the Department of Safe and Drug Free Schools after the middle school shooting in 1998 in Jonesboro, Arkansas, where two students shot and killed four teachers and students. These dollars enabled the county to provide mental health services from outside agencies that worked with the students and school staff throughout the summer months.

As discussed in Chapter 7, FEMA can provide financial assistance in the aftermath of a significant crisis, typically after a natural disaster. The money is generally allocated to provide crisis response services, such as mental health support. For instance, I recall that when the Alfred P. Murrah federal building was bombed in Oklahoma City in April 1995, the school district was able to obtain a FEMA grant. The funds provided the services of 142 counselors, who worked with Oklahoma City schools for over a year.

> I was proud to serve on a national crisis team in the aftermath of the Oklahoma City bombing. I provided consultation to the Oklahoma City school district, and we were able to convince FEMA to fund additional counseling positions in the school district. We felt this was the right move as opposed to making counseling services available in the community, which required students, faculty, and parents to drive across town.
>
> —Scott Poland

An additional federal resource of aid comes from the Victims of Crime Act (VOCA), which was established in 1984. This act provides federal support to state and local programs that assist victims of crime. VOCA uses nontaxpayer money from the Crime Victims Fund (CVF) for programs that serve victims of crime, including state-funded victim assistance grants. A unique aspect of this program is that the funds are derived from fines and penalties paid by convicted criminals (Office of Justice Programs, 2020).

As discussed in Chapter 6, I always recommend that schools apply for a Project School Emergency Response to Violence (SERV; 2014) grant from the USDOE. These short-term grants are typically easy to obtain, and they can offer critical funds to support schools in the aftermath of a severe crisis. Federal assistance can come quickly; however, it typically requires the aid of leaders from your community. Your superintendent should reach out to federal and state representatives (e.g., mayors, governors, senators, city council members) to obtain advice and assistance in accessing financial aid.

Distribution of Funds

Your local banks or savings and loan officer can help your school's administrators to establish accounts, trust, and scholarship funds to manage such donations. A recent example is the effort made by First State Bank of Uvalde, which opened donation accounts for the victims and families impacted by the shooting at Robb Elementary School in Texas in 2022 (Garcia, 2022). Your local United Way organizations may also provide financial aid and, in some cases, they have matched other donations.

A number of individuals should monitor the funds and decide how the money should be spent. Ideally, a committee should include community members, such as parents/caregivers, and school personnel, such as teachers and administrators. The staff and student body should be included in this planning process, and it is suggested that you survey them for their input in how to spend the donated money. Of course, the needs of victims and their families must come first. Spending the remaining donations on a lasting memorial, such as a children's museum or sports facility, will likely satisfy the largest number of people in the community, as members typically like to see a gift of hope for a better future. Refer back to Chapter 8 to review the use of these funds and how they can best be disbursed for memorialization.

Distribution of the funds is a sensitive topic and requires careful planning, for a number of challenges can arise. The example of Uvalde, Texas, highlights some of these issues, including slowed distribution of funds, confusion over who the funds should be distributed to, and what type of help should be funded (Garcia, 2022). It is advised that your school obtain guidance on this matter and should consider consulting with another school in your state or nationally, or with someone who has experienced a severe crisis.

STAY INVOLVED

Even if a national crisis team comes into your school, continue to be an active participant in the crisis response. These teams will always rely on school personnel involvement and often prefer to have the school team leaders guide the response. While the outside crisis teams may have specialty training and expertise, *your* team has the information about the school, its population, the strengths and weaknesses of your school community, details about victims, and much more.

Your participation is an asset to them. National crisis team members must be careful not to be perceived as taking over the school's crisis, and they need to be adept at listening and make efforts to ease their way in.

Additionally, national team assistance is typically time limited and cannot meet the long-term needs of your school. You will need to be in the know of their response efforts in order to be able to perform services without interruption. It is critically important that a national crisis team conduct an exit meeting with school administration and school crisis team members that will go over recommendations and the kind of follow-up the affected school can expect from the national crisis team.

PROVIDE GUIDANCE TO APPROPRIATE ASSISTANCE

Once you have obtained ample outside assistance, your team will need to provide direction on how they can be of support. Helpers should be asked to follow a number of basic principles that will lend best to supportive postvention services (see Table 9.3).

DEBRIEF WITH YOUR HELPERS

Debriefing with your helpers is important, and you should make efforts to have a meeting with them at the end of the day. You will want them to feel connected and supported and to know that they have a space to process what they have witnessed and intervened in. The goals of this meeting include (1) gathering any pertinent information about the needs of the school community, (2) providing a formal thank you for their support and aid, and (3) creating an opportunity for the helpers to unload if needed; remember, they have had a hard day as well.

PROFESSIONAL PERSPECTIVE: Scott Poland

In 1998, I responded to the school shooting that occurred at the Westside Middle School in Jonesboro, Arkansas, where, as mentioned earlier, two students shot and killed four teachers and students. In the aftermath, more than 100 community-based mental health professionals from the local area and beyond arrived to volunteer their help at the school. Given the large number of volunteers and the urgent need to provide aid to the survivors, it was decided that instead of asking the volunteers for their crisis credentials, they would all engage in training on the intervention model developed by NOVA. The training session went well, and the volunteers appreciated the training and the additional skills they gained. The volunteers conducted many processing sessions that were monitored by the NOVA national crisis team. These volunteers were on site for several days. Importantly, at the end of each day, a processing session was conducted with the volunteers to plan for the next day and to thank the volunteers and encourage them to engage in self-care. These debriefings were critical to the intervention process and not only helped the volunteers to best prepare to care for others, but they also provided a sense of connectedness and support for all involved.

TABLE 9.3. Basic Principles for Helpers

- Maintain a calm, warm, nonjudgmental, and sympathetic stance.
- Practice empathetic listening; this is not a time to problem-solve or find solutions. People just need to be heard.
  - Examples:
    - *"Thank you for sharing this with me."*
    - *"I'm so sorry for what you are going through."*
    - *"I'm here to listen to you."*
- Speak little about yourselves; focus on the victims and their feelings.
  - Examples:
    - *"How can I help you?"*
    - *"What are you in need of right now?"*
    - *"How are you feeling?"*
- Allow victims the space to express a range of emotions and stress the normalization of the feelings that victims are experiencing.
  - Examples:
    - *"There is no right or wrong way to feel right now."*
    - *"It is understandable to feel a range of emotions at this time."*
    - *"Try not to judge your emotions, you can feel whatever you need to feel."*
- Remember that there are no magic or right words that can fix this. There are, however, things to avoid saying:
  - Examples:
    - *"I understand . . ."* You really can't understand in this moment.
    - *"I felt the same way when . . ."* Let this person's story be their own.
- Try to instill hope and future thinking.
  - Examples:
    - *"We are going to work together to get through this."*
    - *"Help will be here for you."*
- Help the person to prepare for coping with their reactions; discuss past ways the victim has coped with distress and current sources of strength that they can lean on (e.g., God, family members).
  - Examples:
    - *"You may experience a range of emotions over time, and this is okay."*
    - *"It is important to find sources of strength. What kind of support has gotten you through hard things in the past?"*
- Document every engagement that takes place with a survivor and notify a CRT member if there are any concerns regarding someone who requires a higher level of care.

TAKING CARE OF THE CARETAKER

> I have recognized the critical need to take care of the caregivers. That begins with me when I am a responder and extends to all who are on my team. I must be grounded and present in order to support others. I have great family support for my work and also professionals whom I can go to when the going gets tough.
>
> —CATHY PAINE-KENNEDY

The discussion of debriefing your helpers brings us to the important topic of caring for those who care for others. As crisis responders, the majority of our efforts are geared toward others;

however, just as imperative as it is to provide the right support to others, it is equally as critical to take care of yourself. Vicarious traumatization and burnout in crisis response are very real implications of this work, and you must make efforts to develop helpful coping tools to deal with the stressors of this work. Our experts shared personal ways that they have learned to cope with crisis responding and the related impacts on their well-being.

PROFESSIONAL PERSPECTIVES

How Do You Cope with Crisis Response Work?

Using the methods of relaxation and mindfulness, group support from other professionals, and strong home support. My pets and physical activity have served me well. My NEATY colleagues/friends are there when I need them! I also follow the Israeli BASIC Ph Model of coping activation. Activation of coping resources helps most!

—BILL PFOHL

Having a structure and routine to follow. Having colleagues, including teams, who can help share the burden of the work. Having a caring support system, including my family and colleagues.

—CINDY DICKINSON

The support of my teammates is huge as they really know what crisis response is like. Knowing they have my back and will step in and be there as needed. Being able to debrief with them and process the experience is incredibly helpful as well. Also, being intentional about both my physical and psychological self-care and well-being (doing all the things that we tell everyone to do, i.e., eat healthy foods, hydrate, get enough sleep, exercise, utilize my support systems, say "no," take breaks, laugh, etc.).

—FRANCI CREPEAU-HOBSON

Vicarious trauma is real and doing crisis response work impacts us as professionals. I personally cope by developing an accountability partner relationship with a fellow crisis response colleague. We can debrief with each other and remind and encourage each other to take time for ourselves and do activities that feed our soul and provide time to relax and refresh.

—STEPHANIE CRAWFORD-GOETZ

As one can imagine, it can be stressful to speak with school staff routinely regarding crisis situations—you want to ensure that you are giving campuses helpful information to intervene and keep students safe. I am fortunate to be part of a team with whom I can frequently consult to ensure that we are considering all relevant information and making good recommendations. Having this support helps immensely. On a personal note, I find I need to prioritize getting adequate sleep, both from a stress-management standpoint and to be best prepared to triage concerns.

—MICHELLE PASTOREK

Engage in Self-Care

As a crisis responder, you must be vigilant in practicing appropriate self-care. Self-care does not necessarily mean relaxing or getting a massage (although that can be part of it). Self-care is the practice of doing the right things to best help yourself. Practical examples include nourishing and hydrating your body, getting enough sleep, taking brisk walks, connecting with your loved ones, processing your own trauma with fellow responders, and scheduling time to decompress in the aftermath. Our experts have a wealth of insight regarding the importance of self-care.

PROFESSIONAL PERSPECTIVES

The Importance of Self-Care

. . . While the work [is] incredibly rewarding, it's exhausting work that can really take its toll on you. I had no idea of how draining it could be and how important self-care was.

—FRANCI CREPEAU-HOBSON

The degree of the impact of crisis response on personal mental health [reflects] the critical importance of a personal and professional self-care plan.

—RICHARD LIEBERMAN

One of the things that I have found to be most difficult in crisis intervention is the return to home. Your focus has been totally on the effect of the school and their needs. Also, you were working as part of a team with others. Then you fly home, where hopefully you get a lot of support from your family, but you are expected to immediately go back to work and deal with real life. You return to work on Monday and the typical job issues seem to pale in comparison to the crisis that you've just responded to. I remember returning from leading a national crisis team after a school shooting, and my first morning back at work in my district the phone rang. I answered it to find a parent complaining about the psychological services her child had been receiving. I had to stop myself from throwing the phone across the room because at the moment, the parent's complaint seemed so inconsequential compared to what I had just experienced. Care for the caregiver is critical for local members of crisis teams, as well as those that come in to help at the state or national level. The wise leader of the crisis team would make every effort to support the team members and to encourage them to engage in self-care during the crisis.

—SCOTT POLAND

[Self-care comes in the form of] having a personal self-care plan. Knowing when to say no. Exercise (now, it's a lot of walking). Hanging out with one of the coauthors of this book [and friend, Scott Poland].

—RICHARD LIEBERMAN

The above professional perspectives on self-care offer valuable insight from our experts. Given their significant experience in the field of crisis response, their recommendations for coping and self-care are invaluable and should be implemented in your own life. Self-care practices often bring to mind the age-old example of flight instructions that are given before every flight: if you are traveling with a child, put your mask on first before helping others. Remember, we can't help others without first helping ourselves.

Crisis intervention cannot be done alone; it requires the support of external and internal resources. It is important that your team is well prepared to bring in the support of people from the community, though you must use discernment in the types of aid you choose to include. Thoughtful considerations must occur in relation to funding and the distribution of monies, along with how mental health access is delineated. The guidance offered in this chapter will help your team to best address these concerns in the aftermath of a significant crisis.

Recommended Resources

- **FEMA Recovery Grants (2023):** Grant funds are offered for pre- and postemergency or disaster-related projects. These funds provide support necessary to recovery initiatives, innovative research, and many additional related programs. Found at *www.fema.gov/grants.*
- **National Organization for Victim Assistance (NOVA; 2023):** Provides disaster relief to victims of crime, victims of mass causalities, or survivors of natural disasters in the form of crisis response. Found at *www.trynova.org.*
- **Project School Emergency Response to Violence (SERV; 2014):** USDOE program that provides short-term and long-term fundings for education-related services for local educational agencies and institutions of higher education to help them recover from a violent or large-scale crisis. Found at *www2.ed.gov/programs/dvppserv/index.html.*
- **Red Cross Disaster Relief and Recovery Services (2023):** Provides relief and recovery services to meet the immediate disaster-caused needs of individuals, families, and communities. Found at *www.redcross.org/about-us/our-work/disaster-relief.html.*

FORM 9.1

Screening for Private Providers

Instructions for use: Utilize the following questions as a script for your interview with private providers who may be able to offer mental health support in the aftermath of a crisis. Record the answers in the lines provided.

Review the following questions before accepting the help of private providers:

1. What is your clinical experience in working with adolescents (or the age range of your students)?

   ____

   ____

2. What does your practice specialize in?

   ____

   ____

3. What are your credentials, and what board are you licensed with?

   ____

   ____

4. Do you have any experience working in trauma?

   ____

   ____

5. Have you helped any other schools when there has been a crisis? If so, what did you do?

   ____

   ____

6. What references can you provide?

   ____

   ____

If you are satisfied with the provider's answers and references, you should accept their help. If not, kindly decline their services and obtain the assistance of the security liaison in escorting the individual off the property safely.

CHAPTER 10

Diversity, Equity, Inclusion, and Belonging

Proper school crisis planning cannot take place without consideration of four critical concepts—diversity, equity, inclusion, and belonging (DEIB). The term *diversity* refers to the existence of variations of different characteristics in a group of people. This encompasses a range of factors, including age, race and ethnicity, culture, socioeconomic status, gender identity, affectional orientation, and religious affiliation, to name a few. We have already referenced many of these considerations in the context of specific crises. Such examples include the age and gender differences in trauma impact and reactions, along with higher rates of suicidality in the LGBTQIA+ community. In school crisis intervention, *diversity* relates to the school's recognition of the varied backgrounds, experiences, identities, and expressions and their incorporation of such understanding into school safety and crisis planning. The term *equity* encompasses the school's responsibility to ensure that all school members have equal access to opportunities and resources and the ability to have their needs met. Crisis planning must encompass ideas and strategies that are accessible and developmentally appropriate for all school members. *Inclusion* relates to the school's duty to ensure that all school members, regardless of background and individual attributes, feel integrated within and valued by their school community (Peck, Rosch, & De Sawal, 2022). *Belonging* emphasizes school members' experiences of *feeling* accepted, valued, and understood. A sense of belongingness should naturally occur when diversity, equity, and inclusion are accounted for. In crisis intervention, belongingness is fostered through the assurance that school members' voices and opinions are heard and well represented in safety and crisis planning and that the psychological safety of all are considered.

In this chapter we provide suggestions related to four areas of special consideration that will help facilitate actions to promote DEIB: *age* (i.e., developmental considerations), *cultural impact* (i.e., the influence of one's race, ethnicity, and/or cultural background), *context* (i.e., setting factors, such as prior trauma exposure/experience), and *students with disabilities* (i.e., those with physical, intellectual, and/or neurodevelopmental disorders). Guidance for best practices for crisis planning related to these areas of consideration are reviewed in detail, and specific recommendations for each are offered. Additionally, this chapter provides recommendations for your CRT on how to increase your cultural responsiveness and competence, which will ultimately fulfill the mission of DEIB in your school community.

AGE CONSIDERATIONS

The importance of age and developmental considerations have been discussed throughout this guidebook and are critical aspects of all areas of school crisis intervention. The developmental levels of students have a significant impact on their levels of awareness (i.e., safety matters), reactions (i.e., trauma responses, grief), understanding, and abilities to cognitively and emotionally process crisis events. Aspects of prevention and intervention will differ in many ways based on these levels. It is recommended that your team review age considerations in groups of developmental and grade ranges (e.g., early childhood/preschool, childhood/elementary school, early adolescence/middle school, adolescence/high school). Broad considerations in the context of these ranges include the following:

- Use of developmentally appropriate language (in risk assessments, discussing/processing crisis events)
- Awareness of age-specific needs that relate to risk (e.g., bullying, substance use)
- Awareness of developmental presentations of grief (see Chapter 4, Table 4.1)
- Awareness of trauma impact and reactions by age range (see Chapter 6, Table 6.1)
- Maintenance and provision of developmentally appropriate resources for emotional and psychological aid (e.g., grief books [see Chapter 4, Table 4.5], mental health providers that specialize in working with young children, adolescents, and late teens)
- Intervention strategies (e.g., use of art, journaling, discussion based)

More specifically, consideration of age and development in the prevention context relates to the concepts of school safety and suicide and violence prevention that were reviewed in Chapter 2 (e.g., creating a climate of safety, enhancing the positive social-emotional well-being of students, crisis drills, screenings, and threat assessment). While the guidance in Chapter 2 was provided in a broad sense, it is imperative that these areas are tailored to the developmental needs of your student body. For example, crisis drills must be designed with age ranges in mind, beginning with psychoeducation regarding the need for crisis drills down to the execution of actual drills. Developmental variations of this aspect of prevention would be reflected in the language and content used to describe the need for and implementation of the drills, along with the nature of the drills (e.g., inclusion of more realistic components).

Furthermore, crisis response and interventions must be tailored to developmental levels to ensure appropriateness and effectiveness. Given the range of impact that a crisis can have on an individual depending on their age and developmental level, it is important that your team considers the way each group emotionally and cognitively processes information, particularly in the contexts of stress and trauma. Your SMHP will be a significant resource in the process of adapting intervention strategies. It is also recommended that your team consults with teach-

TABLE 10.1. Key Age and Developmental Considerations in Crisis Intervention

Preschool

Information to remember
- Limited cognitive skills required to understand a crisis
- Do not have the coping skills to deal with crises effectively
- Adults in the environment provide key support and comfort
- Children model adult reactions
- Be aware of concerns of abandonment
- Feelings will often be expressed via behaviors

Interventions to use
- Play activities to facilitate expression of emotions and thoughts that cannot be articulated
- Materials to use: paint, crayons, clay, blocks, puppets, and dolls
- Create stories with toys

Elementary school

Information to remember
- Tendency to be more verbal but are more concrete (vs. abstract) in thinking and processing
- Will ask more questions
- Answer only what they are asking; do not overshare information
- Difficulty in understanding the permanency of death
- Awareness of common fears of death and separation anxiety from family and friends

Interventions to use
- Play activities to facilitate expression of feelings and thoughts
- Planned discussions about fears and worries; normalize feelings
- Try to create increased control (e.g., offering choices)
- Painting or drawing, writing in a journal, reading and/or reviewing stories

Middle school

Information to remember
- Increased sensitivity and understanding about crises
- Limited way of responding to crises
- Show of concern for victims and a desire to help

Interventions to use
- Role-playing games to express emotions
- Journaling
- Group discussion to process and express feelings about crises; normalization of feelings
- Letters to victims and their families

High school

Information to remember
- Usually engage in more abstract and hypothetical thinking
- There is a better sense of the permanence of death
- Tendency to engage in distorted thinking (e.g., "I did something wrong to deserve this")
- You do not have to have all the answers; say, "I don't know" when appropriate

Interventions to use
- Group discussions of thoughts, feelings, beliefs, and concerns regarding the crisis event
- Model coping skills such as problem-solving strategies and relaxation techniques

ers from the grades of each group, as they can offer thoughtful contributions to intervention approaches. Table 10.1 provides a helpful overview of pertinent information related to specific age groups that should be kept in mind when planning for crisis interventions. It also includes a number of brief strategies that can be employed, some of which have been discussed in prior "Ideas for Consideration" sections in earlier chapters.

CULTURAL CONSIDERATIONS

Given the vast ways in which cultural impact can manifest, there are a number of considerations to review. First, you must begin by increasing familiarity with your school community's culture and group identity, as it is a vital part of providing culturally sensitive and effective crisis responses. This practice goes beyond just understanding school demographics; it requires you to develop a deep understanding of diverse backgrounds and how diversity impacts student and family perceptions and reactions. Individual perceptions and responses are heavily influenced by socialization with groups, molding the way an individual perceives and interprets specific contexts (Sue & Sue, 2003). These views will influence a number of aspects in a crisis situation, including individual reactions, vulnerability to trauma, and perception/acceptance/rejection of mental health services (Annandale, Heath, Dean, Kemple, & Takino, 2011; NASP, 2004).

School Demographics

It is recommended that you complete a cultural composition of your student body on an annual basis. You should include details regarding your school's demographics, including their ethnic and linguistic diversity. Another area of diversity that should be explored includes affectional orientation (LGBTQIA+ identifying), given the associated risks for mental health concerns and the benefit of preventative support (see Chapter 5 for information on best supporting this community).

The melting pot status of our country can be easily observed in the diverse population makeup of schools across the nation. In fact, of the 49.4 million students enrolled in public elementary and secondary schools in fall 2020, approximately 22.6 million identified as White, 13.8 million Hispanic, 7.4 million Black, 2.7 million Asian, 2.2 million identified as two or more races, 0.5 million American Indian/Alaska Native, and 180,000 Pacific Islander (National Center for Education Statistics [NCES], 2022). Ethnic diversity is an important consideration in crisis preparedness, and the significant amount of diversity in the student population signals the importance of culturally sensitive services.

An additional school demographic to investigate is linguistic diversity. Language variations are bound to come with ethnic diversity, and it is estimated that as of 2019, approximately 5.1 million students in the United States were enrolled as "English learners" (EL) in the public school system. Among ELs, a range of languages are spoken in their homes, with Spanish being the dominant language, followed by Arabic. English was the third most common home language (105,300 students), which might reflect students who live in multilingual households or those who were adopted from other countries and raised speaking another language but currently live in households where English is spoken. Chinese (100,100 students), Vietnamese (75,600 students), Portuguese (44,800 students), Russian (39,700 students), Haitian (31,500 students),

Hmong (30,800 students), and Korean (25,800 students) are the next most commonly reported home languages of EL students (NCES, 2022). These findings certainly reflect the need for linguistic considerations as you engage in crisis planning.

LGBTQIA+ Population

As mentioned previously, the LGBTQIA+ population presents unique needs in the crisis planning and intervention processes. LGBTQIA+ identifying individuals historically have endured a high level of discrimination and, despite the growing inclusion and acceptance of this culture, they continue to face ongoing harassment and exclusionary behaviors in both the broader society and within schools. Each year hundreds of anti-LGBTQIA+ bills are introduced, with the intent to limit the rights of this population. The proposal (and sometime implementation) of such laws can directly influence school districts and communities, creating challenges such as limited funding for affirming resources and exclusionary curriculum. Experiences and societal messages of discrimination have created ongoing difficulties for this population that strongly intersect with the field of crisis intervention. As discussed in prior chapters, LGBTQIA+ youth are found to be at greater risk for bullying and harassment, mental health concerns, and suicide. Moreover, help-seeking behaviors are influenced by experiences of discrimination and lack of affirming care and resources.

It is imperative that your CRT become well versed in the needs and potential risk factors commonly observed in this population. Efforts must be put into place to create an affirming school environment that fosters a sense of understanding and inclusion. It is recommended that your school's staff and, in particular, your CRT members attend annual LGBTQIA+ sensitivity and diversity training. These workshops will help to increase your staff's awareness, understanding, and competence in working with this population. SMHPs specifically should engage in ongoing training within their field and ensure that they are well equipped to provide affirming care, support, and interventions in times of crisis (e.g., LGBTQIA+-sensitive risk assessments).

Preventive efforts tailored to the LGBTQIA+ population emphasize strategies geared toward creating an affirming school climate. Such efforts include symbolic representations (e.g., pride flags, posters that indicate safe spaces), use of affirming language in forms/documents, offerings of club chapters such as the Gay-Straight Alliance (GSA), incorporation of LGBTQIA+ topics in the curriculum, and strong bullying policies that explicitly prohibit discriminatory language. Risk and threat assessment procedures should be reviewed to ensure that they include inclusive and affirming language and are sensitive to the needs of this population.

Recommendations for intervention approaches with the LGBTQIA+ population emphasize the need for affirming care and support. Those providing interventions must be mindful of a number of important factors, including the following:

- Utilize affirming and inclusive language.
  - Examples:
    - When you don't know someone's pronouns, always default to using gender-neutral pronouns, such as *they/them* pronouns or using a person's name instead of using pronouns.
    - Utilization of the word *person* instead of *man* or *woman*.
    - Utilization of the word *partner* instead of *boyfriend* or *girlfriend*.

- Do not make assumptions about a person's affectional orientation or gender identification; wait for that individual to disclose this to you.
- Be highly aware of nonverbal communication and approach in a nonjudgmental way; many individuals identifying as LGBTQIA+ have encountered significant judgment and discrimination and may be unsure of your level of comfort and acceptance.
- Consider the impact of specific events on LGBTQIA+, such as recent anti-LGBTQIA+ legislation or community violence. Your awareness of these factors will help to enhance your understanding of potential influences of stress and convey an increased sense of safety.
- Your school should maintain an updated list of LGBTQIA+-affirming resources, including mental health providers who are well versed in working with this population, community resources such as nonprofit groups/organizations, LGBTQIA+ crisis hotlines, and online resources and networks.

CONTEXT CONSIDERATIONS

Among context considerations, trauma exposure, experiences, impact, and reactions are of significant interest in crisis intervention. While the topic of trauma has been discussed in each relevant chapter, it has not been considered in the context of diversity and culture. Crisis intervention processes should be tackled with a trauma-informed approach in which a framework is established to relate to and help school members who have experienced negative consequences after exposure to dangerous events. Trauma-informed practices are an important integration of prevention and intervention, as they assist in mitigating the occurrence of future crises and increased risks of traumatization in the aftermath of a crisis. Moreover, they are an excellent way to help facilitate DEIB across your school community.

Incorporation of trauma-informed approaches is an excellent way to strengthen your prevention practices, particularly in areas of school climate and reduction of potential risk factors. NASP has highlighted the benefits of schools becoming trauma-informed, including increased feelings of emotional, social, and physical safety; common understanding of trauma and the impact of adversity on students among school staff; broader access to appropriate mental health resources and services; positive and culturally responsive discipline procedures; and successful community collaborations (Crisis Prevention Institute, 2021). Given the high rates of adverse experiences that students endure (recall the Youth Risk Behavior Survey data from Chapter 1), the use of trauma-informed practices can create a positive impact across the student body.

Having trauma-informed practices in place can also assist in building a strong culturally responsive approach to intervention. In the aftermath of a crisis, it is important to remember that survivors' reactions and recoveries are shaped by their individual backgrounds, beliefs and values, and points of view. Cultural influences vary across group backgrounds, resulting in unique and differing approaches to mental health, death, trauma, grief, and healing. Furthermore, perceptions of help-seeking behaviors and mental health treatment are mixed and have a significant impact on the success of a crisis response.

Intergenerational factors are also an important consideration, including historical influences such as racism, discrimination, war, and internment. Minority groups have long been subject to social and racial inequalities and inequities. People of color have been marginalized in many ways over time, particularly in the areas of availability and access to quality medical and mental health care. These factors contribute to the distrust that is often observed between minority groups and entities that offer assistance, and this distrust should be kept in mind when providing crisis services. Moreover, they create increased risks for retraumatization or higher rates of traumatization in the aftermath of a crisis.

Schools across the nation are increasingly adopting a trauma-informed approach in their practices, although there is yet to be a universal recommendation on how to incorporate and implement this approach. Many state departments of education have utilized SAMHSA's (2015) education-focused resources as guidelines for development, which include manuals, toolkits, and online learning modules (see Recommended Resources). Research on the trauma-informed approach in schools has identified three key categories of content that schools should emphasize: (1) building knowledge (i.e., understanding the nature and impact of trauma), (2), shifting perspectives and building emotionally healthy school cultures, and (3) promoting self-care for educators (Thomas, Crosby, & Vanderhaar, 2019). Specific resources that can be utilized in your training and development of materials are presented in the Recommended Resources section below.

Recommended Resources

- **SAMHSA's Concept of Trauma and Guidance for a Trauma-Informed Approach (2015):** Found at *https://store.samhsa.gov/product/samhsas-concept-trauma-and-guidance-trauma-informed-approach/sma14-4884.*
- **Child Trauma Toolkit for Educators from the National Child Traumatic Stress Network (NCTSN; 2018):** Found at *www.nctsn.org/sites/default/files/assets/pdfs/Child_Trauma_Toolkit_Final.pd.f*
- **Trauma-Responsive Educational Practices Project:** Found at *www.trepeducator.org.*

CULTURAL RESPONSIVENESS

Your mental health training should have already equipped you with an increased level of understanding of diverse backgrounds and their impact on students. In the context of crisis intervention, it is critical that your knowledge goes above and beyond the basics of understanding and that you develop cultural responsiveness in the area of crisis intervention. Cultural responsiveness is the integration and use of knowledge about individuals and groups of people into specific standards, policies, practices, and attitudes used in appropriate cultural settings to increase the quality of services, thereby producing better outcomes (Hernandez, Nesman, Mowery, Acevedo-Polakovich, & Callejas, 2009). You can work to increase your cultural responsiveness in a number of ways, and these efforts should be made in advance of any crisis intervention (see Table 10.2).

The final recommendation regarding continued learning is especially important, and we encourage you to engage in continuing education opportunities in the domain of multicultural competence and intervention services. Training should also be held within your school, in which faculty and staff have opportunities to strengthen their own level of cultural competency. SMHPs are the best individuals to lead these kinds of workshops, and the goals should be to

TABLE 10.2. Strategies to Strengthen My Cultural Responsiveness

- Increase your awareness about your own cultural biases. What are your viewpoints and how has your history impacted your beliefs and preconceptions about others? Do you hold any prejudicial beliefs?
  - Engage in deep self-reflection; explore how prejudice (we all have it) can manifest in your crisis work.
  - Explore your historical experiences with diverse cultures.
  - Become comfortable with your own issues around diversity.
- Obtain an accurate and working understanding of the diversity needs of your student population.
- Maintain an open mind and engage in efforts to continuously learn.

provide foundational knowledge (i.e., terms, demographic data, societal disparities, the concepts of equality and inequity) about multiculturalism. You should encourage school personnel to engage in their own processes of self-reflection, increasing their awareness of cultural biases. Moreover, they should exchange ideas and perspectives about the diverse backgrounds of the school community. These discussions are helpful in creating a more culturally competent staff that will be better equipped to respond to the diverse needs of their student body (Connolly Knox & Haupt, 2015).

WHAT IS YOUR CRT'S ROLE IN CULTURALLY SENSITIVE CRISIS INTERVENTION?

Your CRT's level of cultural responsiveness is an important factor in successful school crisis planning and response. Your team members should be diverse in a number of ways and ideally will represent the ethnic and linguistic makeup of your school community (Allen et al., 2004). If this is not feasible for your team, it is important to establish close relationships with outside resources that can be of aid in a time of crisis. These resources include trusted organizations and agencies that provide culturally sensitive mental health support, cultural and faith-based community leaders, and multicultural television stations, radio stations, and newspapers (Athey & Moody-Williams, 2003).

It is important that the CRT members become attuned to the common cultural issues they may face in crisis responses. Potential issues include communication (decision making and ways to communicate verbally and nonverbally), personal space (appropriateness of physical contact and proximity), social organization (the influences of family, kinships, tribes, and religious, political, and economic organizations), time (variability in interpretation and measurement), and environmental control (belief about external vs. internal control; Athey & Moody-Williams, 2003; Sandoval & Lewis, 2002). All of these factors can impact the effectiveness of your crisis response.

Team diversity training will be helpful with the goal of developing cultural competence and learning about cultural values and traditions, linguistics and literacy, immigration experiences and status, help-seeking behaviors, cross-cultural outreach techniques and strategies, and avoidance of stereotypes and labels (Athey & Moody-Williams, 2003). Your team is encouraged to engage in the same self-reflection and cultural bias exploration that was previously recommended individually for you. Members should examine their own cultures, worldviews, and biases, including how these may affect the provision of mental health services. To ensure continued cultural competence, periodic evaluations of their crisis response efforts should occur. This can include a reevaluation of needs, a review of any barriers that have prevented the provision of services, and the victim response to the culturally sensitive approaches used (NASP, 2004).

CULTURALLY RESPONSIVE CRISIS PLANS

When creating the school's crisis plans, your understanding of the culture and group identity of your school community will be a valuable contribution to its development. Your knowledge will greatly aid in your school's ability to respond effectively with multicultural sensitivity (Annandale et al., 2011; Kemple et al., 2006). There are a number of ways in which SMHPs can incorporate their cultural competence into their crisis plans, school safety, and preparedness. Table 10.3 outlines specific guidance on ways to ensure that your team is employing appropriate and effective services.

CULTURALLY SENSITIVE CRISIS RESPONSE

Only limited guidelines have been provided for culturally sensitive school-based crisis intervention. Most recommendations are formed by combining the two categories of multicultural competence and best practices for school crisis intervention. While knowledge of cultural diversity is paramount, effective responses for diverse populations always consider the individualized experiences, beliefs, norms, values, traditions, customs, and language of each person, regardless of their racial, ethnic, or cultural background. Moreover, your responses must be done in a way

TABLE 10.3. Guide to Completing a Culturally Responsive Crisis Plan

- A needs assessment should be completed in which you obtain information about the culture-related needs of your school community (e.g., interpreter services, religious figures).
- Maintain an up-to-date report of your school community's cultural composition.
  - Include age, gender, race/ethnicity, languages/dialects spoken, refugee/immigrant status, socioeconomic status, percentage of students living in rural versus urban areas, religion, history of trauma, torture, or war experience, and history of racial/ethnic relations within the greater community (Athey & Moody-Williams, 2003).
- Anticipate and identify possible solutions to cultural problems that may arise in the event of a crisis.
- Develop a list of culturally sensitive resources that survivors can be connected to, particularly those in the mental health domain (i.e., therapists who are culturally competent in working with diversity needs). Other examples include interpreters or translators.
- Ensure that you have a current list of the full names of the parents/caretakers of all students, as last names may differ across families.
- Become familiar with the meaning of suffering, pain, and death relevant to the norms of the community's cultural groups (NASP, 2004; Young, 1997).

that identifies, respects, and builds upon the resources and strengths of your school community (Athey & Moody-Williams, 2003; Canada et al., 2007). As suggested in Table 10.3, a needs assessment should be completed in order to complete a culturally responsive crisis plan. An example of such a needs assessment is provided in Form 10.1 at the end of the chapter.

Your response must be tailored to the needs of your school population. One suggestion is the use of "cultural brokers" (e.g., community leaders) from the impacted minority group(s) before, during, and in the aftermath of any crisis event (NASP, 2004). Additionally, community-based groups can create a helpful communication link with the cultural groups that they represent. To ensure an organized response, your team should establish relationships with entities such as civic associations/social clubs, neighborhood groups, faith-based organizations/interfaith groups, mutual aid societies/voluntary organizations, health care and social service providers, and nonprofit advocacy organizations (Athey & Moody-Williams, 2003).

PROFESSIONAL PERSPECTIVE: Scott Poland

Cultural Needs in Crisis Response

It is important that school crisis team members match the affected community regarding race, language, and understanding of culture as much as possible. One thing that we learned from the National Organization of Victim Assistance was the importance of selecting team members that would fit with the affected school community. This recommendation came to fruition when my colleague and fellow expert contributor, Frank Zenere, and I had the opportunity to serve on a team in Red Lake, Minnesota, after a shooting on a local Native American reservation.

What really helped our national team was NASP's offer to assist us in locating a Red Lake Chippewa who was a school psychologist. He was invaluable in helping us to understand the local native customs and the slow pace of life. It was very important to the tribal elders that our team understood and embraced the unique customs of the tribe and supported the community prayer circle. The ceremony included the burning of sage to symbolize prayers being carried to the spiritual maker. Team members were included in the smudging ceremony as a sign of our acceptance as helpers to the community. We learned that the close-knit community felt a shared responsibility for the shooting and viewed the student perpetrator as one of the victims. The tribal elders emphasized the impact of historical trauma on tribal members.

Following a crisis, care should be taken to provide services that are accessible, appropriate, and equitable. NASP has provided helpful tips to ensure that your team can achieve this goal. These strategies, along with other helpful ones that I have gained from experiences, are reviewed in the following section.

Tips for Providing Equitable Care (NASP, 2004)

- Adapt your approach to the varied needs of different cultures; do not use a one-size-fits-all method.
- Always communicate respect and goodwill by dressing appropriately, engaging in rituals, and demonstrating basic manners (i.e., saying please and thank you).
- Be aware of cultural social status and gender conventions. When possible, make attempts to match survivors to responders that their culture will respect.

- Assist survivors in beginning to cope with the impact of the crisis. Help them to reestablish their cultural rituals, customs, and social relationships.
- Explore the survivor's family system; obtain information about the hierarchical structure and dynamics of the person's home, family, and community.
- Ask survivors to try to articulate the type of help they need. Be direct and honest about what your capacity is to help them.
- Acknowledge your differences and limitations (e.g., misunderstandings about customs or language barriers).
- Make every effort to convey an open mind and a genuine interest in learning about the survivor's customs and rituals.
- Ask survivors if they have any specific cultural or religious beliefs that would aid in their coping. This might include going to a place of worship like a church, synagogue, or mosque.
- Refer survivors and their loved ones to the discussed culturally appropriate postcrisis resources.
- Ensure that all materials/information distributed in the aftermath are translated to the languages spoken by those in your school community.
- Organize culturally appropriate memorials and anniversary activities; offer information sheets about these events in order to increase the school community's understanding.
- Offer appropriate linguistic services (i.e., ensure that your responders speak the same language as the survivors).
    - When native speakers are unavailable, interpreters with basic knowledge of crisis response who are also trained to accurately convey the tone, level, and meaning of the information presented in the original language should be utilized (Athey & Moody-Williams, 2003).
    - All interpreters should be sensitive to confidentiality issues.
    - Do not utilize friends and loved ones as interpreters for the survivor.
- Interpersonally, all crisis responders should consider culturally specific communication techniques (e.g., use of eye contact, physical contact and physical proximity, nonverbal communication and expression, integration of food and drink in discussions, the pace of conversation, gender roles).
- Implement culturally sensitive interventions to increase coping in the aftermath, for example, group work, reduction of isolation, relaxation techniques, meditation, education about crisis in culturally relevant terms, and development of individual control.
- Monitor ongoing access to and engagement in needed services, such as therapy.
- Create specific strategies aimed to reach those who are not engaged, along with those whose traditions discourage help-seeking behaviors.

These guidelines and the information discussed in this section will help your team to increase your cultural awareness and competence and to ultimately provide culturally sensitive crisis responses to those in need. Cultural competence is an ever-evolving topic and one in which you will be an ongoing learner and student. Consistent curiosity, research, and conversations are critical parts of the process and will strengthen your practices in crisis intervention with diverse populations.

Recommended Resources

- **NASP's Cultural Competence Resources (2004):** NASP has a wealth of resources that can help you and your team to gain cultural competence in crisis work. Resources cover a number of topics (see below). Found at *www.nasponline.org/resources-and-publications/resources-and-podcasts/diversity-and-social-justice/cultural-competence/culturally-competent-crisis-response.*
    - **Disproportionality**
    - **Social Justice**
    - **LGBTQIA+**
    - **Multiculturalism**
- **SAMHSA's Cultural Competency Curriculum for Disaster Preparedness and Crisis Response:** A database of numerous websites related to diversity factors across the spectrum and their impact on crisis intervention. Found at *www.samhsa.gov/resource/dbhis/cultural-competency-curriculum-disaster-preparedness-crisis-response.*

STUDENTS WITH DISABILITIES

Disabilities are another important diversity factor that must be considered in your crisis planning and response. In the 2020–2021 school year, approximately 7.2 million U.S. students qualified for an eligibility under the Individuals with Disabilities Education Act (IDEA). Specific learning disability was the primary disorder among students. Other common eligibilities included speech impairments, autism, developmental delays, and other health impairments (often attention-deficit/hyperactivity disorder; NCES, 2022).

Students with disabilities have unique needs that can create challenges in the context of a crisis. Given the range of physical and learning disabilities, crisis response cannot be generalized; this population requires thoughtful consideration in order to meet the varied needs. Moreover, the common impairments observed across the spectrum of disabilities can put students at greater risk in a time of crisis (Boon et al., 2011). The nature of crises creates significant challenges for this population, particularly in cases in which the environment becomes unsafe. For example, crises that require swift evacuations can create special difficulties for students with physical disabilities. Unfortunately, the needs of students with disabilities are not often addressed in school safety plans; we strongly recommend that all crisis plans include thoughtful considerations about the needs of this population.

Crisis planning for the special needs population involves the same steps that have been outlined throughout this book, with the addition of increased attention to and concern for functional needs and specific access of one challenge or disability at a time. For example, a student with an intellectual disability will have different needs than a student who is wheelchair bound. It is recommended that your team approach the response planning by grouping needs into clusters. Be sure to consult with the Exceptional Student Education (ESE) department in order to obtain the best guidance for student needs.

Needs Assessment

Evaluating the strengths and needs of students with significant disabilities as they relate to staying safe in the event of a crisis must become part of the annual individualized education program (IEP) process. For students whose crisis-related skill levels are not commensurate with those of peers, a detailed plan for staying safe, teaching the skills to be safe, monitoring progress through instruction, and obtaining opportunities for practicing those skills must be developed and implemented in order to give students the best chance of survival in the event of a school crisis (Clarke, Embury, Jones, & Yssel, 2014).

One of the most important recommendations in crisis planning for students with disabilities is the creation of an individual emergency plan for each student in need. The title for this plan varies across the literature, ranging from Individual Emergency and Lockdown Procedure (Clarke et al., 2014) to Personal Emergency Plan (PEP; Schneider, 2019.) Regardless of the title, these plans are the best way to ensure that individual student needs are considered in the event of a crisis. The points to include in these plans are summarized in the sample plan reviewed in Form 10.2 at the end of the chapter.

Questions to Consider

As you develop a student's personal emergency plan and begin the crisis planning steps, there are important questions that you must consider about each student. The answers to these questions will give you direction on how to best plan for the needs and challenges this population will face in the event of a crisis. The following is a review of pertinent questions to ask yourself, along with helpful solutions to implement (Schneider, 2019).

1. *What is this student's expressive and receptive verbal ability?* Always be mindful of a student's communication abilities and needs. Can the student understand and follow directions? Can they ask for help? Utilize visual supports and assistive communication technology when appropriate. These needs should be included in the individual emergency plan, along with instructions on how to use any assistive technology devices.

2. *Does this student have impulse control issues?* The student's ability to maintain silence, remain calm, and stay in one place during a crisis is important in times of some crises. The provision of a fidget toy in these times can offer distraction and assist in keeping a student's hands and attention occupied. The use of a harness may be necessary in these moments, depending on elopement (i.e., runaway) concerns; however, this must be cleared with the caregivers and your school in advance and recorded in the student's IEP.

3. *Does this student have emotion-regulation concerns?* Many students with special needs have difficulty controlling their emotions, and this can be especially true under times of duress. Emotional outbursts may ensue, including screaming and physical aggression. Develop a list of coping tools that the student can use in times of distress. Collaborate with caregivers/families to generate ideas (e.g., hugging a soft stuffed animal, wearing noise-canceling headphones).

Restraints may be necessary in these instances, although their use is controversial in the ESE world. Restraints should only be used in circumstances in which it is approved by the district and caregivers, and only trained professionals should employ these approaches.

4. *What kind of sensory needs does this student have?* Many students with disabilities, particularly those with autism spectrum disorder, have a number of sensory sensitivities that can create maladaptive behaviors and reactions. In times of crisis, a variety of sensory experiences can occur, from the light and sound of emergency-responding sirens, to the sights and smells that come with natural disasters. Helpful aids to have available include ear and eye protection, advance warnings, reengineered sirens, or alarm devices that would use progressive amplification, taking 20 seconds or so to ramp up to full capacity.

5. *Does this student have physical disabilities or impaired usage of their arms, hands, legs, or torso?* Students may have physical limitations that require the use of aids such as a wheelchair or braces. Plan in advance for all evacuation routes in cases of limited mobility. Customize options for physical responding in times of crisis (e.g., alternatives to ducking under desks or crouching on the floor). Ensure that there are several people who are trained to meet the needs of medically fragile students (e.g., safe lifting procedures).

6. *Can the student cope with crowded halls or rooms?* Crowding can often happen in a crisis situation, and the excess stimulation can trigger disruptive behaviors in children with special needs. One option is to divide the class into various lockdown spots in the classroom (e.g., one group hides in a closet, one group hides behind a desk). The student's evacuation plan should include routes that will allow for the least amount of crowding.

7. *Does the student recognize police, firefighters, or medics as helpers?* Student understanding of emergency-responding personnel as helpers will create a smoother response in the aftermath. The presence of such professionals, like police and firefighters, can help to ease students' anxieties. You should coordinate educational opportunities for students in advance of crises wherein they can meet these types of emergency responders and learn about how they can help in times of need.

Specific Needs Considerations

While crisis preparedness should be individualized, it is also appropriate to utilize diagnostic groups and presentations to guide your planning. With all populations, it cannot be emphasized enough that you must *practice, practice, practice.* All individuals benefit from practicing crisis response drills, and it is particularly helpful for the special needs population, as it helps to mitigate fluency and cognitive deficits, increase predictability, and decrease worries and fears about the unknown. Table 10.4 highlights specific considerations for common special needs that are addressed in the school setting, along with recommendations for best practices in crisis intervention.

Another important part of crisis planning for students with disabilities is student preparedness. This population requires specific instruction in crisis prevention in advance of a crisis (Spooner, Knight, Browder, & Smith, 2012). Your team should disseminate information to teachers that they can use in their classes. Materials should be developmentally appropriate and should always include more images than text. Content should outline information about various crises and coping tools that students can use in the aftermath. Students should become familiar

TABLE 10.4. Disability-Specific Needs and Recommendations

Cognitive impairments/intellectual disabilities

These students may:

- Not understand the crises or their own reactions.
- Respond to traumatic events based more on their observations of adult and peer emotions rather than the verbal explanations they may receive.
- Engage in incongruent emotional expressions (e.g., laughing during a serious time).

Recommendations

- Discussions should be concise, specific, concrete, and developmentally appropriate.
- Visual aids will be helpful when communicating about the crisis.
- Emphasize safety.

Learning disabilities

These students may:

- Not require the supports/accommodation that other students with IEPs do; consider their level of emotional maturity and ability to understand the concepts discussed.
- Have difficulty processing language and applying abstract concepts.
- Be confused by what they see on television; they may have difficulty understanding what happened when, what is likely to happen next, etc.
- Have social difficulties.

Recommendations

- Choose your words with caution; use concrete language.
- Reinforce verbal explanations with visual materials; use maps to help them to understand where the crisis occurred.
- Provide instruction to students on anger control, tolerance of individual differences, and self-monitoring.

Autism spectrum disorder

These students may experience:

- Emotional outbursts and dysregulation
- Behavioral regressions and dysregulation
- Sensory integration issues
- Negative responses to environmental/routine changes
- Difficulty understanding the crisis
- Limited emotional expression and identification in others

Recommendations

- Maintain their routine as much as possible.
- Increase structure and provide clear expectations for behavior.
- Utilize visual aids in all forms of communication, including social narratives that provide a visual representation of what to expect in the case of a school crisis.
- Address sensory needs with headphones, eyewear, weighted blankets.
- Have ample reinforcers available that help to motivate positive behaviors.

(continued)

TABLE 10.4. *(continued)*

Emotional–behavioral disabilities

These students may experience:

- Severe stress reactions following a crisis.
- Limited coping skills.
- Exaggerated symptoms of withdrawal, agitation, feelings of worthlessness and despair, suicidal thinking.
- Increase in nervous behaviors such as thumb sucking, nail biting, and pacing.
- Behavioral issues, such as noncompliance and aggression.

Recommendations

- Incorporate clear and structured routines as soon as possible.
- Maintain any behavioral systems that are in place.
- Model coping tools that students can utilize in times of distress.
- Offer systematic instruction.
- Practice self-management skills.

Visual, hearing, and physical limitations

These students may experience:

- Fear related to their safety and mobility
- Increased fear reactions due to lack of understanding (e.g., a hearing-impaired student cannot hear instructions about the crisis)
- Mobility and physical flexibility concerns
- Vision-impaired: these students cannot pick up on visual cues, such as facial expressions
- Hearing impaired: these students will typically be unable to keep up with the pace of urgent conversations

Recommendations

- Ensure that you convey that the students will be safe; provide reassurance when necessary.
- Use verbal cues to reinforce what you are feeling and seeing. Students may need a verbal description to reinforce what they have heard about the events.
- Ask questions to clarify that the student understands what has happened.
- Be aware of the frustrations that can come with a student's inability to understand.
- Be mindful of the language you use; be very concrete.
- Use visual aids paired with any verbal or signed explanations.
- Provide opportunities in advance for students to explore the facility when it is not in lockdown mode.
- Incorporate braille signage or audible directorial signage.

Sources: Based on Clark et al. (2014); NASP (2002).

with the sounds and sights associated with emergencies (e.g., emergency responders, sirens, flashing lights). Teachers are encouraged to engage students in small-group instruction when reviewing content.

Additionally, each classroom should be equipped with emergency kits that include materials students might need (e.g., medical equipment) and coping tools (e.g., fidget toys). Visual aids should be present, including picture schedules and social narratives. Other items to include are emergency related, such as a flashlight, walkie-talkie, and batteries. These recommendations will help your school to prepare this population for potential crises and will aid in ensuring that your interventions are sensitive to their unique needs. Thoughtful planning and consideration are an imperative part of crisis planning for this population and must be done well in advance of any potential crisis occurrence. The recommendations discussed in this section should be implemented to ensure that your team is using best practices to meet the needs of students with disabilities.

Recommended Resources

- **CDC's Safety Plan Considerations (2024):** Guidelines on how to implement best practices for maintaining safe environments and security for children with disabilities. Includes a number of additional helpful resources. Found at *www.cdc.gov/ncbddd/disabilityandsafety/emergency.html.*
- **NASP's Coping with Crisis—Helping Children with Special Needs (2002):** Guidance on how to best support students with special needs to cope with crisis situations. Found at *www.gcsnc.com/cms/lib/NC01910393/Centricity/Domain/2433/NASP%20-%20Helping%20Children%20with%20Special%20Needs%20Cope%20After%20a%20Crisis.pdf.*
- **NASP's Natural Disasters and Relocated Students with Special Needs (2015b):** Guidance on how to best support students with special needs who have experienced a natural disaster and subsequent relocation. Found *at www.nasponline.org/resources-and-publications/resources-and-podcasts/school-safety-and-crisis/natural-disaster-resources/natural-disasters-and-relocated-students-with-special-needs.*

DEIB is a critical mission that must be incorporated in your crisis planning. Your team's approach to prevention and intervention should be completed with the DEIB tenets in mind so as to follow best practices and avoid any unintended consequences, such as doing more harm. This chapter has covered primary areas of consideration that will aid in incorporating DEIB at your school. However, given the ever-evolving nature of our society and its citizens, it is imperative that you and your school staff make continued efforts to stay informed and updated with the ongoing needs of your individual school community.

FORM 10.1

Needs Assessment Questions for Culturally Responsive Crisis Planning

Instructions for use: Utilize the following tool to assess the cultural needs of your school community. The U.S. Census Bureau provides much of the community information by searching specific zip codes (see *www.data.census.gov*). Record the answers below and utilize the findings to compose a culturally responsive crisis plan. Approximate population data for each category can be recorded as a number (e.g., Ages: 20–30 years old: 1,000 individuals) or as a percentage of the total population of your community/school (e.g., Ethnicities: Latino: 35% of total population).

What are the demographics of my school community?

- Ages: ____________________
- Races: ____________________
- Ethnicities: ____________________
- Languages spoken: ____________________
- Religious identifications:____________________
- Socio-economic statuses: ____________________

What are the demographics of my school?

- Ages: ____________________
- Races: ____________________
- Ethnicities: ____________________
- Languages spoken: ____________________
- Religious identifications:____________________
- Affectional orientation identifications: ____________________
- Religious identifications: ____________________

Additional Questions to Consider

- What type of cultural needs at our school may arise in the event of a crisis?

  ____

  ____

- Are there students who identify as refugees and/or immigrants? **Y/N** If yes, include details regarding demographics and any additional specific needs.

  ____

(continued)

- Have there been any significant historical community events to consider (e.g., violent events, racial/ethnic conflict, acts of terror)? **Y/N**

  ____

  ____

- Do we have staff members who can meet all of the linguistic needs of our students and their family/caregivers? **Y/N** If yes, list staff members who have been identified as willing to assist in translating in the event of a crisis. If no, list the name/contact of translators in the community that can be used.

  ____

  ____

  ____

- Do we have relationships with appropriate religious leaders as matched to the religious identifications at our school? **Y/N** If yes, list the names and contacts. If no, list potential names and contacts and reach out to establish relationships.

  ____

  ____

- Do we have relationships with culturally sensitive resources that are well matched to our school community makeup (e.g., community resource centers)? **Y/N** If yes, include a list of relevant options. If no, develop a list to record here.

  ____

- Do we have relationships established with culturally sensitive mental health professionals in the community? **Y/N** If yes, list the providers. If no, research appropriate providers and begin to establish relationships.

  ____

FORM 10.2

Personal Emergency Plan

Instructions for use: The following plan should be completed for all students with a disability in advance of a crisis. Record the information in the lines provided and save it on file with easy accessibility.

- Student information (age, grade, disability eligibility category)

____

____

____

- Parent/caregiver contact information

____

____

____

- Additional emergency contact (e.g., friends, relatives) in the event that the parents/caregivers are not available

____

____

____

- Communication needs

____

____

____

- Sensory needs

____

____

____

- Medical needs, including medicine and equipment (e.g., epi-pen, wheelchair) and instructions on how to use them

____

____

____

(continued)

- Medical aid (e.g., student therapists, doctors)

____

____

____

- Support people in the student's life (e.g., school aides or staff members, school friends); it is beneficial to have a list of options for supports to utilize

____

____

____

- Student strengths, challenges, and current needs and accommodations

____

____

CHAPTER 11

Ethical and Legal Issues

In the immediate aftermath of school crises, legal considerations are often the last thing on the minds of those intervening. However, all school crises create the very real potential for a slew of legal issues targeted at the school and even worse, directly at *you*. A review of relevant legal cases brings to light that at times, ethical violations on behalf of school personnel have created the potential for culpability on behalf of the school. A review of ethical considerations and the related legal implications is critical, as it can not only help to prevent future crises, but it can also mitigate the risks of your legal responsibility. Schools almost always do things right in a crisis, but a few schools have made mistakes, and we need to learn prevention lessons from those errors.

When reading through this chapter, it is important to keep in mind that we are not attorneys or legal experts and that we cannot provide legal advice. While aspects of cases will be discussed, the related discussions will consist of our opinions on the matters and should not be considered as facts. The opinions expressed throughout the chapter are based on my four decades of working in the field of school crisis and my related involvement in a variety of legal cases. These perspectives are first and foremost provided to help prevent further tragedies, and also to reduce potential liability issues for school personnel. Additionally, it is important to note that many of the cases discussed have been settled out of court. This outcome does not necessarily mean a win for either side; it simply means that the matter was settled outside of court.

ETHICAL CONSIDERATIONS

While it is important for all school personnel to be familiar with their ethical duties, SMHPs who engage in crisis intervention should be *especially* knowledgeable. Their violations of ethics can mean the difference between life and death in a school crisis and, in the legal context, guilty or not. Next you will find a review of ethical considerations in the context of crisis intervention.

Competence

- Being a competent SMHP requires you to have up-to-date knowledge on the risk factors and warning signs of suicide, along with threat assessment procedures.
- SMHPs should engage in regular prevention and intervention training to ensure they are competent in the domains addressed in crisis intervention.
  - Trainings are often not required by school districts but, rather, "recommended"; we *implore* all school personnel to engage in crisis prevention and intervention training, particularly in the areas of suicide and threat assessment.

Do No Harm

SMHPs should make every effort to provide services in their crisis prevention, intervention, and postvention efforts to act appropriately and, in the very least, do no harm in their practices.

Confidentiality

- SMHPs should make efforts to maintain confidentiality. The exceptions to these are suicidal/homicidal ideation and threats of violence toward a specific party. If you suspect any of these, it is imperative that you share this information with their caregivers and other relevant school personnel.
- Remember, the student told you this information because, ultimately, they knew you could help.
- Your school should implement specific guidelines for how you will address student suicidal ideation and violent behavior/threats.

Providing Appropriate Postvention Response

- SMHPs should follow the postvention guidelines outlined in Chapters 4–7.
  - Sadly, these guidelines are not implemented in every school, and we believe it is a number one priority for *all* schools.
- You will need to be on alert to suicidal behavior and traumatic reactions in the postvention processes. All students need assistance in processing their emotions after a crisis.

Ethical violations can result in myriad disciplinary measures. Not only could one result in punishment at your workplace, but it could also result in issues with your school board and district, along with your state licensing board. Moreover, serious ethical violations, such as failure to provide appropriate responses to those in need, can result in grave legal implications. In fact, you may become the target for lawsuits that can leave you vulnerable to legal culpability for crises at your school. *Mares v. Shawnee Mission School District* (2007) is an example of this very issue. This case, along with a number of other relevant legal cases (some of which I have participated in), is discussed in the remainder of this chapter. The hope is that a brief review of these cases will aid in your understanding of your legal responsibilities in crisis intervention and the potential legal implications that come with our profession and, most importantly, help to save a life.

Case Review: *Mares v. Shawnee Mission School District* (2007)

Mares v. Shawnee Mission School District (2007) is a tragic case involving the suicides of two siblings, Jason Mares, age 16, followed by his older brother, Justin Mares, age 18. Both brothers attended the same school. In 2006, a state court ordered the Shawnee Mission School District in Johnson County, Kansas, to stand trial for alleged staff negligence in response to Justin's, the surviving sibling's, needs. Mrs. Mares claimed that the school district did not enact appropriate suicide postvention procedures in the aftermath of Jason's death, resulting in Justin's subsequent suicide. She believed that the implementation of these services would have reduced Justin's risk of future suicide, as he was struggling with the loss of his younger brother. Mrs. Mares attested that in the aftermath of Jason's suicide, she and her family made efforts to connect with Justin's high school principal, to no avail. The school maintained that they were not at fault, as the suicide occurred off campus and that Justin's parents were in the better position to attend to his emotional needs. Ultimately, the case was not pursued in a jury trial and was settled outside of court for an undisclosed amount.

Mrs. Mares's reported lack of postvention services provided raises serious concerns. Only if the case had gone to trial could it be concluded that Mrs. Mares's claims about the school's inappropriate response had been verified and signal potential ethical violations on behalf of the school personnel. In this instance, the appropriate response (based on what was alleged) would have been for Justin's principal and SMHP to make contact with the Mares family to offer their support. Moreover, Justin should have been immediately connected to therapeutic services and suicide prevention programs implemented in the school. While we can't say for certain what the impact would have been, it is hard not to wonder how Justin's grieving process would have differed had he been provided mental health support.

LEGAL ISSUES IN CRISIS INTERVENTION

The following sections review important legal issues related to suicide and school violence, including helpful case reviews and professional reflections. I have had the opportunity to participate in a number of relevant cases, offering my expertise to both plaintiffs and defendants. Additionally, significant legislative responses that have occurred in response to school crises are reviewed.

Suicide

Suicide in the school context can open the door to a myriad of legal concerns regarding the potential liability of the school and district staff, particularly the administrators. Up until the early 1990s, U.S. courts consistently exonerated schools from issues of liability in the aftermath of a student suicide. However, an important ruling in a 1991 appellate case, *Eisel v. Board of Education of Montgomery County*, set a new precedent on this matter.

Case Review: *Eisel v. Board of Education of Montgomery County* (1991)

Nicole Eisel, a 13-year-old middle schooler, died by suicide after making a murder–suicide pact with a peer. Nicole's father sued the school district and two of its school counselors, claiming that they were notified of this pact by Nicole's classmates and that the school failed to report this to the student's parents. He argued that the special relationship the SMHPs had with his daughter placed a duty upon them to share her reported suicidal ideation with her parents. Initially, the lower court ruled that the school had no liability; however, the Maryland Supreme Court reversed this ruling and stated that because the counselors had the potential to successfully intervene, the child's death was foreseeable.

"Foreseeability of harm" (i.e., a reasonable individual could recognize that a student was in an acute emotional state of distress and in danger of suicide) was listed as the most salient factor in determining the school's liability (*Eisel v. Board of Education of Montgomery County*, 1991; Friedlander, 2013). The Maryland Supreme Court held that the state's Suicide Prevention School Programs Act, the school's own suicide prevention policy, and the relationship between school, counselors, and youth created a duty on the counselors' parts to use "reasonable means to attempt to prevent a suicide when they are on notice of a child or adolescent student's suicidal intent" (*Eisel v. Board of Education of Montgomery County*, 1991), including, at a minimum, a report to the student's parents.

While this ruling set a precedent regarding the school's liability, it was not absolute. In fact, 6 years later, the same school district utilized the ruling in their favor, aiding in the exoneration of their liability in a student's suicide. In *Scott v. Montgomery County Board of Education* (1997), a federal appellate court upheld the dismissal of the lawsuit brought on by the mother of a middle school student who had hanged himself. The mother claimed a causal link between her child's suicide and the school psychologist's meeting with him that occurred 2 months prior to his death. The school psychologist indicated that the student was not in distress and did not present an immediate danger to himself or others; therefore, he was not obligated to notify the student's parents. The court dismissed the mother's claims of negligence as educational malpractice and ruled that the facts of the case were not sufficient to claim fault on the school's part (*Scott v. Montgomery County Board of Education*, 1997; Stone & Zierkel, 2012).

Over time, caregivers/families have continued to fight an uphill battle in liability against their school districts, and the courts commonly continue to dismiss school liability in cases of student suicides. The only exceptions are the suits in which there was a clear failure on the school's behalf to notify the caregivers of the potential risk (Stone, 2017). Among these cases, claims of negligence that are grounded in "statutory, regulatory, or district policy for suicidal threats and suicide prevention" (Friedlander, 2013) are most promising to plaintiffs. *Negligence* is a breach of duty owed to an individual involving injury or damage (i.e., suicide) that finds a causal link between a lack of or an absence of duty to care for the student and their suicide (Stone, 2017).

Given that the majority of legal cases have involved failure to notify caregivers when there was a reason to suspect their child was suicidal, one of the primary issues that is considered is the distinction between a *discretionary duty* and a *ministerial duty* for school staff. A discretionary duty allows school personnel, such as SMHPs, to utilize their judgment to make a decision about what to do if a student is suspected of being suicidal. These decisions range from intervention approaches to supervision needs, to administrative and/or caregiver notification.

A ministerial duty, on the other hand, does not give SMHPs any discretionary action in these cases and requires the professional to notify the caregivers in all cases.

Courts must primarily consider whether a student's death by suicide was a direct result of an inadequate response from the school. This decision is complex given the numerous psychosocial risk factors that are associated with youth suicide (e.g., mental health, adverse childhood experiences). As a result, it is quite difficult to narrow down the one causal factor in a child's suicide and thereby a slim chance for a successful outcome for caregivers. Additionally, there are a number of other factors that impact caregivers' chances of successful court outcomes, including the lack of resources, that is, financial means, the lengthy trial periods, and limited evidentiary documentation. For example, bullying is commonly cited as a causal link to a youth's suicide; however, caregivers are often without the necessary documentation to prove that they previously shared their concerns with the school (Friedlander. 2013). More on that later in this chapter.

While it is rare, there are cases in which parents as the plaintiffs have received outcomes in their favor. For example, an appellate court in *Wyke v. Polk County School Board* (1995) reversed the lower court's decision that the school board was not liable for the death of 13-year-old Shawn Wyke. I had the opportunity to participate in this case on the side of the plaintiff.

Case Review: *Wyke v. Polk County School Board* (1995)

> I remember waiting to testify in this case for the plaintiff, and Carole Wyke, the mom of the victim, left the courtroom after she broke down during her testimony. I was asked to help her, and I told her that she had waited 7 years to tell her story and emphasized she could do it.
>
> —SCOTT POLAND

Shawn Wyke was a 13-year-old middle schooler who hanged himself at his home. After his suicide, his family learned that his death occurred two days after two failed attempts were made at school. His mother, Carol Wyke, sued the school district, claiming that the school was liable for her child's suicide. In court, her legal team utilized the "failure to train theory," arguing that the lack of suicide prevention/intervention training for the school personnel demonstrated a direct indifference to their duty to care and protect (Erbacher et al., 2023; *Wyke v. Polk County School Board*, 1995).

The court considered factors of negligence and foreseeability. The jury learned that the school was "somewhat aware" of the attempts that Shawn had made on campus, and they reportedly did not implement any crisis intervention steps, nor did they notify his parents. The court found the school culpable based on their negligence (i.e., lack of intervention and failure to notify) and confirmed foreseeability (i.e., given the prior attempts, Shawn's death was reasonably predictable; Erbacher et al., 2023; Friedlander, 2013; *Wyke v. Polk County School Board*, 1995).

In addition to negligence and foreseeability, *state-created danger* is another legal consideration in the context of school suicide cases. The argument is that schools have the legal responsibility to protect those in their care based on the constitutional rights of the victims. If the school does not implement the appropriate safety policies and procedures, then they could be found at fault for causing danger to the student who died by suicide (Erbacher et al., 2023). It is difficult to successfully argue state-created danger, as plaintiffs must prove four specific factors:

1. The harm that took place (e.g., the student's suicide) was foreseeable and somewhat direct
2. A state entity acted with a degree of culpability that shocks the conscience
3. A relationship between the state and the plaintiff existed such that the plaintiff was a foreseeable victim of the defendant's acts, or a member of a discrete class of persons subjected to the potential harm brought about by the state's actions, as opposed to a member of the public in general; and
4. A state actor affirmatively used his or her authority in a way that created a danger to the citizen or that rendered the citizen more vulnerable to danger than had the state not acted at all (*Sanford v. Stiles*, 2006)

Case Review: *Sanford v. Stiles* (2006)

Michael Sanford was a 16-year-old high schooler who died by suicide in his home in Emmaus, Pennsylvania. An investigation after his death revealed that Michael's guidance counselor, Ms. Pamela Stiles, was reportedly alerted to concerns about Michael's mental health. It was reported that Michael had written a note that included suicidal threats to a fellow peer. This peer became concerned and shared the note with the guidance office. Ms. Stiles immediately met with Michael and completed a risk assessment; Michael denied any suicidal ideation, plans, or intent, including threats of suicide and self-harm. Approximately 1 week later, Michael hanged himself at his home. His mother, Kathleen Sanford, sued the school district under the "state acted danger theory" and claimed that Ms. Stiles was individually culpable of negligence. Ultimately, the District Court determined that the plaintiff's claims did not uphold against the four required factors of state-created danger, and the school could not be held liable. Moreover, they cited that the school was immune from culpability due to their status as a sovereign agent, in which the government offers protection from legal responsibility (*Sanford v. Stiles*, 2006).

The outcome in *Sanford v. Stiles* brings us to another important legal term in the realm of liability: *sovereign immunity*. This is a concept that offers government agencies protection from liability, schools included. Put simply, sovereign immunity means that school districts and their employees cannot be sued. There are exceptions to this, however, and sovereign immunity is waived in which there is clear evidence of negligence. Immunity is also granted to school districts because they are not held liable for any unconstitutional actions of their personnel. Unless the court finds that the school board or administration did not enact or enacted failed policies and procedures (ministerial duty) that violate their duty to protect (state-created danger), or a special relationship existed, their immunity will be upheld for any wrongful actions on behalf of their school personnel (Erbacher et al., 2023). A more recent case, *Gallagher v. Bader* (2016), is an example of this very potential for SMHPs.

Case Review: *Gallagher v. Richard Bader* (2016)

Jay Gallagher, an 18-year-old student in the Loudoun School District in Virginia, died by suicide in early 2016. In the aftermath of his suicide, his parents alleged that Jay's school counselor, Richard Bader, had been aware of Jay's suicidal ideation in the weeks leading up to his death. Postcrisis investigations revealed that Mr. Bader was notified by one of Jay's friends that Jay was expressing suicidal thoughts and experiencing difficulties with his familial relationships. Mr. Bader reportedly followed up with Jay in a face-to-face meeting, during which Jay reportedly denied being suicidal and implored Mr. Bader to not contact his parents. Mr. Bader decided not to notify Jay's parents given the fact that Jay was 18 and that he was so adamant about his privacy.

Three weeks later, Jay died by suicide at home. Jay's parents sued Mr. Bader for $5 million over the allegations that he had failed to notify them of the risk concerns. However, during pretrial motions, the judge ruled that Mr. Bader was allowed to use his discretion (i.e., training and expertise) in how to approach the concern. Moreover, Virginia law only requires parental notification when the harm is imminent. Given the length of time that occurred between Mr. Bader and Jay's meeting and Jay's suicide, the court indicated that there was nothing to suggest an imminent risk that would require immediate intervention. In 2018, Jay's parents withdrew their suit, and the matter was soon after settled outside of court (*Gallagher v. Bader*, 2016).

I was on the side of the plaintiff in the case and noted that the district policy gave no exception for age with regard to parent notification and required SMHPs to notify the building principal when a student is at risk for suicide, which Mr. Bader did not do. The district policy also stressed the importance of taking a peer report that a friend is suicidal very seriously. I felt strongly that Jay's parents should have been contacted and stated, "Your son denied being suicidal but there were concerns expressed by peers that he is suicidal." I also emphasized that suicidal students often deny being suicidal to escape scrutiny and the increased supervision that they know will follow if they admit to suicidal behavior.

Lastly, many attorneys use the "intervening-force" argument to defend the school and its personnel. This theory treats suicide as a superseding and intervening force that disconnects the direct connection between the school's actions, for example, failure to notify caregivers, and the student's suicide. The suicide is therefore caused by the intervening force, rather than the school's possible negligence. This is especially the case in instances in which time has passed between the school's intervention (or lack thereof) and the student's death.

My experience in these cases has taught me that few cases make it to a jury trial. What typically occurs is an out-of-court settlement, in which the school districts' insurance companies opt for a less costly and less public route when compared to all that comes with litigation. Additionally, school districts are often concerned about the potential negative publicity and the stigma associated with lawsuits. Despite this, it should not leave with you the sense that you do not have to worry about the potential legal implications of crisis intervention and suicide. Involvement in any legal battles is complicated, stressful, and costly, although it is something you can attempt to mitigate with your use of best practice.

Bullying and Suicide

> The strong association between bullying and suicide means that when school staff are aware that a student is the victim of bullying, they should not hesitate to ask the student about thoughts of hopelessness and suicide.
>
> —SCOTT POLAND

As discussed in Chapter 5, bullying has been found to be a risk factor for youth suicide, among other serious mental health implications. Given its widespread existence across schools and the associated mental health consequences, many legal suits have been brought against the district and school personnel based on the fact that bullying occurred on school grounds and that its implications are linked to their child's suicide. The school's failure to prevent/intervene in bullying situations has been cited in a number of legal cases.

These cases continue to be unsuccessful, as parents are typically unable to provide evidence of their notifications to the school about their concerns. Issues in these lawsuits have focused on "*in loco parentis*" (to act in place of parents) and whether or not a *special relationship* exists between schools. A special relationship is a legal term that classifies a relationship in which a state entity (i.e., a public school) is required to protect individuals from harm at the hands of private actors. While this may make sense in theory, a special relationship is difficult to prove outside of entities such as foster care, prisons, or involuntary commitment at a state hospital (*DeShaney v. Winnebego County Wisconsin Department of Social Services*, 1989). To date, no court has ruled a school district as liable for student suicide related to the school's failure to intervene to stop bullying; there have only been cases that were settled outside of court.

Case Review: *Witsell et al. v. School Board of Hillsborough County* (2011)

Hope Witsell, a 13-year-old middle schooler, died by suicide at her home in Ruskin, Florida, in 2009. In the aftermath, it was reported that her sister discovered that she had been the victim of intense cyberbullying and harassment at the hands of her peers following the leak of nude photos of herself that she had sent to another student. The photos were circulated throughout Hope's middle school without her permission. Hope's parents alleged that the school social worker met with Hope after a teacher noticed "shallow cuts" on Hope's thigh. During the meeting, the social worker reportedly had Hope sign a "no-suicide contract." The social worker allegedly did not notify any other staff members or Hope's parents about the self-harm concerns. Hope's mother reportedly only learned of the "no suicide contract" after finding it in her bedroom trashcan after her death.

Hope's parents sued the school board under the claim of negligence. I consulted on the case with the Hillsborough County Schools, and my advice was to settle out of court and ensure that no other mental health professionals fail to seek supervision and fail to notify parents of their child being at risk for suicide. I was surprised by the fact that the plaintiff's attorney did not ask for documentation that the social worker was trained in parent notification procedures. I further stressed that written safety plans need to be developed jointly with suicidal students and that "no-suicide contracts" have been criticized because they only focus on what not to do instead of how to keep safe. The school board argued that it was not responsible for an employee who did not follow policy for parent notification. Ultimately, the case was dismissed by the court (*Witsell et al. v. School Board of Hillsborough County*, 2011).

This case, among others, typically calls into question the training that is provided to faculty and staff on bullying and suicide prevention, the policies developed and implemented at school, and the thoroughness of documentation by schools. While schools should not have to pay millions of dollars to grieving parents, there have been a few unfortunate instances in which schools could have been better prepared or intervened more appropriately. As discussed in Chapter 5, it is imperative that schools take the necessary steps to increase their knowledge and implement bullying and suicide prevention programs.

The cases discussed also highlight the very real potential for a SMHP to be left on their own to defend themselves. As reviewed, school districts may claim that they are not responsible for your actions, leaving you as the sole person to fight a suit. This is why it is recommended that all SMHPs carry their own personal liability insurance to ensure that they are well covered in the rare event that legal involvement comes to a head. Should your district offer a union, you can inquire regarding what kind of coverage is provided; however, in my experience, many districts do not have unions and those that do typically focus on teachers rather than SMHPs. Additionally, it is important to reemphasize that SMHPs should always seek supervision and collaboration when intervening in a crisis.

School Suicide Legislation

The major legal implications of youth suicide in the school context certainly justify the need for state laws and mandates targeted at suicide prevention and intervention in the school setting. In the past, districtwide suicide prevention efforts oftentimes only occurred after a tragic student death. Currently, a large number of states require some type of suicide prevention training for their school personnel. However, the programming, efforts, and quality vary state by state (Kreuze, Stecker, & Ruggiero, 2017; Singer et al., 2018). AFSP (2019) reviewed current state laws in the United States, finding varied policies and procedures related to prevention programming. To date, 11 states require mandated annual training; moreover, 20 states (40%) also require mandated training, but without the yearly contingency. Many states without mandated training are making efforts to encourage training throughout school districts; furthermore, many require the provision of suicide prevention and intervention policies and procedures (AFSP, 2019).

Outside of training, legislative responses are typically centered around firearms (see the "Violent Crises and Their Legal Implications" section below for more information), increased prevention/intervention programs in school communities, and support and funding for mental health needs. It is recommended that SMHPs do their best to keep up with legislative changes and requirements in your states. Table 11.1 summarizes some of the key legislative responses that have impacted suicide in the school context.

Lobbyists and advocates for these kinds of legislation report frustrations in their continued efforts, particularly regarding the language used in the adoption of policies and procedures. One critique, for example, are states' usage of the word *recommended* instead of *required* in suicide training for schools (Lieberman & Poland, 2017). Nevertheless, ongoing pursuits for mandated prevention programming and training and increased mental health support are imperative, as they have been demonstrated as significant lifesaving and life-changing legislation.

VIOLENT CRISES AND THEIR LEGAL IMPLICATIONS

School crises that involve violence are subject to similar legal considerations as those associated with a student suicide (e.g., caregiver notification). On the other hand, given the nature of violent crises (i.e., potential for large-scale deaths/injuries), there are unique legal implications that must be considered. Liability continues to be the overarching concern, although the defendants of these cases vary. For example, presently, the family members of the victims from the Sandy Hook Elementary shooting have brought suit against the Remington Arms Company (Altimari,

TABLE 11.1. Significant Suicide-Related Legislation

Garrett Lee Smith Memorial Act (2004)

- First bill signed into law pertaining to suicide prevention among U.S. youth.
- Affirmed suicide as national public health problem.
- Goal is to provide funding to states, tribes, campuses, and behavioral mental health services for grants that support prevention and intervention efforts.
- More detailed information about this bill can be found at *www.congress.gov/bill/108th-congress/senate-bill/2634* (Dodd, 2004).

Jason Flatt Act (2007)

- Passed in the state of Tennessee.
- Requires all educators in the state to complete 2 hours of youth suicide awareness and prevention training each year in order to be able to be licensed to teach.
- Tennessee legislation now serves as the model to introduce the Jason Flatt Act (2007) in other states.
- Founded by the Jason Foundation, a nonprofit agency dedicated to bringing suicide prevention awareness and education to schools.
- To date, 20 states have adopted the act (although each state's requirements vary [AFPS, 2019]) and have been supported by the state's Department of Education and the state's Teacher's Association (Jason Foundation Inc., 2019).
- More information can be found on the Jason Foundation website at *https://jasonfoundation.com*

Suicide Training and Awareness Nationally Delivered for Universal Prevention Act of 2021 (STANDUP Act; 2021)

- Designed to encourage states and tribes to implement and expand evidence-based suicide prevention training in schools.
- The U.S. House and Senate voted unanimously to pass the STANDUP Act and it was recently signed into law.
- Requires that when the Department of Health and Human Services (HHS) awards grants that support mental health needs, they must give preference to state, tribal, and local educational agencies that plan to implement evidence-based suicide awareness and prevention training policies. HHS may also consider suicide rates in the applicable jurisdiction and other factors when awarding the grants.
- HHS must also collaborate with the Department of Education and the Department of the Interior to provide educational agencies with best practices for these training policies (STANDUP Act of 2021, H.R. 586 / S.1543).
- More information about the STANDUP Act can be found on the Sandy Hook Promise (n.d.) website at *https://actionfund.sandyhookpromise.org/issues/mental-health-and-wellness/prevent-youth-suicide/*

2019). They have alleged that the gun company manufactured a weapon that is too dangerous for civilian use, and then glorified its use via aggressive marketing. They claim that this type of marketing is aimed to draw in individuals such as the 20-year-old Sandy Hook shooter, Adam Lanza (Owens, 2019). Just recently, Remington Arms settled out of court for $73 million (Graziano & Wamsley, 2022). Additional relevant liability issues in this context are discussed further here.

Parental/Caregiver Notification

Parental/caregiver notification has been commonly cited in relevant legal cases, including the school's failure to notify caregivers of their child's violent threats or even the provision of crisis intervention services when a need arises. These cases highlight ethical violations that must be avoided. They also raise the concern regarding a SMHP's ability to use their clinical judgment and discretion safely to provide services without the potential risk for legal action in the aftermath. This could be very dangerous for our practice, as it will limit our ability to provide necessary help in a time of an emergency.

The concept of parental/caregiver notification has become increasingly complicated in the last several years, particularly in the context of student privacy in the LGBTQIA+ community. School disclosure of gender identifications and affectional orientations to parents and/or caregivers has become hotly debated in states across the nation. Since 2020, a growing number of states have proposed legislation (some of which have become laws) that require school employees to "out" LGBTQIA+ youth to their parents/caregivers, regardless of the potential consequences that may come (e.g., familial rejection [Movement Advancement Project, 2024]). While the legislation targets LBGTQIA+ youth broadly, much of the laws focus heavily on students who identify as transgender. In response to the concerns for safety of LBGTQIA+ students, the American Civil Liberties Union (2020) published an open letter to school administrators that documented why they believe it is unconstitutional for public schools to disclose such information to parents/caregivers without student permission. Despite this, to date, there are five states that mandate the outing of transgender youth and many others that reportedly promote, though do not require, forced outing (Movement Advancement Project, 2024).

Such issues have made the SMHP's role more complex, bringing new ethical concerns to light and requiring additional thoughtfulness and education. It is recommended that SMHPs ensure that they maintain a current understanding of the laws and regulations of their states, especially given the ever-evolving nature of the ongoing legislation. Furthermore, SMHPs are encouraged to participate in annual training that can equip them with the knowledge and skills to best provide gender-affirming care to students in need. The topic of parental/caregiver notification comes with complicated factors; however, it is important to understand that in the context of risk (e.g., self-harm and suicidality), parental/caregiver notification is critical. The safety of students is the number one priority, and it is imperative that parents/caregivers are informed when there are risk concerns present.

Case Review: *Choquette v. Onsted Community Schools* (2005)

In 2005, 6-year-old Katie Choquette of Onsted, Michigan, reportedly bore witness to the aftermath of a death-by-hanging of a 14-year-old girl. Katie, along with 17 other students, first through sixth grade, were riding the school bus home and witnessed the tragic scene. The following day, the school responded by requiring that all students from the bus attend a group informational/counseling session to process the event. Katie's parents, Judith and Timothy Choquette, claimed that it wasn't until this meeting that their daughter began to understand what she had witnessed and subsequently became traumatized. Moreover, they shared that parental permission was not obtained prior to the meeting and that Katie's teacher had promised not to discuss the suicide unless Katie had brought it up. The Choquettes decided to sue the school, alleging negligence by Katie's teacher and the principal and violation of their civil rights. Ultimately, the court ruled in favor of the school, acknowledging that they did not notify the parents, while affirming their decision to follow protocol of crisis intervention planned by the school psychologist, school counselor, and principal. (*Choquette v. Onsted Community Schools*, 2005).

PROFESSIONAL PERSPECTIVE: SCOTT POLAND

I was on the side of the school in the *Choquette* case, and my perspective is from the work that I completed on this case. I thought that the school was not liable for the claims that Katie's parents alleged. While working on the case, I thought about the potential implications of mandating parental notification prior to crisis intervention. Not only would it be a delay in providing necessary services in an emergency situation, but it could also lead to a general reluctancy for schools to initially involve SMHPs in crises. Given the potential legal responsibility, school administrators may decide to modify their practices and start going to the parents first. The SMHPs that provided the intervention that Katie participated in were well trained in crisis intervention and used best practices. I am a big believer in telling children the truth in developmentally appropriate language. Katie was not identified as having significant problems in the immediate aftermath; those developed much later and, from my perspective, may have been influenced by her parents.

In recent times, there has been a greater emphasis of parental rights in the school context. This is leading many of us in the field to wonder: Will we have to start calling a parent prior to providing crisis intervention services (e.g., a student's teacher dies)? When a crisis presents, I have always gotten involved in helping students first and informing parents later, in a matter-of-fact way. I think of the situation as an emergency and there is a very real need to provide immediate assistance. The quicker those affected get help and know that they are not alone with their reactions, the better the outcome. This need dispenses the requirement for parent permission to work with their child. There is a strong movement toward increasing parent rights in this area in Florida, particularly with groups who seek to target any potential infringements on civil liberties. These movements may prompt schools to think that they need to ask parents before they screen for suicide or help students who are exposed to a tragedy. I hope this won't become the case, but it may be something that SMHPs should discuss with administrators and follow guidelines from their respective professional associations.

School Liability

The issue of liability is typically argued in civil court proceedings; however, in the case of violent crises, criminal court proceedings may occur (e.g., prosecuting a school shooter). Liability issues are generally matters of state law, which is an important consideration given the varied statues across states that create the potential for special duties. School liability cases in this context often utilize the discussed argument of sovereign immunity. Moreover, much like the suits associated with student death by suicide, plaintiff success is difficult to achieve, and most cases are resolved outside of court. The issue of school liability is extremely complex and my involvement in relevant cases has made me acutely aware of the legal risks in this context. While some cases have been clearer in terms of culpability, there are others where the jury's decision was the opposite of my opinions.

Case Review: *Lutz v. Snohomish School District* (2014)

On October 25, 2011, 14-year-old April Lutz and her same-aged friend were reportedly brutally attacked by a female schoolmate at Snohomish High School in Seattle, Washington. The perpetrator, K, who reportedly did not know the victims, stabbed the girls multiple times with a butcher knife stolen from a home. April sustained significant injuries and was left in critical condition; her friend required stiches for deep wounds to her back and arm. Ultimately, K was charged with first-degree attempted murder and second-degree assault and, in March 2012, she pleaded guilty to the charges for which she received a sentence of 13 years in incarceration.

In the aftermath of the attack, records revealed that 6 months prior, K had been expelled from school for threatening to kill a friend's boyfriend by stabbing him. She then completed a weeklong inpatient psychiatric hospitalization and was medically cleared by the psychiatry team to return to school. A transition meeting was reportedly held at school and attended by K and her mother. Upon learning about K's history and the school's knowledge of her prior violent threats, the victims' parents sued the school district for negligence to protect the students. A King County Superior Court jury awarded the families $1.3 million. Other parties who were named in the suit, including the mental-health facility and the attacker's parents, elected to settle out of court (*Lutz v. Snohomish School District, 2014*; Rebik, 2014).

PROFESSIONAL PERSPECTIVE: Scott Poland

I was on the side of the school in the Snohomish case and this perspective is from my time working on the case. I was surprised by the outcome of this case, as I felt that the school had done nothing wrong, given that the actual stabbing was 6 months after K had mentioned stabbing a person who did not even attend her school. She never brought a knife to school before the stabbing, had no discipline issues, and did not even know the girls she stabbed. The plaintiffs' attorney argued that K should have never been allowed to return to school, but she had a right to a free and appropriate education and the threat she made was not against a current student and did not meet the criteria for a substantial threat. Her statement was impulsive and fleeting, the very definition of a transient threat. The school had frequent meetings with K, her mother, and her teachers. Her mother reported that K continued in therapy and was compliant with her medication. The school asked for a release of information to communicate with her private mental health professionals, but K would not grant permission. In the state of Washington, children 13 and older make the decision, not their parents, about record sharing. This presents complications for crisis intervention. Additionally, predicting who will actually carry out an act of violence is difficult in the short term and virtually impossible 6 months into the future, especially when there is no relationship between the perpetrator and the victims.

Other cases demonstrate clear negligence on the school's part, although there are limited examples in which the plaintiffs were able to successfully prove this in a jury trial. I was involved in one of these cases in the recent past.

Case Review: *Cleveland v. Taft Union High School District* (2019)

Sixteen-year-old Bryan Oliver entered his classroom at Taft Union High School in Taft Kern County, California, armed with a shotgun. He opened fired on two of his classmates; his shots missed one classmate and hit another, Bowe Cleveland. While Bowe survived the injury, he suffered from significant medical complications and a tenuous recovery, enduring over 20 surgeries. Oliver was tried as an adult and charged with two counts of premeditated attempted murder, with the potential to spend the rest of his life in prison. The outcome of his initial trial was a mistrial due to a hung jury (Harvey, 2014). Oliver then proceeded to plead no contest to the charges and was subsequently sentenced to 27 years and 4 months in prison (*People v. Oliver*, 2016). Reportedly, he will be eligible for parole in less than 10 years (Strode, 2019).

Oliver's trial revealed that he was a victim of severe peer harassment and bullying, which appeared to be a motive for his attack, targeting two of the boys whom he identified as bullies. Additionally, it was found that Oliver's plans for a previous attack in a school assembly, including a hit list, were leaked to other students and staff members, but only resulted in a five-day suspension. Numerous students, staff, and even parents expressed concern to school officials about Oliver and potential violence over a period of nearly 1 year. Bowe Cleveland sued the school district, claiming that the school was legally responsible for the shooting due to their lack of appropriate intervention following Oliver's initial violent threat and ongoing threats, thereby failing at their duty to maintain a safe school environment. Ultimately, the jury awarded $3.8 million to the plaintiff but the liability was broken into percentages across parties. Specifically, the school administrators were found 35% liable, the school psychologist was found 19% liable, while the perpetrator was found 27% liable and his family members 19% liable. The liability for his family was due to the fact that his mother allowed a loaded unlocked shotgun to be in the home and his older brother was the person who owned the shotgun (*Cleveland v. Taft Union High School District*, 2019).

PROFESSIONAL PERSPECTIVE: SCOTT POLAND

I was on the side of the plaintiff and my perspective is from my time working on this case. It was my opinion that Bryan Oliver exhibited a number of warning signs of violence. Although the school completed an initial threat assessment, it was inadequate, and Oliver continued to engage in threatening behavior; these actions should have necessitated additional threat assessments. Additionally, the counseling services provided to Oliver were insufficient and did not appropriately address his needs. Moreover, the school assistant principal did not take Oliver's issues of bullying victimization serious enough and did not take the appropriate steps to intervene to stop the harassment. I have many thoughts on the case as this is the only one that I know of where school personnel were actually held liable for monetary damages in civil court after a school shooting. It is my opinion that the jury got it right and I am hopeful that this will cause school systems to improve their ability to assess threats of student violence against others more consistently. Moreover, I hope that this case will motivate schools to ensure that they are providing appropriate interventions. If a student is threatening violence toward others, it should always be viewed as a red flag that a student is in need of intervention and support.

Parental/Caregiver Liability

While the individual who commits an act of violence is the one who is prosecuted for the crimes, the liability of these acts can spread far beyond the perpetrator. There are other instances in which the liability of others is targeted in both civil and criminal court. This has become an increasing trend in these types of legal cases, and the question of liability outside of the school often looks to the caregivers. Many cases cite the parents as being negligent and culpable for their children's actions, particularly in the case of school shootings.

> We have a great debate about guns in America but perhaps both sides could agree that if parents do not secure the guns in their homes from their children they should be prosecuted.
>
> —SCOTT POLAND

Case Review: *State of Indiana v. Mary York (2020)*

In December 2019, 14-year-old Brandon Clegg allegedly stole his mother's firearm and forced her boyfriend to drive him to his school with the intent of completing a school shooting. Brandon's mother, Mary York, contacted the police to warn them of his intentions. Brandon arrived at the school and shot at the police, before turning the gun on himself and dying at the scene. No one else was harmed. Investigators found that Brandon had videotaped himself the day before, detailing his plan to complete the shooting. Reportedly, he is shown breaking the lock on the gun safe and stealing a firearm.

Investigators also learned that Brandon had been the victim of bullying and was suffering from mental health issues. Reportedly, he was placed in a 10-day inpatient psychiatric program that his mother terminated early due to lack of insurance coverage and high out-of-pocket costs. Soon after the shooting, Brandon's mother was charged with five counts of felony neglect of a dependent, one count of felony dangerous control of a child, and one misdemeanor count of criminal recklessness. In October 2020, she entered a plea deal and pleaded guilty to all counts, resulting in two and half years of probation (CBS4Web, 2020; Garbe, 2019).

Parental liability can come into play in both criminal and civil suits and can result in serious consequences for the caregivers of youth who engage in criminal acts. Given that the majority of these cases have occurred in the aftermath of a school shooting, we continue to seriously recommend that parents are emphatic about gun safety and to take the utmost caution in their firearm storage. A very recent case involving the parents of 15-year-old, Ethan Crumbley, who shot and killed four peers and injured several others at his high school in Oxford, Michigan, further highlights the potential liability issues that come with improper gun safety and storage in the home. Prosecutors alleged that Mr. and Mrs. Crumbley had ignored significant mental health and behavioral signs that their son was demonstrating. Furthermore, they alleged that Ethan's parents had purchased a firearm for him, the one that was ultimately used in the school shooting. As of April 2024, Ethan's parents, Jennifer and James Crumbley, have become the first parents to be convicted of involuntary manslaughter in connection with a mass shooting by their child. Both parents were sentenced to at least 10 years of prison time (Miller, 2024).

PROFESSIONAL PERSPECTIVE: SCOTT POLAND

I testified the first time before the U.S. Congress in 1999 and emphasized two points: first, the need to reduce gun access for youth and, second, the need for increased mental health services in schools. The issue about guns is not a question of an adult's right to own a gun; it is about the responsibility adults have to secure their guns from a troubled young person. It has been frustrating that many school shootings have occurred in the United States since 1999; however, the case in Oxford, Michigan, is the first time that parents were actually sentenced to jail. The parents of the victims of the Oxford school shooting have indicated that they will now move on to civil lawsuits against the school district. A key point in lawsuits against the school will undoubtably be whether the school did a proper threat assessment that utilized a multidisciplinary team.

School Shootings

In the aftermath of a school shooting, lawsuits come in a variety of shapes and sizes; plaintiffs are typically surviving victims and family members or estates of victims. Defendants can range from the sheriff and their police officers, school resource officers, school administers, caregivers of the shooters, psychotropic drug developers, video or computer game developers, and gun manufacturers and dealers. Case reviews of these kinds of lawsuits in the last 20 years reveal a grim picture for the plaintiffs: they do not typically prevail. These rulings have been upheld repeatedly in both state and federal courts. Time and time again, federal courts use the decision in *DeShaney v. Winnebago County Department of Social Services* (1989), which ruled that under the U.S. Constitution, the state has no duty to protect life, liberty, or property of an individual when the violence is committed by a private individual; thus, the government is not liable when an individual shoots another person. State cases are equally unsuccessful for plaintiffs, and school districts are generally able to cite sovereign immunity (Alexander, 2019).

Parkland

On February 14, 2018, Nicolas Cruz, an expelled student, opened fire on the students and staff at Marjory Stoneman Douglas (MSD) High School in Parkland, Florida. His attack killed 17 people and injured 17 others. This tragedy was particularly impactful to me, as it happened in my very own backyard of South Florida, where I work just miles away from Parkland. Because of my extensive experience responding to many school shootings, I was asked to share my ideas with the leadership team first. My aid resulted in my receiving the Helping Parkland Heal award from the city. In my consultation, I emphasized the following:

1. Broward needed to apply for a USDOE Project SERV Grant (Schools Emergency Response to Violence; 2014) to fund the needed additional mental health positions for the schools. Previous schools that experienced a shooting used the SERV funds to bring trailers to campus, so the increased mental health personnel would have a confidential place to provide support services.
2. Extensive efforts needed to be made to help the school staff prior to students returning to school.
3. The school district should not turn down any sources of assistance, as they are in it for the long haul.
4. A caregiver meeting should be held as quickly as possible to give parents information about how to help their children cope and to prepare parents for the typical reactions that children have to traumatic events. Caregivers need to respond with patience, structure and love.
5. The district should identify one staff member with the right qualifications and background to become the recovery coordinator and that it be made their sole job to chart the course for recovery, not just for MSD but for the entire district.
6. The district should utilize the "Circles of Vulnerability model" (see Chapter 4) to identify staff and students likely to be the most affected.
7. School should resume as soon as staff receive the needed support and should share

that when school is closed for weeks after a shooting, students are largely left isolated and unsupervised, as their caregivers cannot stay home from work for more than a few days.

8. Staff and students in the aftermath of previous school shootings have been frustrated because the counselor assigned to them would change frequently.
9. Everyone needed the opportunity if they wished to talk about the tragedy and the importance of psychological first aid and helping everyone affected to identify their existing sources of support.
10. Students must have the opportunity to talk about the tragedy, write about it, and express their emotions through music and artwork.

Investigations in the aftermath of the shooting revealed a number of concerns. First, video footage surfaced that showed the school resource officer, Scot Peterson, taking position in a building away from where the perpetrator was, where he reportedly remained for over 45 minutes. As a result, Peterson was arrested and charged with 11 violations, including multiple counts of felony child neglect (Reiss & Alonso, 2021). In June 2023, Peterson was acquitted on all criminal charges (Spencer, 2024). The families of the 17 victims have continued to pursue legal action against Peterson in civil court; they are presently seeking an undisclosed amount from Peterson and the Broward Sheriff's Office. In January 2023, a circuit judge ruled that a jury should determine if Peterson demonstrated a "wanton and willful disregard" for the safety of the victims at MSD. The trial is expected to take place at some point in 2024 (Spencer, 2024).

Moreover, it was discovered that the shooter had a history of mental and behavioral concerns that resulted in a previous expulsion and were reported to the police on several occasions. Many caregivers have alleged that in previous years, Broward schools had been encouraged to underreport crimes and that district polices tied the hands of the police. An example of this is the fact that there was not a single trespassing, bullying, or threat reported between 2014 and 2017. The odds of that being the case are unlikely. Student victims attempted to sue the school district, alleging that the school was partially liable for the shooting, given that they had the responsibility to warn the students and faculty about the potential danger of Cruz.

Ultimately, the case was dismissed by a Broward Circuit judge, who stated: "The District, without control over Cruz and without knowledge of a specific threat, did not have the duty to warn the plaintiffs of the actions eventually taken by Cruz" (Heiman, 2021). In 2021, however, a $25 million settlement was reached between the Broward County School District and the families of 52 people killed, injured, or traumatized in the shooting. Additionally, the families were awarded $127.5 million by the Federal Bureau of Investigation for their failure to follow up on tips about Cruz's concerning behaviors that may have prevented the shooting. In criminal court, the perpetrator pleaded guilty to the 34 charges associated with the school shooting. After nearly 6 years, Cruz was sentenced to life in prison with no chance of parole (Thompson, 2024).

The horrific events and aftermath of the Parkland shooting have resulted in a number of legislative pushes. Florida Senate Bill 7026, or the Marjory Stoneman Douglas High School Public Safety Act, was signed into Florida law in 2018, three weeks after the shooting. The bill banned bump stocks and raised the minimum age to purchase a firearm from 18 to 21, among other restrictions. It also allowed teachers who receive training to be armed (Florida Senate Bill 7026, 2018).

School Violence Legislation

The push for school violence legislation began in the early 1990s during a time in which school shootings became an increased concern across the nation. Over time, these legislative efforts have come in waves, typically in the aftermath of serious school crises that have major publicity, such as a school shooting. Legislative responses are primarily centered on gun control and mental health support. These issues are hotly debated in the public service and political worlds and are complicated platforms to effect change. Nonprofit agencies such as Sandy Hook Promise and Everytown Gun Safety are leaders in the legal advocacy work. Table 11.2 outlines a summary of some of the significant legislative responses that have occurred recently.

MITIGATING YOUR RISK FOR LIABILITY

Given the broad range of potential crises and their legal implications, it is impossible to be prepared for all potential risks; however, there are definitely steps that you and your school can take to mitigate these risks. The overarching recommendation is to make every effort to follow best practices in terms of ethics, prevention, intervention, and postvention. Below you will find a list of key steps that should be implemented in order to best mitigate your potential liability in the aftermath of a crisis. These guidelines have been broken down as they apply to you as a practitioner, to your school, and as it relates to school–family involvement.

Strategies for the Crisis Interventionist

- All SMHPs, nurses, guidance counselors, and social workers should obtain personal malpractice insurance. While the school may offer assistance in legal matters, it is up to you to ensure that you have your own protection, as you cannot always guarantee that the school board will provide legal aid.
- Engage in your own professional development in order to stay up to date with current best practices for crisis intervention, particularly in the areas of suicide and threat assessment. Given the limited mandates related to crisis intervention training and the ever-evolving status of the field, it is your responsibility to maintain your competence in the practice of crisis intervention. Attend relevant trainings and professional development workshops on a yearly basis.
- Maintain detailed and up-to-date documentation of *all* crisis services provided. This speaks to the age-old saying "if it wasn't documented, it didn't happen." Ensuring that you have proper documentation throughout your crisis interventions can be a critical aid in the face of a legal issue.
- Always engage in consultation with appropriate colleagues (e.g., administrators, other SMHPs). Multiple heads are better than one in times of crisis and can assist you in reflecting on all of the potential legal and ethical issues that intersect with crises. Document your consultations in your notes.

TABLE 11.2. Legislative Actions Related to School Violence

Claire Davis Safety Act (2015)

- Enacted in 2015 following the shooting at Arapahoe High School on December 13, 2013, after Claire Davis was shot and killed by her schoolmate, Karl Pierson.
- Claire's parents successfully lobbied for a change in the Colorado Sovereign Immunity Act.
- The change creates a right for victims to bring claims against a public school district if they fail to exercise reasonable care to protect students, faculty, or staff from acts committed by another person when the harm is reasonably foreseeable and the victims are on campus.
- More information on this act can be found at *https://cssrc.colorado.gov/claire-davis-school-safety-act* (Claire Davis School Safety Act, n.d.)

Florida Senate Bill 730 (2019)

- Goals:
  - Address the school safety and security recommendations of the Marjory Stoneman Douglas High School Public Safety Commission.
  - Strengthen accountability and compliance oversight authority.
  - Enhance school and student safety.
- Improves student safety by establishing information sharing and reporting requirements for district school boards and charter school governing boards, including responses to emergency situations, safety incident reporting, data collection, and data sharing.
- Provides funding opportunities to enhance school safety and security and to provide additional mental health services to students.
- Requires Florida schools to have threat assessment teams that evaluate threats to others and threats to self.
- A detailed review of the bill can be found at *https://info.fldoe.org/docushare/dsweb/Get/Document-8569/dps-2019-76a.pdf* (SB 7030 Implementation of Legislative Recommendations of the Marjory Stoneman Douglas High School Public Safety Commission, 2019)

Red Flag Laws

- Allows loved ones or law enforcement to intervene by petitioning a court order in order to temporarily prevent the person in crisis from accessing a firearm.
- Nineteen states and the District of Colombia have enacted a form of red flag laws (Everytown, 2022).
- Additional information about Red Flag Laws can be found on the Everytown website at *www.everytown.org/solutions/extreme-risk-laws* (Everytown, 2022).

Bipartisan Safer Communities Act of 2022 (S.2938)

- Firearm regulation and mental health bill passed by the 117th Congress and was recently signed into law in June 2022. Negotiations began after the tragic Uvalde shooting.
- Pertinent school implications:
  - Provides $11 billion for mental health services, increased funding for school-based mental health programs, and investments in pediatric mental health care services.
  - Provides $750 million for state grants to implement crisis intervention order programs; also referred to as *red-flag laws.*
  - Requires expanded background checks for individuals over the age of 21 purchasing firearms.
  - Provides $2 billion for community-based violence prevention initiatives.
- Details from the bill can be read here: *www.whitehouse.gov/wp-content/uploads/2022/06/Bipartisan-Safer-Communities-Act-SAP-1.pdf* (Washington, 2022).

Strategies for the School

- Ensure that your school has a well-trained multidisciplinary team to evaluate threats of violence toward others (see Chapter 2). The team should follow all guidelines from the U.S. Department of Education and their individual state department of education and the state school safety center.
- Provide annual suicide prevention and threat assessment training to your staff. Make this a mandatory part of your staff's training, as it will create foundational knowledge that will help to mitigate potential ethical and legal issues in the time of a crisis.
- Create and/or utilize an anonymous reporting system for students to report threats of violence or suicide.
- Investigate school software programs that monitor student statements on school computers about suicide and violence and alert school administration or local law enforcement.
- Ensure that your CRT's safety plan details best practices for crisis response to all potential crises, especially those that have the potential for death (as documented in Chapters 4–7).
- Utilize the resources at your disposal and always involve the SMHP in any potential crisis. A SMHP will have expert knowledge that will be necessary to the crisis intervention process and will reflect best practices.

Strategies for School–Family Communication

- Notify caregivers in *all* cases of concern of risk for self-harm, suicide, or violence toward others; the only exception to this is if abuse is suspected in the family home. The Department of Children and Families should then become involved.
- Encourage caregivers to be more involved in supervision and awareness with regard to their child's use of technology. Hold an annual seminar at the beginning of the school year to share this message and create a dialogue with families about the importance of being more connected to their children and the potential issues that can arise from technology use.
- Help students and their caregivers understand that even joking about school violence may result in severe consequences. This messaging can also be discussed at the annual family seminar.

We recommend that you take these guidelines seriously and utilize them to inform your practice, as they will help to ensure that you are covered legally and engaging in best practices for your school.

CHAPTER 12

Final Thoughts and Future Directions

This guidebook has provided a variety of recommendations, guidance, and best practices for crisis preparedness, intervention, and postvention services. As mentioned in numerous instances, crisis intervention in the school context is a complex matter and can be an overwhelming practice. It is our hope that this guidebook can assist you in enhancing your understanding and knowledge in the field, and that you will be able to utilize the materials and resources presented in this book to feel better prepared to address the crisis needs of your school community. Crisis intervention is not a black and white approach and requires flexibility, curiosity, tenacity, and courage. As a crisis interventionist, you have taken on a great duty to your school community, and we want to thank you for your committed efforts to the ongoing needs of our nation's students, school personnel, and, as a result, the needs of our broader society.

> Remember that the tragedy cannot remain the story. It must evolve into a narrative about the character of the people who were involved, about their strength and bravery and courage. That will pull us forward because hope must lead the way.
>
> —CATHY KENNEDY-PAINE

As we come to a close, we and our guest contributors leave you with a review of final thoughts from our crisis experts. Their insight into the lessons they have learned and the needs for the future of crisis intervention is invaluable. Moreover, they offer critical suggestions for the changes that should occur in our school systems, along with future directions for school crisis intervention. As leaders in the field, their reflections and recommendations can be considered the most current guiding voices for school crisis intervention.

PROFESSIONAL PERSPECTIVE: Scott Poland

I did a doctoral dissertation on teaching students mathematics and received no training in crisis intervention in neither my doctoral program in school psychology nor the school district where I directed psychological services. Thus, I was very uncertain about what to do when faced with my first school crisis. Crisis intervention in schools changed the direction of my career and my life as many of my closest friends served with me on crisis teams. *Crisis* in Chinese means "danger and opportunity," and my crisis intervention experiences indeed provided me with opportunities that I never could have imagined, such as addressing Congress four times about school violence and suicide prevention. I remember flying to Colorado to help in the aftermath of Columbine and listening to motivational music to convince myself that I could do it and would be able to stay calm and help people. The readers of this book will experience times when they need to give themselves such a pep talk. I am so glad that many of our contributors have stressed the importance of self-care, as it is essential for crisis responders.

School crisis responders must take care of themselves, and they must always be a part of a team. Schools must think about prevention, and students themselves must play a bigger role in school violence and youth suicide prevention. The school shooter or the suicide victim almost always told their friends about their plans. I remember leading a classroom discussion after a gun accidentally discharged in a classroom, severely injuring a student, and I was shocked when many students told me they would not tell an adult if they saw a gun on campus tomorrow. We must end the conspiracy of silence that allows guns on our campuses in the hands of students and homicidal and suicidal behavior to go unreported to adults. Every student needs a go-to trusted adult at school. I am very proud to be a small part of all the crisis prevention and intervention work done by NASP. As an organization, NASP created crisis intervention emergency and support teams and a crisis intervention curriculum to train school personnel. Our current U.S. Surgeon General, in a recent report titled "Protecting the Mental Health of Our Youth," said *we must seize the moment.* I encourage the readers of this book to do just that: seize the moment to increase prevention efforts and crisis intervention readiness in your school.

PROFESSIONAL PERSPECTIVES

Lessons Learned

One of the greatest lessons I have learned is that I have the strength and stamina to address crisis events but must rely on my "support team" of professional colleagues who can help me shore up the efforts. The key is to be prepared, have a protocol or proposed protocol, and remain focused on the task at hand. Sometimes the situation is too close to my personal experience, and it is better to let someone else handle the work. In that case, I can take a different role.

—Cindy Dickinson

Crises are negative, unpredictable, uncontrollable, and highly emotional. Just when you think a response is going well the unexpected will happen. Be ready to pivot. Listen to all voices. The loudest is not always right. You can't do it alone. Construct a network of support prior to a crisis and call on them when needed. Care for the caregivers. It's not over when it's over. Healing takes a long time.

—Cathy Kennedy-Paine

Most people really do get better with time, social support, and a little psychoeducation! Even with mass casualty events, recovery really is the norm. One size really does not fit all. Evaluation and triage are critical to an effective response. This work is NOT for everyone. And sometimes it's really difficult to convey that to those individuals for whom it's not a good fit.

—FRANCI CREPEAU-HOBSON

You are there to provide support and guidance so others can cope. Crises impact goes on for a LONG time! Be prepared! Take care of yourself or this type of responding will catch up with you. One can be vicariously traumatized by this work. Always work with a team (two or more). Crisis response is not for the single responder.

—BILL PFOHL

I've had excellent training over the years and feel that has helped me guide staff when they need to respond to a crisis in their own school. I've also always prayed for guidance before I respond to a crisis and feel this has been crucial for me.

—FULVIA FRANCO

Every situation is different. Prepare, prepare, prepare. Read the literature. Also, go to the site of the crisis if possible before you respond. For example, we visited the site of a tornado that ripped through the community near Kissimmee, Florida, before we went to the impacted school to provide crisis intervention. In this way we could experience the aftermath of the event through all our five senses.

—PHILIP LAZARUS

One of the greatest lessons is appreciation for fellow team members that helps to keep us going through ongoing challenging and distressing circumstances. It also helps to work with many amazing educators in schools where we have responded.

—JEFF ROTH

There are countless, extraordinary stories of resilience and connection that can be told. As a school crisis responder, you win some; you lose some; one foot in front of the other; help as many as you can. Take care of yourself and everyone you love.

—RICHARD LIEBERMAN

I have learned that while the work is challenging, it can be fulfilling and sustainable when you have continual training, the right teams in place, and you remember that you are a part of a process that helps give hope and tools to people who have suffered significant trauma and yet will be able to prevail and be resilient. It is my greatest honor to do this work.

—STEPHANIE CRAWFORD-GOETZ

Each crisis is unique. It is important to listen to the people who are knowledgeable about the school and community and hear their needs while also balancing that with following a fairly consistent response.

—AMANDA NICKERSON

Our experts highlight important lessons learned that reflect many of the recommendations that have been reviewed in this guidebook. It is our hope that these lessons can serve as a guiding light for you and your team as you address your school's safety and crisis prevention and intervention needs. Among the lessons discussed, the most salient takeaways include the following:

- Crisis intervention cannot be successful without appropriate preparation. So many crises are *preventable*. Practice, practice, practice!
- As a crisis interventionist, you are a forever student and must continue to learn and ensure that you are up to date on the most current best practices for crisis intervention in the school context. Engage in annual training and stay up to date with current literature.
- Creation of a diverse and capable crisis team is imperative. Crisis intervention cannot be done alone; lean on your team members and ensure that you engage in consistent self-care practices.
- Our nation's schools need consistent, evidence-based protocols and procedures in place for ensuring a climate of safety, thorough preparedness, mandated staff training, and best practices for intervention and postvention services.

Reflections on lessons learned bring us to consider future directions in crisis intervention. One of the most important recommendations is on the topic of mandated training. As discussed throughout our guidebook and in our experts' reflections, training is a critical component of crisis preparedness and intervention. Even with this knowledge in place, there are limited examples of states or counties where crisis intervention training is mandated for staff. Moreover, the majority of psychology programs have yet to include crisis intervention as one of the primary aspects of their training and curriculum. These aspects of the field must be modified. It is our recommendation that *all* school personnel undergo appropriate and culturally sensitive crisis intervention training. We also stress the importance that *all* psychology training programs should include crisis intervention courses and training as part of their curriculum and practical experience/training. These requirements will ensure that we are creating a strong foundation for crisis intervention services nationwide.

Other future directions to consider relate to the need for ongoing scientific research. As noted many times in this guidebook, crisis intervention is an ever-evolving topic that requires ongoing consideration and changes with time. For example, it is likely that most schools were not prepared for how to handle the significant and complex issues that came with the COVID-19 pandemic, the related school closures, increased mental health concerns, and ongoing trauma exposure across the nation. Even with the best efforts to be prepared, novel crisis situations can occur and will be best handled if your team has already established the foundation of good crisis preparedness and intervention practices.

Much of crisis intervention guidance is based on anecdotal experiences, given the range and variability of crisis contexts. While anecdotal knowledge is invaluable to our practice, the field of crisis intervention would benefit from continued research that provides objective data to support the recommendations and conclusions. Intervention practices should be studied more thoroughly so that our schools can confidently employ plans and strategies that work. Without this, it is difficult for school crisis intervention to continue to evolve with best practices and for practitioners to stay abreast of new developments that will aid in planning for their school setting. Moreover, the hope is that additional scientific research will motivate the federal government to enhance their requirements for a national mandate for crisis training and protocols across schools and provide more funding for this area. We recommend that research focuses on the effectiveness of crisis planning and interventions, including developing more solid conclusions regarding recommended prevention programming. Additionally, our expert contributors have shared their thoughts on what they see as the primary needs for the future directions of crisis intervention.

PROFESSIONAL PERSPECTIVES

Future Directions

We need more research! We have a ton of anecdotal support for school-based crisis response and intervention, but little in the way of hard data that really shows how effective this work can be. I know it's a difficult thing to study, but I would encourage crisis interveners to collect data and disseminate it whenever they respond to show the impact. In the meantime, we need to continue to use our experiences, as well as what is in the professional literature to inform our practice and be comfortable pivoting and making adjustments in how we respond and intervene as appropriate.

—Franci Crepeau-Hobson

Every school team [should] have crisis team training before school years begin, not just fill out a form stating who will be reached in a crisis. Publish ways that students and adults can seek help, not just after a crisis occurs. Examples include tiplines, crisis hotlines, etc.

—Stephanie Crawford-Goetz

Continued training on an annual basis for responders, staff, and administration, debriefing after responding to a crisis, and the importance of a comprehensive prevention, intervention, and postvention model. I'd like to see schools adopt a crisis plan before the start of the school year. I'd like them to be more proactive, instead of reactive.

—Fulvia Franco

Each school is different, and some schools do a better job than others. However, I would like to see school districts in every state mandate training for all their staff in the area of suicide prevention and intervention and in threat assessment. We should have a course or at least part of a course in all school psychology programs that deals with prevention and intervention. Moreover, this type of training should be imperative for all school personnel that are currently in or intend to go into administration. We need to continue to conduct research on the long-term impact of crises on individuals.

—Philip Lazarus

I think the primary prevention and proactive preparation piece is really important. I also recognize that cell phones, text messages, and social media have expanded the challenges and opportunities for crisis response. More training in advance for primary prevention and proactive approaches such as administrators understanding school crisis response and teachers having training in responding to students experiencing emotional trauma and grief. It would be great to have more strong school teams blending with district teams when needed.

—Jeff Roth

I'd like ALL districts to have comprehensive safety plans with written policies and procedures for crisis, bullying, violence, and suicide prevention, intervention, and postvention. Have school psychologists lead the way. Focus on prevention so maybe we don't have to intervene as much.

—Richard Lieberman

My recommendation is that school districts prioritize this work by having a psychological safety team that is well staffed, trained, and supported in developing and maintaining a continuum of services. These services would support students, staff, and families to receive prevention support, invention services, and postvention. For example, this team could support staff navigating child abuse cases, students who are at risk of suicide, and students who may pose threats to others' safety in an effort to prevent the need for crisis response. They would also be a well-versed team to provide a thorough, high-quality crisis response when crises occur. Their work could include professional development, consultation, and direct services. School districts need to have a district crisis team with an experienced leader of this team and a thorough process mapped out for all schools to follow. It would be great for district and school administrators to be required to take crisis training to know better how to work with the crisis teams and to compliment and support them.

—STEPHANIE CRAWFORD-GOETZ

I believe more collaboration with community mental health resources will provide better support for students—more wraparound services. Partnerships between schools, parents/guardians, and the community can help to provide children the care they need, especially after the pandemic.

—MICHELLE PASTOREK

Attending to long-term effects of crises and providing more behavioral Tier 2 targeted or strategic interventions and more Tier 3 intensive intervention for students. CBITS, which stands for Cognitive Behavioral Interventions for Traumatized Students, should be more available in schools. Perhaps this is idealistic thinking, but I think we need a cultural/societal shift in moving from pointing blame when something happens to trying to come together to work to find ways to heal from crisis events (and other events that can be divisive).

—AMANDA NICKERSON

More training: School personnel from the classified employees to the superintendent need to have knowledge about what happens in a crisis, how to support themselves and their students. Not enough schools have this training. More practice: School personnel need to practice emergency drills on a regular basis. More mental health support: All school personnel must recognize the importance of good mental health support for students and staff and promote funding for school-based mental health professionals such as counselors and school psychologists. Schools must lobby for funding for continuous and sustainable crisis and emergency preparedness, response and recovery planning and training utilizing evidence-based models.

—CATHY KENNEDY-PAINE

Prevention efforts are crucial. It appears we only train or respond when there is an actual crisis. Many events can be prevented. I'd like to see crisis response as part of school psychologists' services and training. Have schools seen the value of active responding to a crisis rather than waiting until negative effects become an issue? Also, to have a common language, vision, and response with ALL school personnel from school board to the students and support staff understand what a crisis response is and have the skills to respond.

—BILL PFHOL

While this final chapter signifies the end of our guidebook, it is recommended that the shared reflections be used as a starting point for you and your team. These insights can serve as the building blocks to help your team to structure your crisis preparedness and response plans with the best practices in mind. Moreover, they can assist you in finding the gaps in your approaches and the necessary changes that will aid your team in building the strongest and most thorough practices. As a reminder, the field of crisis intervention is complex and comes with unique professional and personal challenges. It is imperative that collaborative practices become a primary part of your approach, including building strong relationships with your team members and the community in order to ensure that you have the right help for the various crises that you may encounter. We wish you luck and care in your school crisis intervention work, and we emphasize the importance of your work and dedication to this field.

References

Alexander, M. D. (2019). *School liability in school shooting cases.* Springer.

Allen, M., Annandale, N., Gstettenbauer, A., Rutherford, M., Lyman, B., & Conklin, E. (2004). *Providing effective crisis intervention for students and families from diverse backgrounds.* Paper presented at the annual convention of the National Association of School Psychologists, Dallas, TX.

Altimari, D. (2019, March 18). *Sandy Hook families can sue gun manufacturer, rules Connecticut Supreme Court. Governing the future of states and localities.* www.governing.com/archive/tns-connecticut-supreme-court-sandy-hook-families.html.

American Civil Liberties Union (ACLU). (2020). *Open letter to schools about LGBTQ student privacy.* www.aclu.org/documents/open-letter-schools-about-lgbtq-student-privacy.

American Foundation for Suicide Prevention (AFSP), American School Counselor Association (ASCA), the National Association of School Psychologists (NASP), & The Trevor Project. (2019, October 22). *Model school policy on suicide prevention.* https://afsp.org/our-work/education/model-school-policy-suicide-prevention.

American Foundation for Suicide Prevention (AFSP), Suicide Prevention Resource Center (SPRC). (2018). *After a suicide, A Toolkit for Schools* (2nd ed.). https://afsp.org/our-work/education/after-a-suicide-a-toolkit-for-schools.

American National Red Cross. (2022). *Disaster relief.* www.redcross.org/about-us/our-work/disaster-relief.html.

American Psychiatric Association. (2022). *Diagnostic and statistical manual of mental disorders* (5th ed., text rev.). Author.

American Psychological Association. (2009). *Children and trauma.* www.apa.org/pi/families/resources/children-trauma-tips.

American National Red Cross. (2018). *Red Cross training & certification, and store.* www.redcross.org/take-a-class/first-aid/performing-first-aid/first-aid-steps.

American School Counselor Association (ASCA). (2019). *The school counselor and safe schools and crisis response.* www.schoolcounselor.org/Standards-Positions/Position-Statements/ASCA-Position-Statements/The-School-Counselor-and-Safe-Schools-and-Crisis-R.

American School Counselor Association (ASCA). (2022). *School counselor roles & ratios.* www.schoolcounselor.org/About-School-Counseling/School-Counselor-Roles-Ratios.

Anderson v. Snohomish School District No. 201, No. 80218-6-I (Wash. Ct. App. August 24, 2020).

Anewalt, P. H. (2010). Violent, traumatic death in schools and community responses. In N. B. Webb (Ed.), *Helping bereaved children: A handbook for practitioners* (3rd ed., pp. 190–214). Guilford Press.

Annandale, N. O., Heath, M. A., Dean, B., Kemple, A., & Takino, Y. (2011). Cross-cultural sensitivity in state school crisis plans. *Journal of School Violence, 10*(1), 16–33.

Annor, F., Wilkinson, A., & Zwald, M. (2017). Epi Aid #2012-019: *Undetermined risk factors for suicide among youth aged 10–17 years.* https://health.utah.gov/wp-content/uploads/Final-Report-UtahEpi-Aid.pdf.

Arciaga, M., Sakamoto, W., & Fearbry Jones, E. (2010). *Responding to gangs in the school setting.* U.S. Department of Justice, Office of Justice Programs. www.ojp.gov/ncjrs/virtual-library/abstracts/responding-gangs-school-setting.

Aseervatham, V., Born, P., & Lohmaier, D. (2017). Hazard-specific supply reactions in the aftermath of natural disasters. *Geneva Papers on Risk and Insurance Issues and Practice* 42, 193–225.

Athey, J., & Moody-Williams, J. (2003). *Developing cultural competence in disaster mental health programs: Guiding principles and recommendations.* U.S. Department of Health and Human Services. http://media.shs.net/ken/pdf/SMA03-3828/CulturalCompetence_FINALwithcovers.pdf.

Babel, S. (2010, August 21). The trauma that arises from natural disasters. *Psychology Today.* www.psychologytoday.com/us/blog/somatic-psychology/201004/the-trauma-arises-natural-disasters.

Baird, A. A., Roellke, E. V., & Zeifman, D. M. (2016). Alone and adrift: The association between mass school shootings, school size, and student support. *Social Science Journal, 54*(3), 261–270.

Berman, S., Chaffee, S., & Sarmiento, J. (2018). *The practice base for how we learn: Supporting students' social, emotional, and academic development.* National Commission on Social, Emotional, and Academic Development, The Aspen Institute. https://assets.aspeninstitute.org/content/uploads/2018/03/CDE-Practice-Base_FINAL.pdf.

Bilsen, J. (2018). Suicide and youth: Risk factors. *Frontiers in Psychiatry* 9, 540.

Bipartisan Safer Communities Act of 2022, U.S.C., S.2938 (2022).

Bloch, D. A., Silber, E., & Perry, S. E. (1956). Some factors in the environmental reactions of children of disaster. *The American Journal of Psychiatry, 150*, 235–239.

Bonanno, C. M., & Levenson, R. L., Jr. (2014). School shooters: History, current theoretical and empirical findings, and strategies for prevention. *Sage Open, 4*(1), 2158244014525425.

Boon, H. J., Brown, L. H., Tsey, K., Speare, R., Pagliano, P., Usher, K., & Clark, B. (2011). School disaster planning for children with disabilities. A critical review of the literature. *International Journal of Special Education, 26*(3), 223–237.

Borum, R., Bartel, P. A., & Forth, A. E. (2005). Structured assessment of violence risk in youth (SAVRY). In T. Grisso, G. Vincent, & D. Seagrave (Eds.), *Mental health screening and assessment in juvenile justice.* Guilford Press.

Borum, R., Cornell, D. G., Modzeleski, W., & Jimerson, S. R. (2010). What can be done about school shootings? *Educational Researcher, 39*(1), 27–37.

Boston Fire Historical Society. (2021). The story of the Cocoanut Grove fire. Retrieved April 22, 2023, from *https://bostonfirehistory.org/the-story-of-the-cocoanut-grove-fire.*

Brent, D. A., Poling, K. D., & Goldstein, T. R. (2011). *Treating depressed and suicidal adolescents: A clinician's guide.* Guilford Press.

Brock, S., & Jimerson, S. R. (2012). *Best practices in school crisis prevention and intervention* (2nd ed.). NASP Publications.

Brock, S., Lazarus, P., & Jimerson, S. (2002). *Best practices in school crisis prevention and intervention.* Ingram.

Brock, S., Nickerson, A., Reeves, M., Conolly, C., Jimerson, S., Pesce, R., et al. (2016). *School crisis prevention and intervention: The PREPaRE model.* National Association of School Psychologists.

Brock, S., Nickerson, A. B., Reeves, M. A., Conolly, C., Jimerson, S. R., Pesce, R., & Lazzaro, B. (2014). *PREPaRE School crisis prevention and intervention training curriculum* (2nd ed.). National Association of School Psychologists.

Brock, S., Nickerson, A. B., Reeves, M. A., Jimerson, S. R., Lieberman, R. A., & Feinberg, T. A. (2009). *School crisis prevention and intervention (the Prepare model).* National Association of School Psychologists.

Brymer, M., Jacobs, A., Lyane, C., Pynoos, R., Ruzek, J., Steinberg, A., &Watson, P. (2006) *Psychological first aid: Field operations guide* (2nd ed.). National Child Traumatic Stress Network and National Center for PTSD.

Butkus, S. L. (2020). Investigating school shootings from 1996 to 2019 for processes needed to prevent and respond to future school shootings: A case study. Doctoral dissertation, Northcentral University.

Canada, M., Heath, M. A., Money, K., Annandale, N., Fischer, L., & Young, E. L. (2007). Crisis intervention for students of diverse backgrounds: School counselors' concerns. *Brief Treatment and Crisis Intervention, 7*(1), 12–24.

Caplan, C. (1961). *An approach to community mental health.* Grune & Stratton.

Caplan, C. (1964). *Principles of Preventive Psychiatry.* Basic Books.

Carver-Thomas, D. (2022). *Teacher shortages take center stage.* https://learningpolicyinstitute.org/blog/teacher-shortages-take-center-stage.

CBS4Web. (2020, October 14). *Mother of Richmond school shooter pleads guilty to several charges, sentenced to probation.* https://cbs4indy.com/news/mother-of-richmond-school-shooter-pleads-guilty-to-several-charges-sentenced-to-probation.

Center for Substance Abuse Treatment. (2014). *Trauma-informed care in behavioral health services.* Substance Abuse and Mental Health Services Administration.

Centers for Disease Control and Prevention (CDC). (2020a). *Crisis definition.* wwwn.cdc.gov/WPVHC/Nurses/Course/Slide/Unit2_7#:~:text=Crisis%20is%20an%20acute%20emotional,usual%20(Hoff%2C%202009.

Centers for Disease Control and Prevention (CDC). (2020b). *YRBSS.* www.cdc.gov/healthyyouth/data/yrbs/results.htm.

Centers for Disease Control and Prevention (CDC). (2021). *Striving to Reduce Youth Violence Everywhere (STRYVE).* www.cdc.gov/violenceprevention/youthviolence/stryve/index.html.

Centers for Disease Control and Prevention (CDC). (2024a). *Safety plan considerations.* www.cdc.gov/child-development/disability-safety/safety-plan.html?CDC_AAref_Val=www.cdc.gov/ncbddd/disabilityandsafety/emergency.html.

Centers for Disease Control and Prevention. (2024b). *Web-based Injury Statistics Query and Reporting System (WISQARS).* www.cdc.gov/injury/wisqars/index.html.

Centers for Disease Control and Prevention (CDC). (2023). *YRBSS.* www.cdc.gov/healthyyouth/data/yrbs/pdf/YRBS_Data-Summary-Trends_Report2023_508.pdf.

Choquette v. Onstedt Community Schools, No.02-002940 MI. (2005).

Claire Davis School Safety Act. C.R.S. 24-10-106.3 (2015).

Claire Davis School Safety Act, School Safety Resource Center. (n.d.). cssrc.colorado.gov. https://cssrc.colorado.gov/claire-davis-school-safety-act.

Clarke, L. S., Embury, D. C., Jones, R. E., & Yssel, N. (2014). Supporting students with disabilities during school crises: A teacher's guide. *TEACHING Exceptional Children, 46*(6), 169–178.

Cleveland v. Taft Union High School District. No. S-1500-cv-279256 (Kern Cty. Super. Ct. 2019).

Communities in Schools of North Carolina. (2015). *High school gang prevention.* https://cisnc.org/wp-content/uploads/2020/05/HB4-Gang-Prevention.pdf.

Connolly Knox, C., & Haupt, B. (2015). Incorporating cultural competency skills in emergency management education. *Disaster Prevention and Management, 24*(5), 619–634.

Cooper, G. D., Clements, P. T., & Holt, K. (2011). A review and application of suicide prevention programs in high school settings. *Issues in Mental Health Nursing, 32*, 696–702.

Cornell, D. (2018a). *Comprehensive school threat assessment guidelines.* www.schoolta.com/manual.

Cornell, D. (2018b). *School safety.* School Safety Forum, University of Virginia.

Cornell, D. G. (2020). Threat assessment as a school violence prevention strategy. *Criminology & Public Policy, 19*(1), 235–252.

CPR in Schools™ First Aid. (n.d.). https://cpr.heart.org/en/courses/cpr-in-schools-first-aid.

Crisis Connections. (n.d.). *Riding the Waves: Facilitator's guide.* https://www.crisisconnections.org/store/riding-the-waves-manual-1/.

Crisis Prevention Institute (CPI). (2021). *How trauma-informed schools help every student succeed.* www.crisisprevention.com/blog/education/how-trauma-informed-schools-help-every-student-succeed/.

Curran, F. C., Fisher, B. W., & Viano, S. L. (2020). Mass school shootings and the short-run impacts on use of school security measures and practices: National evidence from the Columbine tragedy. *Journal of School Violence, 19*(1), 6–19.

Daniel, S. S., & Goldston, D. B. (2009). Interventions for suicidal youth: A review of the literature and developmental considerations. *Suicide and Life-Threatening Behavior, 39*(3):252–268.

Department of Education, National School Safety Center. (2010). *National school safety.* www.schoolsafety.us.

Department of Homeland Security. (2022). *School and workplace violence.* www.dhs.gov/school-and-workplace-violence.

DeShaney v. Winnebago County Wisconsin Department of Social Services, 489 U.S. 189 (1989).

Dodd, C. J. (2004, October 21). S.2634-108th Congress (2003–2004): Garrett Lee Smith Memorial Act. www.congress.gov. www.congress.gov/bill/108th-congress/senate-bill/2634.

Durlak, J. A., Weissberg, R. P., Dymnicki, A. B., Taylor, R. D., & Schellinger, K. B. (2011). The impact of enhancing students' social and emotional learning: A meta-analysis of school-based universal interventions. *Child Development, 82*, 405–432.

EDSCLS Measures | National Center on Safe Supportive Learning Environments (NCSSLE). (n.d.). https://safesupportivelearning.ed.gov/edscls/measures#Topic%20Areas%20the%20EDSCLS%20Measures.

Eggert, L. L., Thompson, E. A., & Herting, J. R. (1994). A measure of adolescent potential for suicide (MAPS): Development and preliminary findings. *Suicide and Life-Threatening Behavior, 24*, 359–381.

Eisel v. Board of Education of Montgomery County 324 Md. 376, 597 A. 2d 447 (Md Ct. App. 1991).

Epperson, A. (2021, May 5). *Building a positive school climate—#PBIScon21.* PBIS Rewards. www.pbisrewards.com/blog/building-positive-school-climate-pbiscon21.

Erbacher, T. A., Singer, J. B., & Poland, S. (2015). *Suicide in schools: A practitioner's guide to multi-level prevention, assessment, intervention, and postvention.* Routledge.

Erbacher, T. A., Singer, J. B., & Poland, S. (2023). *Suicide in schools: A practitioner's guide to multi-level prevention, assessment, intervention, and postvention* (2nd ed.). Routledge.

Evans, R., & Hurrell, C. (2016). The role of schools in children and young people's self-harm and suicide: Systematic review and meta-ethnography of qualitative research. *BMC Public Health, 16*(1), 401.

Everly, G. S., & Mitchell, J. T. (2016). *Crisis incident stress management: A practical review.* https://cismbookstore.com/sites/cismbookstore.com/files/previews/Preview%209781943001033_WEB.pdf.

Everytown. (2022). *Federal advocacy.* www.everytown.org/federal-advocacy.

Federal Emergency Management Agency (FEMA). (2009). *Guidelines for student/staff sudden death.* https://training.fema.gov/programs/emischool/el361toolkit/assets/suddendeath.pdf.

Federal Emergency Management Agency (FEMA). (2021). *FEMA for kids*. www.fema.gov/blog/fema-kids.

Federal Emergency Management Agency (FEMA). (2022). *Getting assistance after a natural disaster*. www.fema.gov/assistance.

Federal Emergency Management Agency (FEMA). (2023). *FEMA grants*. www.fema.gov/grants.

Fein, R., Vossekuil, B., Pollack, W., Borum, R., Modzeleski, W., & Reddy, M. (2002). *Threat assessment in schools: A guide to managing threatening situations and to creating safe school climates*. U.S. Secret Service and Department of Education.

Finelli, J., & Zeanah, C. H. (2019). Psychopathology in children and their caregivers following America's Hurricane Katrina. In C. W. Hoven, L. V. Amsel, & S. Tyano (Eds.), *An international perspective on disasters and children's mental health* (pp. 233–252). Springer International.

Florida Senate Bill 7026, U.S.C., Ch. 2018-128 (2018).

Florida Senate Bill 730, U.S.C., Ch. 2022-47. (2019).

Fox, J. A., & DeLateur, M. J. (2013). Mass shootings in America. *Homicide Studies, 18*(1), 125–145.

Framework for Evidence-Based Practice. *School Mental Health, 11*(1), 54–71.

Freeman, W., & Taylor, M. (2010, July). *Conducting effective tabletops, drills and other exercises*. Workshop presented at the U.S. Department of Education, Office of Safe and Drug-Free Schools Readiness and Emergency Management for Schools Final Grantee Meeting, Boston. http://rems.ed.gov/docs/Training_FY09REMS_BOMA_TableTopsDrills.pdf.

Freeman, W., & Taylor, M. (2011, August). *Overview of emergency management exercises*. Workshop presented at the U.S. Department of Education, Office of Safe and Drug-Free Schools Readiness and Emergency Management for Schools, Final Grantee Meeting, National Harbor, MD. http://rems.ed.gov/docs/FY10REMS_FGM_NHMD_EMExercises.pdf.

Friedlander, W. (2013). Student suicide and school liability. *American Association for Justice. 49*(12), 55–64.

Gallagher v. Bader. Loudoun County Virginia Circuit Court. No. CL00105423-00 VA. (2016).

Garbe, W. (2019, October 14). Mother who called to warn about Richmond school shooting charged, in custody. *Springfield News Sun*. www.springfieldnewssun.com/news/local/mother-who-called-warn-about-richmond-school-shooting-faces-charges/TG0E7jfaw25A2MOiQ3OThN.

Garcia, U. (2022, August 16). Millions donated after Uvalde shooting still haven't reached victims and families. *Texas Tribune*. www.texastribune.org/2022/08/16/texas-uvalde-shooting-relief-money-victims.

Garcia-Williams, A., O'Donnel, J., Spies, E, Zhang, X., Young, R., Azofeifa, A., & Vagi, K. (2016). Epi Aid 2016–018: Undetermined risk factors for suicide among youth ages 10–24—Santa Clara County, CA, 2016.

Garrett Lee Smith Memorial Act. S. 118 Stat. 1404, 108th Cong., 2nd Session (2004).

Genovario, K. (2013, January 11). *Suspected school shooter Bryan Oliver: Top 10 facts you need to know*. https://heavy.com/news/2013/01/california-school-shooter-bryan-oliver-taft-high-facts/.

Gilliland, B. E., & James, R. K. (1988). *Crisis intervention strategies*. Thomson Brooks/Cole.

Ginsberg, C., & Loffredo, L. (1993). Violence-related attitudes and behaviors of high school students—New York City, 1992. *Journal of School Health*, 63, 438–440.

Gould, M. S., Greenberg, T., Velting, D. M., & Shaffer, D. (2003). Youth suicide risk and preventive interventions: A review of the past 10 years. *Journal of the American Academy of Child and Adolescent Psychiatry, 42*(4), 386–405.

Graziano, F., & Wamsley, L. (2022, February 15). *Families of Sandy Hook victims reach $73 million settlement with Remington*. NPR. www.npr.org/2022/02/15/1080819088/sandy-hook-victims-families-settlement-remington.

Halpoch, A. (2018, August 8). *A mental health crisis continues to unfold in Puerto Rico*. Grist. https://grist.org/article/a-mental-health-crisis-continues-to-unfold-in-puerto-rico.

Harvard Injury Control Research Center. (2019). *Means matter.* www.hsph.harvard.edu/means-matter.

Harvey, K. (2014). *Taft school shooting mistrial: What's next for Bryan Oliver?* KBAK. https://bakersfieldnow.com/news/local/taft-school-shooting-mistrial-whats-next-for-bryan-oliver.

Hazell, P. (1993). Adolescent suicide clusters: Evidence, mechanisms and prevention. *Australian and New Zealand Journal of Psychiatry,* 27(4), 653–665.

Heath, M. A., Ryan, K., Dean, B., & Bingham, R. (2007). History of school safety and psychological first aid for children. *Brief Treatment and Crisis Intervention, 7*(3), 206–223.

Heiman, A. (2021, February 9). *School district had no duty to warn about potential danger posed by MSD shooter: Judge.* NBC 6 South Florida. www.nbcmiami.com/news/local/parkland-school-tragedy/school-district-had-no-duty-to-.

Hernandez, M., Nesman, T. M., Mowery, D., Acevedo-Polakovich, I. D., & Callejas, L. M. (2009). Cultural competence: A literature review and conceptual model for mental health services. *Psychiatric Services,* 60, 1046–1050.

Hill, R. M., Rufino, K., Kurian, S., Saxena, J., Saxena, K., & Williams, L. (2021). Suicide ideation and attempts in a pediatric emergency department before and during COVID-19. *Pediatrics, 147*(3), e2020029280.

Hinduja, S., & Patchin, J. W. (2019). *Cyberbullying identification, prevention, and response.* www.cyberbullying.org.

Hoff, L. A. (2009). *People in crisis: Clinical and diversity perspectives* (6th ed.). Taylor & Francis.

Hope Squad. (2018). https://hopesquad.com.

Howard County Schools, Maryland Civil NO. 201358.

Janosik, E. H. (1986). *Crisis counseling: A contemporary approach.* Jones & Bartlett.

James, N., & McCallion, G. (2013). *School resource officers: Law enforcement officers in schools.* www.fas.org/sgp/crs/misc/R43126.pdf.

Jason Flatt Act, 45 State of Tennessee & 57 (2007).

Jason Foundation. (2019). http://jasonfoundation.com.

Jervis, R. (2018, March 23). "I sit and cry all day": Suicide hotline calls double in Puerto Rico 6 months after Hurricane Maria. *USA Today.* www.usatoday.com/story/news/2018/03/23/mental-health-crisis-puerto-rico-hurricane-maria/447144002/.

Jonson, C. L. (2017). Preventing school shootings: The effectiveness of safety measures. *Victims & Offenders, 12*(6), 956–973.

Judi's House/JAG Institute. (2022). *Childhood bereavement estimation model.* https://judishouse.org/research-tools/cbem.

Katz, C., Bolton, S.-L., Katz, L. Y., Isaak, C., Tilston-Jones, T., & Sareen, J. (2013). A systematic review of school-based suicide prevention programs. *Depression and Anxiety.* (10), 1030–1045.

Kazdin, A. E., Rodgers, A., & Colbus, D. (1986). The Hopelessness Scale for Children: Psychometric characteristics and concurrent validity. *Journal of Consulting and Clinical Psychology, 54*(2), 2.

Kekatos, M. (2022). *1 million have died from COVID in the US. Experts wonder how this seems normal.* ABC News. https://abcnews.go.com/US/us-nearing-million-covid-deaths-experts-normal/story?id=83863055.

Kemple, A. E., Heath, M. A., Hansen, K., Annandale, N. O., Fischer, L., Young, E. L., & Ryan, K. (2006). Cultural sensitivity in school–based crisis intervention. *Communique, 34*(7), 34–37.

Kennebeck, S., & Bonin, L. (2019). *Suicidal behavior in children and adolescents: Epidemiology and risk factors.* UpToDate. www.uptodate.com/contents/suicidal-behavior-in-children.

King, C. A., Foster, C. E., & Rogalski, K. M. (2013). *Teen suicide risk: A practitioner guide to screening, assessment, and management.* Guilford Press.

Kreuze, E., Stecker, T., & Ruggiero, K. J. (2017). State requirements for school personnel suicide prevention training: Where do we go from here? *Adolescent Research Review,* 3, 235–253.

La Greca, A. M., Silverman, W. K., Vernberg, E. M., & Prinstein, M. J. (1996). Symptoms of posttraumatic stress in children after Hurricane Andrew: A prospective study. *Journal of Consulting and Clinical Psychology, 64*(4), 712–723.

Lai, B. S., Auslander, B. A., Fitzpatrick, S. L., & Podkowirow, V. (2014). Disasters and depressive symptoms in children: A review. *Child and Youth Care Forum, 43*(4), 489–504.

Lai, B. S., & La Greca, A. (August 13, 2020). Understanding the impacts of natural disasters on children. *Child Evidence Brief* 8. www.srcd.org/research/understanding-impacts-natural-disasters-children.

Lai, B. S., La Greca, A., Brincks, A., Colgan, C. A., D'Amico, M. P., Lowe, S., & Kelley, M. L. (2021). Trajectories of posttraumatic stress in youths after natural disasters. *JAMA Network Open. 4*(2), e2036682.

Langman, P. (2009). Rampage school shooters: A typology. *Aggression and Violent Behavior, 14*(1), 79–86.

Lazarus, P., Jimerson, S., & Brock, S. (2002). [Review of *Natural Disasters*]. In *Best practices in school crisis prevention and intervention*. Ingram.

Lazarus, P. J., Jimerson, S. R., & Brock, S. E. (2003) *Responding to natural disasters. Helping · children and families. Information for school crisis teams.* National Association for School Psychologists.

Lazarus, P. J., Jimerson, S. R., & Brock, S. E. (2008). *Responding to natural disasters: Helping children and families information for school crisis teams.* National Association of School Psychologists.

Lazarus, P. J., Suldo, S. M., & Doll, B. (2021). *Fostering the emotional well-being of our youth: a school-based approach.* Oxford University Press.

Lazarus, R. S. (1993). Coping theory and research: Past, present and future. *Psychosomatic Medicine*, 55, 234–247.

Lieberman, R., Poland, S., & Cassel, R. (2008). Best practices in suicide intervention. In A. Thomas & J. Grimes (Eds.), *Best practices in school psychology* (pp. 273–288). National Association of School Psychologists.

Lieberman, R., Poland, S., & Cowan, K. (2006). Suicide prevention in the schools. *Principal Leadership*, 7(2), 11–15.

Lieberman, R., Poland, S., & Kornfeld, C. (2014). Best practices in suicide intervention. In P. L. Harrison & A. Thomas (Eds.), *Best practices in school psychology: Systems-level services* (pp. 273–288). National Association of School Psychologists.

Lieberman, R., & Poland, S. (2017). [Review of *Suicide Prevention Legislation: What School Psychologists Need to Know and Do*]. *Communiqué, 46*(3), 8. www.nasponline.org/publications/periodicals/communique/issues/volume-46-issue-3/suicide-prevention-legislation-what-school-psychologists-need-to-know-and-do.

Lifesaving Naloxone. (2022, September 7). CDC. www.cdc.gov/stopoverdose/naloxone/index.html#:~:text=What%20is%20naloxone%3F.

Limacher, U. (2020). *How to deal with different coping styles.* Ute's International Lounge & Academy. https://utesinternationallounge.com/how-to-deal-with-different-coping-styles.

Lindemann, E. (1944). Symptomatology and management of acute grief. *American Journal of Psychiatry 101*, 141–148.

Lutz v. Snohomish School District. No. 18-1-01670-8 WA. (2014).

Make Our Schools Safe. (2018). https://makeourschoolssafe.org.

Mares v. Shawnee Mission School District. Johnson County Kansas District Court. No. 06CV00160 (2007).

Mason, V., Andrews, H., & Upton D. (2010). The psychological impact of exposure to floods. *Psychological Health and Medicine, 15*(1), 61–73.

McEvoy, A. (1998). *When disaster strikes: Preparing schools for bus accidents, murders, suicides, tornadoes, and other community catastrophes.* Learning Publications.

McMyler, C., & Prymachuk, S. (2008). Do "no suicide" contracts work? *Journal of Psychiatric and Mental Health Nursing, 15*, 512–522.

Miller, D. N., & McConaughy, S. H. (2005). Assessing risk for suicide. In S. H. McConaughy (Ed.), *Clinical interview for children and adolescents: Assessment to intervention* (pp. 184–199). Guilford Press.

Miller, L. (2024). A handgun for Christmas: Why were James and Jennifer Crumbley found guilty for their son's mass shooting? *New York Magazine*. https://nymag.com/intelligencer/article/oxford-school-shooting-ethan-crumbley-parents.html.

Milman, O. (2020, October 6). *California wildfires spawn first "gigafire" in modern history*. www.sfgate.com/california-wildfires/article/Record-breaking-August-Complex-Fire-threatens-15566912.php.

MindWise Innovations. (2019). *Suicide prevention programs overview*. www.mindwise.org/what-we-offer/suicide-prevention-programs.

Moffitt, M. (2020, September 14). *August complex fire threatens Emerald Triangle, U.S.'s largest cannabis region*. www.sfgate.com/california-wildfires/article/Record-breaking-August-Complex-Fire-threatens-15566912.php.

Morrison, J. (2007). Social validity of the critical incident stress management model for school-based crisis intervention. *Psychology in the Schools*, 44(8), 765–777.

Movement Advancement Project. (2024). *Equality maps: Forced outing of transgender students*. www.mapresearch.org/equality-maps/youth/forced_outing.

Mughal, S., Azhar, Y., & Mahon, M. M. (2022). *Grief reaction*. StatPearls.

Najarian L., Goenjian A., Pelcovitz, D., Mandel, F, & Najarian, B. (2001). The effect of relocation after a natural disaster. *Journal of Traumatic Stress, 14*(3), 511–526.

NASP School Safety and Crisis Response Committee. (2018). *Recovery from large-scale crises: Guidelines for school administrators and crisis teams* [Handout]. Bethesda, MD: National Association of School Psychologists.

National Association of School Psychologists (NASP). (2002). *Coping with crisis—Helping children with special needs*. www.gcsnc.com/cms/lib/NC01910393/Centricity/Domain/2433/NASP%20-%20Helping%20Children%20with%20Special%20Needs%20Cope%20After%20a%20Crisis.pdf.

National Association of School Psychologists (NASP). (2004). *Culturally competent crisis response*. www.nasponline.org/resources-and-publications/resources-and-podcasts/diversity-and-social-justice/cultural-competence/culturally-competent-crisis-response.

National Association of School Psychologists (NASP). (2013). *Conducting crisis exercises & drills: Guidelines for schools*. www.nasponline.org/resources-and-publications/resources-and-podcasts/school-safety-and-crisis/systems-level-prevention/conducting-crisis-exercises-and-drills.

National Association of School Psychologists (NASP). (2015a). *Addressing grief*. www.nasponline.org/resources-and-publications/resources-and-podcasts/school-safety-and-crisis/mental-health-resources/addressing-grief.

National Association of School Psychologists (NASP). (2015b). *Natural disasters and relocated students with special needs*. www.nasponline.org/resources-and-publications/resources-and-podcasts/school-safety-and-crisis/natural-disaster-resources/natural-disasters-and-relocated-students-with-special-needs.

National Association of School Psychologists (NASP). (2015c). *Preventing suicide: Guidelines for administrators and crisis teams*. www.nasponline.org/resources-and-publications/resources-and-podcasts/school-climate-safety-and-crisis/mental-health-resources/preventing-youth-suicide/preventing-suicide-guidelines-for-administrators-and-crisis-teams.

National Association of School Psychologists (NASP). (2015d). *Preventing youth suicide*. www.nasponline.org/resources-and-publications/resources-and-podcasts/school-climate-safety-and-crisis/mental-health-resources/preventing-youth-suicide.

National Association of School Psychologists (NASP). (2015e). *Responding to school violence prevention: Guidelines for school administrators and crisis teams*. Author.

National Association of School Psychologists (NASP). (2015f). *Threat assessment for school administrators & crisis teams*. www.nasponline.org/resources-and-publications/resources-and-podcasts/school-climate-safety-and-crisis/systems-level-prevention/threat-assessment-at-school/threat-assessment-for-school-administrators-and-crisis-teams.

National Association of School Psychologists (NASP). (2016). *School violence prevention*. Author.

National Association of School Psychologists (NASP). (2017a). *Large-scale natural disasters: Helping children cope* [Handout]. Author.

National Association of School Psychologists (NASP). (2017b). *Relocating to a new school: Tips for families* [Handout]. Author.

National Association of School Psychologists (NASP). (2017c). *Resources to assist states/territories recovering from natural disasters* [Handout]. Author.

National Association of School Psychologists (NASP). (2018a). *School safety and crisis*. www.nasponline.org/resources-and-publications/resources-and-podcasts/school-safety-and-crisis.

National Association of School Psychologists (NASP). (2018b). School Safety and Crisis Response Committee. (2018b). *Recovery from large-scale crises: Guidelines for school administrators and crisis teams* [Handout]. Author.

National Association of School Psychologists. (2020a). *Preparing for infectious disease epidemics: Brief tips for school mental health professionals* [Handout]. Author.

National Association of School Psychologists (NASP). (2020b). *Responding to a mass casualty event at a school: General guidance for the first stage of recovery* [Handout]. Author.

National Association of School Psychologists (NASP). (2021a). *Bullying and prevention*. www.nasponline.org/resources-and-publications/resources-and-podcasts/school-safety-and-crisis/school-violence-resources/bullying-prevention.

National Association of School Psychologists (NASP). (2021b). *PREPaRE training curriculum*. www.nasponline.org/professional-development/prepare-training-curriculum.

National Association of School Psychologists (NASP). (2022a). *NASP adopts resolution regarding policing in schools*. www.nasponline.org/about-school-psychology/media-room/press-releases/nasp-adopts-resolution-regarding-policing-in-schools.

National Association of School Psychologists (NASP). (2022b). *State Shortages Data Dashboard*. www.nasponline.org/about-school-psychology/state-shortages-data dashboard.

National Center for Education Statistics. (2022). *Racial/ethnic enrollment in public schools*. U.S. Department of Education, Institute of Education Sciences. https://nces.ed.gov/programs/coe/indicator/cge.

National Child Traumatic Stress Network (NCTSN). (n.d.). *About child trauma*. www.nctsn.org/what-is-child-trauma/about-child-trauma.

National Child Traumatic Stress Network & National Center for PTSD (2018). *Child trauma toolkit for educators*. www.nctsn.org/sites/default/files/assets/pdfs/Child_Trauma_Toolkit_Final.pdf.

National Education Association. (2018). *School crisis guide*. www.nea.org/sites/default/files/2020-07/NEA%20School%20Crisis%20Guide%202018.pdf.

National Institute of Mental Health. (2022). *Suicide*. www.nimh.nih.gov/health/statistics/suicide.

National Save and Sandy Hook Promise. (2022). *Students Against Violence Everywhere (SAVE) Promise Club*. www.sandyhookpromise.org/our-programs/save-promise-club.

National Weather Service. (n.d.). *A guide to developing a severe weather emergency plan for schools*. www.weather.gov/media/grr/brochures/swep.pdf.

Nickerson, A. B., Savage, T. A., & Woitaszewski, S. A. (2015). School crisis prevention and intervention: Emergency preparedness and response. In R. H. Witte & G. S. Mosley-Howard (Eds.), *Mental health practice in today's schools: Issues and interventions* (pp. 399–417). Springer.

Norman, M. (2010). The psychological impact of natural disasters in school. In V. O. Pang, Fernekes, W. R., & Nelson, J. L. *The human impact of natural disasters: Issues for the inquiry-based classroom*. National Council for the Social Studies.

Office of Justice Programs. (2019). *Gang violence prevention.* U.S. Department of Justice. https://ojjdp.ojp.gov/programs/gang-violence-prevention.

Office of Justice Programs. (2020). *OJJDP Statistical Briefing Book.* U.S. Department of Justice. https://ojjdp.ojp.gov/statistics.

Office of Justice Programs. (2022). *Crime victims' fund.* U.S. Department of Justice. https://ovc.ojp.gov/about/crime-victims-fund.

Oliver, J., & Ryan, M. (2004). *Lesson one: The ABCs of life.* Fireside.

Ornes, S. (2018, August 14). How does climate change influence extreme weather?: Impact attribution research seeks answers. *Proceedings of the National Academy of Sciences of the United States of America.*

Osman, A., Gutierrez, P. M., Bagge, C. L., Fang, Q., & Emmerich, A. (2010). Reynolds Adolescent Depression Scale—Second Edition: A reliable and useful instrument. *Journal of Clinical Psychology, 66*(12), 1324–1345.

O'Toole, M. (2000). *The school shooter: A threat assessment perspective.* U.S. Department of Justice Office of Justice Programs. www.ojp.gov/ncjrs/virtual-library/abstracts/school-shooter-threat-assessment-perspective.

Owens, T. (2019, March 14). *Sandy Hook parents can now sue gunmaker of rifle used in school shooting.* VICE. www.vice.com/en/article/wjmybb/sandy-hook-parents-can-now-sue-gunmaker-of-rifle-used-in-school-shooting.

Parkinson, D., & Zara, C. (2013). The hidden disaster: Domestic violence in the aftermath of natural disaster. *Australian Journal of Emergency Management, 28*(2), 28–35.

Paul, L. A., Felton, J. W., Adams, Z. W., Welsh, K., Miller, S., & Ruggiero, K. J. (2015). Mental health among adolescents exposed to a tornado: The influence of social support and its interactions with sociodemographic characteristics and disaster exposure. *Journal of Trauma Stress, 28*(3):232–239.

Peck, A., Rosch, D., & De Sawal, D. (2022). Student belonging: A critical pillar in the scholarship of diversity, equity, and inclusion in campus activities. *Journal of Campus Activities Practice and Scholarship, 4*(1), 5–11.

People v. Oliver, F071129 (Cal. Ct. App. Jun. 30, 2016).

Pfefferbaum, B., Jacobs, A. K., Griffin, N., & Houston, J. B. (2015). Children's disaster reactions: The influence of exposure and personal characteristics. *Current Psychiatry Reports, 17*(7), 56.

Pitcher, G., & Poland, S. (1992). *Crisis intervention in the school.* Guilford Press.

Poal, P. (2009). Introduction to the theory and practice of crisis intervention. *Quaderns de Psicologia* (19), 121.

Poijula, S., Wahlberg, K. E., & Dyregrov, A. (2001). Adolescent suicide and suicide contagion in three secondary schools. *International Journal of Emergency Mental Health and Human Resilience 3,* 163–168.

Poland, S., Lieberman, R., & Niznik, M. (2019). Suicide contagion and clusters—Part 1: What school psychologists should know. *NASP Communiqué, 47*(5), 21–23. https://nsuworks.nova.edu/cps_facarticles/1709.

Poland, S., & Ferguson, S. (2021a). *Lessons learned from school shootings: Perspectives from the United States of America.* Springer International.

Poland, S., & Ferguson, S., (2021b). Youth suicide in the school context. *Aggression and Violent Behavior,* 5(16).

Poland, S., & McCormick, J. (1999). *Coping with crisis: Lessons learned.* Sopris West.

Poland, S., & Poland, D. (2017). *The Montana Crisis Action School Toolkit on suicide.* https://saom.memberclicks.net/assets/SAM_unpublished_links/CAST-S 2017 FINAL_revised.pdf.

Posner, K., Brent, D., Lucas, C., Gould, M., Stanley, B., Brown, G., et al. (2009). *Columbia Suicide Severity Rating Scale (C-SSRS).* Research Foundation for Mental Hygiene.

Project SERV. (2014). *Programs: Project School Emergency Response to Violence (SERV).* U.S. Department of Education. www2.ed.gov/programs/dvppserv/index.html.

Quinnet, P. (1995). *QPR for suicide prevention.* QPR Institute.

Rathner, J. L. (2018, November). *Taking care of emotional health after a hurricane.* Laborer's Health and Safety Fund. www.lhsfna.org/taking-care-of-emotional-health-after-a-hurricane.

Reardon, S. (2015, August 24). Hurricane Katrina's psychological scars revealed. *Nature.* www.nature.com/articles/524395a#/ref-link-1.

Rebik, R. (2014, April 16). Jury: Snohomish School District must pay stabbing victims $1.3 million. Q3Fox News. *www.q13fox.com/news/jury-snohomish-school-district-must-pay-stabbing-victims-1-3-million.*

Reeves, M. A., Conolly-Wilson, C. N., Pesce, R. C., Lazzaro, B. R., Nickerson, A. B., Feinberg, T., & Brock, S. E. (2012). Providing the comprehensive school crisis response. In S. E. Brock & S. R. Jimerson (Eds.), *Best practices in school crisis prevention and intervention* (2nd ed., pp. 305–316). National Association of School Psychologists.

Reeves, M. A., Nickerson, A. B., Connolly-Wilson, C. N., Susan, M. K., Lazzaro, B. R., Jimerson, S. R., & Pesce, R. C. (2011). *Crisis prevention and preparedness: Comprehensive school safety planning* (2nd ed.). National Association of School Psychologists.

Reiss, R., & Alonso, M. (2021, August 20). *Judge says case against former Parkland school resource officer Scot Peterson can go to trial.* CNN. www.cnn.com/2021/08/20/us/parkland-shooting-scot-peterson-charges/index.html.

Ridout, K. K., Alavi, M., Ridout, S. J., Koshy, M. T., Awsare, S., Harris, B., & Iturralde, E. (2021). Emergency department encounters among youth with suicidal thoughts or behaviors during the COVID-19 pandemic. *JAMA Psychiatry, 78*(12), 1319–1328.

Rosenfeld, L. B., Caye, J., Ayalon, O., & Lahad, M. (2005) *When their world falls apart: Helping families and children manage the effects of disasters.* NASW Press.

Roth, J., & Fernandez, B. (2018). *Perspectives on school crisis response: Reflections from the field.* Routledge.

Rudd, M. D., Mandrusiak, M., & Joiner, T. (2005). The case against no-suicide contracts: The commitment to treatment statement as a practice alternative. *Journal of Clinical Psychology, 62*(2), 243–251.

Safe and Sounds Schools (2015). *Straight A school safety model.* www.safeandsoundschools.org.

Safe Crossings Foundation. (n.d.). *Tools and resources for professionals.* https://safecrossingsfoundation.org.

Sandoval, J., & Lewis, S. (2002). Cultural considerations in crisis intervention. In S. E. Brock, P. J. Lazarus, & S. R. Jimerson (Eds.), *Best practices in school crisis prevention and intervention* (pp. 293–308). National Association of School Psychologists.

Sandy Hook Promise Action Fund. (n.d.). *Prevent youth suicide.* https://actionfund.sandyhookpromise.org/issues/mental-health-and-wellness/prevent-youth-suicide.

Sanford v. Stiles, 456 F.3d 298 (3rd Cir. 2006).

Sastry, N., & Gregory, J. (2014). The location of displaced New Orleans residents in the year after Hurricane Katrina. *Demography, 51*(3):753–775.

Save the Children. (2007). *Legacy of disasters: The impact of climate change on children.* https://resource-centre.savethechildren.net/library/legacy-disastersthe-impact-climate-change-children.

SB 7030 Implementation of Legislative Recommendations of the Marjory Stoneman Douglas High School Public Safety Commission. (2019). https://info.fldoe.org/docushare/dsweb/Get/Document-8569/dps-2019-76a.pdf.

Schneider, T. (2019). *Next level crisis planning for students with disabilities.* Campus Safety. www.campussafetymagazine.com/news/next-level-crisis- planning-for-students-with-disabilities.

School Threat Assessment Consultants, LLC. (2022). *Training in school-based assessment.* www.schoolta.com.

Scott v. Montgomery County Board of Education, No. 96-2455 U.S. App LEXIS 21258 (4th Cir. 1997).

Shear, M. K. (2012). Grief and mourning gone awry: Pathway and course of complicated grief. *Dialogues Clinical Neuroscience, 14*(2):119–128.

Sherman, J. (2022). *The evolution of Rule 9.130 and appellate review of sovereign immunity.* www.floridabar.org/the-florida-bar-journal/the-evolution-of-rule-9-130-and-appellate-review-of-sovereign-immunity/.

Shneidman, E. (1973). *Deaths of man.* Quadrangle Books.

Should we change how we teach run, hide, fight? (n.d.). Vector Solutions. www.vectorsolutions.com/resources/blogs/should-we-change-how-we-teach-run-hide-fight.

Singer, J. A., Erbacher, T. E., & Rosen, P. (2018). School-based suicide prevention: A framework for evidence-based practice. *School Mental Health*, 1–18.

Sokol, R. L., Heinze, J., Doan J., Normand, M., Grodzinski, A., Pomerantz, N., Scott, B. A., et al. (2021). Crisis interventions in schools: A systematic review. *Journal of School Violence, 20*(2), 241–260.

SoulShoppe. (2021). *Trauma-informed activities for students.* https://soulshoppe.org/blog/2022/09/19/trauma-informed-activities-for-students.

Spencer, T. (2024). *Lawsuit against Parkland school deputy over 2018 mass shooting can go to trial: Judge.* NBC 6 South Florida. www.nbcmiami.com/news/local/lawsuit-against-parkland-school-deputy-over-2018-mass-shooting-can-go-to-trial-judge/3202574/

Spies, E., Ivey-Stephenson, A., VanderEnde, K., Lynch, S., Dean, D., & Gleason, B. (2104). *Epi Aid 2015-003: Undetermined risk factors for suicide among youth, ages 10–24 Fairfax County, VA, 2014.* www.fairfaxcounty.gov/health/sites/health/files/assets/images/suicide-epi-aid-final-report.pdf.

Spooner, F., Knight, V. F., Browder, D. M., & Smith, B. R. (2012). Evidence-based practice for teaching academics to students with severe developmental disabilities. *Remedial and Special Education, 33*(6), 374–387.

Stanaway, C. (2020). *The stages of grief: Accepting the unacceptable.* University of Washington, Counseling Center. www.washington.edu/counseling/2020/06/08/the-stages-of-grief-accepting-the-unacceptable/.

STANDUP (Suicide Training and Awareness Nationally Delivered for Universal Prevention) Act of 2021, H. R. 586 / S.1543.

Stanley & Brown. (2021). *Stanley-Brown Safety Plan.* https://bgg.11b.myftpupload.com/wp-content/uploads/2021/08/Stanley-Brown-Safety-Plan-8-6-21.pdf.

State of Indiana v. Mary York, 89D01-1910-F5-000113 (Wayne Sup Crt. 2020).

STEPS (School Toolkit for Educators to Prevent Suicide). (2021). www.nova.edu/suicideprevention.

Stern, J. (2013, June 24). *Apple's Siri can be first call for users thinking of suicide.* ABC News. http://abcnews.go.com/Technology/apples-siri-now-prevent-suicides/sotry?id=19438495.

Stone, C. (2017). *Ethics and the law* (4th ed.). American School Counselor Association.

Strode, M. (2019, July 17). Bowe Cleveland awarded $3.8 million in damages for 2013 Taft school shooting. *Bakersfield Californian.* www.bakersfield.com/news/bowe-cleveland-awarded-3-8-million-in-damages-for-2013-taft-school-shooting/article_10c515c0-a820-11e9-b492-7783a9cd6c21.html.

Substance Abuse and Mental Health Services Administration. (2009). *SAFE-T Pocket Card: Suicide assessment five-step evaluation and triage for clinicians.* www.store.samhsa.gov/product/safe-t-pocket-card-suicide-assessment-five-step-evaluation-and-triage-clinicians/sma09-4432.

Substance Abuse and Mental Health Services Administration. (2012). *Preventing suicide: A toolkit for high schools* (HHS Publication No. SMA-12-4669). https://store.samhsa.gov/product/Preventing-Suicide-A-Toolkit-for-High-Schools/SMA12-4669.

Substance Abuse and Mental Health Services Administration. (2022a). *988 Suicide Crisis and Lifeline.* www.samhsa.gov/find-help/988/faqs.

Substance Abuse and Mental Health Services Administration. (2022b). *Disaster Distress Helpline.* www.samhsa.gov/find-help/disaster-distress-helpline.

Substance Abuse and Mental Health Services Administration. (2022c). *Earthquakes.* www.samhsa.gov/find-help/disaster-distress-helpline/disaster-types/earthquakes.

Substance Abuse and Mental Health Services Administration. (2022d). *Tornadoes.* www.samhsa.gov/find-help/disaster-distress-helpline/disaster-types/tornadoes.

Substance Abuse and Mental Health Services Administration. (2022e). *Wildfires. www.samhsa.gov/find-help/disaster-distress-helpline/disaster-types/wildfires.*

Substance Abuse and Mental Health Services Administration, National Center for Trauma-Informed Care. (2015). *Trauma-informed approach.* www.samhsa.gov/nctic/trauma-interventions.

Sue, D. W., & Sue, D. (2003). *Counseling the culturally diverse: Theory and practice* (4th ed.). Wiley.

Suicide Prevention Lifeline. (2019). https://suicidepreventionlifeline.org.

Suicide Prevention Resource Center. (2019). *Preventing suicide: The role of high school teachers.* www.sprc.org/settings/schools.

Suicide Prevention Resource Center. (2021). *Best practices and recommendations for reporting on suicide.* https://reportingonsuicide.org/wp-content/themes/ros2015/assets/images/Recommendations-eng.pdf.

Talbott, L., & Bartlett, M. (2012). Youth suicide postvention: Support for survivors and recommendations for school personnel. *Alabama Counseling Association Journal*, 38(2), 104–119.

Tang, B., Liu, X., Liu, Y., Xue, C., & Zhang, L. (2014). A meta-analysis of risk factors for depression in adults and children after natural disasters. *BMC Public Health, 14*(1), 623.

Thomas, M. S., Crosby, S., & Vanderhaar, J. (2019). Trauma-informed practices in schools across Two Decades: An interdisciplinary review of research. *Review of Research in Education, 43*(1), 422–452.

Thompson, J. (2024, March). To stop a shooter. *The Atlantic.* www.theatlantic.com/magazine/archive/2024/03/parkland-shooter-scot-peterson-coward-broward/677170.

The Trevor Project. (2021). *Model school district policy on suicide prevention: Model language, commentary, and resources.* www.thetrevorproject.org/wp-content/uploads/2021/08/Model_School_Policy_Booklet.pdf.

Trotta, D. (2019). *Florida teachers can arm themselves under new gun bill.* Reuters. www.reuters.com/article/us-usa-guns-florida/florida-teachers-can-arm-themselves-under-new-gun-bill-idUSKCN1S74GZ.

Underwood, M. M., & Dunne-Maxim, K. (1997). *Managing sudden traumatic loss in the schools.* University of Medicine and Dentistry of New Jersey, New Jersey Adolescent Suicide Prevention Project.

Uscher-Pines, L. (2009). Health effects of relocation following disaster: A systematic review of the literature. *Disasters, 33*(1), 1–22.

U.S. Department of Agriculture. (n.d.). *Safe and effective wildfire response.* www.fs.usda.gov/managing-land/fire/response.

U.S. Department of Education. (2014). *Guiding principles: A resource guide for improving school climate and discipline.* www2.ed.gov/policy/gen/guid/school-discipline/guiding-principles.pdf.

U.S. Department of Education. (2019). *Parent and educator guide to school climate resources.* www2.ed.gov/policy/elsec/leg/essa/essaguidetoschoolclimate041019.pdf.

U.S. Department of Education, REMS Technical Assistance Center. (2006). Emergency exercises: An effective way to validate school safety plans. *ERCMExpress, 2*(3), 1–4.

U.S. Department of Homeland Security. (February 2007). *Homeland security exercise and evaluation program. Vol. I: HSEEP Overview and Exercise Program Management.* https://hseep.dhs.gov/pages/1001_HSEEP7.aspx.

U.S. Department of Veterans Affairs. (2014). *PTSD: National Center for PTSD.* www.ptsd.va.gov/.

U.S. Surgeon's General Advisory. (2021, December 7). *Protecting youth mental health.* www.acf.hhs.gov/cb/news/surgeon-generals-protecting-youth-mental.

Uscher-Pines, L. (2009). Health effects of relocation following disaster: A systematic review of the literature. *Disasters. 33*(1):1–22.

Vaillancourt, K. M., & Gibson, N. A. (2014). model school district policy for suicide prevention. *Communique, 43*(2), 24–27.

Vermont School Safety Center. (2017). *Vermont school crisis guide.* https://schoolsafety.vermont.gov/planning/vermont-school-crisis-guide.

Vernberg, E. M., Silverman, W. K., La Greca, A. M., & Prinstein, M. J. (1996). Prediction of posttraumatic stress symptoms in children after hurricane Andrew. *Journal of Abnormal Psychology, 105*(2), 237–248.

Victor, D. (2017). Hurricane Andrew: How the *Times* reported the destruction of 1992. *New York Times.* www.nytimes.com/2017/09/06/us/hurricane-andrew-florida.html.

Vujanovi, A., & Gallagher, M. (September 6, 2017). *Psychological impact of natural disasters in adults.* University of Houston. www.uh.edu/class/news/archive/2017/august-september/natural-disasters-impact-adults.

Washington, D. (2022). Executive Office of the President, Office of Management and Budget. www.whitehouse.gov/wp-content/uploads/2022/06/Bipartisan-Safer-Communities-Act-SAP-1.pdf.

Wilke v. St. Vrain Valley School District. Civil Action No. 15-cv-01925-RPM (D. Colo. Jul. 27, 2017).

Williamson, E. (2021, May 1). A search for remembrance after the Sandy Hook Massacre. *New York Times.* www.nytimes.com/2021/05/01/us/politics/newtown-sandy-hook-elementary.html.

Wilson, S. J., & Lipsey, M. (2007) School-based interventions for aggressive and disruptive behavior. *Update of a Meta-Analysis, 33*(2), 130–143.

Witsell et al v. The School Board of Hillsborough County, No. 8:11-cv—00781 (M. D. Florida 2011).

Woodrow Cox, J., Rich, S., Chiu, A., Thacker, H., Chong, L., Muyskens, L., and Ulmanu, M. (2022). Explore the *Washington Post*'s database of school shootings. www.washingtonpost.com/graphics/2018/local/school-shootings-database.

Wyke v. Polk County School Board. U.S. Middle District Court Florida. No.91-1457-CIV-T-24C (1997).

Wyman, P. A., Brown, C. H., Lomurray, M., Schmeelk-Cone, K., Petrova, M., Yu, Q., & Wang, W. (2010). An outcome evaluation of the sources of strength suicide prevention program delivered by adolescent peer leaders in high schools. *American Journal of Public Health, 100*(9), 1653–1661.

WYTV Staff. (2021, June 4). Hurricane dangers: Flooding. Grey Mediabook Inc., Station. Retrieved May 22, 2022, *from www.wtvy.com/2021/06/04/hurricane-dangers-flooding.*

Yellow Ribbon International for Suicide Prevention. (2021). https://yellowribbon.org.

Young, M. (1997). *The community crisis response team training manual* (2nd ed.). National Organization for Victim Assistance. www.nasponline.org/NEAT/neat_cultural.html.

Zhang, A., Musu-Gillette, L., & Oudekerk, B. A. (2016). *Indicators of school crime and safety: 2015* (NCES 2016-079/NCJ 249758). U.S. Department of Justice.

Zhe, E. J., & Nickerson, A. B. (2007). The effects of an intruder crisis drill on children's self-perceptions of anxiety, school safety, and knowledge. *School Psychology Review,* 36, 501–508.

Index

Note. *f* or *t* following a page number indicates a figure or a table

D

P

R

S

T

U

V

W

Y

Z